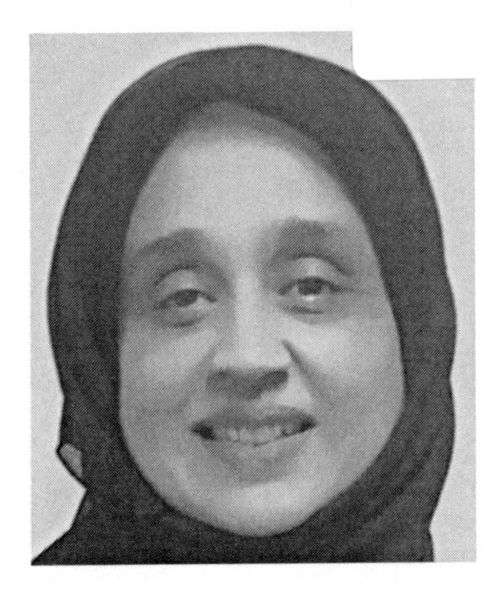

Syeda Faiqa Mazhar's academic journey has gone through many transitional phases. She achieved an M.A. degree in English Language and Literature to add to her M.Phil./Ph.D. research studies. During this phase of life, she discovered her passion for post-colonial literary discourses. This led to exploring themes of race, borderland, and identity with an exclusive focus on Nobel laureate South African writer Nadine Gordimer's fiction. This book is an outcome of Dr. Mazhar's post-doctoral project conceived and researched during her Visiting Research Fellowship at the Institute of Commonwealth Studies, School of Advanced Study, University of London, United Kingdom.

SYEDA FAIQA MAZHAR

Nadine Gordimer's Fiction

Transitional Phases in South African History, Politics and Society

AUSTIN MACAULEY PUBLISHERS™
LONDON • CAMBRIDGE • NEW YORK • SHARJAH

A CIP catalogue record for this title is available from the British Library.

ISBN 9781035800827 (Paperback)
ISBN 9781035800957 (Hardback)
ISBN 9781035800834 (ePub e-book)

www.austinmacauley.com

First Published 2023
Austin Macauley Publishers Ltd®
1 Canada Square
Canary Wharf
London
E14 5AA

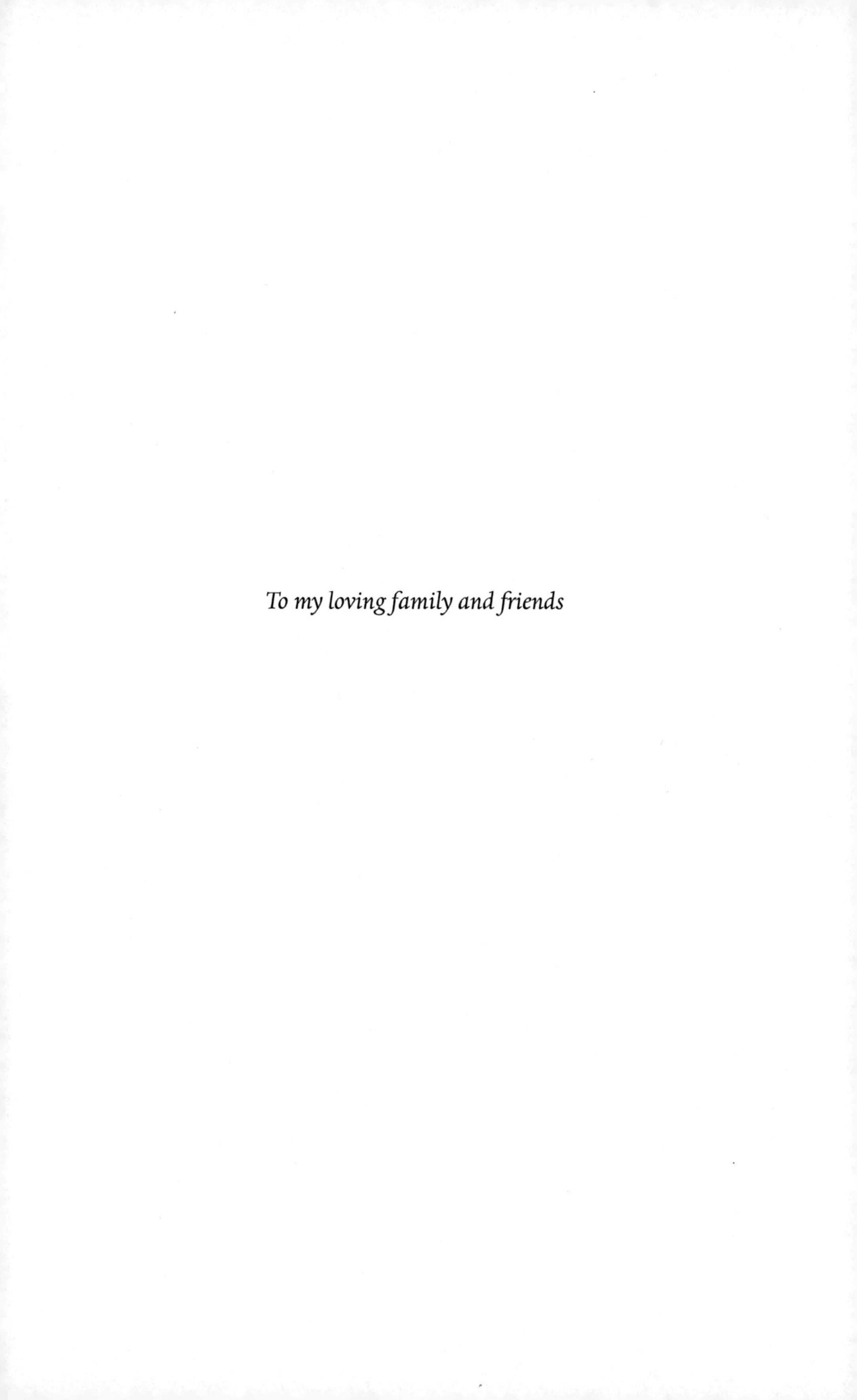

To my loving family and friends

Acknowledgements

I remain immensely grateful to Nadine Gordimer for her exceptional kindness during my informal visit to her house in Johannesburg.

Deep gratitude to Professor Shaista Sonnu Sirajuddin (Department of English Literature, University of Punjab, Pakistan) for introducing me to the world of literary research studies.

I am hugely indebted to my mentors—Dr Balasubramanyam Chandramohan (Senior Research Fellow, Institute of Commonwealth Studies, School of Advanced Study, University of London, United Kingdom), and, Professor Christopher Heywood (Honorary Senior Research Fellow, University of Sheffield, United Kingdom) for their wholehearted support and continual interest in this project, and their contribution in comments on the manuscript. Without their splendidly acute editorial eye and vigilant supervision, this book could have never been written.

Many thanks to Keith Hollinshead (Emeritus Professor of Public Culture, University of Bedfordshire, United Kingdom) for making me understand post-colonial theorist Homi Bhabha's coined metaphors.

I am immensely grateful to Geffrey Haresnape (Emeritus Professor of English and Creative Writing, University of Cape Town, South Africa) and his wife Leslie Haresnape, Indian-born South African writer Ahmed Essop and his wife Fareeda Essop, Yusuf Abrahams (Director of Marketing, Communication and Development, Cape Peninsula University of Technology, South Africa) and his wife Cass Abrahams, and, the Afrikaner couple and business entrepreneurs Nora and Erhardt for their input and exceptional hospitality.

Deep thanks to Philip Murphy (Professor of British and Commonwealth History and Director, Institute of Commonwealth Studies, School of Advanced Study, University of London, United Kingdom) for his moral support in completing this project.

I would like to warmly thank academics and people of other backgrounds who provided insights into South African society and Gordimer's work.

Resources at the British Library and in the libraries at Senate House, SOAS University of London, and the University of Bedfordshire as well as at the University of Stellenbosch, Cape Town, and Johannesburg were of immense help.

I thank Maria Brink and Hanna Botha, the librarians at the University of Stellenbosch, and Tanya Barben, Special Collections librarian at the University of Cape Town for their time and efforts to discover the research material related to my area of work.

I thank Santa Joubert and Jonathan Paton—with both of whom I stayed in Stellenbosch and Johannesburg—for their hospitality and efforts to meet South Africans of diverse backgrounds which helped to understand better the view of South Africa that appears in Nadine Gordimer's fiction.

I am grateful to Ghulam Akbar (Chief Editor, Daily National Herald Tribune, Islamabad, Pakistan) for his time and effort to proofread drafts of this book and provide an objective reader's response on the quality of my narrative.

I am grateful to Sir Anwar Pervaiz (Chairman, Bestway Foundation, London, United Kingdom) for his generous financial support in conducting this research study.

Lastly, I am grateful to my family, friends, and colleagues for their support, patience, and confidence in my research project.

Syeda Faiqa Mazhar (Ph.D.)
12 October 2023

CONTENTS

PREFACE

This author study projects my passion for the style and subject of writings by South African political activist and 1991 Novel Prize in Literature recipient, Nadine Gordimer (1923–2014). I discovered her writings during my post-graduate research studies in 1994; the first story I read was 'Amnesty' (1991) which fascinated me to the extent that I chose to review it as part of my coursework assignment. A comparative study of short stories written by Gordimer and British-Zimbabwean writer Doris Lessing (1991–2013) was the focus of my M.Phil. dissertation in 1996.

I was awarded Ph.D. in 2008 for investigating a methodological perspective on Gordimer's fiction that has not been explored before: the thesis established a connection between the recurring theme of borderland in Gordimer's fiction and the post-colonial notion of *third space* propounded by Indian critical theorist, Homi Bhabha (1949-to date). Though Bhabha coined the above metaphor in his work, *The Location of Culture* in 1994 —decades after Gordimer presented her theme of borderland, there is an amazing similarity that projects Gordimer ahead of her time to visualise a society without the prevailing race and social classifications worldwide and in South Africa in particular.

A study visit to the South African cities of Stellenbosch, Cape Town and Johannesburg in 2005 led to experience, at close quarters, the subtle social divisions not only between but also within the white South African community and also amongst the non-white peoples of the land: the Afrikaners (the Boers—descendants of Dutch, French and German settlers), the English (British settlers), the Coloured (people of mixed European and African or Asian ancestry) and the black world (the non-Bantu Khoisans—descendants of San—Bushman and Khoikhoi—Hottentots, and Bantu-speaking Africans); a rainbow nation as described by South Africa's first black Anglican Archbishop, Desmond Mpilo Tutu (1986–1996), a cohesive creole society as noted by Professor Heywood in *A History of South African Literature* (2004).

Life in Stellenbosch and Cape Town reveals the traditional divide of South African society into Afrikaner, the Coloured and the black worlds. In an Afrikaner-dominated town, the Stellenbosch Museum displays Afrikaner society and culture since the Dutch settlers came to South Africa in the seventeenth century. In Cape Town, the District Six Museum and the Bokaap area where the slaves of Indian, Indonesian, Mauritian and

Madagascarian origins inhabited in the past and which became home to the Cape Coloured Muslim community, are in complete contrast with the white suburbs of the city. The townships in Stellenbosch, Cape Town and Johannesburg remain as permanent features which reveal the social divide between the relatively rich whites and the poor blacks in South Africa.

Though apartheid—meaning apartness in the South African Afrikaans language—that sanctioned a rigid racial segregation policy in 1948 no longer legally exists in South Africa and the African National Congress has been in government since 1994, memories of apartheid are still alive in the minds of South Africans who lived through those times and have much to tell: the colour bar or apartheid is indeed a story of the past in South African society but it has left a majority of the inhabitants in deep poverty and economic deprivation which would take time to heal. Courtesy, academics, and people of other facets of life whom I met in South Africa and who provided insights into South African society and Nadine Gordimer's writings; the topics under discussion were racism, the Afrikaner community, apartheid, liberalism, and the reception of Gordimer's work. This exercise helped to understand better the view of South Africa that appears in Nadine Gordimer's fiction.

This face-to-face interaction with South Africans of various backgrounds in Stellenbosch, Cape Town and Johannesburg has provided further strength to my findings that I discovered reading Gordimer's fiction such as the complexity and the resulting dilemma of the liberal society in its South African world. Despite the divisions of liberals into militant, left and progressive groups which had made them, in Gordimer's description, borderland characters in their liberal world too, the liberals in twentieth-century South Africa did provide space to people of a different colour to come closer to each other, the experience which was null and void under the then prevalent apartheid system of life. They were, indeed, the in-between society between Afrikaner nationalism and Africanism that Gordimer attempts to project in her fiction. A detailed record of meetings and interviews in Stellenbosch, Cape Town and Johannesburg is documented in the Memoir sections of this book.

I met Gordimer in Johannesburg, though for a short while, this interaction with her was no less than an interview; the whole episode of this dramatic meeting is recorded in the last Memoir section. As an exceptional personal courtesy, she admitted me to her house for a brief photo session. I was amazed to discover different shades of her personality; the detachment in her attitude and the arrogance in her way of talking exist side by side with the lively and caring sides of her character. Meeting

Gordimer in person reminded me of my M.Phil. dissertation (Punjab University 1996) which I wrote on the development of style in her shorter fiction. How close I was in my deduction then: her changing perception of the world is integral to the development of her detached style of writing. Her fiction is, indeed, a reflection of each facet of her life.

The Africana section of the library at Stellenbosch University owns valuable letters exchanged between Gordimer and the Afrikaner poet, Matheus Uys Krige (1910–1987) during their earlier days of writing. They reveal how Gordimer was at the forefront of organising a campaign in favour of freedom of expression for the writers in South Africa. She attempted to motivate people from different backgrounds to raise their voices against censorship of writings by the apartheid government during the 1950s and 1960s. These letters inform about the reception of Gordimer's work inside as well as outside South Africa and reveal that Gordimer found it difficult to get her work published in the early days of her writing. Selected copies of these letters are displayed in the Appendix section of this book.

As compared to Stellenbosch University where I could locate three dissertations written on Gordimer fiction, the Archive section in the library at the University of Cape Town had a record of fifteen theses written on Gordimer and a collection of her PEN (the Writers' Association in London since 1921 to promote friendship and intellectual co-operation worldwide) letters. There, I also found out that The National English Literary Museum at Grahamstown (the old settlers' town—Eastern Cape) has more related material in this regard.

In the library at Witwatersrand University, I came to know that Gordimer had sold all her original manuscripts to Indiana University in the United States. However, some of her research work including two interviews with Gordimer, newspaper cuttings about the Central African Federation in the 1970s, the role of the Congress of Democrats and the African National Congress (ANC) in the apartheid era, documents relating to the *Drum* (a literary forum for humour, satire and protest by the black writers) and the Institute of Race Relations, and, a Guide to the Gordimer's papers in the Lilly Library, Indiana University, Bloomington, Indiana 1994 are available at the Department of Historical Papers in the library at Wits University, Johannesburg.

Amongst others that have notably contributed and hugely assisted in my appreciation of Gordimer as a post-colonial writer and an anti-apartheid activist over the decades in line with the development of the South African literary scene: some notable social and political minds are Aime Cesaire's *Discourse on Colonialism* (1950), Octave Mannoni's *The Psychology of Colonisation* (1956), Frantz Fanon's *Black Skin and White Masks* (1967) and *The Wretched of the Earth* (1963), Albert Memmi's *The Coloniser and the Colonised* (1974), Edward Said's *Orientalism* (1978) and *Culture and Imperialism* (1993), Benedict Anderson's *Imagined Communities* (1991), D W Winnicot's *Playing and Reality* (1971), Georg Lukacs' *The Historical Novel* (1962), Abdul R JanMohamed's *Manichean Aesthetics: The Politics of Literature in Colonial Africa.* (1983), Homi Bhabha's *Nation and Narration* (1990) and *The Location of Culture* (1994), Christopher Heywood's *A History of South African Literature* (2004), Peter Vale, Lawrence Hamilton and Estelle H. Prinsloo's edited work *Intellectual Traditions in South Africa: Ideas, Individuals and Institutions* (2014), together with Gordimer's non-fictional writings and interviews.

Post-doctoral Visiting Research Fellowship (2016–2017) at the Institute of Commonwealth Studies, University of London, United Kingdom provided an opportunity to put together decades of my academic research on Gordimer's fiction. The book explores her personal development and her emergence as a major literary figure amongst other contemporary writers who raised their voices against prevalent discrimination and injustices in their societies. As part of the trend, Gordimer has, indeed, not only extensively written about her South African society but has also aesthetically recorded its transitional phases in her short stories and novels.

A world free of complexities, one must strive for—has been Gordimer's message for humanity that she gracefully articulated in her fiction. This publication is my tribute to her writings which create awareness of the racial prejudice that triggered exploitation and discrimination in society, both in South Africa and worldwide. It is, indeed, the root of not only psychological misery but also physical abuse of the human race to date.

Abbreviations

Title	Short Stories
Abroad	'Abroad'
AE	'Alternative Endings'
Amnesty	'Amnesty'
Beethoven	'Beethoven Was One-Sixteenth Black'
DD	'Dreaming of the Dead'
Era	'Which New Era Would That Be?'
FDL	'For Dear Life'
Fools	'Fools'
FS	'The First Sense'
Home	'Home'
Jump	'Jump'
KF	'Keeping Fit'
Lion	'A Lion on the Free Way'
Magician	'The African Magician'
Meet?	'Is There Nowhere Else Where We Can Meet?'
Once Upon	'Once Upon a Time'
PT	'Parking Tax'
Some Monday	'Some Monday for Sure'
Train	'The Train from Rhodesia'
TS	'The Third Sense'
Woe	'Ah, Woe Is Me'

Title	**Novels**
BD	*Burger's Daughter*
CBC	*Cry the Beloved Country*
CMNM	*Call Me Not a Man*
Cons.	*The Conservationist*
CP	*The Colour Purple*
Get	*Get A Life*
Guest	*A Guest of Honour*
HG	*The House Gun*
JP	*July's People*
LBW	*The Late Bourgeois World*
LD	*The Lying Days*
Loving	*Occasion for Loving*
LT	*Life Times*
None	*None to Accompany Me*
Present	*No Time Like the Present*
PU	*The Pick Up*
RB	*The River Between*
RTHC	*Roll of Thunder, Hear My Cry*
Something	*Something Out There*
Sport	*A Sport of Nature*
Strangers	*A World of Strangers*
Story	*My Son's Story*
TP	*Train to Pakistan*
TW	*Turbott Wolf*

INTRODUCTION

To understand the reality of apartheid in South Africa, one needs to come to grips with the complex culture of physical and mental borders generated by colonialism for centuries. There is a disturbing history behind the prevalent power politics and race relations worldwide. In this regard, Nadine Gordimer's fiction is an artistic record of the transitional phases of South African society — from resistance to struggle and then to liberation from apartheid.

Complexities

Colonialism—a policy of political and economic subjugation of peoples and resources of foreign lands by the powerful nations of the world—dates back to antiquity when empires were built by the Egyptians, Greeks, Romans, and the Phoenicians (ancient Semitic civilisation). Modern colonialism that began in 1500 after the discoveries of Africa in 1488 and of America in 1492 continued this practice of dominance and generated physical and mental barriers between people of different races in the world; such level of interaction eventually divided society into the *Self* (the coloniser) and the *Other* (the colonised) polarities, activating racial discrimination to the extent that the former considers the latter as chattels, even not human beings! The brutal death of George Perry Floyd, a 46 years old African-American in the custody of white policemen in Minneapolis, the United States of America on 25 May 2020, and the 30 January 2021 social media insult with monkey emojis targeting 23 years old Black-British footballer of Premier League Club Manchester United, Marcus Rashford are those blunt reminders of the racial prejudice that began centuries ago and exists in different forms and manifestations till to date: 'Jakedteddybear FFS this banana peeler should leave. Just leave... go back to the zoo you do a better job there...football ain't your thing.' (Instagram, Saturday 30 January 2021) Marcus responded to this abusive comment:

> Humanity and social media at its worst. Yes, I'm a black man and I live every day proud that I am. No one, and no one comment, is going to make me feel any different. [...] I have beautiful children of all colours following me [...] Beautiful colours that should only be celebrated. (Twitter, Saturday, 31 January 2021)

Coincidentally, my residence in London comes under the Metropolitan Housing Association that was created in 1963; it was originally called the Metropolitan Coloured Peoples Housing Association and was founded in the 1950s by Lady Molly Huggins, wife of a former Governor of Jamaica (then a British colony) who pioneered the provision of homes for people from ethnic minorities. As a settler in the United Kingdom since 1997, my experience of marginalisation as belonging to one of the ethnic communities—Asian/British Pakistani—has contributed to making connections with Nadine Gordimer's attempt to go in the beyond—the borderland world that she creates in her fiction—to understand the impact of racism in South African society and worldwide, challenge it and find a solution.

'The problem of the twentieth century is the problem of the colour-line,—the relation of the darker to the lighter races [...] in Asia and Africa, in America and the islands of the sea,' acknowledges African-American civil rights activist, William Edward Burghardt Du Bois (1868–1963) in his book *The Souls of Black Folk* (1903, 1–2). The term *colour line* was originally used by African-American social reformer Frederick Douglass (1818–1895) in his article 'The Colour Line'—published in *North American Review* in 1881—as a reference to the racial segregation that existed in the United States of America; Douglass was a firm believer in the equality of all peoples—white, black, female, natives or immigrants. Similarly, Du Bois stood for the equal rights of people of colour everywhere, particularly Africans and Asians in colonies. Founding member of the National Association for the Advancement of Coloured People (NAACP) in 1909, he was also an advocate of Pan-Africanism—a twentieth-century worldwide political and cultural black power movement that aimed to unite all indigenous and diaspora ethnic groups of African descent.

Du Bois borrowed the term *colour line* to represent racial discrimination and legalised segregation prevalent in American social and political life. His aim was 'to make it possible for a man to be both a Negro and an American, without being cursed and spit upon by his fellows, without having the doors of opportunity closed roughly in his face.' (ibid) For Du Bois, being both American and black is a unique identity that had been a handicap in the past but could be a strength in the future. He believed that African-Americans should embrace their African heritage while contributing to American society as 'the destiny of the race could be conceived as leading neither to assimilation nor separatism but to proud, enduring hyphenation.' (Lewis, 1993, 194–195):

> He would not Africanise America, for America has too much to teach the world and Africa. He would not bleach his Negro soul in a flood of white Americanism, for he knows that Negro blood has a message for the world. (Lewis, 1993, 143–145)

The message is to recognise the genius and humanity of the black race: Du Bois begins each chapter in *The Souls of Black Folk* with two epigraphs—one from a white poet, and one from a black spiritual—to demonstrate intellectual and cultural parity between black and white cultures.

Similar to Du Bois's protest against racism, African-American writer Mildred DeLois Taylor (1943–to date) in her 1977 Newbery Award-winning novel, *Roll of Thunder, Hear My Cry* (1976) focuses on the discrimination in education and employment faced by African-Americans in the southern states of Georgia, Alabama, Mississippi and Louisiana; these American states are called the Cotton States because of cotton plantations (17th-20th century) and chattel slavery (1776–1865), and, have been major sites of economic ruin and racial tension due to successive governments white supremacy policy and denial of political rights and economic opportunities to black citizens of America.

Taylor draws on her family history in *Roll of Thunder, Hear My Cry* and explores the life of African-Americans who are persecuted for the colour of their skin. Born in Jackson, Mississippi in 1943, Taylor is the great-granddaughter of a former slave who was the son of an African-Indian woman and a white landowner. The story in the novel is set in the cotton-growing farmlands in Mississippi almost 100 years ago and chronicles the story of an African-American Logan family who struggles against the chilling hatred and violence that surrounds them. Cassie Logan, the nine-year-old perceptive daughter of the Logan family questions the unfairness and injustices of the society they live in. Her mother, Mary Logan makes Cassie aware of the realities of intolerance:

> The whites preached that black people weren't really people like white people were, so slavery was alright. They also said that slavery was good for us because it taught us to be good Christians—like the white people. [...] But they didn't teach us Christianity to save our souls, but to teach us obedience. They were afraid of slave revolts and they wanted us to learn the Bible's teaching about slaves being loyal to their masters. But even teaching us Christianity didn't make us stop wanting to be free [...] (RTHC, 140)

Through Cassie's eyes, Taylor touches on the insidious power of white supremacy that permeates everything—from the inequalities of the education system to the corruption and rule even the basic needs such as shopping. At school, Cassie and other black children are provided worn-out textbooks; outdated castoffs from the white school with a chart that says only white kids used these books up until they were in bad condition, indicating their future uses are intended only for black students. Mary glues a piece of paper over the chart containing this racist information.

During a visit to the shops, Cassie is appalled by Barnett Mercantile, the white shop owner's behaviour who makes her and other black customers wait and serve the white clients first; Cassie reminds Barnett that they have been waiting for an hour; he tells her in racist terms to continue waiting. On another occasion, Cassie is horrified when her grandmother forces her to apologise for accidentally bumping into a white girl of her age, Miss Lillian Jean Simms. Cassie is made aware by her mother:

> White people may demand our respect, but what we give them is not respect but fear. What we give to our own people is far more important because it is given freely now you may have to call Lillian Jean 'Miss' because the white people say so, but you'll also call our own young ladies at church 'Miss' because you really do respect them. (RTHC, 142)

Even though the Logan family rails against the injustices of the society in which they live, they instil in their children a fierce sense of pride in themselves. In *Roll of Thunder, Hear My Cry* Taylor provides a true account of the deep-seated racism of the time, and highlights the significance of land possession for African-Americans in the last sentence of the novel: Cassie 'cried for T.J. For T.J. and the land'. (RTHC, 305); T.J. Avery, son of the sharecropper Avery family on the plantation gets convicted for burglary and murder of the white racist shop owner, Bernett. As regards the land, the Logan family bought two hundred acres of land in 1887, and then another two hundred acres in 1918 on a mortgage. Through his banking influence, the white landowner Harlan Granger made the Logan family pay the mortgage in full within a week even though the latter had four more years to pay it. Cassie's uncle from Chicago, Hammer Logan sells his car and other belongings to allow the Logans to pay their mortgage. Despite the end of slavery in 1865, the whites continued to control the blacks through intimidation in the United States of America. That is why, black nationalist and the founder of the Universal Negro Improvement Association and African Communities League (UNIA), Marcus Mosiah Garvey (1887–1940) established a steamship corporation, the Black Star Line in 1919 and the Negro Factories Corporation in 1920 to finance the African-American community to achieve economic independence that ensures greater protection from discrimination and provides the foundation for social justice.

As compared to Du Bois who propagated racial integration, Garvey opposed the social and economic integration of the white and black races. Garveyism promoted racial separatism and stressed black racial purity; UNIA stood for the pride and purity of race and denounced miscegenation. Garvey supported the Back to Africa movement believing Africa was the natural homeland of the African diaspora. He was influenced by the pure African blood idea propagated by Liberian black writer, Edward Wilmot Blyden (1832–1912) who articulated a notion of African Personality and the uniqueness of the African race in his work. Blyden believed in Ethiopianism, a 19th-century religious movement that strengthened Africans' faith in their heritage of ancient Egyptian and Ethiopian empires and their civilisations which had been undermined by the Europeans during colonisation. The Biblical reference, 'Princes shall come out of Egypt; Ethiopia shall haste to stretch out her hands unto God' (Psalm 68:31) gave the blacks hope to unite, control, and govern their lands and cultures. In this context, Blyden publicly supported Zionism, a political organisation established in 1897 that led to the creation of a Jewish state of Israel in 1947. Similarly, Garvey stood for collaboration between black and white separatists because of the shared common goal: the purification of both races.

I remember my youth days in Pakistan where I was born and grew up with a societal prejudice as a girl: white is beautiful. The colour of the skin as *white* was and still has been classified as a sign of beauty in the fashion arena; women of all backgrounds make an effort, though futile, to treat their darker complexions; beauty creams and bleach products have been engaged by the cosmetic manufacturers worldwide to attract women of darker complexion to buy their products which would get them a white complexion. This psychological complex of people towards the darker colour of their skin reveals the devastating impact of colonialism: exploitation, enslavement, and unequal social relations; racial discrimination depends on visible difference, and the colour of the skin proves a convenient 'signifier of discrimination'. (Bhabha, 1983, 31). As per Bhabha's notion of mimicry, the colonised, that is, the Other is drawn to mirror the customs of the coloniser, that is the Self, such an attempt is futile and leads to the possibility of protest as the former becomes both resemblance and menace to the latter. That is why, Mary Logan in *Roll of Thunder, Hear My Cry* feels the need to explain to her child, Cassie that 'white is something just like black is something. Everybody born on this earth is something and nobody, no matter what colour, is better than anybody else.' (RTHC, 139)

African-American writer Alice Malsenior Tallulah-Kate Walker (1944–to date) in her 1983 Pulitzer Prize for Fiction winner and National Book awarded novel, *The Colour Purple* (1982), highlights this colour complexity that exists in her African-American world. Set in 1930s rural Georgia, the story in the novel focuses on the life of African-American women in the Southern United States and addresses their exceedingly low position in American social culture. In one of the letters to her sister Nettie, the black protagonist Celie reveals:

> They say everybody before Adam was black. [...] the Africans throwed out the white Olinka peoples for how they look [...] the missionaries tried to make them put on clothes [...] white person can tell they naked, but black people cannot be naked because they cannot be white. (CP, 231–232)

In reply, Nettie informs Celie about her housemate Tashi who is conscious of the 'scarification marks on her cheeks: Americans would look down on her as a savage and shun her':

> [...] black people did not truly admire black-skinned black people like herself, and especially did not admire black-skinned black women. They bleach their faces, she said. They fry their hair. (CP, 235)

Earlier, Nettie had written to Celie:

> It is the picture in the bible that fool you [...] Christ had hair like lamb's wool. Lamb wool is not straight, Celie. It isn't even curly [...] we are black [...] we and the Africans will be working for a common goal: the uplift of black people everywhere. (CP, 113–115).

Sadly, most black women to date are not comfortable with their natural bushy African hair and hide it with smooth silky wigs to look acceptable and fashionable. Garvey denounced such Eurocentric beauty standards amongst blacks and found them as an impediment to black self-respect.

In this context, the 22nd Prime Minister of Pakistan (2018–2022), Imran Khan argues in his memoir, *Pakistan: A Personal History* (2011) that colonialism has wrought lasting damage by destroying the self-esteem of the subjugated people; the inferiority complex that is ingrained in a conquered nation results in its imitation of some of the worst aspects of the conquerors, while at the same time neglecting its great traditions. Similarly, West Indian French philosopher, Frantz Fanon (1925–1961) in *The Wretched of the Earth* (1961) describes the nature of colonialism as essentially destructive; its societal effects—the colonial identity and the systematic denial of all attributes of humanity—were harmful to the mental health of the natives or the *Other*.

One finds a resemblance between the real story (25 May 2020) of the white policeman kneeling on George Floyd's neck and the painting inscribed on the Royal Star medal of the highest British chivalry award—the Order of Saint Michael and Saint Goerge: an Angel—a white man standing on the neck of Devil—a black man; a display of deeply embedded notion of white superiority over other races in the world. Albert John Mvumbi Luthuli (1898–1967), South African Zulu tribal chieftain and the first African person to win the 1960 Nobel Peace Prize for his role in the non-violent struggle against apartheid, documents in his autobiography *Let My People Go* (1962): 'We Africans are depersonalised by the whites, our humanity and dignity are reduced in their imagination to the minimum. We are boys, girls, kaffirs, goof natives and bad natives.' (1962, 6)

In this context, Polish-British writer Joseph Conrad (1857–1924) was criticised by Nigerian writer Chinua Achebe (1930—2013) for dehumanising Africans in his novella *Heart of Darkness* (1899); Achebe calls Conrad 'a bloody racist' for presenting Africa as 'a metaphysical battlefield devoid of all recognisable humanity, into which the wandering European enters at his peril.' (1989, 1–20) Africa is perceived as a place of darkness in the novella, even though Charles Marlow, the English protagonist as the captain of a river steamboat for an Ivory trading company, discovers through his experience of a voyage in the Congo River that there is little difference between civilised people and those described as savages. Achebe challenges the incorrect depiction of Africa as the antithesis of Europe and civilisation which ignores the artistic accomplishments of the Fang people—the central African ethnic inhabitants of Congo.

South African writer, Beverley Naidoo (1943 to date) similarly condemns such projection of Africans as disgraceful demeaning them as if they are a little better than animals. This dehumanisation is achieved with physical and mental violence by which the coloniser inculcates a servile mentality upon the colonised. Therefore, Fanon suggests violent resistance to colonialism as a mentally cathartic practice that purges colonial servility from the native psyche and restores self-respect to the subjugated. In *Manichean Aesthetics: The Politics of Literature in Colonial Africa* (1983), Kenyan postcolonial critical theorist, Abdul R. JanMohamed (1945-to date) focuses on the African reaction to colonial images of Africa and its inhabitants which consequently has built an antagonistic relationship between colonial and African literature.

German philosopher Karl Heinrich Marx's (1818–1883) scientific explanation of society and economy is productive in understanding the nature of racism worldwide. Marxism—a collective name for the critical theories about society, economics and politics as propagated by Marx—asserts that the capitalist economic system is the root cause of the class conflict in human societies because it creates a ruling rich class (the bourgeoisie) which is allowed to control both the means of production and the working labour class (the proletariat). This paves the way for class antagonism and economic inequality which in turn influence social relations, political institutions, legal systems, cultural systems, and ideologies. Like Marx, Du Bois stressed that capitalism is a primary cause of racism and that socialism is a better path towards racial equality than capitalism. A political-economic capitalist phenomenon, the Western powers established colonies in Asia, Africa and the Americas in the sixteenth century; the French, the Dutch, and the British empires flourished in the seventeenth century followed by the Russian, the Ottoman, the Austrian, the German and the Belgian empires in the eighteenth century. Although this process of establishing colonial empires slowed down due to the American Revolutionary War (1775–1783) and the Latin American wars of independence in the nineteenth century, western powers managed to explore, conquer and exploit large areas of the world. The socio-economic Marxist dialectic that favours socialism and the establishment of a classless communist society thus views colonialism as a form of exploitation an instrument of wholesale destruction, dependency and systematic exploitation producing distorted economies, socio-psychological disorientation, and massive poverty.

Whether it was Africa or the Arab world, Asia or the Americas, native cultures and languages had always been undermined and undervalued by colonisers. Born in Calcutta and educated in England, the English journalist Mark Tully (1935-to date) records in the introduction to his book *No Full Stops in India*:

> The best way to destroy a people's culture and identity is to undermine its religion and its language. We, the British, did that as India's rulers and we continue to do that as part of the dominant culture of the world now. [...] we did not attempt to convert India into Christianity. But we did create the impression that our religion was superior to Hinduism. (1992, 4)

Like the Greek Empire of Alexander (336–323 BC), the British Empire (1707–1997) encouraged the spread of the English language, religion, science, and philosophy throughout its colonies. To promote European literature and science, the first governor-general of British India, Lord William Henry Cavendish-Bentinck (1774–1839) implemented the English Education Act of 1835 making English the medium of instruction and replacing Persian with English as the language of the higher courts.

Like the Greeks, the English considered their own culture superior to all others; they referred to people speaking foreign languages as barbarians, dismissing foreign languages as inferior mutterings. Set in Mano Majra, a fictional border village between Pakistan and India in *Train to Pakistan* (1956), Indian writer Khushwant Singh (1915–2014) describes this colonial perception in the character of an uneducated villager Juggut Singh: 'For him, education meant knowing English. Clerks and letter writers who wrote Urdu or Gurmukhi were literate, but not educated.' (TP, 108–109)

My personal experience is no different in this regard: As part of Lincoln University, United Kingdom collaboration with Saudi Arabia's Education Ministry, I was based in Al-Aflaj, Laila Town, Saudi Arabia in 2014 to teach English Language and Skills Learning programmes to Saudi students; in comparison to qualified tutors of different ethnic backgrounds like myself, white English teachers—regardless that they didn't speak queen's English—were extended much higher respect, were cherished and valued by the students and staff even at the college in Saudi Arabia desert. The colonial phenomenon has left deep-rooted prejudices in people's minds all over the world.

Prominent British Orientalist, William Jones' (1746–1794) philological work challenges this notion of Western superiority over other languages and cultures. His translation of Hindu hymns into English is one of the first popular incarnations of Eastern mythology. He found value in the heritage of the colonial *Other* and propagated the genetic relation between the Indo—European languages: Sanskrit, Greek and Latin languages have a common root, and that indeed they may all be further related, in turn, to Gothic and the Celtic languages as well as to Persian. His legacy as a linguist and scholar of native myth is an example of the shifting nature of colonial relations during the Romantic era (1800–1890) which showed a greater sense of respect for indigenous culture than the attitudes of earlier periods. His work is considered an early example of what English poet, Lord Byron (1788–1824) came to term Orientalism (the East) or what Khushwant Singh calls 'mysterious':

> Proof? We do not go in such pedestrian pastimes as proof! That is Western. We are of the mysterious East. No proof, just faith. No reason: just faith. Thought, which should be the sine qua non of a philosophical code, is dispensed with. We climb to sublime heights on the wings of fancy. We do the rope trick in all spheres of creative life... We explain the unattractive by pretending it is esoteric...there does not seem to be a code either of man or of God on which one can

> pattern one's conduct...In such circumstances, what can you do but cultivate an utter indifference to all values? (TP, 171–172)

Similar mental probing happens in Gordimer's fiction which activates an awareness amongst her white characters of their *Self*—the superiority that could be challenged and exposed. Gordimer confronts and discards her colonial Manichean heritage: the white society's patronising or abhorrent attitude to the blacks and the former's parasitic dependency on the latter. Manichaeism was a dualistic religious movement founded in Persia in the third century (AD) by a Persian prophet Mani known as the apostle of light and supreme Illuminator. Manichaeism propagated a primaeval conflict between light and darkness according to which a moral course of action involves a choice between a good—spiritual world of light, and an evil—material world of darkness. Gordimer is conscious of the nurturing of such ideological bankruptcy in her white colonial society: the *Self* (white) recognises its truth as good and the objective certainty of its existence as superior only through the negation of the *Other* (the black) as evil and inferior. In her fiction, Gordimer questions this assumed moral superiority of her white society and recognises the need for redefining the relationship between the *Self* and the *Other.* A white person born in South Africa where Manichean dichotomy is prevalent, and her relationship with the non-white South Africans an experience of a stranger, Gordimer realises that the enormous economic and political distance between the white and the non-white communities can only be bridged if both take their attitude apart and assemble afresh their ideas of themselves.

In this context, Gordimer deliberately situates her fiction within a space—a borderland—between apartheid theory and actual practice, between liberal pretence and actual callowness, and repeatedly examines the conflict between the wish to abandon and gratify personal desires and the sense of obligation towards others which ultimately forces her protagonists to protest and struggle. Gordimer's fiction simultaneously reveals the absence of and the desire for a viable, humane, and just interracial community that would free the inhabitants of South Africa from the contradictions of prevalent Manichean society. Her portrayal of black characters as distinctly different but dramatically equal to her white protagonists is an attempt to indicate a way forward in the future race relations between the white and the non-white communities in South Africa.

Motivated by my bureaucrat father—Syed Mazhar Ali Shah—and his love of the English language, I was naïve to believe, though not anymore, that English is the only language that has and can produce the best literature in the world. My father did his Master's degree in English Literature, has served in the British set provincial civil service of Pakistan, has written books and poetry, and is a newspaper columnist in both English and Urdu languages. Though the British colonial rule ended in 1947, the English language and culture are, to date, in comparison to the national language and local traditions, considered superior and followed by the elite class to divide and rule people in the sub-continent. In Khushwant Singh's words: 'We were slaves of the English, now we will be slaves of the educated Indians—or the Pakistanis.' (TP, 48). Tully observes that 'colonialism teaches the native elite it creates to admire—all too often to ape—the ways of their foreign rulers' (1992, 3):

> The upper echelons of Indian society regard English as one of the greatest gifts of the British. [...] The elite are not concerned that English has impoverished Indian languages and stood in the way of the growth of an indigenous national language. They insist that English must be preserved as the common language of multilingual India, even though less than 3 per cent of the population have even a basic understanding of it. (1992: 7–8)

For years, the English language curriculum was not upgraded by the Pakistan Education Ministry and the masses learned the language that was introduced by the British colonisers to communicate with subordinate classes of the society; the template to write a formal letter started with a phrase *Dear sir or madam, I beg to state that I need...*selected, calculated, controlled words and sentences in a servile language. Scholar of Latin American colonial discourses, Kathryn Joy McKnight in *Afro-Latino Voices: Narratives from the Early Modern Ibero-Atlantic World: 1550–1812* (2009) documents a similar formatted letter written by an Afro-Iberian woman in 1600, requesting her colonial master, the King of Spain's permission to emigrate from Europe to Spain and reunite with her daughter:

> I, Francisca de Figueroa, mulatta in colour, declare that I have, in the city of Cartagena, a daughter named Juana de Figueroa; [...] I must write to Our Lord the King to petition that he favour me with a licence, [...] I beg your Lordship to approve, and order it done. (2009, 59)

Francisca repressed her native African language and spoke her request in Peninsular Spanish, the official language of colonial Latin America. Caribbean writer, Derek Walcott (1930–2008)—the 1992 Nobel Prize

Winner—identifies this deep colonial damage: we are all strangers; our bodies think in one language and move in another. East African writer Ngugi wa Thionga's characterisation of Miriamu—a complex black female personality in his novel *The River Between* (1965) is an appropriate example in this regard: 'One could tell by her eyes that this was a religion learnt and accepted; inside the true Gikuyu woman was sleeping.' (RB, 34). Set in colonial Kenya when the British introduced Christianity and exploited the country, the novel presents a story of a struggle between two Kenyan villages over differences in faith. Miriamu retains her Gikuyu tribal spirit side by side with her Christian faith; a devout convert, she follows her husband Joshua who renounces tribal rituals and traditions in colonial Kenya and is dedicated to converting his people to Christianity that would save them from hell. 'Perhaps that was what was wrong with Joshua. He had clothed himself with a religion decorated and smeared with everything white. He renounced his past and cut himself away from those life-giving traditions of the tribe.' (RB, 141)

Focusing on the traditions of his Nigerian tribal Igbo society, Achebe similarly describes the effect of Christian influences and the clash of Western and traditional African values during the colonial era in *Things Fall Apart* (1958); the novel chronicles traditional Nigerian life and the repression of the Igbo language as well as the destruction of the native culture by the British colonisation in the nineteenth century. Whereas Jamaican writer Erna Brodber (1940–to date) debates the whitewashing and distortion of black history through religion and colonialism in a story of a young woman's cultural and spiritual struggle in colonial Jamaica in *Myal* (1988). Enough to pass for white, the light-skinned protagonist, Ella returns to Jamaica after an unsuccessful marriage abroad, zombified and devoid of any black soul. The Afro-Jamaican religion Myal which asserts that good has the power to conquer all is invoked to heal her from a mysterious illness; she has suffered a breakdown after her white American husband produced a black-face minstrel show based on the stories of her village and childhood. As a colonial experience, a sense of chaos prevails towards the end in all these stories which is captured in the presentation of the role of missionaries and the white cultural superiority complex, local responses and the divide in local reactions, the disunity amongst the colonised which benefits the coloniser to expand and rule, perceptions of each other's traditions, and colonised people's sensitivity to their culture and traditions.

Influenced by the language of the coloniser and semi-legendary ancient eighth-century (BC) Greek epic poem, Homer's *Iliad*, Walcott wrote an epic poem *Omeros* (1990) in English mimicking the *Iliad*. He defends his love of the English language by stressing the need to salvage the best of other cultures and make something new after the past slavery and colonial times. On these grounds, Sir Syed Ahmed Khan (1817–1898), an Indian Muslim social reformer in nineteenth-century British India founded an Anglo-Oriental college in 1875 (later converted to Aligarh University in 1920). It was India's first centre of Islamic and Western-style scientific education with instruction given in Oxford English.

However, there are intellectuals like Ngugi wa Thionga (1938–to date) who have challenged the supremacy of the language and culture of the coloniser and the logic that the English language and literature have a wider audience. In *The River Between,* Ngugi makes his protagonist Waiyaki get a piece of advice from his father Chege, an elder in the tribe: 'Learn all the Wisdom and all the secrets of the white man, But do not follow his vices. Be true to your people and the ancient rites.' (RB, 20) Ngugi has renounced his Christian name James Ngugi and stopped writing in English because English is not an African language so it cannot be part of the African experience. He now writes in his native Gikuyu and Swahili languages and advocates to promote African culture and literature. On similar grounds, South African academic and writer, Njabulo Simakahle Ndebele (1948-to date) creates an awareness of the changes in civilisation as regards race, ethnicity and identity in his story 'Uncle' from the collection *Fools and Other Stories* (1983); the musician uncle teaches his nephew about their African roots by explaining about hieroglyphics: 'This is the Egyptian language [...] in this language Mshana is written all the ancient wisdom of Africa. Know that. From Egypt, we gave our glory to the world. Now it is time that we got it back.' (Fools, 10)

In this atmosphere when black voices like Ngugi stress the need to protest and demand exclusive focus on native languages and literature, white South African writer, Gordimer attempts to define and defend the significance of English writing in African literature:

> My own definition is that African writing is writing done in any language by Africans themselves and by others of whatever skin colour who share with Africans the experience of having been shaped, mentally and spiritually, by Africa rather than anywhere in the world. One must look at the world from Africa, to be an African writer, not look upon Africa from the world. (Gordimer, 1972)

Gordimer was a big supporter and promoter of black writers in English both at home and worldwide. She argues that the origins of modern African literature cannot be traced back to African languages only:

> [...] the whole negro race wherever in the world history had dispersed that race-negritude, with which modern African literature began, originated not in Africa, but across the world, in the Caribbean. Its creators, Aime Cesaire, and others descended from African slaves, had never set eyes on Africa; Africa had passed, along with their African names, religions, and languages out of living memory, generations before. (ibid)

Gordimer's defence of African literature written in languages other than native, including her writings in English, projects her sense of belonging to her South African world. She attempts to transcend the Manichean dichotomy of her South African society—beyond the polarities of the superior *Self* and the inferior *Other*, though utilising the language of the coloniser to tell, inform and get her message across worldwide.

Being her mother tongue and the language of the affluent white South African class, the English language provided Gordimer with a platform to comment on the moral distance of most of her white community from the problems of the deprived natives; her substance is African. Through her sensitive gaze on the everyday lives of common South Africans, Gordimer perceives and records many facets of the human psyche; with her articulation of words and detached observation, Gordimer creates a mirror that captures the existing colonial currents of South African life. Aware of psychic repression, she attempts to unmask the unconscious aspects of colonial mentality and makes her characters appalled by various aspects of racism. When one reads Gordimer's fiction, one gets fascinated by her selection of themes and style of narration; she doesn't let one escape or ignore the grinding reality of South African life: apartheid.

Politics

What was so special about the white settlers in South Africa? Was it the colour of the skin or the application of the intellect for commercial gains or a lack of confidence in their own culture or the competition amongst the European races to colonise? What made them aware of their identity crisis in the African world? Nadine Gordimer, the white South African intellectual, through her fiction, attempted to approach these questions by portraying her white society as insignificant amongst other inhabitants in the large African landscape: she was a woman in conflict with the society of her birth and education, and, confronted the outrages committed against non-white South Africans by her white colonial and post-colonial society; systematic humiliation of non-white peoples at the hands of whites in Africa continued even after British abolished the slave trade in 1833 and even after Abraham Lincoln abolished chattel slavery in the United States of America in 1865.

Land possession lies at the heart of South Africa's colonial history and heritage of inequity. In 1652, the Dutch East India Trading Company established a refreshment station in Cape (South Africa) for passing ships. In 1657, farms were allocated to free burghers (seventeenth-century white settlers) in the surrounding Cape areas which displaced the Khoikhoi natives from their land and consolidated European land possession; the agricultural settlements of the Boers economically dislocated the pastoral Khoikhoi who were forced to serve as servants due to their loss of grazing land. Since then, indigenous lands were expropriated from their rightful owners by the white settlers—often without compensation such as The Native Location Act 1879 by the British colonisers which was the first step towards systematically depriving natives of their land that ultimately led to their impoverishment and marginalisation in South African society.

Amongst other discriminatory laws against blacks, the most severe was the Natives Land Act 1913 which codified injustice by preserving 87% of the land for the exclusive use of the white minority and 13% for use by 80% of the black population. The Act prevented blacks from purchasing, leasing or using land, except in the reserves or Bantustans—the allotted black location or territory. The Act effectively meant that access to land and other resources depended upon a person's racial classification. This legislation caused endemic overcrowding, extreme pressure on the land,

and poverty. At the birth of South African anti-apartheid revolutionary Nelson Mandela (1918–2013), the natives controlled only 7% of the land in South Africa.

Cecil Rhodes Statue—University of Cape Town (2005). 10 years later—the statue was removed on 9 April 2015 following a decolonisation protest (Rhodes Must Fall Campaign on 9 March 2015).

Racism in South Africa was not confined to the prejudice of the white settlers against the natives, it also emerged in cultural differences between the Afrikaners and the English settlers. Cecil John Rhodes (1853–1902)—an English mining magnate, an ardent imperialist and a white supremacist, and the Prime Minister of Cape Colony (1890–1896)—believed that the Anglo-Saxon race is destined to greatness: 'I contend that we are the first race in the world and that the more of the world we inhabit the better it is for the human race.' (Stead, 1902, 58). The British took over the control of the Cape colony in 1806 and introduced the first rudimentary rights for the Cape's non-white population; the Cape colony elected its first parliament in 1854 based on the multi-racial Cape Qualified Franchise; Cape European residents qualified as voters based on a universal minimum level of property ownership. The Afrikaners despised the English for the abolition of slavery and resented social change as well as the imposition of the English language and culture. To create a white country for themselves, the Afrikaners disrupted the centuries-old rhythm of the native life, similarly, the English conquest devalued the Afrikaners' culture and disturbed their master-servant relationship with the natives of South Africa.

Mistrust of the British colonial rule, resentment against taxation and economic hardships led the Afrikaners to migrate and search for new grazing lands; after the Great Trek by wagon (1835–1840), the Afrikaners settled inland, forming the Boer republics of Transvaal and Orange Free State. The discovery of diamonds in 1867 and gold in 1884 led to the struggle between the white settlers and the natives and between the Afrikaners and the English to control these important economic resources. The Boer Republics successfully resisted British encroachments during the first Anglo-Boer War (1880–1881) but the British defeated them in the second Anglo-Boer War (1899–1902). In reconciliation and to maintain white supremacy rule in South Africa, both the English and the Afrikaners united under a Union (self-governing dominion of the British Empire) in 1910—the former to progress as the master of industry and the latter in control of political power.

Long before this formation of the Union of South Africa with the Cape and Natal colonies, and, the Boer republics of Orange Free State and Transvaal, the English introduced discriminatory rules and legislations such as the Pass Law 1906 which meant that blacks could not be employed by any white farmer, minor or industrialist without a pass. In 1907, the house/hut tax was levied on all members of the population which compelled the black population to seek work in white-owned businesses. General Louis Botha (1862–1919), the second Anglo-Boer War hero and the first Prime Minister of the Union (1910–1919) introduced a policy of formal segregation curtailing the rights of the black majority. The Mines and Works Act of 1911 legislated that black workers could only be engaged as cheap semi-skilled labourers and effectively prohibited them from seeking skilled work. In 1914, The National Party under its Boer founder and the third Prime Minister of the Union (1924–1939), General J. B. M. Hertzog (1866–1942) dedicated itself to racial separation and the belief that eligibility to vote as a right belongs to whites only and electoral privileges are not to be extended to blacks. Racism and segregation thus increasingly restricted the lives of black South Africans; slavery was replaced by Master and Servant laws that preserved a social hierarchy in which race closely corresponded to class. Apartheid was a product of these earlier racial prejudices and policies imposed by European and British settlers; from the colonial occupation of the Cape in 1652 and following land dispossession, economic impoverishment, and exclusion from the citizenship of blacks through the creation of the Union of South Africa and the segregation period (1910–1948) are the historical roots of apartheid in South Africa.

Afrikaner Army General J M B Hertzog Statue in Union Building—Pretoria (2005)

Gordimer's fiction provides a platform to explore the hollowness of apartheid in South Africa that legalised the colonial concepts of the *Self* and the *Other* as a definite and absolute reality. Both her short stories and novels challenge the notion of physical and cultural boundaries that colonialism had promoted and question the generated social and political Western ideas of racial divisions in the colonised world. For instance, eighteenth-century English physician Charles White (1728–1813) promoted institutional racism by formalising his theory that all organisms—from plants to animals to humans—are created in gradations. Therefore, non-white races are inferior and primitive due to their skin pigmentation, and women resemble the darker races because their bodies reveal areas of darker pigmentation. The nineteenth-century pseudo-scientific studies of racial hierarchical ideology perceived African women's genitals as of mandrills, baboons, and monkeys, differentiating colonised Africans from what was viewed as the features of the evolutionarily superior, European woman. The question of biological racial difference contributed to the emergence of the *Self*—the coloniser as superior, and the *Other*—the colonised as inferior in culture and civilisation.

German philosopher, G.W.F. Hegel's (1770–1831) master-slave dialectic also shed light on the colonisers' attempt to assert a superiority and inferiority relationship between the races based on this argument: the objective and subjective states of consciousness assimilate and realise the self as a foreign object. Each can choose to ignore the other, in which case no self-consciousness forms and each views the other merely as an animated object rather than an equivalent subject. Known for his absolute idealism, Hegel argues that cultures have stages in the course of the historical unfolding of the Absolute, and those cultures which lag in their development, need Christian-European stewardship to mature towards civilisation. In the Scramble for Africa (1870–1914), the native empires of the Ashanti (Ghana) and the Benin (Nigeria), and, the African kingdoms of Dahomey (Benin), Buganda (Uganda) and Kongo were annexed by the European colonisers under the pretext that these native African civilisations required, in Hegel's terminology, Christian-European stewardship. In 1883, French academic artist, William Adolphe Bouguereau (1825–1905) painted a white woman with several white and black children clinging to her titled, 'The Motherland and her dependent colonial offspring.' This self-claimed superiority and motherhood continue to exist in the form of Commonwealth nations in the contemporary world, though it had previously generated a set of unequal relationships between the colonisers and the colonised.

In this context, French Orientalist, Joseph Ernest Renan (1823–1892) in *La Réforme intellectuelle et morale* (1871) asserts that both the coloniser and the colonised have an assigned cultural identity, a social place, and an economic role within an imperial colony:

> The regeneration of the inferior or degenerate races, by the superior races is part of the providential order of things for humanity; Nature has made a race of workers, the Chinese race, who have wonderful manual dexterity, and almost no sense of honour; govern them with

> justice, levying from them, in return for the blessing of such a government, an ample allowance for the conquering race, and they will be satisfied; a race of tillers of the soil, the Negro; treat him with kindness and humanity, and all will be as it should; a race of masters and soldiers, the European race; Let each do what he is made for, and all will be well. (Williams and Chrisman, 1993, 175)

With this prejudiced mindset, the European powers justified their colonisation of the Far East and the Scramble for Africa; Belgium, Britain, France and Germany proffered theories of national superiority that justified colonialism as delivering the light of civilisation to unenlightened colonised peoples. In the Introduction to his book, *The Heart of India* (1996), Tully writes:

> Britain ruled India, but it did not colonise it. The British Raj did not encourage settlers. Settlers might set a bad example and 'go native', destroying the carefully nurtured image of difference, and hence the superiority, of the British race. The Raj, it was thought, depended on that image of superiority to enable it to rule so many with a few. (vii).

German Nazi theorist, Alfred Rosenberg (1892–1946) promoted his master race ideology on claims that the natives of Atlantis—a mythical Greek island—were a powerful white race of blond supermen who conquered Northern Europe where their descendants still live. Rosenberg termed them Aryan. With secrets of civilisation that they had achieved through superior muscle, intellect and science, the Aryans are destined to uplift barbarians and the primitive nations of the world; Rosenberg placed blacks and Jews at the very bottom of the ladder while at the very top stood the white Aryan race. Such a self-ascribed civilising mission led the colonisers to believe that their race and culture have a higher purpose in life which gives them the right to colonise other peoples, in service to the noble idea of civilisation and its economic benefits.

To make sense of the idea of 'higher' and 'lower' cultures, the founder of the doctrine of positivism that determines a systematic and hierarchical classification of all sciences into five groups—astronomy, physics, chemistry, biology, and sociology, French philosopher Auguste Comte (1798–1857) divided civilisations into the Primitive, the Barbarian, and the Civilised; society undergoes three phases, the first is Theological stage in which man's place in society and society's restrictions upon man are referenced to God; he believes in a supernatural and in whatever he is taught by his ancestors. Secondly, the Metaphysical stage involves investigation because people start reasoning and questioning; this stage of the investigation is the beginning of a world that questions authority and religion. Lastly, the Positive or scientific stage is when people find solutions to social problems and bring them into force despite the proclamations of human rights or prophecy of the will of God. Science providing answers, however, makes the whole argument of European cultural superiority questionable; it becomes difficult to accept that what had been considered primitive and barbarian in the East, and Africa in particular, had already evolved in the West at the time of European colonisation! The fact is that long before the modern colonisation, civilisations of North America, Australia, and New Zealand did exist and flourished like the Mughal Empire in India and the Incas in the Americas. Colonialism, therefore, was not an extension of civilisation as ideologically believed by the colonisers to justify their self-ascribed superiority, both racial and cultural over the colonised people. To consider European civilisation as superior to other cultures is, therefore, a fallacy.

In concordance with the French philosopher, Michel Foucault's (1926–1984) concept of inseparable power-knowledge binary relation, that is, power produces reality through accepted forms of knowledge, Palestinian American postcolonial intellectual, Edward Said (1935–2003) challenges the West representing the East as backward, inferior, irrational, savage, haunting, wild and uncivilised in comparison to the former as superior, progressive, rational and civil—the reason associated with the West only. Focusing mostly on East Asia and the Arab world in *Orientalism* (1978), Said presents the Western representation of the *Other* as a system of knowledge that leads to stereotyping: construction of the identities of colonised people and land as undeveloped, primitive, and immature; the colonisers rejected cultural compromises with the colonised people because they were convinced of their superiority and their ordained mandate to rule. English writer of adventure fiction, Henry Rider Haggard (1856–1925) in his imperialist romance *King Solomon's Mines* (1887) portrays his white protagonists, the three Englishmen on a treasure hunt, as the statues of conscience and bravery against the wild African life: the selected race who must become a guide to the barbarians of the world. Set in the exotic African landscape, the protagonists develop a friendship with Ignosi, the rightful African King of Kukuanaland and help him not only regain his throne but abolish witch-hunts and arbitrary capital punishment in his kingdom. This creation of a dominant and subordinate dynamic—the us-and-them paradigm—allowed colonisers to reinforce a physical mapping of the world, creating a visual separation between *us* and *them*; the Europeans used a set of rules in their formation of boundaries which led to ethnocentrism; portraying their ethnicity as central whereas the unexplored areas were mapped as blank spaces—renamed and redefined to control colonised people and their lands. In this context, the Othering is a tool that provides a separate entity to persons or groups who are labelled as different or not normal. It is the creation of those who discriminate to distinguish, label, and categorise those who do not fit in their societal norm. In response to this visual coding of difference and identity formation through the *Self* and the *Other* trajectories, Achebe's *Things Fall Apart* (1958) is the pioneer novel in English which—according to Wole Soyinka, the first sub-Saharan African recipient of the 1986 Nobel Prize in Literature—'spoke from the interior of the African character, rather than portraying the African as an exotic, as the white man would see him.' (2001, 28–29). Translated in more than fifty languages, *Things Fall Apart* deals with the misconception that African culture is savage and primitive and portrays Western culture as arrogant and ethnocentric which attempted to invade African culture and civilisation in the colonial era.

The roots of twentieth-century politics in South Africa lie in previous centuries, especially the nineteenth century. This was the time when racial discourse emerged, and social imagination was driven towards activism in resistance to colonialism. At the end of the nineteenth century, the doctrine of white superiority was asserted and to a great extent enforced in practice throughout the world; the superiority complex of pseudoscientific ideology that whites are biologically and intellectually superior to non-white peoples led white intellectuals to allow their fellow beings to commit harsh cruelties towards the non-whites which are amongst the heaviest counts in the indictment against humanity. For instance, savage atrocities were committed by the Belgian colonisers in Congo (1885 to 1908); countless natives were killed, tortured, and mutilated; the right hand of the native was cut off as punishment for not fulfilling the given labour task. Another example is the detention of the Kikuyu tribe in concentration camps by the British colonisers in Kenya (1920–1963); millions of natives were systematically tortured and assaulted during the Mau Mau war of independence from the British rule (1952–1960). On another occasion, the British did not provide food supplies to India during the Second World War and let millions of natives die in Bengal (1943–45), to mention a few.

Following the defeat of far-right Nazi Party leader and Chancellor of Germany, Adolf Hitler (1889–1945) and his ambitions of creating a blue-eyed blond hair master race, South Africa was the only avowedly and systematically racist minority government remaining in the world after the Second World War. Its laws, policies and practices were not only crushingly oppressive to most of its citizens but they also constituted a standing insult to the rest of the human race who allowed this phenomenon to continue for such a long time. Gordimer's fiction reveals a certain consciousness of that attitude, that is, awareness of the excess of the German Nazi history (1920–1945) repeating itself in twentieth-century South Africa. Experimenting with the form of language, she constructs her plots by transforming history into fiction, though history itself is fiction and debatable. The historical event is represented in a discourse that is somehow beyond control, though it initiates unique meaning, allowing Gordimer to go beyond the historical hypothesis, and serves to create, to invent and even to guess in her imaginary plots the future of South Africa. The characters get introduced to a different perspective on their South African lives, that is, the black-and-white society between white and black people in South Africa. Gordimer stitches together history, imagination, fact, and fiction to describe her South Africa.

Borders

A world of physical borders and mental barriers existed and still exists between and within communities all over the globe. For instance, Japanese racial segregation of the *Buraku* community in Japan. During the feudal Tokugawa era in the seventeenth century (1603–1868), the *Buraku* community, also known as *Eta*—meaning 'unclean'—were involved in occupations like leather-making which were thought to be unclean by the Buddhists and Japanese indigenous religion *Shinto* followers; they believed that anything which involved the taking of life was unclean. Since then, discrimination against the *Buraku* community codified to distinguish them as *Eta* and *Hinin*—meaning 'non-person'; the *Etas* were forced to dispose of dead cattle or take work as animal hide tanners and other leather-related crafts whereas the *Hinin* became security guards and executioners. Specific rules were established limiting the types of clothes and hairstyles that Buraku could wear, rendering them easily identifiable. Buraku people were prohibited from entering towns at night or frequenting certain religious sites. Their gravestones were also marked with names connecting them to slavery or cattle. The *Buraku* system was officially abolished by the Emancipation Edict of 1871, and successive governments introduced reforms to counter this discrimination against the *Buraku* community in Japan.

The Hindu caste system propagated racial segregation for more than two thousand years in the Indian sub-continent. It divided the Hindu community into four occupational groups (varnas): the *Brahmins* (priests and teachers), the *Kshatriyas* (rulers and soldiers), the *Vaisyas* (merchants and traders), and the *Shudras* (labourers and artisans). A fifth category 'untouchable' or *Dalit* fell outside this varna system and was placed at the very bottom of this caste hierarchy. These differences in status were justified by the religious doctrine of karma, a belief that one's place in life is determined by one's deeds in previous lifetimes.

Economically marginalised, the *Dalit* community both in India and Nepal suffered social ostracization and punitive violence; they were not allowed to cross the line dividing their area of living from that occupied by higher castes. They could not visit the same temples, or drink from the same cups in tea stalls. They were forbidden from performing marriage or funeral rites in public areas and, in some areas, from speaking to members of upper castes. They lived in extreme poverty, without land or opportunities for better employment or education; their jobs included the most menial tasks as human waste disposal, clearing carcasses, leather workers, street sweepers, cobblers; *Chamars* as drum beaters, beggars, hawkers and shoemakers, *Pallen* as landless labourers, *Dhobis* as washers, *Coolies* as porters and *Dasis* as house servants.

Dalit children made up most children sold into bondage to pay off debts to upper-caste creditors. Countless *Dalit* girls were ceremonially dedicated or married to a deity or a temple. Once dedicated, they were forced to become prostitutes for upper-caste community members, and eventually auctioned into an urban brothel. Along with those from the prostitution caste, *badi,* most *Dalit* women and girls got driven to prostitution also due to exploitative wages and little subsistence earnings. The practice of untouchability and the imposition of social barriers on persons because of birth into a particular caste was abolished in the constitution of India in 1950 which paved the way for the implementation of a policy of quotas in education and government jobs to uplift the social and economic status of Dalit Community in India. Whereas Nepal's 1990 constitution prohibited discrimination based on caste, religion, race, sex, and ideology.

Similarly, the successive governments in Sri Lanka launched development and social welfare programmes to integrate the Sinhala lower caste *Rodiya* and Indian-origin untouchable Tamil communities into mainstream society. The Prevention of Social Disabilities Act 1957 made it an offence in Sri Lanka to deny access to various public places to persons because of their caste. The 1978 constitution prohibited discrimination on the grounds of caste, including caste-based restrictions on access to shops, public restaurants, hotels, places of public entertainment, and places of worship of one's religion.

As an aspect of a feudal society, the majority Sinhala community in Sri Lanka segregated people according to their descent and blood or according to their hereditary roles and functions. The *Rodiyas* or *Rodi*—meaning filth—in the Sinhalese caste system were condemned to a degraded life; they were denied land, and work and excluded from villages and communities, forcing them into street begging, scavenging, and roving. The *Rodiyas* were made to only wear caste-specific attire, restricted from schools and public facilities, segregated at gravesites, and made to drink out of disposable coconut shells from local teashops so as not to contaminate the glasses of others. They resided in segregated communities with little to no interaction with upper castes.

Whereas the minority Tamil community in Sri Lanka segregated its people into ones with ancestors in the country and others with Indian origin, that is, the untouchables who were brought from India by the British colonial government in the eighteenth century as captive labour to work in plantations and as domestic, and attendants; *Pallas* and *Nalavas* work on upper-caste land for wages whereas *Paraiyars* are predominantly engaged in unclean sanitation work. These Indian-origin Tamils were oppressed and faced severe social discrimination; a person of higher-caste would not touch food offered by an untouchable and the intermarriage between upper-caste and lower-caste persons was socially discouraged. Though the untouchables had resided in the country for more than a century, they only became citizens through registration; they were denied the right to citizenship by descent to which the rest of the Sri Lankan population were entitled.

Rules of racial segregation rigidly structured the societies in Africa such as the *Wolof* community—the largest ethnic group in West African country Senegal. *Wolof* Senegalese are divided into two main racial groups, the superior and noble, *Geer* and the inferior and lower caste, *Neeno*. The former comprised farmers, fishermen, warriors, and animal breeders whereas the latter comprised artisans *(Jeff-lekk)*, griots and jesters *(Sab-lekk)*, and servants and courtesans *(Noole)*. The artisans are further divided into four sub-castes: blacksmiths or jewellers, shoemakers, woodcutters, and weavers. Beneath the *Neeno* is the category of *Jaam* or slaves—like Dalits in India—who are deemed to be outside the grouping system.

Like *Neeno* in Senegal, *the Osu* ethnic group of the *Igbo* community in another West African country Nigeria suffered marginalisation, were shunned as pariahs, and denied social equality. They were considered inferior beings because their ancestors were offenders who were cast away to avoid the anger of the earth Deity and to prevent the spread of abomination amongst the people of the land; these outcasts were either sold to slavery to other men or were delivered to be enslaved to certain deities who were believed to ask for human sacrifice during festivals to clean the land from the abomination. Mostly landless, the *Osu* people were allowed only to marry within their caste and were buried in separate cemeteries. A marriage to an Osu by a non-Osu was condemned by society whilst children of such a union were ostracised and mistreated. Since the 1950s, both Senegalese and Nigerian governments abolished these prevalent segregated systems and introduced constitutional reforms that prohibit all acts of racial, ethnic, and religious discrimination and provide equal protection of the law to all citizens regardless of race, religion, sex, or origin.

Besides West African *Fulani, Mandinka, Soninke* and *Halpular* communities in Africa, caste-based divisions were central to several ethnic groups in other parts of Africa such as Burkina Faso, Mali, Cameroon, Mauritania, Guinea, Guinea Bissau, the Ivory Coast, Gambia, Sierra Leone, Liberia, Burundi, and Mauritius. The Arab and Afro-Mauritanian groups distinguished their community members based on caste such as a slave distinction for Arabic-speaking Sub-Saharan African origin—*Haratin* (black Moors).

At a time when racial groupings and practices had been outlawed and banned through national and international constitutional guarantees, and legislations enforced to tackle human rights violations worldwide, the South African Population Registration Act of 1950 made it incumbent upon all South Africans to register themselves as members of any one of the classified groups, Europeans, Bantu, and Coloureds. As a product of racist thinking, this stereotyping created stigma, social distance, and terror amongst different races in South Africa. Like a caste system, Apartheid was created in layers—layers within layers: white versus black; Coloured versus black, Indian versus black with further sub-classifications in each grouping. This has, in Gordimer's words, 'undermined our ability to grow as a people, to adapt to the changing demands of society and to deal with the challenges of living together as people of different backgrounds and cultural identities.' (Villa-Vicencio, 1996, 110) Gordimer called herself 'a white African' to identify with the black struggle and opt out of apartheid classifications. (Villa-Vicencio, 1996, 104)

Since the colonisation in the sixteenth century, the racial grouping of South African people followed the organised practice of European settlers in South Africa and other continents. Numerous race classifications are peculiar to South Africa. Numerous terms have acquired special and generally racist meanings. The main examples are Coolie, Kaffir, Coloured, Bantu, Native and African. All these have been replaced, initially by non-white and later by black. Though the subsequent polarisation between Coloureds and blacks, and, Indians and blacks and the granulation of these differences are missing in her stories and novels, Gordimer's fiction does show her sensitivity to this field.

The usage of the word *Coolie* dates back to 1548. It originates from two different words, Koli which was the name of an aboriginal tribe in Gujarat, India, and the Tamil word, Kuli which means hire. By 1819, it was used for a porter, bearer or other unskilled labourers in South Africa. The term appeared in provincial regulations which were introduced in 1827 in Cape Town to establish control on rates of pay and working hours for Coolies. In 1831, a Tariff of Coolie Hire was introduced, followed by a list of classifications in 1855; Coolies were then 477 in number in the Classified Census of Cape Town (1854) list.

The term Coolie became more specialised after 1860 when Indian Coolies were imported from India to work on the sugar plantations in the Natal province in South Africa. The term Kaffir Coolie was in vogue to describe black casual labourers till 1861. In 1866, a Coolie Certificate was introduced to list new categories such as wharf Coolie, fish Coolie and market Coolie. In 1868, Chinese workers were imported to work as miners in the diamond mines. After 1870, the Indians and the Chinese worked as labourers but only the Indians were termed as Coolies.

According to the *South African Concise Oxford Dictionary* (2002), a Coolie was an unskilled native labourer in Eastern countries. Although it was used for a porter employed on the statutory tariff in South Africa, it had a derogatory connotation when referring to Indians, not necessarily labourer or menial; by 1955, Coolie was used for all Indians whether merchants or barristers. In 1967, the Asians bitterly resented the labelling Coolies for them just as the blacks objected to their description as Kaffir. By 1971, to say that a Coolie is a South African Indian was an insult to the Indians. The word was used in colonial times to hurt and to give offence. In the short story 'Abroad' (1972), Gordimer describes this complexity in the attitude of her white protagonist who reluctantly agrees to share a room in the hotel with an Indian.

In twentieth-century South Africa, Europeans were identified as people with a white complexion in South Africa. The term white was defined as a 'person who in appearance obviously is, or who is generally accepted as white, but does not include a person who, although in appearance a white person, is generally accepted as a Coloured person.' So 'a person who in appearance is a white person shall for the Act be presumed to be a white person until the contrary is proved.' (Suzman, 1960, 354) In the novel, *The Conservationist* (1978), Gordimer satirises the terms of the classification by leading her white protagonist to sexually involve with a pale black girl who looks whiter than the usual olive colour.

The whites in South Africa were divided into two main groups, English-speaking and Afrikaans-speaking. The former stood for whites whose mother tongue was English whereas the latter were termed Afrikaners, a term that replaced Boer by the Dutch settlers for themselves. In Gordimer's novel, *The Late Bourgeois World* (1966), the parents of the protagonist's husband belong to these groups. As the English term, African represented dark-skinned Negroid people, the blacks had reservations about the coinage of the term Afrikaner by the Afrikaans-speaking whites who 'refused to be assimilated into African culture and believe that geography is all that they need to justify the label "Afrikaner".' (Mphahlele, 1962, 14)

Recognising the blacks' support for the usage of the term African for themselves only, the Afrikaans-speaking whites avoided the statutory recognition of the term so as not to endanger the credibility of the terms Afrikaner or Afrikaans. In Afrikaans, the distinction swart mense (black people) anticipated the modern term black but was restricted to South Africans of Negroid (Niger-Congo speaking) type. Instead, the term Bantu which means people was adopted by the Afrikaners for the classification of the Negroid people of Southern and Central Africa. They were subdivided according to their community origins: North Sotho, South Sotho, Swazi, Tsonga, Tswana, Venda, Xhosa, and Zulu. Bantu was also utilised as a collective name for the languages spoken by these groups.

The term native was in common use for the description of blacks before the formation of the Union of South Africa in 1910. The ANC was named as South African Native National Congress at its foundation. A native in South African terminology means 'any member of an aboriginal race or tribe of Africa'. (Suzman, 1960, 348) In the vocabulary of nineteenth-century South Africa, the term negro or nigger, meaning a member of the dark-skinned indigenous peoples of Africa, was in extensive use for the description of a black person. Alongside, the term Kaffir from Qafir, for any heathen or non-believer in Arabic, was used initially for the Xhosa people but later it was extended to all black groups.

The usage of all these terms for the identification of blacks by the Europeans carried offensive connotations and were objectionable on political and linguistic grounds in twentieth-century Africa. The replacement term Bantu was no better substitute for the former terminology. Blacks preferred to be called black which meant a member of any but the white group; Africanism excluded Indians and Coloureds but the Black Consciousness Movement in the 1960s was keen to incorporate them as blacks. (February, 1981, 130) Since then, Indians and Coloureds identified themselves as blacks.

Coloured referred in colonial times to a person who is not white or a native. It was used by the whites for a person of mixed ancestry speaking either Afrikaans or English as a mother tongue, and for Indonesian Muslim immigrants. The Coloureds were sub-divided according to their community origins: Griqua, Chinese, Cape Coloureds, that is, the product of miscegenation in Western Cape since the arrival of the Dutch in 1652 till the present, other Coloureds who were not included in the Cape Coloured group (the Cape Coloureds formed African Political Organisation in 1902 and enjoyed limited voting rights till they were removed from the common electoral roll in 1956. As compared to other Coloureds, they were educated and had more opportunities to contribute towards the betterment of their community), Malay who were the descendants of Javanese political prisoners, removed to South Africa by the Dutch East India Company in the seventeenth century, skilled Indonesian Muslim craftsmen as well as free slaves who embraced Islam, and other various groups of Asian descent. Referring to all these different racial groups as Coloured in The South African Population Registration Act of 1950 was a racist move by the Afrikaner government. These groups preferred to be named South Africans rather than Coloureds which carried an insulting and negative connotation.

Apartheid and the historical scenario

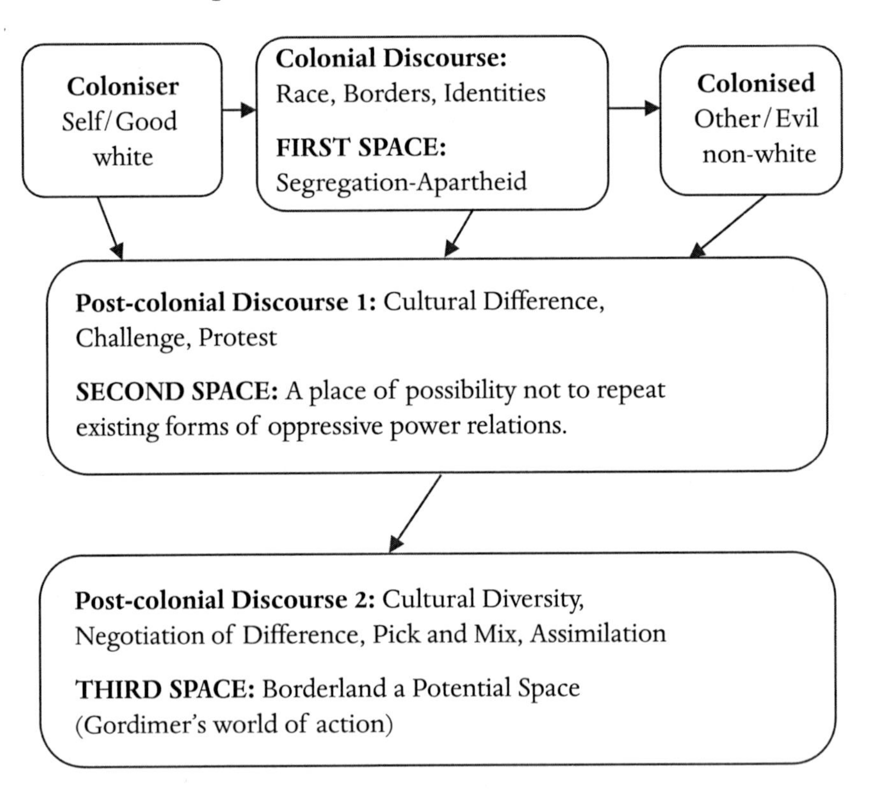

What is so unique about racial segregation in South Africa is that it kept clinging to the colonial discourse of cultural differences and separateness of communities in the form of apartheid till the end of the twentieth century. By that time, the rest of the world had already entertained post-colonial discourse of cultural diversity and multiculturalism paving the way for the third possibility—a hybrid society.

The concept of borderland finds much recognition in colonial and post-colonial societies respectively. As colonial civilisation tended to produce definite boundaries, the white colonisers treated the non-white peoples of the colonies as the *Other* to socially construct them as removed, distant and lesser individuals who were serviceable to cater to the former's needs, values and interests thus destroying the latter's self-esteem once for all; to establish traditions of mastery and control involved the setting up of boundaries which required inventing of traditions of subordination as well as all sorts of fixities of identity in the colonial world. South Africa stood out as the only country in which racism had been established to an extent rarely known before, codified and brutally enforced: this goes back to segregation under the Constitution of South Africa in the 1910 Act of Union and Dominion status under the Statute of Westminster 1930 which brought independence from British colonial rule but that gave suffrage and power to white South Africans only, and, then the 1948 election which imposed apartheid—segregation by political as well judicial decision, socially implying contempt for non-white South Africans.

This discriminatory attitude of the white South African minority towards the majority non-white South African community has been debated in literary circles worldwide but not so openly within South Africa. Key concepts like Diaspora (dispersion of people from their original homeland), Fanonism (anti-colonial liberationist critique), Imperialism (expansion by conquest), Manicheanism (good and evil dichotomy), Mimicry (imitate to ridicule), Negritude (an affirmation of the value of black or African culture and identity), Orientalism (a representation of Asia/East embodying a colonialist stereotyping attitude), Transculturalism (extending through all human cultures), to mention a few, influenced the post-colonial intellectual arena: the French psychoanalyst Octave Mannoni (1899–1989) challenged and attributed complex to the coloniser, the Afro-Caribbean French poet Aime Cesaire (1913–2008) focused on the power of colonialism to exploit and dehumanise, the West Indian French philosopher Frantz Fanon (1925–1961) stressed self-liberation and spoke of remapping class divisions, the Jamaican British cultural theorist Stuart Hall (1932–2014) recognised the colonial experience as one which breaks one down and creates identity crisis, the Palestinian American cultural critic, Edward Said (1935–2003) challenged West representing East, the Indian Marxist philosopher Ajaz Ahmed (1932-to date) described post-colonialism as a new form of colonialism, and Indian literary theorist Gayatri Chakravorty Spivak (1942-to date) critiqued race with nationality and supported rewriting of history and silenced voices, and, many more.

However, in South Africa, discourses on race, borders and identities have been entertained in fictional writings which can easily be traced back to the earliest period of British colonisation of the African land.

South African Literature

Known as the father of South African poetry, Thomas Pringle (1789–1834) was the first English writer who described the South African landscape, native peoples, and living conditions in his writings. In a journalistic form, South African English writings first appeared on the literary horizons in the eighteenth century, mostly non-fictional in the shape of diaries, chronicles of white missionaries, memoirs, and traveller's tales about the unique African world. Fictional realism in the pastoral tradition appeared in Olive Shreiner's *The Story of an African Farm House* (1881), the first South African novel in English. Shreiner (1855–1920) addresses discourses of race and gender through the themes of love, marriage, and motherhood: the tragic view of life derives from despair about the efficacy of the liberal impulse; the female protagonist Lyndall revolts against oppression by her shallow white frontier society.

Continuing the pastoral tradition, Pauline Smith (1882–1959) captures the poor life of the Afrikaners in the South African landscape in *The Little Karoo* (1925); her stories focus on the hard life that the Afrikaners had to bear due to economic depression after the conflicts with the natives and the British occupation. The same theme is later approached by Doris Lessing in *The Grass Is Singing* (1950); the novel presents a detailed picture of poverty which was then prevalent amongst white farmers in Africa. Lessing (1919–2013) brings into light the psychological impact of constant economic hardships and the contradictions which existed between the English and the Afrikaners over their sense of identity and belonging to Africa.

Sarah Gertrude Millin (1889–1968) and William Plomer (1903–1973) deal with the theme of racism innovatively. Both Millin's *God's Step Children* (1924) and Plomer's *Turbott Wolf* (1929) stand as politicised literature, the former focuses on the theme of miscegenation whereas the latter presents social realism as a mode of protest against racism. The white protagonist Reverend Andrew Flood in *God's Step Children* — a missionary marries a native Hottentot woman who gives birth to their racially mixed child. The Reverend is disappointed at the futility of his efforts as he doesn't succeed in converting the natives to Christianity, even though he has mingled himself with their ways of life. Whereas *Turbott Wolf* presents miscegenation not as a problem to be solved, but as a solution to South African problems. The protagonist Friston, a missionary is obsessed with a vision:

> Mostly of the future South Africa [...] I look forward to the great compromise between white and black: between civilisation and barbarism, between the past and the future, between brains and bodies [...] between habit and instinct. (TF, 102)

Friston goes mad in the end as he cannot stand up to his vision in real South African life; miscegenation meant mixing what should not be mixed—displaying the prevalent rigid South African racial framework.

Adding to social realism his liberal humanist standpoint, Alan Paton (1903–1988) continued this tradition of protest literature in *Cry the Beloved Country* (1948). Here, a Zulu parson Stephen Kumalo comes to Johannesburg and finds that the environment has forced his sister Gertrude to become a prostitute and his son Absalom a murderer. The pastor's sufferings epitomise the sufferings of his race: native crime due to social instability, moral issues due to the disintegration of the tribal system, and flight to urban areas due to the degrading of the land reserved for the natives. The novel is a social protest against the structures of society that would later give rise to apartheid. At the same time, the novel mocks the prevalent Christian spirit:

> The truth is that our Christian civilisation is riddled through and through with dilemma. We believe in the brotherhood of man, but we do not want it in South Africa [...] believe in help for the underdog but we want him to stay under. (CBC, 238)

The Christian traditions in South Africa emerged in three ways: the Dutch Reformed Church tradition which the Afrikaners followed, the Anglican Church across the Protestant-Catholic divide that the English-speaking community believed, and the missionary tradition that is rooted in independent indigenous churches as followed by Kumalo in the novel. The missionary education in Africa is questioned in Ngugi's *The River Between* as well:

> Waiyaki knew that not all the ways of the white man were bad. Even his religion was not essentially bad. [...] But the religion [...] had to be reconciled to the traditions of the people. [...] A religion that takes no account of people's way of life, a religion that did not recognise spots of beauty and truths in their way of life, was useless. [...] It would

> only maim a man's soul, making him fanatically cling to whatever promised security, otherwise, he would be lost. (RB, 151)

Amongst others, Dan Jacobson (1929–2014) combined social realism and political awareness with the pastoral tradition in *The Trap* (1955) and *A Dance in the Sun* (1956). It appears that South African writing had always been influenced by the politics of race: Roy Campbell (1901–1957), Herman Charles Bosman (1905–1951), Van der Post (1906–1996), Gay Butler (1918–2001), John Coetzee (1940-to date), Athol Fugard (1932-to date), Andre Brink (1935–2015), and, Beverley Naidoo (1943-to date), to mention a few, in their respective capacities, attempted to describe and question South African life they lived. Gordimer was no different from her predecessors. She combined the vision of early writers and created a mode of urban realism to record the frustrations, insecurities, and humiliation that South Africans suffered in their daily lives due to segregation and apartheid. Chronologically, Gordimer's fiction emerged from twentieth-century South Africa and was immersed in it. The theme of borderland in her fiction is like a no-mans-land to project a society—the South African society which had all other doors of expression closed to it and grappled with the threats of cultural domination and political oppression.

Writing by non-white writers in South African English literature had been sparse before the 1950s. Whatever little that was produced such as RRR Dhlomo's *An African Tragedy* (1928)—the first novel in English by a Zulu writer, and, Solomon Tshekisho Plaatje's *Mhudi* (1930), heavily relied on English models nurtured by mission schools. Dhlomo (1901–1971) followed the tradition of social realism whilst Plaatje (1876–1932)—the founder member of the South African Native National Congress (SANNC) which became the African National Congress (ANC), built his fiction on romance tradition. During the 1950s, the *Drum* encouraged writing by black writers such as Ezekiel Mphahlele (1919–2008), Can Themba (1924–1968), Lewis Nkosi (1936–2010), Nat Nakasa (1937–1965); they followed American models of writing, and their fiction was impressionistic, racy but readable.

By 1960, several non-white South African writers had emerged on the literary scene: Alex La Guma (1924–1985), Bessie Head (1937–1986), Mongane Serote (1944-to date), Njabula Ndebele (1948-to date), Zoe Wicombe (1948-to date), Mda Zakes (1948-to date), and Peter Abrahams (1919–2017)—the first coloured novelist in English, to mention a few. These writers actively took part in the anti-apartheid struggle; La Guma acknowledged racial segregation as an important problem that defined his artistic vision (1975, 17). Although there was a barrier between the white and non-white peoples in South African society, and they looked at each other through a 'keyhole' (Mphahlele, 1962, 14), Gordimer with her privileged white eyes found room for dealing with issues of rigid boundaries in her fiction.

Along with the theme of racial conflict or the colour bar that dominates South African literature, there exists a powerful sense of the place:

> [...] the feel of a vast and varied canvas [...] can smell the location streets, the rich suburban gardens, the limitless veld [...] The writing, whether political or not, is all intensely South African, close to the earth, written in a language which seems, almost as much as in the days of Olive Shreiner, to have come out of the landscape. (Gordimer, 1967,12)

To entertain the English 'themes of intimate relationships, sensitive childhoods, fantasy or nostalgia' was not possible for South African writers because 'people out there seem always larger or smaller than life, as in a Dickens' novel. Every African writer is faced with the bizarre backcloth of location life, a territory as full and dangerous as Shakespeare's London.' (ibid) The single point of focus in South African literature, therefore, has always been how the white and non-white races view each other and what has been their identity in each other's world: from Shreiner to Gordimer, and from Plaatje to Abrahams, for instance, both white and non-white South African writers deal with the question of identity-crisis and project modern literary consciousness of South Africa, that is, the search of an African image and the white settlers' belonging to Africa. Nadine Gordimer set out to find alternative ways of conveying her perception of the process which gave birth to the Afrikaner culture which was ruthlessly overprotective of its identity in the alien world of black South Africa. Gordimer provides an extraordinary and unique insight into the historical experience of the period in which she had been writing: movements of protest against the 1948 election and the recognition of its roots in segregation, active resistance, and her withdrawal from the Liberal Party after the Sharpeville massacre of the blacks in 1960, and new anxieties after the democratic elections of 1994.

Through her postcolonial gaze, Gordimer sets out the historical background that in her opinion, had led to the makings and later to the changes in the white consciousness of the views about the apartheid system; South African society had a layer of borders and boundaries between its peoples since the colonial times. There had been already a boundary of religion and tribalism between them and on top of this, another boundary was imposed in the form of apartheid which was a total transgression. There was a strong reaction but people reacted in their ways. The white South Africans took the whole system of life for granted which had marginalised them in every way. Though materially and physically privileged, they were isolated from other communities in South Africa. Gordimer shows this alienation of the white community in every phase of her fiction. During the Black Consciousness Movement in the 1970s, black writers were under pressure to leave the writers' organisation of which Gordimer and other whites were members too; the alternatives were to become a white organisation or to disband. Though Gordimer chose the latter, she experienced a sense of isolation because of her colour. She recalls:

> [...] while I understood why this separation had to take place—those black people had to free themselves from their so-called tutelage by whites and to test their muscle both intellectually and on the streets—I was nevertheless deeply hurt. I felt rejected and abandoned. (Villa-Vicencio, 1996, 106)

Gordimer admits that it was 1984 Nobel Peace winner, Sir Desmond Mpilo Tutu (1931–2021), a known South African Anglican cleric, anti-apartheid and human rights activist who made her understand her situation:

> His words are still with me: 'Nadine,' he said, 'you must realise that you feel like this because you have established a relationship with black people. For whites who do not have a real relationship with blacks, there is no hurt involved, there is no one to feel isolated from. Your very sense of rejection is your affirmation.' (ibid)

Restricted social identity based on colour was a dilemma of all South Africans which Gordimer addressed and challenged through a dual development of physical and mental borderlands in her fiction.

Physical borderlands are developed through the plot in her fiction; there are places, frontiers, and landscapes where the action is developed across the racial divide in South African life. Mental borders are presented in psychological processes which lead her characters to break down in shame and guilt and achieve transformation in their view of themselves as well as in their South African life. A continual interaction between these physical and mental borderlands contributes towards finding a new perspective upon Gordimer's fiction. Quite contrary to the physical and mental barriers which were enforced by apartheid in South African society, Gordimer's borderland opens avenues for discovering new identities which are worked out of the conflicts in the characters' lives. It provides a space for them to socialise across the racial spectrum as equals. Gordimer once stated:

> I've written usually about the borderland, the kind of frontier where black and white do meet, [...] more or less as equals, though you can never be equal in an unequal society, you cannot make up by any kind of personal ethics for the set-up around you [...] half-world where people do meet—black and white—and because of the general set-up around them, and other inequalities forced upon them, they tend just to go past, just miss [...] the moment of communication that doesn't quite come off [in the South African world]. (Terkel, 1962, 19)

Textual evidence of the theme of Borderland

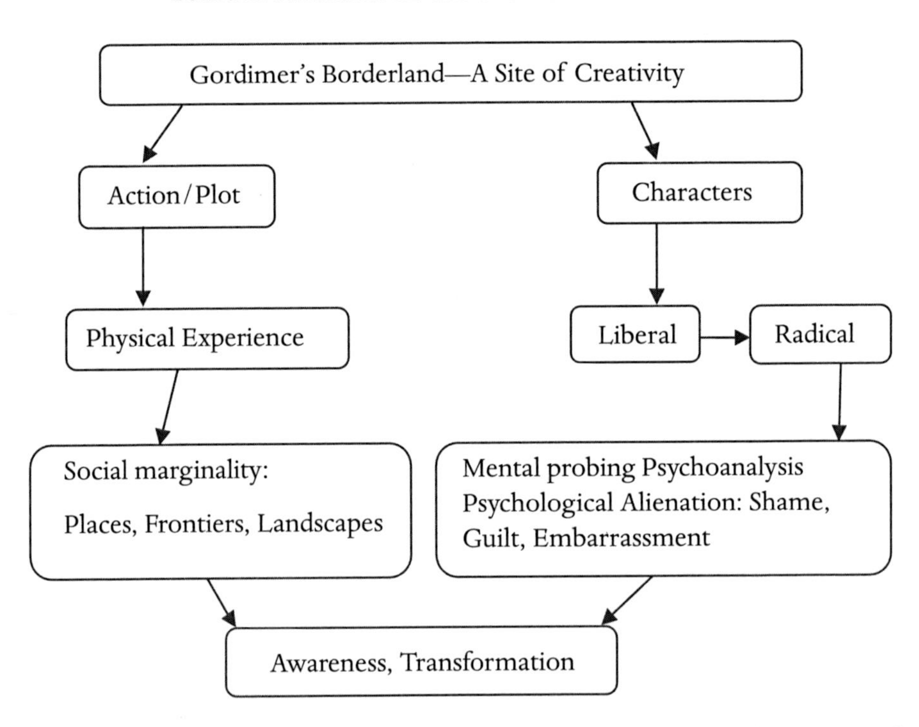

This sparsely populated frontier in Gordimer's fiction provides a ground for the characters to focus on discovering the reality of apartheid in their South African world; the border leads the characters to confront the most feared and hated aspects of their selves such as their moral distance from each other's life in South Africa. Like a little house on the prairie, Gordimer utilises the space of borderland in her fiction as a site of adventure as well as phantasmatic for her characters, attaining new avenues of knowledge and understanding of the apartheid situation in their South African world.

Although Gordimer presents her characters as living in an immobile world, transformation takes place in their experience of the South African situation. Their moderate and liberal stand on segregation develops into a conservative and radical approach to the struggle against apartheid; in the South African context, the connection between the notion of borderland and the liberal community is obvious as both represent the in-between society in Gordimer's fiction. Though quite limited and marginalised, her liberal characters get a space to experience life on both sides of the polarised South African world in her fiction. Such paradoxical characterisation depicts Gordimer's marginal position in her South African society as apartheid 'placed' people 'into conceptual and moral ghettos' (Villa-Vicencio, 1996, 105). Being white, Gordimer revealed her experience of the limitations in South African society by admitting that despite her efforts, her consciousness had the same colour as her face. (Gordimer, 1979, 162) Gordimer belonged to a privileged white Jewish class in South Africa, though her privilege had its limitations too. If it made her powerless and paralysed on one hand as belonging to one particular section of South African society, on the other hand, it provided her with the option to stay back and struggle under apartheid restrictions, whereas others like Alex La Guma (1925–1985), Dennis Brutus (1924–2009), and many other white and black writers and activists had to leave their land to espouse the causes of the deprived non-white South African masses.

The Third Space

An analytical study of Gordimer's fiction in three phases as compiled in this book has established a striking link between her presentation of the borderland in her fiction and the post-colonial theorist and critic, Homi Bhabha's interpretation of the notion of borderland in his work, *The Location of Culture* (1994). Bhabha exclusively defines his notion of borderland in several ways such as the third space, the interstices, and the domain of the beyond, to mention a few. For Bhabha, a boundary is not only a spatial fact with sociological effects but also a sociological fact that forms space. It defines at once territorial limits and socio-cultural space; such spaces are locations where new forms of identity may be articulated. These are the passages between fixed identifications that prevent identities from settling into 'primordial polarities' thus opening the possibility of cultural hybridity. (Bhabha, 1994, 3–4) Known for jargon and specific words, Bhabha elaborates his thoughts on cultures, diaspora, and belonging in a language that is 'poetic' whilst disputing the notion of plain language in cultural studies:

> When scientists write in their papers about their experiments, they use the terms they need to use. [...] Cultural theorists and philosophers, on the other hand, are more often faced with demands to speak in plain language. [...] I bring upon myself the responsibility to do the best I can to convince people that there is a purpose in my using terms, or a turn of phrase or even a literary style that they may not encounter. (Bhabha, 2019)

Bhabha's notion of cultural hybridity defines that world cultures do not stay in one form and are malleable entities endlessly being shaped. One can also notice a sense of worldliness and rootedness in Bhabha's work, especially the interplay between the global and the local. Born and brought up in a Parsi family in Mumbai, India, Bhabha has an experience with migration that runs in his family history. The Parsis are descendants of Persian Zoroastrians who follow Mazdayasna—the teachings of the Iranian prophet Zoroaster that date back to the second millennium BCE. This world's oldest continuously practised religion is a multi-faceted faith focused on a dualistic cosmology of good and evil with a benevolent deity of wisdom as its supreme being; its main features—messianism, judgment after death, heaven, and hell—influenced later religious and philosophical systems. Zoroastrianism served as the state religion of the ancient Iranian empires for more than a millennium. Following the Muslim conquest of Persia in the 7th century (633–654), the Parsis migrated from Iran to the Indian sub-continent to avoid religious persecution. Relatively a small community, the Parsis have been an affluent and self-supporting minority worldwide.

Bhabha grew up in a family which was cosmopolitan and was strongly rooted socially and culturally in Mumbai which was then a bustling multicultural metropolis—a city of hope, quite the opposite world to the current Hindu nationalism which has become a rising trend in the 21st century India. In this regard, the United States of America is one other example that supported retrograde visions of national greatness that involve the subjugation—in Bhabha's coined term—'degradation' of the Other, that is, minorities, migrants, and dissidents. (ibid) To highlight that violence and discrimination are carried out in many forms, Bhabha reflects on Nazi Germany's degradation of Jews in the 20th century when the latter's rights were stripped, and they were subjected to the slow torture of detention. In the same way, the 45th President of the USA (2017–2021), Donald Trump's slogan, *Make America Great Again* revived the same ideology in the 21st century:

> [...] *great* refers to majoritarian sovereignty and the possibility of nationalist-populist alliances; *again* references a revanchist temporality of degradation that goes full animal by legitimating a mythical return to a state of racial purity; a closed-in cultural homogeneity; a sexuality that is deeply regulated; a walled insecurity of territorial sovereignty. [...] we need a new language. In the place of discrimination, [...] we should speak instead of *degradation* [which] deals in images; it deals in the language of abuse; it deals in incivility. While discrimination casts racial violence as a bug in the system, degradation suggests that in certain hands, it can be a feature. (ibid)

Taking the example of Trump's treatment of refugees from Central America, Bhabha is critical of the idea of closing the border and rejecting the migrants by the countries which have used migrant labour for their economic ends, or waged war in other countries and destroyed their local infrastructure. According to Bhabha, a humane immigration policy would approach the subject from the standpoint of the migrants, and the risks and challenges they face in their daily lives. Bhabha believes that people of different cultures around the world can and have lived well together despite various inequalities of race, society, and livelihood. 'I owe a huge debt to London for making it possible to be both a public intellectual and an academic.' (ibid) Bhabha migrated from India to the United Kingdom in the early 1970s where he studied, taught, and drew the attention of academics for his postcolonial thoughts on ambivalence, mimicry, and cultural hybridity. Bhabha moved to the United States in the early 1990s where he wrote and published *The Location of Culture.* In this book, Bhabha propounds borderland as an aesthetic discipline and a place of creativity which provides a 'third space' to attain new avenues of knowledge and understanding of the individual's identity in a society. (Bhabha, 1994, 1). Through cultural and psychological dimensions, it explores this space in an individual's life that leads him or her to discover a different perspective on life. In his earlier work, *Nation and Narration* (1990), whilst talking about margins in a minority discourse, about the space of people and halfway populations, and discussing the cultural temporality of the nation as a social reality, Bhabha emphasises to rethink questions of identity, social agency, and national affiliation because these entities are open to a continuous process to redefine themselves. According to Bhabha, a boundary is an in-between space that brings into light the articulation of ethnocentric ideas so that people who believe in them can have an opportunity to initiate new identities for themselves.

Gordimer's fiction presents this 'third space' through borderland situations in which her characters acknowledge new sensibilities about themselves and their South African world. Through moments of transit, Gordimer makes them aware of a liberal's marginal position in radical South Africa; they approach issues related to identity and its limitations in their South African world. Gordimer characters can be labelled as types such as the liberals in South Africa, yet she involves several voices in the narration of her plots such as the construction of the action of the story in first-, second- or third-person narration simultaneously in her fiction. In this context, Bhabha's *Nation and Narration* explores how the story of a nation is narrated and interpreted by various voices and in various contexts in society. Similarly, Gordimer is very much conscious of the teller of the story who has the responsibility to interpret her views on the South African world.

This space finds its way into Gordimer's fiction in different forms, frequently appearing as a theme and at times, taking control of the text or appearing as a trait or a flaw in characters' personalities; it exists in the construction of plots such as places or physical spaces where the main action of the story takes place. Geographically, one can find similar locations in South Africa such as the Eastern Cape which was, historically, the meeting and confronting place between Europe and Africa—the bordering that separates and connects at the same time. In this sense, Gordimer's borderland acts as a liminal space and emerges in the form of crossing physical frontiers and mental barriers which existed in South African society at the time. She constructs the theme of borderland in her fiction through borderland engagements of cultural differences which perplex her characters' understanding of the South African world. They realign the boundary between their private and public lives in their effort to challenge the apartheid system and the standards of the Afrikaners' identity in South African society; the characters see how the white South Africans, in their act of essentialising blackness, misbehave towards non-white South Africans. The borderland in Gordimer's fiction becomes a 'connective tissue' which not only constructs the difference between the white and non-white worlds but also recreates a new self thus resonating with Bhabha's 'breaking of a time barrier of a culturally collusive present' (Bhabha, 1994, 3–4).

Analytical framework of the third space

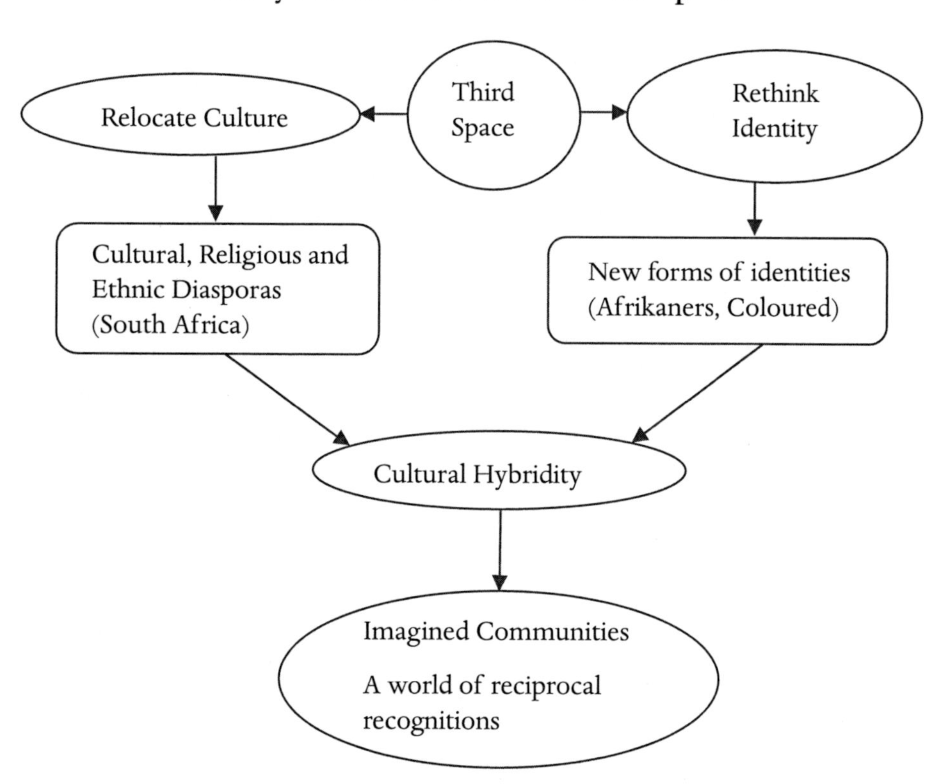

Bhabha's notion of borderland is productive in exploring Gordimer's fiction, though she presented her theme of borderland decades before

Bhabha interpreted his definition of the concept in *The Location of Culture* (1994). However, it is complex to justify its credibility in the South African context. It provides spaces for individuals to grow into new identities as opposed to the barred South African society that allowed no room for its people to cross over physical and mental borders. In South Africa's multi-ethnic society, borders adopt many dimensions, one of which was the separate development of its white and black communities during the apartheid era. In South African society, the notion of borderland has a lot to do with the economic, political, and cultural limits and this confinement produces anxiety about limits in the forms of madness and hallucination in Gordimer's characters' lives. Anxiety, alienation, and horror—the nub of a psychic trauma—which results from the encounter between two very different cultures, surface again and again in Gordimer's fiction to define how racial differences, both real and imagined, have an impact on a range of activities in her characters' lives inside as well as outside the borderland in South African society.

Bhabha's conceptual metaphors such as third space, identity and hybridity, and the interaction of fiction and society, get themselves articulated in different forms in the theme of borderland in Gordimer's fiction but his other concepts such as stereotyping find no room in her fiction. Gordimer's characters are types who go through a transformation, so they cannot be associated with the process of labelling identities which the term stereotyping stands for. On the contrary, it is applicable in the South African context because people's identities were labelled in South Africa into white, black, Coloured, and Indian groups; these terms were in common use and had specific connotations in South African society and history. This study, therefore, takes account of a shift in Gordimer's lexicon for ethnic identities in her fiction; her vocabulary went through a transformation over some time in South African society, from her earlier use of the terms native and Coloured to her later description of African characters as black in her fiction. However, to a great extent, Gordimer presents her characters as individuals in groups such as the black, the white, the Indian and the Coloured. The black became the mark of identification for both the blacks and the Coloureds in the later era of twentieth-century South Africa; the Coloureds became blacks when the former joined hands with the political campaigns of the ANC (African National Congress) and the PAC (Pan Africanist Congress) in the 1970s post-Soweto liberation struggle.

As a personal response by Gordimer to the world of power and politics in South Africa, the book examines the three phases of her fiction—protest, struggle, and liberation era. In all these phases of her writing, she has focused on narratives of personal relationships and borderland society in a variety of ways; the dual development of physical and psychological processes is a central narrative strategy that determines a link between chronology and the presentation of borderland in her fiction. Anticipating Bhabha's formulation of the notion of borderland in Gordimer's fiction develops a new methodological perspective on her fiction. It helps to think about the relationship between fiction and theory that works effectively in the application of Bhabha's notion of borderland to Gordimer's presentation of the theme of borderland in her fiction. Bhabha approaches the notion of borderland as an entry into a transitional zone which is an important aspect of Gordimer's fiction. To discover Gordimer speaking Bhabha's language makes her presentation of the theme of borderland significant in the fictional world.

Author in the queue to speak with Homi Bhabha—University of Cambridge (2003)

Author in conversation with Homi Bhabha

PART 1: THE THREE PHASES

Three historical periods emerge in Gordimer's fiction—the early protest era which is mostly autobiographical or biographical such as The Lying Days *(1953) and* Burger's Daughter *(1979), the middle era of struggle and prophecy such as* The Late Bourgeois World *(1966),* A Sport of Nature *(1987), and* July's People *(1981), and, the later period of liberation when Gordimer includes themes other than apartheid in her fiction such as her thrillers,* The House Gun *(1998) and* The Pick Up *(2001). A chronology of contemporary South African history can be traced in the plot and characterisation that stands out as an integral part of Gordimer's fiction.*

Resistance, Struggle and Liberation

Nadine Gordimer focused on moral and racial issues in her fiction. All her life, as an uncompromising realist, Gordimer searched for truth and reality in man's relation to man, nature and God. She lived through apartheid, fully supported the anti-apartheid struggle, encouraged writings by black writers, and did not go to exile, though she travelled internationally to speak out against discrimination and political repression in South Africa. Gordimer questioned the liberal English attitude towards general life and local affairs in particular. She presented ideals that were very similar to those of black South Africans who hoped and strove for a better and just future in South Africa.

In line with notable South African writers such as Olive Schreiner (1855–1920) and Sol Plaatje (1876–1932), Bessie Head (1937–1986) and J M Coetzee (1940-to date), Gordimer's fiction presents her resistance to colonial ideology in South Africa. She was a writer in conflict with social conditions during the transition from segregation and apartheid to democratic rule in South Africa. Gordimer was born on 20 November 1923 and bred at Springs in the Transvaal (now Gauteng), a centre of a gold mining town in the east of Johannesburg. She was aware of her split historical position: a white person having a privileged life in South Africa, recognised by a literate elite, particularly the privileged international readership and yet supporting the causes of the deprived black South African masses. New York's famous publisher Simon and Schuster published her first novel. Gordimer's short stories were published in the USA magazines: the New Yorker, the Yale Review, and the Virginia Quarterly Review. She was the first South African to win the Nobel Prize for Literature in 1991. She received honorary doctorates from fifteen academic institutions and was a Fellow of the Royal Society of Literature. She was the recipient of prestigious literary awards in South Africa, Britain, France, Italy, Germany, and the United States of America: CNA Literary Awards, the W.H. Smith Literary Award, the James Tait Black Memorial Prize, the Booker Prize and the Grand Aigle d'Or. Her books have been translated into thirty-one languages and are the subject of leading studies by literary scholars.

Although Gordimer was officially and socially cut off from other ethnic groups in their struggle against racial and economic inequality, she identified herself with the cause of black South Africans through her fiction. Gordimer declared her position:

> Few of the white people in my stories belong to that group of white South Africans who visualise and accept freedom for South Africa in terms of a black majority government elected by an unqualified franchise. I do. [...] some perfectly ordinary day, for sure, black South Africans will free themselves and rule themselves. (1976, Introduction, *Some Monday,* xi-xiii)

It is amazing to notice that Gordimer was born in the same year—1923—when the South African Native National Congress (formed in 1912) became the African National Congress (ANC). Gordimer joined ANC when it was listed as an illegal organisation by the South African government in 1961; she secretly sheltered ANC leaders in her own home to aid their escape from arrest by the government; she was close friends with Nelson Mandela's defence attorneys—Bram Fischer and George Bizos—during his trial in 1962; she helped Mandela edit his famous speech 'I Am Prepared To Die,' given from the defendant's dock at the trial; she testified at the 1986 Delmas Treason Trial on behalf of 22 South African anti-apartheid activists; she also testified in the Pretoria Supreme Court in 1988 in mitigation of sentence for Terror Lekota and 10 others found guilty of terrorism. When the ANC was unbanned in 1990, she became a card-carrying member. Gordimer was one of the first people Mandela wanted to see on his release from prison after twenty-seven years in 1990.

Gordimer's interest in racial and economic inequality in South Africa can be traced back to her adolescence when she was raised in a secular household by her Jewish parents; an Eastern European Orthodox Jew, Gordimer's father, Isidore Gordimer belonged to a poor family in Latvia, left school at the age of eleven to learn the skill of watch mending which became the source of his livelihood. He knew not a word of English when he arrived in South Africa at the age of thirteen. Whereas Gordimer's mother, Hannah Nancy Myers was born in England to an established Anglo-Jewish family and had come to South Africa with her parents when she was six years old. Hannah despised her husband Isidore's background as her attitude to Jewishness was the product of several generations of middle-class Anglo-acculturation; no Kosher restrictions were observed, and bacon was consumed. Except for Isidore, none in Gordimer's family—Hannah (the wife), Betty (the elder daughter) and the youngest Nadine practised Jewish religion nor ever attended synagogue even on religious days. Inspired by Franz Kafka (1883–1924), the Jewish German writer's 47 pages long autobiographical letter to his abusive and narcissistic father 'Letter to His Father' (1919), Gordimer's short story 'Letter from His Father', published in the American literary magazine *The Three Penny* in 1984, is a remarkable fusion of realism and fantastic that reflects her Jewish experience:

> You go on [...] about my use of vulgar Yiddish expressions [...] your Judaism was highly intellectual, nothing in common with the Jewish customs I was taught to observe in my father's shtetl, pushing the barrow at the age of seven. [...] Your Judaism was learnt at the Yiddish Theatre. [...] Right, towards the end you studied Hebrew [...] The latest book about you says you were in revolt against the shopkeeper mentality of your father's class of Jew; but it was the shopkeeper father, the buttons and buckles, braid, ribbons, ornamental combs, press-studs, hooks-and-eyes, boot laces, photo frames, shoe horns, novelties and notions that earned the bread for you to dream by. You were anti-Semitic, Franz; if such a thing is possible as for a Jew to cut himself in half. For you, I suppose, anything is possible.

Nadine was brought up as a South African of purely English cultural background and learned about Judaism later in life when she studied comparative religion as an adult. Gordimer had a prickly relationship with the organised Jewish community, though both her husbands were Jewish; she married the dentist, Gerald Gavronsky in 1949 from whom she had a daughter, Oriane Gavronsky; three years later after her divorce in 1952, she married the German-Jewish refugee art dealer, Reinhold Cassirer from whom she bore a son, Hugo Cassirer.

Gordimer defined herself as 'a South African rather than as a South African Jew' (Shimoni, 2003, 4); she identifies herself as being Jewish through birth but has no religious belief. For her, being a Jew is like being black: 'It's something inside you, in your blood and in your bones.' (Gordimer, 2005). That is why Gordimer has never counted Jewishness as a factor in shaping the liberal values that made her an opponent of apartheid:

> I don't think that my Jewishness is an influence, and I get rather annoyed when people say that my opposition to racism comes from being Jewish. It's a terrible deflection if you have self-interest in acting against racism. (Shimoni, 2003, 96)

Her support for the black struggle against discrimination had nothing to do with her being Jewish: '[...] you don't have to be a Jew, to be appalled, as long as there is a living memory, by the Holocaust. And that you don't have to be black in order to be appalled by apartheid.' (Frazer, 2014, 12). Gordimer expressed an even-handed humanism throughout her literary career. Social conscience does not come from being part of a persecuted race; not all Jews in South Africa were opposed to apartheid, despite the racial discrimination they have suffered as a people; the attitude of Gordimer's father was wholly compliant with white racist norms, though being an example of former victims of racism but still adopting the same racist attitude towards others. In her story, 'My Father Leaves Home' (1991), Gordimer captures this arrogant attitude in the character of a father who has emigrated from an East European village—the Old World of anti-Semitism—without any sensitivity towards the anti-black racism in South Africa.

However, there were other South African Jews who endured imprisonment, banning and exile for their commitment to the black liberation struggle: out of two white prisoners of conscience condemned to life imprisonment in 1963–64 Rivonia Trial—Bram Fischer and Denis Goldberg—one was a Jew; Denis and Jews like him had not suffered the racial discrimination suffered by blacks. The source of moral values thus emerges from the collective wisdom and consciousness of humankind: whatever religious or ethnic background, people have an equal responsibility to fight what is evil:

> [Human compassion] is certainly not the exclusive possession of any one ethical tradition or religious heritage. Our values emerge from the many different streams of what we call civilisation. There is a blending of sources and traditions in human history from which people in different contexts and parts of the world can and often do draw. (Villa-Vicencio, 1996, 112)

Growing up in the prejudiced white middle-class life in Springs, reading and writing as a child helped Gordimer develop her imagination. She had an unusual childhood due to the unhappy marriage of her parents. Her mother dominated the home environment and removed her from her school, the Convent of Our Lady of Mercy in Springs because of a supposed heart ailment. Gordimer spent the years between eleven and sixteen mainly isolated from her peers. She became deeply involved in reading and writing and at the age of thirteen had a story published in the children's section of the *Sunday Express,* a Johannesburg weekly newspaper. When she was fifteen years old, her first adult story 'Come Again Tomorrow' was published in *Forum*, a liberal South African magazine.

A raid by the police who confiscated letters and diaries from a servant's room in her family home was Gordimer's first-hand experience of repression as a teenager. Later, as a student at the University of Witwatersrand, and the house of her first publisher, Lulu Friedman in Johannesburg, Gordimer had a chance to meet fellow professionals and anti-apartheid writers across the racial divide; she was simultaneously being drawn into the world of black friends and colleagues. A crucial point of transition was her contact with *Drum*, a popular black-oriented magazine, and her literary involvement with black writers, musicians, journalists, poets, critics and artists in the 1950s; this exposure to the cosmopolitan and bohemian life of Johannesburg and in particular, the life of Sophiatown—one of Johannesburg's black townships provided her emotional and intellectual awakening and brought her, 'as she puts it, out of whiteness into humanity':

> [Till then] Racism was invisible to me. [...] I realised that the segregation of my life as a white person from black people was not an act of God. [...] not a cosmological given. [...] not inevitable. It was man-made. [...] I discovered the extent to which I had been denied life by the laager into which I was born. [...] life is more than the narrow white perception on which I was raised. Once the illusion that those who differ from us are inferior is shattered, a whole new dimension to life opens up before us. We no longer reduce what it means to be human to our understanding of humanity. (Villa-Vicencio, 1996, 109)

Gordimer witnessed government repression and confronted the outrages committed by the white society against the peoples of Black, Coloured and Indian backgrounds: the government policies about land ownership and representation 1946; Native Land Acts of 1913 and 1936 had restricted the land ownership by blacks—classifying 70 per cent of the population to 'reserves' or townships which equates to only 13.70 per cent of the total land at most; under the apartheid laws of South Africa, the Black Reserves formed the basis of the tribal homelands. Besides this, the blacks were eliminated from the common voters' roll in Cape Province and were instead placed on a separate roll to elect seven white members to the Parliament. The apartheid platform codified and expanded on such laws and legislation which already existed in every sphere of South African life since Segregation under the Constitution of South Africa in the 1910 Act of Union; independence from British colonial rule in 1930 gave suffrage and power to whites only which was unchanged until the early 1980s.

In this regard, a large body of Gordimer's fiction depicts characters with this social climate of apartheid and the related upheavals in South Africa. Her fiction has described landmarks in the people's resistance and struggles against apartheid until South Africa became free from its shackles with the first general election in 1994. The historical landmarks were the legalisation of apartheid after 1948, the Sharpeville incident in 1960, the Soweto Uprisings in 1976 and the underground struggle of the ANC and the adjacent movements of the 1960s, the general election in 1994 and the corruption and the power struggle amongst the democratic leadership after the 1994 elections. These political developments found a central place during events in the characters' lives in Gordimer's fiction. These historical times are projected chronologically, providing a link between the resistance, the struggle, and the liberation phases of South African history. From 1948, Gordimer's fiction falls into three main phases:

1. Protest against the 1948 election and recognition of its roots in segregation.
2. Active resistance after the Sharpeville massacre and Gordimer's withdrawal from the Liberal Party in 1960, and,
3. New anxieties after the democratic election of 1994.

In her fiction, the emphasis falls on society in general, and not any race in particular, even though the Afrikaner as such is seldom referred to, either directly or through the characters, and then usually in uncomplimentary terms. She touches upon the colour question but mainly as part of the views held by the section of the community she portrays. From her earlier accounts of a segregated society and then apartheid government to the following democratic rule in South Africa, her novels and selected short stories explore the crises that led to the formation of South African literary consciousness, notably the rise of the apartheid government in 1948, the Sharpeville incident in 1960, the Soweto uprisings in 1976, and the abolition of apartheid in 1994.

Gordimer's novels, *The Lying Days* (1953), *A World of Strangers* (1958) and *Occasion for Loving* (1963) present the protest era—phase one—when South Africans resisted the legalisation of apartheid in every sphere of life. It brings into light the Sharpeville incident of 1960 when the black activists, after the killing of sixty-nine black demonstrators by the police, started moving away from their policy of peaceful struggle against apartheid. The Sharpeville demonstration was in protest against the Pass laws

(Identity Cards) which made it compulsory for all people other than the whites to keep a reference book: it stood for racial identification and therefore, for racial discrimination. After the Sharpeville tragedy, Gordimer announced: 'I used to regard myself as a liberal, but now I regard myself as a radical.' (Cassere, 1972, 56) The Sharpeville massacre and the arrest of her best friend, Bettie du Toit in 1960 became the defining moments after which Gordimer became active in South African politics. A semi-autobiographical, *The Lying Days* charts the growing political awareness of a young white middle-class woman, Helen, towards the racial division in the life of a South African gold-mining town. It depicts the opening of her world in Johannesburg and her gaining enlightenment about apartheid through friendships across the racial divide. Gordimer also introduces a theme in this novel that is repeated in many of her later novels—either committing oneself to struggle for a new and just society by remaining in South Africa or deciding to leave.

A World of Strangers was banned by the apartheid government for twelve years. It presents an outsider's view of South Africa: Toby Hood, an English agent of a publishing company comes to South Africa and experiences alienation and social severance in his relationships across the racial divide. *Occasion for Loving* puts apartheid and love squarely together; the protagonist, Ann Davis, is married to Boaz Davis, an ethnomusicologist, but she is in love with Gideon Shibalo, an artist with several failed relationships. Ann Davis is white, and Gideon Shibalo is black, and South Africa's government has criminalised such relationships!

This early phase of Gordimer's fiction emphasises the importance of personal relationships and individual fulfilment; personal relationships across the colour line are projected as solutions to the racial tensions in South Africa. But the Sharpeville massacre made Gordimer realise that liberalism in South Africa 'has been too ready to compromise, to see both sides of the question, too polite, too much of a gesture, not enough of a commitment, not radical enough, that is why it has never delivered goods.' (Schwartz, 1977, 93) The projection of the consciousness that liberalism is too moderate to resolve the opposing notions of nationalisms of the time—white supremacism, and, Africanism, that is, an ideology of African nationalism propagated by a South African activist Anton Muziwakhe Lembede (1914–1947)—draws a line between her early and later fiction.

By now, Gordimer had achieved international literary recognition. In the year 1961, she received the W.H. Smith Commonwealth Literary Award, a major international recognition. Her following novels present the period of commitment after the Sharpeville tragedy: *The Late Bourgeois*

World (1966), *A Guest of Honour* (1970), *The Conservationist* (1974), and *Burger's Daughter* (1979). This struggle era—phase two—focuses on the events that led to the black uprisings at Soweto in 1976 when the activists raised their voices against apartheid through the underground movements—where the characters carry out the underground missions. Gordimer's fiction articulated the frustrations and aspirations of South Africa's urban society, during that period. Like a duck that appears quite calm whilst floating on the surface of the water but is quite active underneath as her invisible feet move forward and backwards to keep their movement intact on the water, the underground activists struggled against apartheid in the pre-Soweto era. In *The Late Bourgeois World,* Elizabeth a young white South African woman lives through a struggle, privately as a wife and a mother, and publicly as a liberal standing by her revolutionary husband Max. As a member of a communist cell, Max makes a bomb, blows up a post office, and is caught and sentenced. He gets his freedom by becoming a state witness, and in the end, commits suicide. *The Late Bourgeois World* was banned for a decade by the South African government.

However, Gordimer collected international literary prizes for her next two novels. James Tait Black Memorial Prize was awarded for *A Guest of Honour* in 1971, and The Booker Prize was awarded to Gordimer for *The Conservationist* in 1974. *A Guest of Honour* appeared on the literary scene in the period of silence before the black uprisings; it presents the story of a central African country going through a period of turmoil after getting its independence from the British colonials. The character Evelyn James Bray, an English Liberal and a close contact of the People's Independence Party attempts to sort out differences and grievances between the characters, Mweta and his rival Shinza, but he ends up being beaten to death. Gordimer presents an imaginary experience of power and independence by the blacks and rivalries between them. Whereas *The Conservationist* explores Zulu culture and the world of a wealthy white industrialist through the eyes of Mehring, the antihero. Mehring seeks to conserve nature to preserve the apartheid system, keeping change at bay. When an unidentified corpse is found on his farm, Mehring provides it with a proper burial but the dead person's image continues to haunt, a reminder of the bodies on which Mehring's vision is built.

Written in the aftermath of the Soweto uprisings, *Burger's Daughter* (1979) was banned by the South African government after its publication; the Publications Committee Appeal Board reversed the censorship of *Burger's Daughter* six months later, determining that the book was too one-sided to be subversive. Gordimer responded to this decision in her essay 'Essential Gesture' (1988), pointing out that the board banned two books by black authors at the same time it removed the ban on her work. The novel presents the story of an Afrikaner woman, Rosa Burger who examines her relationship with her father, a martyr to the anti-apartheid movement. The child of two Communist and anti-apartheid revolutionaries, Rosa finds herself drawn into political activism. Gordimer described the novel as a coded homage to Bram Fischer, the lawyer who defended Nelson Mandela and other anti-apartheid activists.

In phase three, Gordimer's fiction projects the liberation era when freedom from apartheid was being prophesied or even predicted in an independent South Africa. In *July's People* (1981), Gordimer visualises a brutal South African revolution against the apartheid government, in which white people are hunted down and murdered by black people. The characters Maureen and Bamford Smales, an educated white couple, hide for their lives with July, their long-time former black servant. The novel plays off the various groups of July's people: his own family as well as the Smales family in the village. The story examines how people cope with the terrible choices forced on them by violence, race hatred, and state laws and officials. *July's People* was banned under apartheid and faced censorship under the post-apartheid regime; in 2001, the provincial education department removed *July's People* from the school reading list, describing the novel as deeply racist, superior, and patronising, a characterisation that Gordimer took as a grave insult, and that many literary and political figures protested. Gordimer's activism was not limited to the struggle against apartheid. She resisted censorship and state control of information and fostered the literary arts. She refused to let her work be aired by the South African Broadcasting Corporation because it was controlled by the apartheid government. Gordimer also served on the steering committee of South Africa's Anti-Censorship Action Group. She was a founding member of the Congress of South African Writers and was also active in South African letters and international literary organisations; she was the Vice President of International PEN.

One after another, Gordimer's novels *A Sport of Nature* (1987), *My Son's Story* (1990) and *None to Accompany Me* (1994) contained historical accounts of contemporary South Africa, reflecting an increasing pressure on the South African regime to go beyond liberalism and to move towards a radical political system. Set in 1960s South Africa, *A Sport of Nature* is a narrative about a white liberal Jewish woman Hillela who is growing up into a radical person during this period in the era of the Sharpeville massacres and thereafter. In parallel, there runs a story of her private life; Gordimer names her protagonist Hillela after the Babylon era Jewish religious scholar Hillel the Elder (110 BCE-10 CE) to evoke the latter's much-preached holy book Talmud's Rabbinic moral golden rule: treat others as you want to be treated.

Set in 1980s South Africa, *My Son's Story* presents the story of a black schoolteacher named Sonny, and his family, and the effect upon their private and public lives during their struggle to be free of apartheid. In *None to Accompany Me,* Gordimer presents the character Vera Stark, who is a white lawyer committed to the struggle against apartheid. She represents blacks in their fight to reclaim the land. The story in these narratives is spread over a period going back to the 1960s and it deals with the experience of victory by the blacks in their struggle against apartheid. Their confidence in themselves is further reiterated in Gordimer's post-apartheid novel *The House Gun* (1998): it describes the strength of character of a black barrister who defends a white man in a case of murder; it follows the story of a couple, Claudia and Harald Lingard, dealing with their son Duncan's murder of one of his housemates. The novel treats the rising crime rate in South Africa and the guns that virtually every house keeps as well as the legacy of South African apartheid and the couple's concerns about their son's lawyer, who is black. The novel was optioned for film rights to British television Granada Productions.

A shift in action and characterisation in Gordimer's post-apartheid fiction marks a boundary between her fiction written during and after the apartheid era. In *The House Gun,* Gordimer explores other avenues of human life such as a court trial for murder. Set in the era of black majority rule in South Africa, the action in the novel reveals a change in Gordimer's presentation of her South African society. Gordimer accepts:

> As for retrospect as a valid critique, I realise it (to make sense of life) has no fixed existence but represents my own constantly changing effort to teach myself how to make out of words a total form for whatever content I seize upon. (1975, 9)

Berlin and Johannesburg: The Wall and the Colour Bar was a documentary film that Gordimer made in collaboration with her son Hugo Cassirer in the post-apartheid era. The action in this film is set in Johannesburg and Berlin, the 'two cities in which a wall has come down' but 'with a difference'. (Brink, 1998, 419–420) It existed in Berlin for thirty years but in South Africa, for centuries. So the new South Africa without the wall has become an interesting place to discover the life of the *Other*. This is substantiated in the award-winning 2001 novel, *The Pick Up* (2001) in which Gordimer focuses, for the first time in her writing career, on a character and a family who are of the Muslim faith. It tells the story of a couple in South Africa, Julie Summers, a white woman from a financially secure family, and Abdu, an illegal Arab Muslim immigrant from the Far East. After Abdu's visa is refused, the couple returns to his homeland, where Julie is the alien. Her experiences as an alien in another culture form the heart of the work. The novel considers the issues of displacement, alienation, of separation, class and economic power, religious faith, and the ability of people to live, and to love, across these divides. Themes related to race and identity thus recur in Gordimer's post-apartheid fiction, though in different forms.

Since the fall of apartheid and South Africa's first democratic elections in 1994, Gordimer has been active in the fight against the spread of HIV/AIDS, addressing a major public health crisis in South Africa. In 2003, she rallied twenty Nobel Prize and other award-winning writers, including the Israeli writer Amos Oz (1939–2018), and, American writers of Jewish background, Susan Sontag (1933–2004) and Arthur Miller (1915–2005) to collaborate on a short-story anthology *Telling Tales* (2004); published in twelve countries and launched at the United Nations on the World AIDS Day (1 December 2004), *Telling Tales* was an effort by Gordimer to raise funds for South Africa's Treatment Action Campaign for HIV/AIDS prevention and care. On this issue, she was critical of the South African government, noting in 2004 that she approved of everything President Thabo Mbeki had done except his stance on AIDS.

In her last two novels, *Get a Life* (2005) and *No Time Like the Present* (2012), Gordimer presents contemporary South Africa juxtaposed in a story about human fear of destruction, contamination, alienation, and solitude, and presents a sharp psychological insight into political complexities of the liberation era respectively. *Get a Life* is a story of a man undergoing treatment for a life-threatening disease. Whilst drawn from personal life experiences, the novel also continues Gordimer's exploration of political themes. The protagonist is an ecologist, battling with the installation of a planned nuclear plant. But he is at the same time undergoing radiation therapy for his cancer, causing him personal grief and, ironically, rendering him a radioactivity health hazard in his own home. Here, Gordimer again pursues the question of how to integrate everyday life with political activism. Similarly, the novel, *No Time Like the Present* which is set in contemporary South Africa tells the story of a couple; the character Steven Reed is a lecturer of Chemistry, and his black lawyer wife Jabulile Gumede. They move to live in a suburb; the new status makes them aware of the fact that freedom that was fought for—is created but still challenged by political and racial tensions in South Africa.

Gordimer's novels can be divided into four categories, autobiographical or biographical such as *The Lying Days* (1953) and *Burger's Daughter* (1979), historical such as *The Late Bourgeois World* (1966) and *A Sport of Nature* (1987), prophecy such as *July's People* (1981), and thrillers such as *The House Gun* (1998) and *The Pick Up* (2001). Gordimer wrote one novella, *Something Out There* (1984) which is ironic as well as a symbolic presentation of the ANC's sabotage movements in South Africa. In her novels, Gordimer utilises the themes and patterns which she has rehearsed in her short stories. For instance, the theme of the master-servant relationship in *The Lying Days* (1953) and *July's People* (1981) is explored before by Gordimer in 'Ah, Woe Is Me' (1949). Similarly, Gordimer follows a pattern in her short stories such as in 'The Train From Rhodesia' (1949) where the action becomes alive with the protagonist's experience of a moment or a set of events that pricks her conscience and breaks her down in shame and embarrassment. The characters such as Helen in *The Lying Days* (1953), Toby in *A World of Strangers* (1958) and Maureen in *July's People* (1981) undergo this mental probing. Gordimer admits: 'I have a theory that a writer is always writing the same story—like a mosaic, a jigsaw puzzle that is put together.' (Cassere, 1972, 57) So a pattern is followed by Gordimer in her plots and characterisation that can be traced in a variety of ways in her short stories and novels.

Gordimer's fiction first appeared on the literary horizon in the form of short stories which cast back on her experiences as a child and young woman growing up in a mining town on the East Rand. For instance, 'The Umbilical Cord' (1949), 'The Prisoner' (1953), 'The Defeated' (1953), 'Charmed Lives' (1956) and 'The Termitary' (1980). This mining town near Johannesburg, as it features in her fiction, is the canvas upon which Gordimer portrays idiosyncratic characters such as Van in 'The Last Kiss' (1960), Uncle Chookie in 'Clowns in Clover' (1956) or the deaf watchmaker Simon Datnow and the drunken Dr Connor in 'Charmed Lives' (1956). Besides, there are short stories in which Gordimer describes the lifestyle of affluent white people. Most of them are South Africans, South Africans abroad or foreign visitors to South Africa. For instance, 'Enemies' (1956), 'Face from Atlantis' (1956), 'Out of Season' (1956), 'The Path of the Moon's Dark Fortnight' (1960), 'Native Country' (1965), 'Otherwise Birds Fly In' (1972), 'Time Did' (1980), 'A Mad One' (1980), and 'You Name It' (1980), wittily probe into social pretensions of these well-to-do characters. They become targets of Gordimer's satirical and ironic observation:

> My approach in these stories, as in any other, is that of irony. I would say that in general, in my stories, my approach as a short story writer is the ironical one and that it represents the writer's unconscious selection of the approach best suited to the material. (Gordimer, 1976, 11)

There are a substantial number of these kinds of stories in all her collections which point to the spiritual impoverishment of the affluent characters and lay bare the shallow and empty lives most of these people pursue. Gordimer admits:

> My method so often has been irony, I find irony very attractive in other writers, and I find life full of irony, my own life and everybody else's; somehow one of the secret locks of the personality lies in what is ironic in us. (Gardner, 1981, 110)

Sarcasm was a dominant element of her short stories till the 1970s, as in 'The Train from Rhodesia' (1949), 'Enemies' (1956), 'The Last Kiss' (1960), 'The African Magician' (1965), and 'Abroad' (1972). This ironic element is superseded by a symbolic and graphic presentation of South African life in her later short stories like 'A Lion on the Free Way' (1980), 'For Dear Life' (1980), 'Siblings' (1980), 'Jump' (1991) and 'Amnesty' (1991).

Amongst the large body of Gordimer's short stories, some narratives depict characters with the social climate of apartheid and the related upheavals in South Africa such as in 'Is There Nowhere Else Where We Can Meet?' (1949), 'Ah, Woe is Me' (1949), 'The Train from Rhodesia' (1949), 'Which New Era Would That Be?' (1956), 'The Smell and Death of Flowers' (1956), 'The African Magician' (1965), 'Some Monday for Sure' (1976), 'A Lion on the Free Way' (1980), 'Keeping Fit' (1991), 'What Were You Dreaming' (1991), 'Jump' (1991) and 'Amnesty' (1991). In these stories, the action becomes alive with the protagonist's experience of a moment or a set of events that pricks his or her conscience and breaks him or her down in shame and embarrassment. For her protagonists, this mental probing is a state of great potential—a necessary stage to a greater awareness; the character undergoes a dynamic process which, in turn, presents him with another perspective on himself and his South African life.

As compared to her short stories where the focus is on the experience of the very moment, Gordimer expands on it in her novels to present the effects on characters' lives: they transform and look for a change in their South African society, as Helen does in *The Lying Days* (1953). At the same time, after confronting the most feared and hated aspects of the inner self, Gordimer's protagonist, Toby in *A World of Strangers* (1958) finds an opportunity to achieve a healing unity for the peace of his mind towards the end of the novel. The form of the novel allowed Gordimer more space to present the lives and actions of her characters who are placed in situations of physical or moral difficulty in South Africa such as Jessie in *Occasion for Loving* (1963) and Elizabeth in *The Late Bourgeois World* (1966). There is direct involvement with the exigencies facing characters in these novels who are either living through or who are closely tied to the political realities in South Africa.

Physical and psychological situations are thus permanent features of Gordimer's fiction. Her short stories and novels present racial experiences from childhood and interracial relationships to political activism through these encounters in her characters' lives as in *The Lying Days*. The action develops across a kind of frontier that allows her characters to experience life that exists across the racial divide as in *A World of Strangers*. The impact of social, administrative, political, economic, linguistic, physical, and geographical borders is projected in several ways and on a range of activities in characters' lives in Gordimer's fiction such as in the stories 'Is There Nowhere Else Where We Can Meet?' 'Ah. Woe Is Me', and 'The Train for Rhodesia'. A clearly defined physical and mental world of barriers is present in her early fiction. In her later fiction, the construction of a marginal situation or a liminal state in characters' lives defines for them the future course of their commitment towards the struggle against apartheid as in *The Late Bourgeois World*, *Burger's Daughter,* and *A Sport of Nature.*

Within this narrative strategy, the theme of borderland is presented through complex characterisation, the selection of titles, and the language which contributes towards discovering a continual pattern in Gordimer's fiction. It is developed dually: a physical borderland, that is, deployment of frontiers and landscapes revealing social marginality, and mental borders, that is, the themes of madness, shame, embarrassment, and guilt leading to psychological alienation. As apartheid generated restricted social identities in South Africa, the notion of borderland provided Gordimer with a space to escape from her rigid hierarchical society, making this marginal space of the frontier a site of creativity for her. She gives a vivid account of this process of alienation and social severance in her fiction. She works both within and beyond the colonial experience to question the myth of an unbridgeable gap between the black and the white races. For her, there are two Africas: the country which has always belonged to African communities, and the veneer the white colonial has imposed upon it.

Gordimer belongs to neither in any real sense. This marginality enables her to act as an observer; suffering through conditions of social inequality in their lives, her characters in 'Is There No Where Else We Can Meet?' (1949) and in *Occasion for Loving* (1963) observe that white denial of the black community is the common root of fear and alienation between them. At crossing physical and psychological borders such as colour and language barriers, her characters such as Toby in *A World of Strangers*, Elizabeth in *The Late Bourgeois World*, and Maureen in *July's People* discover their marginal positions in South African society. The tensions in these characters' lives arise out of the conflicting pulls and pushes of individual free will on the one hand and environmental determinism on the other. At the same time, the titles of these novels comment on the working of a transitional world that is in action in Gordimer's fiction. Physical situations develop in parallel with psychological encounters in action and characterisation in her fiction.

Through various angles of their study of her fiction, researchers have recognised Gordimer's description of the urgencies and difficulties which people faced under apartheid in South Africa. For instance, Robert Haugh in *Nadine Gordimer* (1974) argues about her ability to sustain a tense dialectic between the personal and the political in her fiction. His study proposed that Gordimer had increasing difficulty in integrating her primary interest in the personal with a set of political themes in her fiction. In contrast, Michael Wade developed a new perspective on her fiction by interpreting this element as significantly sustained by Gordimer. In *White on Black in South Africa* (1993), Wade finds Gordimer's fiction addressing those mythic structures or ideologies which were used to maintain white South African visions of themselves and which rendered white South Africa visible to itself. Wade's study also evaluates the place of Jewishness in Gordimer's fiction.

For Stephen Clingman, Gordimer writes not just of the events and movements of South African history but also of what it has been like to live through them. He sees her fiction as a reflection of Gordimer's changing apprehension of social and historical developments in South Africa. His study *The Novels of Nadine Gordimer: History from the Inside* (1986) discovers the role of physicality as fundamental to resistance against oppression; since apartheid was dividing according to the body, only the whole body can function as a sign of reintegration. A whole body, he argues, is resurrected from a past state of fracture. He finds that Gordimer's fiction presents the history of South Africa as experienced by individuals who are themselves products of history in all its complexity and contradictions.

Andrew Vogel Ettin's approach to Gordimer's fiction is the reverse of Clingman's. For him, Gordimer always tells the same story which revolves around the politics of the family, the sensuous experience, and issues of social identity. In *Betrayals of the Body Politic: The Literary Commitments of Nadine Gordimer* (1992), Ettin finds patterns of imagery as a major strength in her fiction and discovers the role of sexuality as a way out from the family into social freedom. However, Gordimer's general distaste for feminism is persuasively read as the product of her firm socio-economic grasp: she rejects feminism as elitist in the racial situation in South Africa.

> I take the political context of the South African situation seriously. Black women in South Africa have more in common at the level of oppression and deprivation with black men than they have with white women. [...] vast gap in the experiences of black and white women [...] who claim to be feminists continue to do all they can to curtail black political and economic advancement. [...] I fundamentally believe that the concerns of women should be included in the struggle for an inclusive culture. Culture must be gender inclusive as well as racially inclusive. (Villa-Vicencio, 1996, 111–112)

John Cooke in *The Novels of Nadine Gordimer: Private Lives/ Public Landscapes* (1985) addresses the significance of Gordimer's unusual childhood and adolescence in her fiction. He argues that Gordimer has endowed her private history with public associations to liberate herself from familial restraints, symbolising a challenge to the dominant political order. Cooke discovers the South African landscape as a driving force for Gordimer to develop the narrative in her fiction.

The narrative voice, not generally discussed by Clingman and Ettin, is a special emphasis of Judie Newman's study. She explores the relationship between gender and genre in Gordimer's fiction. She argues in *Contemporary Writers: Nadine Gordimer* (1988) that Gordimer's fiction subverts Eurocentric conventions by establishing a counterpoint between male and female protagonists, white and black interpreters and by employing double plots which readjust the relationship between social context, text, and subtext, by the reconstruction of the implied reader and, by interrogating the language of South African cultural voices. Newman builds on work done by Clingman and Cooks but takes a post-structuralist approach; where Clingman sees South African history as the conditioning force behind Gordimer's fiction, and where Cooke sees the nature of Gordimer's relation with her mother as the crucial determinant,

Newman argues that Gordimer's intersection of racial, colonial, and sexual themes, with an increasingly sophisticated focus on gender, takes her work into a reassessment of narrative realism. Newman argues that Gordimer's deconstruction of realism as a way of knowing South African reality opens a new route to cultural and political decolonisation. Her reading resonates interestingly with that offered by Abdul JanMohamed in *Manichean Aesthetics* (1983), where the interest is specifically in the deconstruction of some of the binary oppositions that underpin the colonial enterprise.

David Ward in *Chronicles of Darkness* (1989) finds in Gordimer's fiction a steady movement away from chronicle to prophesy. Although he heralds her for acute, almost lyrical sensitivity and richness of style and detail in her fiction, he addresses the coolness of her tone; for Ward, Gordimer's detachment is a fault neither of the writing nor the writer herself, but an aspect of her ability to produce her narrator as *Other*, alienated not just from the presented world but also from the pre-existing ways of seeing reality. Besides these major approaches to Gordimer's fiction, Dorothy Driver, Lars Engle, Christopher Heywood, Graham Hugun, Karan Lazar, Brian Macaskill, Brighton Oledi, Sheila Roberts, Rowland Smith, and Susan's Winnett have contributed similar critical perspectives on Gordimer's fiction. These researchers have looked at Nadine Gordimer's fiction in several ways but the theme of borderland in her fiction has not been fully explored before this study.

During my lifetime, I have dedicated myself to this struggle of the African people. I have fought against white domination, and I have fought against black domination. I have cherished the ideal of a democratic and free society in which all persons live together in harmony and with equal opportunities. It is an ideal which I hope to live for and to achieve. But if needs be, it is an ideal for which I am prepared to die.

(Nelson Mandela, The Rivonia Trial, Pretoria Supreme Court, 1964)

The Birth of Apartheid

Nadine Gordimer wrote eleven collections of short stories, thirteen novels, and a novella during the years 1949 to 2012. In these fictional publications, she portrayed the rise and fall of apartheid in South Africa. For instance, the Nationalist Party of Afrikaners which institutionalised apartheid through laws and legislation in every sphere of South African life came to power in 1948. (Schrire, 1992, 223) Gordimer's first collection of short stories *Face to Face* was published in 1949. Since then, her fiction has described landmarks in the people's resistance and struggle against apartheid until South Africa became free from its shackles with the first general election in 1994. Gordimer published *None to Accompany Me* in the same year.

In *The Mind of South Africa: The Story of the Rise and the Fall of Apartheid*, the South African journalist Allister Sparks (1933–2016) presents South Africa as a 'honeycomb of cellular group ghettos, full of ghetto attitudes of 'us' and 'them', in which white and black are bound together in a web of mutual destructiveness. Apartheid, brutalising the whites as it destroys the self-esteem of the blacks, robs both of their humanity.' (1990, 217–218) Gordimer presents this mutual destructiveness in 'The Train from Rhodesia' (1949) and *The Conservationist* (1978). These narratives focus on the moral distance of the white people from suffering black South Africa and describe the effects on communication with each other.

The first territorial segregation took place when early Dutch colonists grew 'a bitter almond hedge' around their occupied African land to separate their living area from the rest of the black area, marking a boundary between the two worlds. (Sparks, 1990, xvii) For almost three centuries, this process of marking boundaries to limit the movements of the black people into white areas was practised by the white settlers in South Africa, eventually producing the apartheid system. The Land Act (1954) required a vacant strip of five hundred yards between any black quarter and the white town it served. Gordimer makes her protagonists in *The Lying Days* (1953) and 'Keeping Fit' (1991) conscious of this fence between Van Riebeek's white descendants and the black people of Africa through their casual visits across the boundary. Bulldozing Sophiatown, a township in the west of Johannesburg and building a white suburb in its place, and replacing the black people to South Western townships, later called Soweto, was apartheid's first large-scale undertaking in twentieth-century South Africa. Sophiatown was considered by the Afrikaners as a 'black spot' in a 'white area', partly because it housed a new kind of black lodgers who were second and third-generation city people, detribalised, modern, working-class people, aspirant artists, politicians, writers, musicians, prostitutes, pimps, con men, shebeen queens, and gangsters; people discovering and creating a new world, suffering under its burdens but hugely stimulated by the adventure of it. (Sparks, 1990,188)

This was the place where South African Anglican Archbishop Desmond Mpilo Tutu (1931–2021) grew up, white liberal writers like South African writer Athol Fugard (1932 to date) spent time, anti-apartheid activist and the founding member of the Liberal Party, Alan Paton's (1903–1988) black protagonist looks for his lost son in *Cry the Beloved Country* and Gordimer's white liberal protagonist pays visits in *A World of Strangers*. The underlying objection was against the owning of houses and land by blacks. Gordimer describes the social and economic impact of such encroachment and displacement through borderland situations in her characters' lives such as in *My Son's Story* (1990) and *None To Accompany Me* (1994).

This development continued the colonial past. Discrimination against the black people flourished under the political alliance of the South African party and the English Labour party with the Afrikaners' National party in 1924 and continued to progress under the coalition between these political parties to form the United party in 1934. British settlers worked along with the Afrikaners' style of segregation after they arrived in 1820 and accepted it as part of the natural order of things. The new industries needed cheap black labour after the 1870s for their Industrial wealth. Gordimer describes this hypocrisy of the industrial magnate class in the characterisation of life at the High House in *A World of Strangers* (1958).

The new government of 1948 legally generated a radical and programmatic restructuring of intermixed South African society, which was becoming daily more integrated economically, by dividing it into separate living areas, separate towns, separate economies, separate nations, total separation. The blacks were to be separated not only from the whites but also from the Coloureds, Indians, Chinese and to a lesser extent from one another according to their ethnic classification such as Zulu, Xhosa, Sotho, and Tswana. The Race Classification Act 1950 required every citizen to be registered according to his or her racial group. The Native Laws Amendment Act 1952 limited the blacks' right to live in the urban areas and moved the native owners out of their ancestral lands.

The long-established Pass laws were hardened in 1952, prohibiting the black people from moving about the country to sell their labour on a free market and classified those who were unemployed as vagrants. The Bantu Education Act 1955 was introduced with an inferior education policy to give inferior education to the blacks with the purpose to produce a subordinate class. The Mixed Marriages Act 1949 prohibited mixed marriages and made sexual relations between consenting adults of different skin colours a criminal offence in 1950. In almost all phases of her fiction such as in *Occasion for Loving* (1963), 'Town and Country Lovers' (1980) and *The Pick Up* (2001), Gordimer focuses upon physical relations across the racial spectrum to question the validity of such a rule of law in the real human world.

In 1959, the Afrikaner government introduced a new apartheid policy, calling the blacks different people and thus justifying their need for different treatment. The black people could build their homelands in the black regions which were called Bantustans. The claim was that these were no longer inferior but only different: separate developments with separate freedoms. Gordimer captures this climax of apartheid in her symbolic presentation of the appalling social and economic divisions in white and black life on a South African farm in *The Conservationist* (1978). The strip of bare veld which separated the farm from the black quarters is more than just a physical barrier. It is a mental barrier, too. Apartheid laws prescribed inequality, so that was what its courts enforced; in *Burger's Daughter* (1979), the protagonist's father is charged with treason by a South African court of law for challenging Afrikaner nationalism. Gordimer's *None to Accompany Me* (1994) focuses on such sacrifices through her characters' struggling lives, both on physical and psychological levels, till the apartheid era ended.

A Marxist tendency to reconstruct the past based on economic evidence finds its way into Gordimer's fiction. Reversing Hegel's formulation that the world is governed by thought, that the process of history is the gradual dialectical unfolding of the laws of Reason, and that material existence is the expression of an immaterial spiritual essence, Marx argued that all mental or ideological systems are the products of social and economic existence. (Marx, 1961, 170) The material interests of the dominant social class determine human existence, individual and collective. In this framework, a legal system like apartheid policy is not the pure manifestation of human or divine reason, but a reflection of the interests of the dominant white class in the colonial and post-colonial periods of history; in comparison to African nationalism with an overlay of Marxism stood for communism, Afrikaner nationalism favoured free market. Bhabha in *The Location of Culture* investigates several issues such as liberation from colonial oppression, and cultural differences which can be applied to texts such as Gordimer's fiction and struggles against oppression such as apartheid in South Africa. In his study, Bhabha looks at post-coloniality as continuity rather than rupture between the era of colonialism and the contemporary period, which he refers to as the ongoing colonial 'present'. (1994, 6–9) Similarly, apartheid is an extension, a continuity of the colonial set up which is the basis of physical and psychological borders in South African society. And which Gordimer deals with by focusing upon the social marginality and the psychological alienation that apartheid generates in the lives of her characters in her fiction.

The African National Congress (ANC) was founded in 1912 under the influences of Gandhi's philosophy of non-violence, and the black American struggle in the early 1900s, which advocated black advancement within the framework of segregation rather than confrontation with the system; the civil rights movement (1896–1954) was primarily a nonviolent struggle for civil rights and equality under the law to all Americans. Influenced by Martin Luther King (1929–1968), an African-American civil rights activist, and the Russian writer Leo Tolstoy's (1828–1910) ideas of nonviolent resistance, Mohandas Karamchand Gandhi (1869–1948), an Indian lawyer and a civil rights activist in South Africa (1893–1914) helped found the Natal Indian Congress in 1894. He adopted his methodology of *Satyagraha* (devotion to the truth) and nonviolent protest for the first time when the Transvaal government promulgated a new Act in 1906, compelling registration of the colony's Indian and Chinese populations.

Like the black maid in 'Ah, Woe Is Me' (1949) who works to educate and give a better life to her children, the ANC put its faith in the white man's professed commitment to Christian charity, democracy, and justice, but to no avail. South Africa's first black national trade union leader, Clements Kadalie's (1896–1951) industrial and commercial unionism in the 1930s brought a surge of militancy for a short period. Gordimer reflects on the era of strikes in the childhood experiences of her protagonist in *The Lying Days* (1953); although it is a matter of change of diet for the mineworkers in the novel, it reminds the protagonist of the past strikes about which she had heard from her father in her childhood. Gordimer's fiction describes this aspiring black life in her characterisation of the educated black victims in *A World of Strangers* (1958) and *Occasion for Loving* (1963). Her characters in *The Lying Days* (1953) are disillusioned as nothing brings about their long-awaited future. The ANC's Defiance Campaign (1952) on Gandhian principles of civil disobedience, strikes, boycotts and stay-at-homes, was committed to the goals of national freedom and political independence. The ANC, the Indian Congress, the Coloured People's Congress, a white organisation named the Congress of Democrats, and the non-racial Congress of Trade Unions participated in the national convention that published the Freedom Charter in 1955. The Liberal Party and the United Party did not attend, though they were invited. Gordimer presents this vision in *A Sport of Nature* (1987).

The assertion that South Africa belonged to all is presented indirectly in Gordimer's *A Guest of Honour* (1973), which portrays an independence struggle in Central Africa. In South Africa, the more radical Africanist group broke away from the ANC in 1959 to form the Pan-Africanist Congress, the PAC. It accused the ANC of allowing Africa to be swamped by foreign ideologies, for succumbing to the influence of its white and Indian sympathisers and having been taken over by communists for their extra-African purposes. (Schrire, 1992, 225) In *A Guest of Honour*, Gordimer explores a similar scenario in Zambia, an independent African country.

The Sharpeville massacre (1960) changed the course of action; the white police ruthlessly crushed a black demonstration held against the unjust Pass laws. Like the Jallianwala Bagh (Amritsar, India) massacre of peaceful demonstrators by the British soldiers in 1919 which marked a turning point to pave the way for Indian nationalism and the struggle for independence from Britain, the Sharpeville incident dashed all the hopes of achieving a common non-racial society through peaceful and legal means. Gordimer's *The Late Bourgeois World* (1966) outlines the blacks' approach towards committing violence in their struggle to change their society to one that is non-racial. In 1961, the ANC and the PAC were banned as unlawful organisations. The ANC worked underground; Nelson Mandela became the leader of the National Action Council which demanded a national convention to establish a new Union of all South Africans before the whites declared South Africa a whites-only republic on May 31, 1961. The ANC decided to abandon its policy of non-violence and switched from strategies of non-violence to those of guerrilla struggle. This entailed abandoning its Gandhian commitment to avoid harming human life. Mandela formed the guerrilla-armed wing of ANC, and the PAC formed an armed wing called Poqo—meaning pure and alone—which called on the masses to kill and drive out the white bosses and take over their homes. The possibility of a political solution to the racial conflict was replaced by the certainty of confrontation. Gordimer records this underground struggle of the activists in *July's People* (1981), *Something Out There* (1984) and *A Sport of Nature* (1987) thus revealing her concern and affiliation with the resistance politics in protest of apartheid in South Africa.

Liberalism in South Africa was preoccupied with two main issues, race relations and the rule of law. A philosophy belonging to the eighteenth-century period of Reason and Enlightenment, it cherished certain democratic rights as essential: freedom of conscience, speech and of the press, and equality before the law. In South Africa, it developed out of a white minority who upheld this humanist spirit—the freedom of the individual against political, social, and economic domination; a small group of the United Party (1934 merger of two Afrikaner political parties—the 1914 National Party and the 1910 South African Party) dissidents founded the Liberal Party in 1953. The founding members included Margaret Ballinger, Alan Paton, Leo Marquard, Oscar Wolheim, Leslie Rubin, Peter Brown, H. Selby Msimang, Leo Kuper and Hilda Kuper. The party was in direct conflict with the South African government due to its opposition to apartheid and criticism of the erosion of human rights by legally allowing detention without trial and arbitrary suppression of political opposition.

The liberals in South Africa were against all types of isms whether it was Afrikanerism, Africanism or Communism, and aimed to work towards the elimination of racial discrimination in South Africa. They first favoured a non-racial but qualified franchise for the blacks but later advocated political equality for all before the law. (Schrire, 1992, 224) Initially, the Liberal Party supported a qualified franchise but the Sharpeville massacre in 1960 and the consequent state of emergency changed its outlook; the liberals then stood unequivocally for a democratic non-racial South Africa, with one man, one vote as its franchise policy.

Gordimer's fiction deals with the plight of the liberal community in twentieth-century South Africa. *The Lying Days* (1953), *A World of Strangers* (1958) and *Occasion for Loving* (1963) focus on the liberal voice that adhered to the principle of humanism in its protest against apartheid. These novels have traced changes in liberal attitudes from the period of passive resistance to apartheid in the 1950s and then to the era of armed opposition and struggle, beginning in the 1960s. They provide an insight into what had been happening in the lives of liberals with the rise to power of the National Party in 1948 and the establishment of the Liberal Party in 1953. Gordimer's characters who are determinedly concerned with private relationships in these novels cannot escape an intrusion from the political situation in their relationships with people across the racial spectrum. They suffer alienation and marginalisation for their accommodating attitudes and question the validity of their liberal values in South

African society. This changing consciousness of the liberals appears most clearly in *The Late Bourgeois World* (1966). It projects the early post-Sharpeville era when the underground struggle began to overthrow the apartheid government in South Africa. The Sharpeville incident (1960) marked a watershed in South African life and a change in Gordimer's approach to apartheid. She stated: 'I used to regard myself as a liberal, but I now regard myself as a radical.' (Cassere, 1972, 56) Gordimer turned away from liberalism because 'it has never delivered the goods. Too ready to compromise, to see both sides of the question, too polite: too much of a gesture, not enough of a commitment, not radical.' (Schwartz, 1977, 93) It could not succeed in front of a cherished political system that advocated white supremacism in South Africa and offered political stability and economic security to the white minority only. Sparks noted that it failed in South Africa because it was not acting 'as an inspirational force that could lead to constructive action but a sterile dogma that concealed an unconscious attachment to the status quo.' (1990, 259)

The liberals were divided into various groups such as left-wing liberals who were also militant, right-wing liberals who later called themselves progressive liberals and who were able to survive under the apartheid regime. The world of liberals as described by Gordimer in her fiction represented the border between the polarised worlds of the whites and the blacks in South Africa. Whether it is the protagonist with his liberal humanism in *A World of Strangers* (1958) or the protagonist with his militant spirit in *The Late Bourgeois World* (1966), the liberals played the role of a bridge in South African society which adjoined two parallel worlds but never succeeded in uniting them. A recession in open black politics resulted from the ban on major black political parties in the 1960s; the Liberal Party provided a joint platform to people from all communities to keep the protest alive under its banner. But the Improper Interference Act (1968) prohibited this by outlawing multiracial political parties. The black, Coloured, and Indian members had to quit the Party for the sake of its survival which disillusioned many liberals of its integrity in the South African world. Gordimer's move away from the politics of liberalism is reflected in her developing concern with the struggle of black nationalists in her fiction.

Steve Biko (1946–1977) a young medical student at the University of Natal and an anti-apartheid activist, rejected liberalism as an ideology and propounded a new doctrine in 1969 which said that black liberation could be achieved only by the black people themselves and had to begin with breaking free of the shackles of psychological inferiority. In Biko's view, apartheid was 'an eyesore spoiling an otherwise beautiful view', for the liberals to 'take their eyes off' whenever they wished to. (Biko, 1978, 22) Biko resented the problem that the whites dominated the liberal organisation and imposed limits on the militancy they believed in. The whites protested orally, almost ritually, but that was as far as they were prepared to go. This state of liberal affairs is epitomised by Gordimer in *Occasion for Loving* (1963) in the failure of the relationships between the white and the black characters in the novel. Biko's movement changed the direction of the blacks' move towards violent means to liberate South Africa from the white minority rule. Gordimer generates this spirit of Black Consciousness in her fiction. It is inculcated in the black characters' sense of confidence in them such as the protagonist's father in *My Son's Story* (1990), the protagonist's servant in *July's People* (1981) and the protagonist's lawyer in *The House Gun* (1998).

A relation between the fictional world and its historical period in South Africa is explicit in Gordimer's fiction. Her short stories and novels describe the changes in social mood from the time of passive resistance against apartheid in the 1950s to the armed opposition and struggle after 1960. With historical specificities and cultural diversities of the South African world, she focuses upon social and cultural displacements to raise her voice against the polarisation of society into white, black, Coloured and Asiatic groups in South Africa as in *A World of Strangers*, *The Conservationist* and *July's People*. Her fiction depicts this consciousness of her era thus telling the history of South Africa in chronological order.

This presentation of history in Gordimer's fiction can be divided into three main parts: the protest era, the struggle era, and the liberation era. The legalisation of apartheid after 1948, the Sharpeville incident in 1960, the Soweto Uprisings in 1976 and the underground struggle of the ANC and adjacent movements between the 1960s and the general election in 1994, found a central place during events in characters' lives in Gordimer's fiction. They chronologically project these historical times, providing a link between the resistance, the struggle, and the liberation phases of South African history. In the protest era, resistance is focused on limited mixed gatherings and relationships of characters across the racial spectrum. This social framework appears in *A World of Strangers* (1958). The struggle era appears in *The Late Bourgeois World* (1966) and *Burger's Daughter* (1979). A South Africa free from the shackles of apartheid appears in *A Sport of Nature* (1987) and *None to Accompany Me* (1994).

Gordimer's fiction is historical in the sense that it unfolds the story against the backdrop of a specific event such as the failure of liberalism exposed in *A Guest of Honour* (1973); liberalism cannot bring emancipation for black South Africans, therefore, a radical change must be pursued. Whereas in *Burger's Daughter* (1979), a rejection of liberal society is presented in the protagonist Rosa's association with the prison community. However, there is a difference in the presentation of psychological effects on characters after their experiences in these three historical eras as recorded by Gordimer in her fiction. In the protest era, the focus is on the experience of apartheid such as in the short story, 'Ah, Woe Is Me' (1949) and the novel, *The Lying Days* (1953). In the struggle and the liberation eras, a process of transformation is added, to capture the changed lives of the characters in novels such as *Burger's Daughter* (1979) and *My Son's Story* (1990). These historical eras altered the presentation of the characters and society's development in Gordimer's fiction.

Issues related to apartheid get special attention in Nadine Gordimer's fiction. Attention to other systems such as slavery, genocide, assimilation, and labour differentiation in colonial societies worldwide, as it appears in the South African writer Njabulo Ndebele's *Rediscovery of the Ordinary* (1991) find little room in her writings, though these movements encouraged the survival of indigenous cultural and literary expression. In the South African context, social differences, and legally enforced separation between the white and the black people created physical borders and mental barriers between them. The concept of borderland is important here as it categorically deals with the severe physical impact of apartheid on its white and black communities; it affected them to live in separate units and classes, and generated fear and a sense of alienation towards each other as in *The Lying Days* and *Occasion for Loving*. This regulated a restricted social experience and identity in twentieth-century South Africa, imposing different types of borders based on colour. However, there is a difference between the notion of borders that was at work or which existed in South African society under apartheid and Gordimer's presentation of the theme of borderland in her fiction during the apartheid era: in the South African context, it divided people into white, black, Coloured, Indian and Asiatic communities whereas, in Gordimer's fiction, it creates a space for these people to see beyond their restricted identities and discover a new perspective upon themselves as well as on their South African life.

Hungarian philosopher Georg Lukacs' (1885–1971) Marxist critical theory of reflection describes a text as a reflection of a kind of system that was gradually unfolding: a narrative reveals or ought to reveal underlying patterns in the social order and provide a sense of wholeness of existence with all its inherent contradictions, tensions, and conflicts. Similarly, Gordimer's fiction is concerned with the content of South African life from which emerges a sense of order within the complexity and subtlety of lived experience; all the contradictions and tensions of social existence are realised in a formal whole in her fiction. Like Homi Bhabha who addresses the issue of how a nation's history is narrated and interpreted through different voices in the literature (*Nation and Narration* 1990), Gordimer's fiction presents the unspoken and unrepresented past which haunts the present, thus signifying the relationship of the arts with the social reality of life. In Gordimer's words: 'In the writing, I am acting upon my society, and in the manner of my apprehension, all the time history is acting upon me.' (Gordimer, 1975, 13) Gordimer stitches together history and imagination, fact, and fiction, black and white to build a narration that aims to chronicle, with poetic license, the epic of South African history.

Segregation (1488–1948)

B.C. San (Bushman) and Khoikhoi (Hottentots) resided in an area now known as South Africa.

A.D. Bantu-speaking African farmers migrated to the eastern part of present-day South Africa.

1488 Portuguese explorers discovered the Cape of Good Hope. Africans settled in Transvaal, Orange Free State, Natal, and Eastern Cape.

1652 Dutch East India Company established a station in Cape Peninsula. Dutch, German and French Huguenot immigrants settled in the Cape and merged later to become Afrikaners (called Boers by the British). Slaves were imported from the East Indies, Madagascar and other parts of Africa, and indigenous San and Khoikhoi died off or were assimilated.

1760 First Pass Laws were introduced. All slaves in the Cape were required to carry documents designed to control the movement of the population.

1795 British captured Cape Colony from the Dutch.

1816 Zulu kingdom rose under Shaka.

1820 English immigrants settled in the Eastern Cape.

1834 British abolished slavery throughout the empire.

1836 Afrikaner farmers, rejecting British rule, made Great Trek into interior South Africa.

1838 Afrikaners defeated Zulus in Natal.

1841 The first African secondary school, Lovedale Missionary Institution was established in Eastern Cape.

1843 British annexed Natal.

1852 British recognised Transvaal and Orange Free State as independent Afrikaner states.

1853 The non-racial qualified franchise was established in Cape Colony through British influence.

1860 Indentured labourers were brought from India by the British to work on Natal sugar plantations.

1867 Diamonds were discovered in the north of Cape Colony, near Kimberley.

1877 British annexed Transvaal.

1878 Xhosa were defeated by the British in frontier wars in Eastern Cape.

1879 British defeated Zulus and annexed Zululand.

1880 First Anglo-Boer War took place in which Transvaal Afrikaners regained their independence.

1884 First African edited newspaper started.

1886 Gold was discovered in the Witwatersrand.

1894 Natal Indian Congress (NIC) was formed under Mohandas K. Gandhi who lived in South Africa from 1893 until 1914.

1898 Afrikaners defeated Venda, the last independent African kingdom.

1899 The second Anglo-Boer War took place in which Afrikaners were defeated. Transvaal and Orange Free State became self-governing British colonies.

1902 Cape Coloureds formed the African Political Organisation.

1909 Africans held the South African Native Convention to protest racial segregation in the proposed constitution.

1910 Union of South Africa was formed as a self-governing British dominion with parliament limited to whites. General Louis Botha, leader of the Afrikaner-English coalition and supported by General Jan C Smuts became the first Prime Minister.

1912 The first national African political movement under the South African Native National Congress began to overcome ethnic divisions and oppose racial segregation.

1913 Native Land Act limits land purchases by Africans: 70 per cent of the population to reserves which equals 7 per cent of the land.

African reserves form the basis of today's tribal homelands.

1914 Afrikaners formed the National Party under General J B M Hertzog to oppose Botha and Smuts. Afrikaner nationalists opposed South African armed forces fighting in WW1 on side of Britain.

1915 South Africa conquered the German colony of South-West Africa (Namibia).

1916 South African Native College was opened in Eastern Cape.

1919 Smuts became Prime Minister. South African Native National Congress campaigned against Pass Laws.

1920 The first nationwide mass movement for Africans, the Industrial and Commercial Workers' Union was formed. League of Nations granted South Africa trusteeship to govern South West Africa.

1921 South Africa Communist Party (SACP) was formed.

1923 South African Native National Congress was renamed the African National Congress (ANC).

Nadine Gordimer was born in Gauteng, an East Rand mining town outside Johannesburg.

1924 General Hertzog became Prime Minister in coalition with the English-speaking Labour Party.

1925 Afrikaans was recognised as the second official language after English.

1930 White women were enfranchised.

1931 All property and literacy tests were removed for white voters. Britain recognised South Africa's legal sovereignty within the Commonwealth.

1934 Hertzog and Smuts joined forces to form the United Party. Afrikaner nationalists under Dr D F Malan established the National Party.

1936 Native Land and Trust Act increased African reserves from 7 to 13.7 per cent of all land. Africans were removed from the common voters' roll in Cape Province and were placed on a separate roll to elect seven whites to Parliament. All African Convention was held to protest this creation of the national advisory Natives' Representative Council.

1937 **Gordimer published her first short stories in 1937 at the age of 15. Her first published work was a short story for children, 'The Quest for Seen Gold' which appeared in the Children's Sunday Express. 'Come Again Tomorrow' another children's story appeared in Forum.**

1940 Pass Laws were suspended in all major towns during WW2.

1943 ANC called for a non-racial franchise. Youth League was formed and led by Nelson Mandela and Oliver Tambo. The Non-European Unity Movement began which advocated non-collaboration with all segregated bodies.

1946 Natal Indian Congress (NIC) and Transvaal Indian Congress (TIC) began a passive resistance campaign to protest policies on land and representation. About 70 thousand African mineworkers went on strike. Natives' Representative Council adjourned indefinitely.

1948 The National Party of Afrikaners introduced apartheid which was codified and expanded through laws and legislation in every sphere of South African life.

This early phase of Gordimer's writing has its significance because of her exploration and experimentation with the form and subject matter of her fiction. For instance, the theme of apartheid that Gordimer presents in her early short stories such as 'Is There Nowhere Else Where We Can Meet?' 'Ah, Woe Is Me', 'The Train From Rhodesia', and 'Which New Era Would that Be?'—discussed in detail later—recurs in her early novels, The Lying Days, A World of Strangers, *and* Occasion for Loving. *In comparison to her short stories where the focus is on the experience of the very moment such as in 'The Train From Rhodesia', Gordimer presents the effects of apartheid on the characters' lives in* A World of Strangers *and* Occasion for Loving: *after confronting the most feared and hated aspects of the inner self, Gordimer's protagonists transform and look for a change in their South African society. If Gordimer presents harsh encounters between the characters in brevity in her short stories, the novel allows her more room to depict the social climate of apartheid and the related upheavals in South Africa in a succession of intimate glimpses of her South African world.*

Phase One: Years of Liberal Protest

In the 1950s, the short story was the most sought-after literary form because of the rise of popular tabloids and small literary magazines such as the *Drum*, *Fighting Talk* and *New Age*. Their emergence partly filled the gap created by the dearth of local publishing houses in South Africa with strong interests in literature during that period. Also, the form of the short story appeared well-suited to social conditions of duress; its brevity can contain many of the brief, harsh borderland encounters of South African life. Therefore, short stories are a dominant form of writing in Gordimer's early fiction. Although Gordimer did not have the same publication constraints that the *Drum* generation had, a linear pattern of writing appears in her approach to fiction. Like Alex La Guma, she finds space for direct racial confrontation in the form of short stories first. This is replaced in the form of novels in the later years of her writing.

Nadine Gordimer's story 'Is There Nowhere Else Where We Can Meet?' from the earliest collection *Face to Face* (1949) explores the working of a borderland where things happen that make devastating as well as transforming impressions on the main character's mind. The story describes a threatening encounter between a white girl and a black man in their daily South African life. When the story begins, the white girl is treading her way on a path that she knows well. She notices the presence of 'a native in a red woollen cap' at the far end of the same path; he is gazing at the direction he has come from. As she approaches him, his appearance reveals to her his poverty: 'His one trouser leg was torn off above the knee, [...] The eyes were red [...] strong smell of old sweat [...]' (*Meet?*, 15) Whilst passing by each other, both pretend that they have not seen each other but then the white girl realises that the black man is hurriedly approaching her. She turns back and finds him right behind her in a position to attack her. She is frightened:

> For a moment it was Fear itself that had her by the arms, the legs, the throat; not fear of the man, of any single menace he might present, but Fear, absolute and abstract. (*Meet?*, 16)

As she observes that his 'one foot, cracked from exposure until it looked like broken wood, moved, only to restore balance in the dizziness that follows running', he grabs her by the shoulder. The smell of his body 'choked her—It was an old pyjama jacket, not a shirt'—she realises about his dress at a close glance. In the struggle, the white girl drops her bag and parcel on the ground. The black man gets hold of them before she restores her balance. The white girl runs away and reaches the road on the other side of the fence that she climbs and behind which she feels that she is safe. The fence in this story is symbolic of boundaries and borders which demarcate social and economic divisions between the white girl and her black attacker:

> A little way on there were houses, with gardens, post-boxes, a child's swing. A small dog sat at a gate. She could hear a faint hum, as of life, of talk somewhere, or perhaps telephone wires. [...] (*Meet?* 16–17)

The white girl realises that she fears the black man for nothing. He has been in desperate need of food and shelter. Here, the path that exists closer to the fence provides a moment of intense communication that the white girl and the black man live through at the same time, thus revealing to the white girl her low level of understanding of the black man's world: 'What did I fight for? Why didn't I give him the money and let him go? [...] she [...] went down the road slowly, like an invalid [...]' (*Meet?* 17–18) Taken over by the experience of fear in the violent attack, the white girl becomes aware that she should have responded differently.

The action in this story is developed in a setting that makes the impact of apartheid visible to the white sensibility. It disturbs the white girl to realise, after living through the experience of violence, that though her black attacker is a native of South Africa, his presence as a human being has never been recognised in her society. The title of the story, 'Is There Nowhere Else Where We Can Meet?' poses the question of whether it will ever be possible for racial groups in South Africa to come to know about each other's life to understand the real problems of the other's world.

'Ah, Woe Is Me' is another story from the same collection *Face to Face* (1949) in which the central character, through her humility towards her black housemaid, discovers a conflict between her white sensibility (or lack of it) and African life. Sarah, a fat 'light yellow-brown' middle-aged woman works as a housemaid in a white family where she is known for her good cooking and polite manners. Her frequent utterance of—'Ah, woe is me'—amuses the white mistress and her family, though it is Sarah's comment on her struggling life: 'You got to live in this world the way it is, she said.' The white mistress finds Sarah ambitious in her attempt to 'want' her three children, Robert, Janet, and Felicia 'to know their place':

> Her Mission School education, with its tactful emphasis on the next world rather than this, had not made her dangerous enough or brave enough or free enough or even educated enough to think that any place was the place for her children [...] her believe that there was a place for them; not a share in the White Man's place, but not no place at all, either; a place of their own. She wanted them to have it and she wanted them to stay there. (*Woe*, 24)

In her attempt to discipline her children for a better place in life, Sarah first sends them to school in the Location and then moves them to a boarding school in Natal. She shares her pride and satisfaction with the white mistress at her children's progress at the boarding school, though they can only visit her once a year because she cannot afford the travel fare to bring them home frequently.

The white mistress finds Sarah's children extremely quiet and introverted in their manners. Once she gives Sarah some sweets to be sent to the children at the boarding school. In return, she receives a polite letter of thanks from Janet but to her surprise, the letter does not reveal 'the slightest hint of any pleasure that the gift might have brought'. (*Woe, 25*) On one other occasion, when Sarah's children are at home with their mother for their yearly vacations and can stay in the black quarter with the white mistress's permission, the white mistress gives a water pistol to Robert but she never sees him playing with it. She is unable to understand Robert's attitude who took the toy 'as if it were a penance'. (*Woe*, 26) The white mistress simply cannot entertain the idea that Sarah's children cannot afford to be virtuous without the fulfilment of basic needs; a little education has given them some manners but it cannot guarantee any protection of their self-respect.

Sarah wants her children to earn respect and honour in life but her struggle and her commitment cannot save her and her children from their impending fate and misery. She gets sick and has to leave the job at the white mistress's house. She moves to the Location and earns her living on the part-time washing that she can do at home. Her children are shifted back to the school at the Location as Sarah can no longer afford to pay for their education and lodging at the boarding school. But Sarah doesn't lose heart. She still believes that she can educate her children better with her Mission school education.

Through her children's visits from time to time, the white mistress comes to know about Sarah's deteriorating health and notices the bad condition of the children's lives in poverty. Helping Sarah's family with a bit of money and some old clothes, and her inquiry from Sarah's children about their progress in school always make the white mistress think:

> I always had the curious feeling that they were embarrassed, not *by* me, but *for* me, as if their faces knew that I could not help asking the same questions, because the real state of their lives was unknown and unimagined by me, and therefore beyond my questioning. (*Woe*, 27)

When she comes to know through another servant at her house that Sarah's husband has also lost his job and Robert has started working on a dairy to support the family, she sends a message for Sarah to say, 'is there anything I can do to help?' The messenger comes back with an answer that is delivered in an arrogant and restrained tone: 'Her husband has got another job.' To be led to feel as if they don't need her help offends the white mistress: 'As if I was incapable of understanding anything told me once.' (*Woe*, 28)

Next time, when Janet visits the white mistress, she looks poorer and much quieter than before. The white mistress has to dig out the information from her: Felicia is married, Robert is working and Janet herself has stopped going to school because she has to look after her sick mother. She offers Janet a cup of tea with bread and gives her some money and old clothes. Janet cannot bear the pain of suffering this time and lets her feelings go in public by weeping bitterly in front of the white mistress. In return, the white mistress didn't know how to react: 'What could I do for her? What could I do? Here…I said, here—take this, and gave her my handkerchief.' (*Woe*, 30) Although the white mistress's standard of humility towards Sarah and her family ends here, it reveals to her the level of the social and economic divide that exists between her and Sarah's world and which is huge enough to keep both at a distance from each other.

In this story, Gordimer makes the white mistress aware of her moral distance from the real problems in Sarah and her family's life through her attempt to keep a goodwill relationship with them. Whereas in the story 'The Train From Rhodesia', from the same collection *Face to Face* (1949), Gordimer's central character is appalled to find her husband in full appreciation of the African wooden craft without any recognition and respect for the black craftsman or the vendor who has made them into 'a beautiful piece of work'. (*Train*, 47) The action of the story is set in a railway station—a place of departure or arrival, or transit for the white woman in this story. For her, the station becomes a stop-over enabling her to experience the exploitation of African life in the hands of her white community. In this setting, 'native vendors' come up to the train to sell African handicrafts to the white travellers. The white woman indicates to her husband her liking for a wooden lion which 'is carved out of softwood.' She finds it too expensive to pay 'three and six' pence for the item and lets the bargain go. She goes back to her compartment but her husband keeps on bargaining with the old vendor over the price of the wooden lion. When the train starts moving, the native seller agrees to 'one-and-six' pence and is led by the white woman's husband to complete the deal by running alongside the train. Instead of getting happiness at the possession of the wooden lion, the white woman is embarrassed at her husband's act of 'bargaining' for 'fun':

> Why didn't you buy it in the first place? If you wanted it, why didn't you pay for it? Why didn't you take it decently [...] why did you have to wait for him to run after the train with it, and give him one-and-six? One-and-six! (*Train*, 46–7)

She feels that her husband has done something irresponsible and disrespectful. To bargain for a few pennies is an embarrassment for the young woman:

> The heat of shame mounted through her legs and body and sounded in her ears like the sound of sand pouring. [...] She sat there, sick. [...] the discovery of a void [...] the physical state of the young woman is in complete harmony with her mental condition. (*Train*, 47)

The experience of the purchase has knocked at the door of her conscience but she finds herself helpless to do anything about it. The story is narrated in a very compact form. The whole action takes place in the train's stop-over for a few minutes at a station. The train enters the platform from a 'red horizon' suggesting something inevitable is going to happen: 'Creaking, jerking, jostling, gasping, the train filled the station.' (*Train*, 43) Both at the arrival and departure time, the train 'called out to the sky, I'm coming, I'm coming; and again, there was no answer.' Like the train on the platform, the white woman is not able to find an answer to the pricking of her conscience; feelings of shame are 'cast' over her 'like a skin'. (*Train*, 47)

From the action and characterisation in these stories, it becomes evident that Gordimer focuses on that rare experience that makes a lasting impact on her characters' lives. In 'Which New Era Would That Be?' from the collection *Six Feet of the Country* (1956), Jake Alexander, a Coloured man, part Scottish, part African, owns a printing business in a 'run down' area in Johannesburg. His shop which is situated in a 'New Era Building' acts as a borderland where Jake entertains people across the 'colour bar'. (*Era*, 71–72) He 'had decided long ago that he would take the whole business of the colour bar as humorous.' (*Era*, 76)

So he has 'strange friends' such as Alister Halford, an Englishman who has been in South Africa for eighteen months as a correspondent for a newspaper in England. Both Jake and Alister get along with each other because they gain 'nostalgic pleasure' from adventures like slipping into 'bars of the shabbier Johannesburg hotels' and many times, they get away with it. This attitude has the effect of making their friendship less self-conscious than is usual between a white man and a Coloured man' in South Africa:

> [Alister] had accompanied Jack to a shabeen in a Coloured location, where it was illegal for a white man to be, as well as illegal for anyone at all to have a drink [...]. (*Era*, 75)

When the action of the story begins, Jake and his five friends, Themba, Klaas, Albert, Billy and Maxie Ndube are having their drink in 'secret' because 'black men've got to drink in secret'. (*Era*, 80) Except for Billy and Maxie who are black men, the rest of Jake's friends are Coloureds. Themba with his 'large yellow hands' is Coloured like Jack but with a different ancestry:

> Themba, a Coloured—a mixture of the bloods of black slaves and white masters, blended long ago, in the days when the Cape of Good Hope was a port of refreshment for the Dutch East India Company. (*Era*, 73)

Klaas is a 'yellow' skinned man with hair 'like ginger-Coloured wire wool' but he shares his roots with Albert:

> Klaas and Albert had in their mixed blood some strain of the Bushman, which gave them a batrachian yellowness and toughness, like one of those toads that (prehistoric as the Bushman is) are mythically believed to have survived into modern times (hardly more fantastically than the Bushman himself has survived) by spending centuries shut up in an air bubble in a rock. (*Era*, 73)

The Population Registration Act (1950) required racial classification of all South Africans. (Suzman, 1960, 354) Jake and his party of five men are educated Africans for whom such classification means nothing. They are, however, against the progressive attitude of the whites towards the blacks like them such as Jennifer Tetzel, a white assistant director of a rehabilitation scheme for 'a desolate slum' on the Cape Flats in the bush outside Cape Town:

> Jack knew the type well [...] Congress of Democrats and other organisations where progressive whites met progressive blacks. These were the white women who, Jack knew, persisted in regarding themselves as your equal. *'That was even worse,'* he thought, *'than the parsons who persisted in regarding you as their equal'*. (*Era*, 71–72)

In 1953, the left-wing whites of the United Party dissidents formed the Congress of Democrats in sympathy with the ANC. (Schrire, 1992, 224) Jake did not approve of these whites who identify themselves with the black man's 'feelings'. He believes:

> [The white man cannot understand] the humiliation of the black man walking the streets only by the permission of a pass written out by a white person, and the guilt and swagger of the Coloured man light-faced enough to slink, fugitive from his own skin, into the preserves—the cinemas, bars, libraries—marked 'EUROPEANS ONLY'. (*Era*, 71–72)

Jennifer accompanies Alister in one of his occasional visits to meet Jack and his party at the garage. In her conversation, Jennifer shares her experience of living in the Cape Flats with Maxie who, in his capacity as an organiser of African trade unions, has also stayed in the same slum for quite a time before moving to Johannesburg. Both know George Elson, a white lawyer who is arrested for his participation in anti-colour bar movements. Maxie recalls some of his experiences of life with George which amuses everybody in the shop except Jennifer. Maxie says that whenever he has accompanied George to visit the white officials, George is told that 'your boy can wait outside'. (*Era*, 74) Once the tea is served in two different mugs in a white manager's house, one in a tin and the other in a China cup. George takes the tin mug for himself. At lunchtime, the white manager directs Maxie to have his food alone on the stoep. Another incident that Maxie narrates makes everybody laugh. As Maxie doesn't have an African accent, a white girl, Peggy fancies his voice on the phone but when she sees him, she is embarrassed: her face is 'red' at shaking hands with a black. Here, Jennifer makes a comment which surprises Maxie:

'It's hard to be punished for not being black. [...] Really, I assure you it is.' (*Era*, 80)

Before her departure, Jennifer tells Maxie that although she respects his narration of the incidents about the colour bar, she doesn't believe his story about his being served lunch on a stoep in the white manager's house. For her, Maxie has invented something 'about' the white man. (*Era*, 81–82) When Jennifer and Alister are gone, Jake kicks the chair hard on which Jennifer had been sitting to let out his anger and mistrust for her sincerity towards them. Jennifer's very presence in the shop has been an irritation for Jake who 'felt suddenly, after all, the old gulf opening between himself and Alister.' (*Era*, 77)

In this story, the action develops in a situation in which the white and the black characters meet each other across the usual master-servant relationship that was prevalent in South African society. Their efforts towards such relationships are hindered by the working of apartheid that keeps on intruding in their everyday contact with each other. Like the title 'Is There Nowhere Else Where We Can Meet?' the title of this story 'Which New Era Would That Be?' raises a question, as posed by Jennifer at the beginning of the story and to which Alister has no clear answer:

> [Alister] had known whether the reference was to the discovery of deep-level gold mining that had saved Johannesburg from the ephemeral fate of a mining camp in the nineties, or to the optimism after the settlement of labour troubles in the twenties, or to the recovery after the world went off the gold standard in the thirties—really, one had no idea of the age of these buildings in this run-down end of the town. (*Era*, 70–71)

However, Jake and his party of black and Coloured friends represent a world in which racial categorisation is not acceptable to educated Africans like them. Nor will they agree to the white man's participation in the struggle against apartheid in South African society.

Similar situations and psychological encounters between the white and the black characters are the gist of action in Gordimer's other early short stories too, but with a difference. If stories like 'Is There Nowhere Else Where We Can Meet?' (1949) and 'Which New Era Would That Be?' (1956) describe a strong sense of alienation between the white and the black worlds, stories like 'The Smell of Death and Flowers' (1956) pinpoint the difficulties which times of oppression and resistance create in people's lives in South Africa. In stories like 'The Catch' (1953), 'Amateurs' (1953), 'The Soft Voice of the Serpent' (1953), 'Six Feet of the

Country' (1956) and 'Happy Event' (1956), Gordimer deals with issues related to social identity and marginality through characters' physical and psychological encounters with the reality of their everyday South African life such as the existence of no-man's land between the white houses and black quarters in 'Happy Event'. Besides, there are stories in which Gordimer reflects upon the childhood and youth experiences of a young person growing up in South Africa such as in 'The Umbilical Cord' (1949), 'A Present for a Good Girl' (1949), 'The Last of the Old Fashioned Girls' (1949), 'The Prisoner' (1953), 'The Defeated' (1953), 'Charmed Lives' (1956), 'Clowns in Clover' (1956) and 'A Bit of a Young Life' (1956). Gordimer's early short stories are especially interesting because of their diversity in form and content. Also, major social, economic, and political issues of the country are given a central place in her short stories such as in 'Ah, Woe Is Me' and 'Which New Era Would That Be?' The stories which depict social climate and related upheavals in South Africa become a microcosm of the course of action that Gordimer follows in almost all her novels.

Gordimer's early novels *The Lying Days* (1953), *A World of Strangers* (1958) and *Occasion for Loving* (1963) present the protest era when South Africans resisted the legalisation of apartheid in every sphere of life. It brings into light the Sharpeville incident of 1960 when the black activists, after the killing of sixty-nine black demonstrators by the police, started moving away from their policy of peaceful struggle against apartheid in South Africa. The Sharpeville demonstration was in protest against the Pass laws which made it compulsory for people other than whites to keep a reference book: it stood for racial identification and therefore, for racial discrimination. In *The Lying Days*, this change in direction from protest to resistance politics is projected in the protagonist's observation of the black activists who stop coming to the group discussions that had been organised by the social welfare community in Johannesburg. In *A World of Strangers*, it is presented in the polarisation between white supremacism and Africanism in South African society. The oscillation of the protagonist between the poor black world at the locations and the white rich world of Johannesburg describes the social climate of South African society at the time of the Sharpeville tragedy. As the thread of communication is missing due to the intrusion of apartheid in their South African lives, Gordimer's characters go through a process of alienation and social severance in their relationships across the racial spectrum in *Occasion for Loving*. It explores the immediate post-Sharpeville time when the divide between the white and black nationalisms seemed irreconcilable. Gordimer's early fiction emphasises the importance of personal relationships and individual fulfilment; personal relationships across the colour line were projected as solutions to the racial tensions in South Africa. The projection of the consciousness that liberalism is too moderate to resolve the opposing nationalisms of the time—white supremacism and Africanism—draws a line between her early and later fiction.

The plot in these early novels is built through the characters' attempt to cross over the social barriers of their South African society into those borderland places such as mixed gatherings and parties where they can meet people across the racial spectrum as equals. The action, there, becomes alive with the intrusion of apartheid in their borderland relationships with each other. They break down in shame and embarrassment at the futility of their efforts of building bridges across the racial divide. But at the same time, this mental probing drives them to commit themselves to the struggle against apartheid in their South African society.

The action in *The Lying Days* (1953) develops in three parts, the Mine, the Sea, and the City, providing insights into Helen Shaw's life as a child, a teenager, and a young woman. It depicts a sensual and intellectual emergence of a young white girl into womanhood in a profoundly divided society; Helen finds it difficult to stay intact in her relationship with her parents with whom she spends her childhood in a gold mining town near Johannesburg. She forms friendships with individuals who represent divisions in South African society: Joel Aaron, a young Jew, Mary Seswayo, a black girl whom Helen meets in her student life at the university in Johannesburg, and Paul Clark, a white welfare officer with whom she shares a flat in Johannesburg before leaving South Africa for Europe.

During her casual visit to a native compound in her childhood, Helen discovers a world that is ugly and does not exist in books:

> I have never read a book in which I myself was recognisable; in which there was a 'girl' Anna who did the housework and the cooking and called the mother and father Missus and Baas; in which the children ate and lived closely with their parents and played in the lounge and went to the bioscope. [...] The sedate walk of two genteel infant Tories through an English Park was other world enough for me. (LD, 20–21)

The story in the novel develops in a setting that is South African. Whilst walking along the 'white corrugated tin fences' (LD, 14) which separate the white living area from the rest of the mining town, the 'niggers' (LD, 35) become a focus of Helen's attention: she finds the mine boys 'something to laugh at in their blankets and their clay-spiked hair' and also 'they spoke and shouted in a language you didn't understand and dressed differently in any old thing.' (LD, 14) Helen notices that 'the skin of the natives' feet was like bark, the nails like thorn.' (LD, 23) But Helen feels a 'tingling fascination' for the 'real world' of the Location: peeping through the window of a native general store, she finds her finger wanting to hold 'the dustiness, the greyness, the scavenged collection of tooth and claw and skin and sluggish potion' displayed inside the shop. (LD, 23) Helen shows 'a longing of affection for the tortoiseshell which was to me a creature in itself.' (LD, 22) But her absorption in the native world is short-lived. As she makes her way towards the Recreation Hall in the white living area, she completely forgets about her visit to the compound. She gets mixed up with the familiar society of her privileged white world: 'I was quite one of them.' (LD, 25) Despite the acquired familiarity with the native world, the child in Helen finds herself very much part of the patterns of her white world.

However, her adulthood 'adventure' (LD, 327) of the Location upsets Helen. She sees the magnitude of the 'difference' that exists between the white and the black standards of living in South Africa:

> A difference so great that the whole conception of charity must be changed. [...] a whole population, the entire black-skinned population on whose labour the city rested, forced to live in slums because there was nowhere else for them to live, too poor to maintain themselves decently because no matter what their energy, their skill, their labour was not allowed value above subsistence level. (LD, 239)

It disturbs Helen to know how much people could be distant from each other's economic insecurities as well as how much the whites in South Africa are sheltered from the reality of the masses. As a child, it 'amused' Helen to find her mother communicating with their gardener, Paul 'as if he were a friend' (LD, 34) but as she grows up, Helen finds it difficult to digest her mother's hypocrisy and moral distance from real problems in a black person's life. Helen disapproves of her mother's level of communication with Anna, the black housemaid in their house:

> Making use of Anna as a friend and conveniently ignorant yes-woman, elevating her to the status of a confidante, and at the same time pushing her, along with her whole race, into a categorical slough—of moral, spiritual—everything—inferiority. (LD, 124)

As Anna has 'never known a sufficiency of ideas', she is very 'calculated' in 'absorbing' the 'personal homespun philosophy' of Helen's mother; it irritates Helen to notice 'that's how my mother likes it' to communicate with Anna. (LD, 123)

Later, Helen discovers a similar response in her parents' attitude towards her friend, Joel. If Helen's mother keeps a pleasant distance from Joel, Helen's father treats Joel as someone coming from a different background of life—'a cultured native'; he builds his conversation with Joel always adding phrases like 'your people' and 'the customs of your people' to make sure that he is an outsider. (LD, 120) This makes Joel conscious of his identity as a Jew. Whereas Helen finds it difficult to go out for a dance with him:

> The difference of nationality—between us—as it existed in the minds and emotions of our parents, mind, not as we conceived it—was a conscious taboo. Friendship was all right, it took place in the mind, in the interchange of speech and the world; but touch, an embrace between you and me—emotional contact reaches back into the family. It's very old, very deep, very senseless; and harder than you think to overcome. (LD, 359–360)

The taboos of their families hold both Helen and Joel back from building a relationship with each other. Similarly, in her attempt to stay friends with Mary, Helen wishes her to be 'less harassed and flattened' (LD, 170) in their contact with each other. But for Mary, the experience of racial prejudice in Helen's society is too blunt to ignore:

> You want to give a nice plump person to practicing cannibals and tell them that they mustn't eat him because it's like eating themselves. But they're used to eating people. They haven't had their ideas of diet changed yet, like you have. (LD, 203)

Helen finds Mary very conscious of her position as a black person amongst the white students in the University: 'No airiness could take from that quiet, serious little figure the consciousness of privilege that sent it, alone, [...] to be swept aside with errand boys and cooks and street cleaners, still alone.' (LD, 132) Helen questions the wide distance that exists between her and Mary's life:

> These differences in the everyday living out of our lives—could they end there? Or out of them did we love, want and believe. And so could the formula of our loving, wanting, believing, be the same? (LD,176)

It embarrasses Helen to find Mary too humble towards her: 'She was horribly grateful. I felt like a bossy missionary presenting a Bible to a little savage who has no shoes and chronic hookworm.' (LD,142) In the same way that Anna never disagrees with what Helen's mother says, Mary is very careful not to miss 'a single word' (LD, 123) from the lectures delivered in the class. Helen observes:

> The life of an African—especially of her generation, passed into a sort of ghetto vacuum between the tribal life that is forgotten and the white man's life that is guessed at—it's the practical narrow life of poverty. All the kinds of poverty there are: money, privacy, ideas. (LD,133)

But once 'the moment of ease' (LD, 203) is achieved between her and Mary, Helen sees a different person in her: 'She was not humiliated; in fact I had never seen her so confident, so forgetful of herself, of what she inherited in disabilities before the fact of me.' (LD, 202) They then speak to each other as equals. Helen shares with Mary her disgust over her mother's behaviour for not letting Mary come to their house for a week or so: 'We've got a room that isn't inside and isn't out. But they were afraid to have you, even there.' (LD, 201) Helen finds herself helpless in front of such 'taboos' (LD, 169) which contribute to the ending of her friendship with Mary:

> I tried hard with Mary. They try with justice, with declarations of human rights, with the self-abnegation of Christ. Love one another It becomes nonsense when you decree it. An absolute, like black and white, that has no corresponding reality in the merging, changing outlines of living. (LD, 229)

It further upsets Helen to find her white friends in Johannesburg conscious of the racial prejudice in their 'slightly uncomfortable, impermanent-looking' lives: 'Nothing infuriates your servant more than the idea that you've lowered yourself to eat with a non-European.' That is why 'whenever John wants to bring Nathoo Ram home for dinner I [Jenny Marcus] have to let Hilda go off.' (LD, 162–163) The Welsh and Marcus families find Helen's 'acquaintance' with Mary 'damaging' for race relations: 'She will become a teacher and a bourgeois and feel herself a little nearer to the whites instead of closer to the blacks.' Helen finds this attitude of her white society hard to digest: 'A sudden sense of my own climate blowing upon me.' (LD, 164) It finally makes her feel like a 'stranger' (LD, 274) in her world.

In Helen's character, Gordimer presents the disappointment of South Africans who looked for a revolutionary change: in reality, there was 'nothing to do, nowhere to go, no hope of change.' (LD, 263) Helen finds Paul getting frustrated with the inefficiency of the welfare committees to fulfil the basic needs of the blacks. It puts off Sipho, 'the man of peace, the disciple of Gandhi' (LD, 329) from coming to the group discussions organised by the social welfare community. His murder in the riots at Alexandra leaves the black community in a mood of violent resistance against the government. Helen waits 'for calamity to come down':

> We wanted a quick shock, over and done with, but what we were going to get was something much slower, surer, and more terrible: [...] *apartheid* in public transport and buildings, the ban on mixed marriages, the Suppression of Communism bill, the language ordinance separating Afrikaans and English-speaking children in schools, the removal of Coloured voters from the common electoral roll and the setting aside of the Supreme Court judgment that made this act illegal—passionately debated in Parliament with the United Party and Labour Party forming the Opposition, inevitably lost to the Government before the first protest was spoken. (LD, 255)

This describes the atmosphere of the 1950s when all efforts to resist the apartheid policy of the Afrikaner government came to a standstill: 'Nothing's happened. Of course nothing happened.' (LD, 255) In 1953, the Public Safety Act empowered the government to declare stringent states of emergency and authorised severe penalties for protestors, virtually eliminating passive resistance as a tactic. (Schrire, 1992, 224) In the same year, the United Party dissidents formed the Liberal Party which favoured qualified franchises for the blacks in South Africa. The liberals found themselves caught between the growth and success of Afrikaner nationalism and the emerging forces of African nationalism. Association and identification with African nationalism were increasingly made difficult for them through legislation in 1956 by the Afrikaner government which proscribed any form of political or intimate social liaison between white and black people in South Africa. Helen reflects in *The Lying Days*:

> Something had been working in me—the slow corrosive guilt, a guilt personal and inherited, [...] which, admitted or denied, is in all white South Africans. The Nationalist farmers who kicked and beat their convict African labourers had it and it was in me. Like an obscure pain we can't confess we clutch to it this counter-irritant, or that. [...] With kicks and curses, you may keep the guilt at a distance, [...] (LD, 211–212)

This penetration of political awareness in her personal life makes Helen realise the impossibility of standing aside: 'Paul and I had talked about the strike. It was something that belonged right in our lives, it wasn't a piece we'd read in the papers or a mild interest justifying someone's pretensions to liberalism.' (LD, 353)

The consciousness of marginalisation develops a kind of fear in Helen: 'The fears, like an invasion of strangers, which now, never left me.' She fears losing her boyfriend Paul. She avoids entering into arguments with him as she wants to 'hold together the torn and tearing garment' of her relationship with him. In her depressed state of mind, Helen thinks: 'How was it possible, then, that the difficulties of this work, affecting him, should throw our relationship out of balance?' (LD, 296) As a social welfare officer, Paul is involved in sorting the blacks' everyday problems in his area. He is offended by the Afrikaner government's ban on mixed marriages and restrictions on socialisation between the white and the black people in South Africa. It disturbs Helen to find herself unable to involve herself with Africa and its people. She struggles to stay with Paul but it becomes impossible for her to avoid 'the loneliness that is a failure to connect'. (LD, 332)

Experiences of fear and alienation contribute to Helen's decision to break away from her South African life. In her childhood, her mother avoids leaving her alone in the house 'because there were native boys about'. (LD, 14) But the experience of the black boys during her visit to the compound makes Helen discover that they are 'harmless'. She questions: 'Was there something to be afraid of?' (LD, 18) Helen realises that it is the fear of their 'mysteriousness' (LD, 14) that has kept her away from knowing them. Later in her adult life, Helen experiences this kind of fear at her first contact with Mary: 'We were afraid of each other, she of the lion-mask of white mastery that she saw superimposed on my face, I of the mouse-mask of black submission with which I obscured hers.' (LD, 127) Helen also comes across a forceful presence of fear and alienation during her journey back from the poor Location in the town:

> I was afraid. There was nothing to be afraid of in the people, no menace in their shouts or their looks: like their shacks, their bodies, they were simply stripped of gentleness, of reserve, all their bounds were trampled down, and they only moved or cried out in one need or another, like beasts. Yet I was afraid. The awfulness of their life filled me with fear. (LD, 177)

Helen leaves South Africa because 'it's a stage most of us get to' where people like her long 'to get out to the wide open spaces, I suppose'. (LD, 367) Living through physical and psychological worlds of barriers in her South African society makes Helen aware of apartheid as 'the huge central problem of our country in our time': she admits that it is 'something that oppressed me not only in my intellect since I had grown old enough to have a concept of man's freedom, but in my blood.' (LD, 262) The title of the novel, *The Lying Days* sums up Helen's experiences of growing from childhood into adulthood:

> Though leaves are many, the root is one; Through all the lying days of my youth I swayed my leaves and flowers in the sun; Now I may wither into the truth.

Gordimer quotes these lines from the Irish poet W.B. Yeats' (1865–1939) collection of verses *The Coming of Wisdom with Time* (1910) as the epigraph of the novel. For her, they signify the completion of a physical and psychological process that leads Helen to grow out of the sham and lies of her youth days. Her adolescence years—the transitory time between puberty and adulthood—provide a physical space for Helen to understand the working of apartheid in her South African life.

Describing an insider's view of the South African world in *The Lying Days*, Gordimer presents an outsider's approach to South Africa in *A World of Strangers* (1958). The action in the novel begins with the visit to South Africa by Toby Hood, the English agent of a publishing company based in England. As a young man, he is 'tired' of 'the atmosphere of ideological flux' in his British life in which he has passed the period of his adolescence: 'My interest in [...] now that man-ordained barriers of race, creed, class and colour were breaking up, was as great as that of my mother [...]' (Strangers, 30–32) So without a desire to become 'a voyeur of the world's ills and social perversions' (Strangers, 33), Toby discovers Africa and its people on Mombasa seaport: 'Heavy, mild and brutish faces, on which emotions settle momentarily [...] an involuntarily twitch that is nothing more conscious than the reaction of a muscle'.

(Strangers, 7) Although Toby is conscious of his attitude as 'Sinbad the Sailor' (Strangers, 18) on his way to South Africa, he is irritated by the appalling distance of his white companions on the ship as well as their approach to 'explore' Africa 'as we go'. (Strangers, 8) He shows his dislike for their high English voices and upper-middle-class manners. He finds it difficult to digest one of the white passengers' 'amused bewilderment' at the passive-looking African waiter on the ship: 'Pangas and burnings—And look at that. Wouldn't want to harm a fly.' (Strangers,17) Amongst other white passengers, there are Mrs Turgell and her daughter, Rina who are interested only in exploring the natural beauty of the Mombasa land and show their fascination for the gemstones and the elephant tusks they find in the shops on the port. Toby is appalled by Mrs Turgell's attitude towards life in Africa. She says: 'You must have an active and not a contemplative nature, to take Africa. [...] The people are quite terrible. [...] Awful food. [...] Nothing to talk of but crops, female complaints, servants. Ugly, ugly. Nothing but ugliness'. (Strangers, 15)

Mrs Turgell cannot face the reality of her married life on a farm in Zimbabwe, then Rhodesia. She finds an escape in spending most of her time in Europe. For her, 'warmth and beauty and physical happiness' (Strangers, 4) lie in Italy. She looks forward to going back to Europe in a few weeks. Toby finds it strange that Mrs Turgell always needs a 'sedative' (Strangers, 16) as she gets nearer to her short stay in Africa. Toby feels sick at this 'spoilt' attitude of hers towards her African life: 'Husband, marriage, reality took the discreet disguise of "Africa". Poor devil of a husband, working his farm to foot the bill at the Pensione Bandolini.' (Strangers, 24–25)

Toby feels embarrassed at the arrogance and detachment of his white companions on the ship: 'Were these the sort of people Africa gets? Christ, poor continent!' (Strangers, 25) In comparison, he feels a powerful sense of place; the blacks become a focus of his attention. He perceives the natives in animal imagery. In the teashop, Toby cannot stay away from looking at an African waiter for his 'sweaty monkey-face' which has 'innocent ancientness'. (Strangers, 17) Although Toby projects himself as a man with no 'colour prejudice' (Strangers, 204), still, he finds himself noticing a difference in his contact with black people later in Johannesburg: 'Those other faces, dark faces, other hands, dark hands, emerging from the same old coat sleeves, made a difference.' (Strangers, 79) He is struck by the educated, Steven Sitole's 'sauntering' conversation with him: 'It was the first word a black man spoke to me that wasn't between master and servant.' At the same time, Toby finds Steven's appearance as a 'pleasant, light colour of polished wood and his hair was like wool embroidery.' This describes a sense of mystery about the black world in Toby's mind, though in England, he has known a few Africans who belong to the 'gargoyle class' (Strangers, 80).

The main action in *A World of Strangers* is set in Johannesburg where Anna Louw, an Afrikaner lawyer and activist, introduces Toby to a world in which people get together and make friendships across the racial divide. Such gatherings help Toby to overcome his feelings of strangeness about the black world. His visit to a party of mixed races makes him see how much colour and social barriers count for keeping both the white and the black people far away from knowing each other. Toby discovers:

> There are too many landscape painters here. They don't know how to deal with man, so they leave him out. Or if they do put him in, they use only the picturesque aspect—they treat a face or a figure as if it were a tree. (*Strangers,* 81)

On his very first visit to a party of mixed races, Toby is moved by 'the ordinary pattern' of the people gathered and symbolises it as 'remarkable' in its composition like an 'Oriental rug': 'The scrolls and flowers that you expected to see were also found to be people, animals, jokes and legends; things that, in real life, are not found together, cheek by jowl in the space of one experience.' (Strangers, 79) The 'voluntary context' (Strangers, 80) of such meetings provides Toby with an opportunity to make acquaintances amongst blacks like Steven who has returned from England, and, Sam, a struggling musician. He goes to shebeens with Steven together and gets happiness from their private adventures in each other's world.

In his friendship with Steven, Toby notices a certain kind of arrogance in Steven's personality that he has acquired through the experience of his stay in England for some time. It infuriates Steven to see Sam composing his musical work 'in collaboration with a white man':

> It was also more of a white man's idea of what a black man would write, and a black man's idea of what a white man would expect him to write, than the fusion of a black man's and a white man's world of imagination. (Strangers, 201)

Sam is calculated in absorbing the ideas of the white man. He is conscious of his ability to find his place in the white man's world whereas Steven wishes him to produce his original work without being flattened by the contact with the white world. It disturbs Steven to find Sam thanking the 'whites' for giving him a 'chance to work' with them. (Strangers, 202)

He calls Sam a 'fool': 'All they want to do is pick his brains and pinch his music.' (Strangers, 204) Steven has a deep mistrust for the white community in South Africa. At the same time, he gives an impression to his friends that he is 'a white man in a black man's skin' or as if he 'cared damn all for the African people'. (Strangers, 153) But Toby can relate to what Steven is all about: 'We did not understand each other; we wanted the same thing.' (Strangers, 96) Both Toby and Steven prefer to stay away from the politics of South African life, yet their lack of commitment towards the struggle against apartheid cannot guarantee their freedom of 'private life'. (Strangers, 185)

During his stay in Johannesburg, Toby visits his mother's friend, Marion Alexander who lives in the 'High House' (Strangers, 45), and his black friends in the townships. He finds the line of demarcation that exists between the lavish white life and the poor blacks:

> While I had kept going, simply carried along, I had not consciously been aware of the enormous strain of such a way of life, where one set of loyalties and interests made claims in direct conflict with another set, equally strong; where not only did I have to keep my friends physically apart, but could not even speak to one group about the others. (Strangers, 246)

It disturbs him to find a particular kind of distance from the black people in everyday life of the High House: their conversation 'hardly seemed to be concerned with the same country or spoken by people in the same situation as the talk I heard in Sophiatown or in houses where black and white people met.' (Strangers, 198) At the same time, it becomes difficult for him to stay unmoved by the experience of his visit to the Location where Sam lives. Despite the 'difference between what was well-paid for blacks and what was well-paid for whites', Sam struggles to maintain a high standard of life for his family. But his attempt to live 'an ordinary way of living' becomes a 'showplace' for other blacks on the Location. (Strangers, 125) There comes a time when Sam has to sell his much-loved Morris car to meet the family financial requirements. He reveals: 'Toby, man, the black skin's not the thing. If you know anybody who wants to know what it's like to be a black man, this is it. No matter how much you manage to do for yourself, it's not enough.' (Strangers, 243–245) There is less opportunity to live a life of one's own choice in South Africa because 'the pressure is too strong'. (Strangers, 116) However, 'across the breach of the town between white man and black' life (Strangers, 240), Toby finds it difficult to put up with the worry that Cecil Rowe, a white acquaintance, has about having 'not enough money to live decently' in South Africa: 'She began to talk of what she would do if she had money, if she didn't have the child, if she lived in Europe.' (Strangers, 191) Cecil finally marries a wealthy man, Guy Patterson 'in her greed and fear of life'. (Strangers, 249) Toby cannot do much about Cecil's racial prejudice about communicating with a black person as an equal: 'You mean you can actually sit down to dinner with them and it doesn't seem any different to you?' Cecil shudders at the thought of 'touching' a black skin: 'Her hand came out in the imaginary experiment and hesitated, wavered back.' (Strangers, 250–251) She feels very strange at Toby's socialising with the blacks. Earlier, Cecil is unable to understand the senselessness of a communal black cleaner, William who celebrates Christmas by smoking 'dagga' [marijuana] in an ample quantity: 'What other country is there where you'd have a thing like that on your doorstep? What a Christmas for anybody! Nothing but a beast! How can you live with savages around you!' (Strangers, 191) Toby is embarrassed at Cecil's distant attitude towards the suffering man. She offers coffee to William who is unconscious to make him come out of his misery. Toby finds himself listening to William's grunts along with Cecil in 'a kind of shameful fascination'. William's 'bestial and wretchedly human' sound, as if 'a monstrous serenade from some medieval hell' generates fear in Toby:

> It was all the cries we do not cry, all the howls we do not howl, all the bloody furies in our hearts that are never, must never be, let loose. Even I was afraid, hearing it: not of the man, but of a stir of recognition in myself. (Strangers, 190)

This experience of fear of the black life that white people like Cecil live within their South African life, leads Toby to understand the resulting sense of alienation that exists across the colour divide. When Toby is lost for some time during a hunting expedition, he comes across a strong consciousness of the colour bar in the attitude of a black servant who accompanies him in the bush:

> He did not look at me or at anything; his isolation came to me silently; I was aware of it then, but it must have existed all the time, while we ate and we drank and we sang and we cursed, in our camp. I offered him a cigarette but he would not take it from the packet and he cupped his hands and I had to drop the cigarette into them. Loneliness gathered with the chill, a miasma of the ancient continent; he and I

> were in hand's reach of each other, like people standing close, and unaware of it, in a fog. (Strangers, 232)

Despite Toby's attempt to chat with him, the African servant prefers to keep silent in his company, keeping himself at a distance from the white man. Through this oscillation between the rich white society and the poor black world, Toby discovers a void that exists between both worlds: 'I passed from one world to another—but neither was real to me. For in each, what sign was there that the other existed?' (Strangers, 186)

A strong sense of alienation towards the white society at the High House overcomes Toby: 'I had not been to the Alexanders' for weeks. I couldn't go there anymore, that was all.' (Strangers, 246) Toby is hurt by the fact that the 'taboos' of this white society have no room for relationships with the blacks like Steven and Sam. He wonders what to write in letters to his family and friends in England about the state of his life in South Africa:

> Could I tell them how pleasant it was to be lulled and indulged at the High House? Could I explain the freedom I felt where I had no legal right to be, in that place of segregation, a location? I suppose that to have a 'life out there', a real life in Johannesburg, you'd have to belong in one or the other, for keeps. (Strangers,193)

The divide between the white and the black nationalisms seems irreconcilable to Toby when he notices that the idea of 'calling for unity between English and Afrikaans-speaking whites instead of a divided people' is acceptable in the High House white gentry and that 'the squabbling of the two white peoples was simply picayune; dwarfed by the towering bout between black and white.' (Strangers, 199) A disruption in his contact with the rich white class at the High House and a discontinuity in his friendships with Anna, Steven, and Sam makes Toby realise 'the awful triumphant separateness' of apartheid in South Africa: 'You couldn't really reconcile one with the other, the way people were, the way laws were, and make a whole.' (Strangers, 193) Under apartheid, both the white and the black people needed a 'permit' (Strangers, 184) to visit each other's worlds. Toby gets upset by the white caretaker's objection to entertaining 'kaffirs' in his rented flat 'unless they're in the capacity of servants'. (Strangers, 206) The racial prejudice of the white caretaker is too blunt to ignore for Peter, one of the black men present inside Toby's flat. Opposite to Peter's reaction, Steven is remote in his response to this insult: 'His voice was passionless and removed; I heard it like the voice of someone not present, a voice in one's brain.' (Strangers, 205–206) Toby becomes very sad after this direct encounter with apartheid and realises that 'private livers', like Steven and himself, become hunted people: 'You must protest, defy, non-cooperate. And all these things you must do; you can't leave it all in the infinitely more capable hands of the public livers.' (Strangers, 115) Steven's death in a car accident 'provided a check, a pause' to Toby 'when the strain of the kind of life I had been living for months broke in upon me.' (Strangers, 240) His death makes him conscious of the fact that 'he was in the bond of his skin, and I was free; the world was open to me and closed to him; how could I recognise my situation in his?' (Strangers, 246). The title of the novel, *A World of Strangers* concludes Toby's physical and psychological experiences of the South African world: although both white and black people live together in South Africa, they are strangers in each other's world: 'What I had known of Steven, a stranger, living and dying a life I could at best only observe; my brother.' (Strangers, 240)

Oscillating between the white and the black South African society followed by the failure of personal relationships across the racial divide reveals to Toby the necessity of a commitment towards the struggle against apartheid. Sam, however, is not sure of Toby's decision: 'Who knows with you people, Toby, man? Maybe you won't come back at all. Something will keep you away. Something will prevent you, and we won't.' But Toby is in 'peace' with himself at the time of his departure from South Africa: 'The two pieces of newspaper rested in my wallet in polarity'—one is about Anna being arrested for a treason charge and the other clip is about Cecil being married to a wealthy man.' (Strangers, 254) This keeping of two different clips of information beside each other in Toby's wallet suggests that individual Afrikaners like Anna are the committed reformers and the English-speaking whites cared only for wealth and fashion in their South African lives. The epigraph of the novel forecasts the rise of a revolutionary spirit in people's attitudes who were against apartheid:

> I want the strong air of the most profound night to remove flowers and letters from the arch where you sleep, and a black boy to announce to the gold-minded whites the arrival of the reign of the ear of corn. (Spanish poet Federico Garcia Lorca 1898–1936)

The action in *A World of Strangers* develops through Toby's friendships and relationships across the racial divide. The meetings between the white and the black characters in mixed gatherings or parties are the spaces that act as a bridge to cross over and socialise beyond the racial divide that existed in their South African society.

Like Toby's visit to South Africa in *A World of Strangers*, the action in *Occasion for Loving* (1963) is set in a framework of an English couple, Ann Davis and Boaz Davis' adventurous visit to South Africa. As guests of an English-speaking South African couple, Jessie Stilwell and Tom Stilwell, they come to make acquaintance with Gideon Shibalo, a black painter, and a friend of the family. Ann and Gideon fall in love with each other and towards the end of the novel, Ann decides to leave South Africa after deserting Gideon for good. As when one throws a stone in a pool of water, it splashes and creates a disturbance in the water, similarly, this visit of Ann and Boaz and then their abrupt departure from South Africa gives Jessie a window onto the strange attitudes of her white community towards the blacks in South Africa.

Accompanying Ann and Boaz to an African dance programme, Jessie finds the appearance of black dancers wild, dancing in front of the white crowd who are amused by their strange display of themselves:

> With bits of Coloured rag tied to old bathing-trunks, lemonade bottle-tops making do for anklets around the legs [...] and, in their hands, cow-skin shields and wooden assegais, the black men went through the savage motion of warring [...] dreadful sighing grunt that belongs to the ecstasy of death dealt out. (Loving, 36)

Jessie suddenly becomes aware of her childhood sensibility of the black life: 'You know, the mine boys were not human to me.—Like a cage full of Coloured parrots, screeching at the zoo. I watched them dancing and I walked home and forgot about them.' (Loving, 35) Jessie finds herself comparing the blacks to animals. This childhood recollection of the wild native world makes Jessie recognise a persistent race consciousness between the white and the black people in South Africa. As an adult, she again finds herself watching the 'terrible fetish-faces of medicine men's masks' and the 'ugly faces of all clowns' in the African dance programme. (Loving, 36) She notices their voices 'like the trumpeting of an elephant or the panting that follows the lion's roar'. This impression of the black performers in her mind brings an 'unspeakable sadness' to her: 'Her consciousness of self was lost, as it sometimes was when she was surrounded by the common mystery of human faces.' The performance of the black dancers 'mummed an ugly splendid savagery, a broken ethos, well lost' which brings 'heavy, cold tears' to Jessie's eyes. (Loving, 37) Later, Ann comes across a similar experience in her sexual contact with

Gideon. At touching him, she is troubled by 'the dark positiveness of his skin, the mattness of it, the variations like markings shading one part of his body in difference from another.' (Loving, 181) In return, Gideon is no less confused than Ann: 'He lost himself, his confusion in the confusion of her face.' (Loving, 181) However, such a strong experience of colour consciousness makes Jessie cry during the African dance programme. She knows that 'they were not tears of sentiments. They came from horror and hollowness':

> Now and then the parody of the white man's voice [...] sent a murmur of delighted recognition through the white audience, who did not know in what light they were being represented, but were glad to be mentioned anyway. (Loving, 36–37)

Jessie is deeply affected by this detached fascination with the white crowd's response to the African dance show. In Gordimer words:

> Too many whites still regard culture as synonymous with European culture, seeing indigenous music, dance, and oral tradition as a lower form of existence, which needs to be tolerated rather than something of beauty which can enrich and empower our common future. (Villa-Vicencio, 1996, 110)

Ann is interested in knowing 'savage rites, secret ceremonies' whilst Boaz is occupied with the worry that the ancient musical instruments which are used in the show are not preserved by the black artists as they should be. (Loving, 39) Jessie is appalled by Ann and Boaz's distance from the black performers who, in turn, also keep up a reserved manner: 'Ann was taking photographs of the warriors with feather-duster tails. They lined up for the photographers like children in a class. "Come on!" she wheedled. "Let's have some life." But they only stood more stiffly to attention.' (Loving, 38) To justify this lack of understanding and distance which exist between the white and the black people, Tom, the lecturer in history, earlier comments: 'They did not yet know each other well enough to talk all at once.' (Loving, 15) Tom 'hoped to write a history of the African sub-continent that would present the Africans as peoples invaded by the white West, rather than as another kind of fauna dealt with by the white man in his exploration of the world.' (Loving, 14) Jessie observes Ann's excitement at 'being amongst good-natured strangers'. (Loving, 31) Ann meets them in public places like 'Lucky Star' or 'Tommie's' where 'Coloured and white people mixed'.' (Loving, 100) She makes acquaintances with the blacks with a sense of adventure towards the native life: 'The surge of feeling against the barriers of colour was the ethos of the decade in which she had grown up; her participation in it was a substitute for patriotism rather than a revolt.' (Loving, 89) However, Ann shows no commitment in her socialisation with the blacks whom she helps in arranging an art exhibition; nor does she stay faithful in her love affair with Gideon Shibalo. This makes Jessie very critical of Ann's casual attitude towards real African life: 'In a whole year, has she ever really *said* anything, except "It was marvellous fun" [...]' (Loving, 205)

Ann is fascinated by her physical relationship with Gideon although 'making love to Shibalo was breaking the law.' (Loving, 153) But her adventurous love affair with Gideon crumbles after the experience of her running away with him. Despite her intimate relationship with Gideon, Ann feels strange and alienated during the journey to his native land. Ann tells Jessie: 'When the man in the garage looked at Gid, and I stood next to him seeing Gid at the same time, it wasn't the same person we saw...' (Loving, 270) For the white owner of the garage, Gideon was 'madam's boy'. (Loving, 225) The simplest mechanics of daily South African life part them during their attempt to live together as lovers. In the tea houses, they break their journey to get food and some rest on their way to Lesotho, then named Basutoland, and in their short stay in an African village, they encounter a barrier that restricts them from meeting as equals. During her stay with Gideon in the traditional African village, Ann finds the teacher who provides them with lodging embarrassed for not having the type of food which Ann might have fancied as a white person. Ann finds him very much conscious of the laws which restrict the whites and the blacks from any kind of social and public meetings in South Africa. The fear of persecution finally drives the teacher to ask Gideon and Ann to leave the village. Instead of following their planned journey to Lesotho, this experience of poverty and fear in the South African world leads Ann to take refuge with Gideon in Jessie's holiday resort at Natal. Even there, Ann and Gideon cannot be allowed to be seen together as lovers because it will upset the 'peace of mind' of the black servant, Jason, to see a white woman sleeping with a black man. (Loving, 205) Also, Jessie is conscious of the white residents of the holiday resort who have been objecting to the blacks' presence on the beach; she finds them suggesting that some part of the beach should be allotted to them. On returning from her holiday, Jessie receives a letter from the agent of her holiday resort, pointing at her daughters who are seen playing with Gideon on the beach. Jessie questions the agent's account of the complaint that is made by 'certain local residents': 'Why is one always having to be so ashamed for these people—why do they have to spit on everything.' (Loving, 285)

Besides experiencing a sense of alienation, fear is one other significant factor that contributes to Jessie's understanding of apartheid in her South African life. She is disturbed by the experience of her visit to the township where Gideon lives. Jessie observes:

> When they were children, they were cold and hungry, and when they were old they were cold and hungry again; and in between was a brief, violent clutch at things out of reach, or the sad brute's life of obliviousness to them. That was the reality of the day, for the time being. (Loving, 270)

Jessie is frightened 'at the idea of being allied to this life': 'She fought it, denying its validity, but fear doesn't lie down at the bidding, like a dog.' Jessie wants to share with Ann her experience of the huge difference between the white and the black standards of life which cannot be avoided, 'not even for love, that is supposed to cast it out.' (Loving, 270) Ann's going back to Europe with Boaz instead of carrying on her journey to Johannesburg with Gideon strengthens Jessie's belief that Ann has wanted Gideon drowned during one of his last lonely ventures on the beach. Tom's justification for Ann's attitude towards Gideon, 'but what could the bloody woman do, if she didn't want him or couldn't face wanting him' upsets Jessie, but to no purpose: 'She didn't have to stick to him to harm him; it was done already.' (Loving, 279) Jessie is very bitter to realise that Ann abandons Gideon because 'she did not love him across the colour bar'. (Loving, 268) Boaz also cannot tolerate Gideon 'like any other man' because 'Gideon isn't a man, won't be, can't be, until he's free'. (Loving, 271) During Ann's stay with Gideon in the native life, Boaz is worried only about Ann who might get picked up by the police and end up in jail with Gideon. After meeting Gideon for the first time, Boaz reveals his inhibition towards the man by calling him 'black bastard—All that filthy cock, man'. (Loving, 167) He ends up taking advantage of 'Gideon's skin' by refusing to treat him like any other man. And the pity is that 'Gideon knows it', Jessie observes. (Loving, 271–272) Just as Jessie's shaking hands with Jason at the end of her holiday leave the poor servant confused for a while, Ann and Boaz's goodwill treatment of Gideon takes him nowhere but to a secluded life away from the white world. It is painful for Jessie to see Gideon drunk with the impression after his 'experience of the disastrous love affair' with Ann that every white woman is a 'bitch'. Jessie loses Gideon's company as a family friend, thus revealing the 'failure' of 'personal relations against the distortion of laws and society' in which people live in South Africa:

> They continued to meet in a friendly fashion, sometimes in the Lucky Star, occasionally at the houses of friends, but the sense of his place in the Stilwells' life and theirs in his that she felt that night never came again. So long as Gideon did not remember, Jessie could not forget. (Loving, 288)

From the beginning of this novel, Jessie is conscious of the capacity of apartheid to break and pull people apart from each other. That is why, when Boaz talks to her about his ambition to work freely in Africa, Jessie questions him to clarify whether he wishes to work with the Africans 'without hurting them' or 'without being hurt by them' or 'without responsibility'. (Loving, 12) Jessie knows that the fascination of the white community with the African world is short-lived:

> We don't see black and white and so we all think we behave as decently to one colour face as another. But how can that ever be, so long as there's the possibility that you can escape back into your filthy damn whiteness? How do you know you'll always play fair? (Loving, 271–272)

Boaz who seems to be dedicated to the recovery of ancient African musical instruments and Ann who claims to be passionately in love with Gideon leave South Africa without saying goodbye to Gideon. Jessie is embarrassed at such arrogant attitudes of her white community towards Africa and its people. In the same context, earlier, it is difficult for her to come to terms with her father, Bruno Frecht's 'theatrical behaviour' towards the native life; despite living all his life amongst the blacks, Bruno is 'markedly a stranger in South Africa; his thirty or forty years as a chemist on the South African mines were brushed away and his foreign identity—a Swiss German, a man of Europe—reasserted itself.' (Loving, 76–77) Jessie knows that Ann can abruptly depart from the African world because 'she is white, she could go, and of course, she went'. (Loving, 279) Jessie sadly admits that the break-in relationships occurs across the racial divide because 'none of us knows how much getting free of the colour bar means to us—none of us'. (Loving, 253) At the beginning of the novel, Gordimer quotes Albert Camus (1913–1960), the French philosopher and the 1957 Nobel Prize in Literature recipient:

> [...] servitude, falsehood, and terror...these three afflictions are the causes of silence between men, obscure them from one another and prevent them from rediscovering themselves in the only value which can save them from nihilism—the long complicity between men at grips with their destiny.

Alongside, Gordimer also quotes the 1929 Nobel Prize in Literature laureate, the German novelist Paul Thomas Mann (1875–1955): 'In our time, the destiny of man presents its meaning in political terms.' Jessie is aware of this fact in her South African life because her privacy gets invaded every time she attempts to stay away from what happens around her. (Loving, 12) The title of the novel, *Occasion for Loving* reflects how Gordimer's characters find and then miss the opportunity of coming closer to each other; they are socially marginalised in their contact with the world they live in. In the same way that Helen in *The Lying Days* goes away from Joel, Mary and Paul, and Toby in *A World of Strangers* loses contact with Anna and Steven, Jessie's friendship with Gideon breaks down in *Occasion for Loving*. The more apartheid put barriers in these characters' relationships across the racial spectrum, the more they felt a need to make connections with each other. Paralysis of conversation steps in, driving powerfully the need for self-expression in these characters. Helen longs for 'wide open spaces' (LD, 367) though Toby finds one: 'The only way to do that was to do what Anna Louw had done—make for the frontier between the two, that hard and lonely place as yet sparsely populated.' (Strangers, 193) However, failure across the racial divide leads Jessie to see the futility of any such attempt: 'So long as the law remained unchanged, nothing can bring integrity to personal relationships.' (Loving, 279) This interweaving of history into fiction is presented through a framework of circumstances and situations which in turn, provides a space to Gordimer's protagonists for living through a life that could be non-racial. But soon they realise that 'all this that was real and rooted in life was a void before the clumsy words that reduced the delicacy and towering complexity of living to a race theory.' (Loving, 216)

Occasion for Loving is an appropriate point of departure from the rhythm in which Gordimer has produced her earlier novels; both *The Lying Days* and *A World of Strangers* explore characters' lack of social commitment to the issues of race and identity in their South African life whereas *Occasion for Loving* focuses on the process of alienation and social severance which apartheid created in the lives of people in South Africa. Jessie's memory of a woman who 'was sewing without any thread in the needle' describes it the best: 'It flashed in and out of the stuff, empty, connecting nothing with nothing.' (Loving, 44)

In her early fiction, Gordimer projected a tingling fascination for the real South African world. Through meditations over the landscape, Gordimer attempts to look at the position of whites in South Africa, the strangeness of their being there. She brings into question the entire values of the white colonial minority settled in South Africa. Her characters, like Jessie in *Occasion for Loving*, draw moral strength from the landscape that exists around her. She gains a kind of relief in the company of her garden plants; she feels 'a wordless empathy' for them. (Loving, 9) Jessie doesn't fancy the shabby wallpaper in her sitting room: 'We don't see why we should ape Europe…' (Loving, 13) For her, decorating walls with paper is a European tradition that looks out of place in South African life. On her holiday in Natal, the seaside landscape reminds Jessie that this place has once been 'Shaka's country' but now various races from different origins have become the occupiers of the land. (Loving, 189) Nearly in all her early narratives such as 'Ah. Woe Is Me', Gordimer has questioned the entire system of values of the white minority settled in South Africa and described a conflict between white sensibility and African culture.

Researchers have approached Gordimer's early fiction in several ways, pointing to diversity in the subject and form of her fiction. For instance, Stephen Clingman (1986) finds *The Lying Days* autobiographical in form and John Cooke (1985) notes that this quality is missing in the novels written after *The Lying Days*. Besides the autobiographical aspect, Gordimer records the South African history of her times in her fiction. Clingman's analysis that 'a related feature of white consciousness explored by the novel [*The Lying Days*] is its cultural alienation from its local environment' (1986, 31), can be extended to other early texts such as *A World of Strangers* and *Occasion for Loving*.

This 'historical consciousness' (Clingman,1986, 43) of white South Africa runs side by side with a personal exploration of characters' lives in Gordimer's early fiction. In his study, Dominic Head calls *The Lying Days* and *A World of Strangers* 'novels of learning'. (1994, 48) This can be true for most of Gordimer's early fiction such as 'Ah, Woe Is Me' and *Occasion for Loving*; the characters in these short and long narratives go through a process of breaking down after the experience of apartheid. This leads to change and transformation in their perspective on their selves as well as the world around them. Gordimer reveals in an interview:

> […] people like myself have two births, and the second one comes when you break out of the colour bar. It's a real rebirth when you

> break out of your background, the taboos of your background, and you realise that the colour bar is not valid and is meaningless to you. (Terkel, 1962, 16)

Here, the Dutch-German-French ethnographer and folklorist, Arnold van Gennep's (1873–1957) model of 'rites of passage' is fruitful to understand the development of the plot and mental processes in characterisation in Gordimer's fiction. According to Gennep, initiation rites are of two types, physical puberty leading to physical maturity, and social puberty leading to social maturity thus marking the transition from one stage to another. (1960, 10–11) A similar process is at work in the characters' lives in Gordimer's early fiction; they go through rites of passage to find a 'sense of place' (Clingman, 1986, 44) for themselves. For instance, through physical and mental encounters of apartheid in their South African lives, the characters in 'Ah, Woe Is Me' and *Occasion for Loving* become aware of the inevitable discrepancy between the liberal attitude of white South Africa and the decencies implied in the whites' way of life. Gordimer describes the 'white ethics' that had been prevalent in South Africa: 'They tell them [their children] to behave decently, to be kind, and honest, and so on [...] it does not extend to humanity in general; it does not extend across the colour bar'. (Terkel, 1962, 29) In her essay, 'Where Do Whites Fit In?' (1959) too, Gordimer presents her disillusionment with liberal strategies of opposing apartheid and for achieving black liberation in South Africa. This appears indirectly in her characters' attempt to apply a personal standard of values in their relationships across the racial spectrum in Gordimer's early fiction. A personal liberal attitude conflicts with the world of apartheid, and the characters' failures confirm the liberal failure in South African society.

By the early 1960s, Gordimer had exhausted humanism as a discourse. Like Gennep's 'rites of passage', a process of transition is explored in *The Lying Days*, followed by liberal humanism in *A World of Strangers*, and leading towards the failure of socialised humanism in *Occasion for Loving*. In his study of Gordimer's fiction, Abdul Jan Mohammed explores the distinction between different phases of Gordimer's fiction. For him, *The Lying Days, A World of Strangers* and *Occasion for Loving* constitute a 'bourgeois phase' which is succeeded by the 'post-bourgeois phase' of *The Late Bourgeois World, A Guest of Honour* and *The Conservationist*. (1988, 88) Gordimer's early fiction is distinctive as compared to the middle and later periods of her work; it records a moment of transition for the South African liberal world.

Gordimer presents this moment of transition for the liberal world through the working of physical borderland situations together with psychological borderland encounters. *The Lying Days*, *A World of Strangers* and *Occasion for Loving* are 'frontier' (Clingman, 1986, 71) texts suggesting a strong pull towards a transition from one state of life to another. The characters in these novels are physically led to frontier places or borderland situations in which they find a world of friendships other than the master-servant relationship between the white and the black people in South Africa. There, they break down with shame and embarrassment at noticing the indignities that the blacks suffer. Toby in *A World of Strangers* discovers a huge social and economic void through his oscillation between the rich white class and poor black South Africa. His experience of hypocrisy in the white class resembles the experience of the protagonist in 'The Train from Rhodesia' in which she feels ashamed of her husband's act of bargaining for fun with the black vendor. Similarly, it hurts Jessie in *Occasion for Loving* to find Ann having an adventurous love affair with Gideon without loyalty and commitment towards him. Such attitudes lead to the creation of a wall, a barrier that separates these characters in their relationships with each other. The resulting break in communication is a recurring theme in Gordimer's early fiction.

The notion of borderland as defined in the work of Bhabha, is indeed, productive in approaching Gordimer's early fiction and exploring the complexity of the apartheid situation in South Africa; the theme allows Gordimer an aesthetic space to discuss issues related to race consciousness and identity between the white and the black South Africa in her fiction. In Bhabha's terms, her characters 'locate' a culture for themselves in this 'moment of transit where space and time cross to produce complex figures of difference and identity, past and present, inside and outside, inclusion and exclusion.' (Bhabha, 1994, 1) Helen in *The Lying Days* lives through a traumatic terrain of apartheid experiences. These lead her to 'rethink questions of identity, social agency and national affiliation' with her South African world. The handling of a theme close to Bhabha's borderland in Gordimer's fiction provides, in Bhabha's words, a 'terrain for elaborating strategies of self-hood—singular or communal—that initiate new signs of identity and innovative sites of collaboration, and contestation, in the act of defining the idea of society itself.' This 'third space' allows Gordimer's characters to observe and comment on their South African society. The plots in *The Lying Days*, *A World of Strangers* and *Occasion for Loving* are developed in borderland places and situations which lead the characters, in terms anticipating Bhabha's formulation, to 'move away from the singularities of 'class' and 'gender' and create in them 'an awareness of the subject positions—of race, gender, generation, institutional location, geographical locale, sexual orientation—that inhabit any claim to identity' in their South African world. In their respective capacities, Helen, Toby, and Jessie grow out of the 'exploratory' and 'restless movement' after the visit to the 'borderland' world in their South African society. (Bhabha, 1994, 1–2)

As a method, the notion of borderland clarifies Gordimer's construction of the theme of borderland in her fiction. It allows room for the interaction of physical borders and psychological barriers. In 'Is There Nowhere Else Where We Can Meet?' the attack by the black man is the point of meeting—the physical borderland—which brings him in contact with the white girl on the path. At that stage, no civilised meeting is possible. Such physical situations and psychological encounters in her characters' lives allow Gordimer to focus on those moments and processes that are produced in the articulation of social and economic differences in society. Gordimer's early fiction sets a pattern in the presentation of the theme of borderland that is followed in the later periods of her fiction. The construction of physical borderland situations and psychological borderland encounters continues in the pattern of dual development in action and characterisation but with a difference.

Resistance (1949–1963)

1949 The Mixed Marriages Act (1949) prohibited mixed marriages and made sexual relations between consenting adults of different skin colours a criminal offence.

Voting rights of the Indians and the Coloureds were abolished, and the ANC adopted the Programme of Action calling for boycotts, strikes and civil disobedience.

Gordimer's first short stories collection *Face to Face* published.

1950 The Population Registration and Race Classification Act (1950) required every citizen to be registered according to his or her racial.

The Group Areas Act (1950) required segregated residential and business areas for whites, Coloureds, and Asians.

1951 The Bantu Authorities Act (1951) abolished the Natives' Representative Council to establish a basis for ethnic government in the black reserves or homelands.

1952 The Native Laws Amendment Act (1952) limited the blacks' rights to live in the urban areas and moved the native owners out of their ancestral lands.

The Defiance Campaign (1952) on Gandhian principles of civil disobedience, strikes, boycotts and stay at home was committed to the goals of national freedom and political independence.

The long-established Pass laws were hardened, prohibiting the blacks from moving about the country to sell their labour on a free market, and classified those who were unemployed as vagrants.

1953 The United Party dissidents formed the Liberal Party, favouring a non-racial but qualified franchise for the blacks and left-wing whites formed the Congress of Democrats in sympathy with the ANC.

The Separate Amenities Act (1953) was introduced.

The Public Safety Act (1953) empowered the government to declare stringent states of emergency.

The Bantu Education Act (1953) imposed the government's control over schools for black children.

Gordimer's first novel *The Lying Days* and second short stories collection *The Soft Voice of the Serpent* published.

1954 The Land Act (1954) required a vacant strip of five hundred yards between any black quarter and the white town it served.

1955 In alliance with Indian, Coloured, and white organisations, the ANC endorsed the Freedom Charter.

The Bantu Education Act (1955) was introduced with an inferior education policy for blacks with the purpose to produce a subordinate class.

1956 The Coloureds were removed from the common voters' roll and placed on a Separate roll to elect four whites to represent them in the Parliament.

Nelson Mandela along with 154 others arrested on charges of treason.

The enactment of the Riotous Assemblies Act (1956) prohibited public meetings of 12 or more persons. It also prohibited the formation of racially mixed unions and required existing mixed unions to split into segregated unions or form segregated branches of white executives.

Gordimer's third short stories collection *Six Feet of The Country* published.

1957 The blacks in Johannesburg waged a bus boycott against an increase in the fare which ended successfully after three months. Thousands of blacks demonstrated in Cape Town against the government's decision to bar blacks from white church services.

1958 **Gordimer's second novel *A World of Strangers* published.**

1959 Former United Party members formed the Progressive Federal Party, favouring non-racial qualifications for a franchise. The Africanists, who opposed the inclusion of whites, broke away from the ANC and formed PAC (Pan-African Congress).

The Bantu Self-Government Act (1959) discontinued the representation of blacks by whites in Parliament.

The idea of separate development was introduced by the government for the blacks to build their homelands in the black regions called Bantustans.

1960 The Sharpeville massacre took place in which the police killed sixty-nine black demonstrators and injured many more who were protesting against the Pass laws.

Gordimer's fourth short stories collection *Friday's Footprint* published.

1961 South Africa became a Republic.

The ANC and the PAC were banned as unlawful organisations.

The ANC abandoned its policy of non-violence: Umkhonto we Sizwe (Spear of the Nation) launched a sabotage campaign.

1962 Poqo (Africans alone), an armed offshoot of the PAC attacked whites; Mandela was sentenced to five years in prison for inciting workers and leaving the country without a passport.

The Sabotage Act (1962) was introduced to provide for prolonged detention without trial.

1963 **Gordimer's third novel *Occasion for Loving* published.**

The legalisation of apartheid in the 1950s and the 1960s led Gordimer to present a frontier society in her early fiction. This scenario is inculcated in the rise of a liberal world in her early novels. Through the same canvas, Gordimer focuses upon the shift from a peaceful struggle against apartheid towards a radical solution to the injustices in her later fiction. This scenario is captured in the rise of a radical society of people in her novels The Late Bourgeois World *(1966),* A Guest of Honour *(1973),* The Conservationist *(1978) and* Burger's Daughter *(1979). These novels deal with the struggle era when the activists raised their voices against apartheid through underground movements such as in* The Late Bourgeois World *(1966) where characters carry out the underground missions that banned their movements. This is followed by* A Guest of Honour *(1973), about a new political life of an African country that, after getting independence from its colonial white masters, finds itself in political turmoil in the hands of its black people. The construction of this imaginary novel was possible only in the period of silence before the black uprisings at Soweto in 1976.*

Phase Two: Commitment After Sharpeville

Like a duck that appears quite calm whilst floating on the surface of the water but quite active underneath as her invisible feet move forward and backwards to keep its movement intact on the water, activists in South Africa struggled against apartheid in the pre-Soweto era. *The Conservationist* (1978) portrays the period just before the black uprisings at Soweto. It is manifested in the trap which is laid by the police to catch the protagonist in his sexual contact across the colour line. In *Burger's Daughter* (1979), Gordimer sums up this struggle against apartheid through the story of an Afrikaner family. Through the 1960s and 1970s, when overt political activity seemed impossible, Gordimer's fiction of the struggle era articulated the frustrations and aspirations of South Africa's urban society.

The action in Gordimer's early fiction becomes alive with the protagonist's experience of a moment or a set of events that prick his or her conscience or break him or her down in shame and embarrassment. This mental probing reappears in Gordimer's later fiction. It leads them to go through dynamic processes like those followed in the early fiction but here they are dealt with in a new way. The experience of the South African world presents the 'round' (Forster, 1927, 77) or complex protagonists of *The Lying Days, A World of Strangers* and *Occasion for Loving* with new perspectives on themselves. The new development in the later fiction is the presentation of characters who are *abstractions* set in a larger and more committed political framework. This change in characterisation projects Gordimer's transformed consciousness towards revolutionaries and opponents of apartheid in her South African world. Besides, Gordimer's early novels presented the increasing impoverishment of the liberal ideology in South African society and how it proved itself inadequate to meet the historical realities of South Africa. This failure of liberalism finds its deepest expression in her middle novels. They present an increasingly radical stance towards the struggle against apartheid in South Africa. This new stance separates Gordimer's *The Late Bourgeois World, A Guest of Honour, The Conservationist* and *Burger's Daughter* from her early novels.

The theme of borderland in Gordimer's short stories of the struggle era takes on a new form. In the early fiction, the characters transform themselves after their encounter with apartheid in the South African world. The plot here is constructed through borderland situations which make the characters conscious of their identity and marginality in South African life. For instance, in 'Good Climate, Friendly Inhabitants', from the collection *Not for Publication* (1965), a middle-aged white woman is rescued by a black man from exploitation by a younger white man with whom she had a physical relationship for some time. Gordimer creates a link between the black man and the white woman both through the communication they share and through the marginal social positions they occupy. In stories like, 'A Chip of Glass Ruby', from the same collection *Not for Publication* (1965), Gordimer attempts to examine acts of political resistance in South Africa through the context of a marriage. An Indian woman, Mrs Bamjee is a political activist for the rights of the blacks in the story. Her husband is upset at her arrest; he goes through a process of suffering and anxiety which makes him realise his wife's value as a person, not only to himself and the family but also to the wider community.

Similarly, in 'Some Monday for Sure', from the same collection *Not for Publication* (1965), Josias's optimistic spirit at his partially successful hold-up of a truck carrying dynamite is set against the hardships and disappointments which he and his wife Emma face during the process of their political involvement. The story suggests that the struggle for South African liberation will not be without enormous pain to individuals—the trials the couple go through in their love for each other and their hope and effort for a better South Africa. Except for a few narratives such as 'Son-in-law', 'A Company of Laughing Faces', 'The Pet', and 'Tenants and the Last Tree-House' (1965) which describe petty incidents of everyday life, most of the short stories, from the collections *Not for Publication* (1965), *Livingstone's Companions* (1972) and *A Soldier's Embrace* (1980), present history and identity issues through borderland situations in characters' lives such as 'Native Country' (1965), 'A Hunting Accident', 'Oral History', and 'You Name it'. (1980)

In 'The African Magician', from the collection *Not for Publication* (1965), the story revolves around European passengers returning to African colonies with their wives and children from their home in Belgium. Their 'white' boat makes a stopover at river stations in the Congo River. (*Magician*, 247) The white passengers notice a huge difference between their luxurious life on the boat and the 'stopping places': 'Our contribution to the shore [...] which were not industrialised [...] looks as strange as a space-ship from Mars might set down in a city.' (*Magician*, 251) A white passenger who looks forward to his retirement in two years comments on Africa: 'Lot of Bloomin' nothing, eh? Country full of nothing. Bush, bush, trees, trees.' (*Magician*, 246) The main action in the story is set in magic shows which are organised for the entertainment of white passengers on board at a stopover. A black magician performs magic tricks at eighty francs for the white 'gentlemen' and seventy francs for the white 'ladies'. The white audience don't find the black magician impressive and complain: 'It's too much, too expensive.' [...] 'You can't charge eighty francs for only half an hour. Is this all he knows?' (*Magician,* 254) They feel cheated and fooled by the black magician:

> [...] it was a matter they prided themselves on—not to be done down, even by blacks, whom they didn't expect to have the same standards about these things and whom they thought of as thievish anyway. (*Magician,* 255)

Most of the white audience is not willing to patronise or 'make special allowances for these people, simply because they were black':

> For them, blacks are people who [...] managed to scramble aboard, to our eyes dressed in their sleek wet blackness, hid their penises between their closed thighs with exactly that instinct that must have come to Adam when he was cast out of the Garden. [...] If they chose, as they had, to enter into activity governed by Western values, whether it was conjuring or running a twentieth-century state, they must be done the justice of being expected to fulfil their chosen standards. (*Magician,* 251-255)

However, one young white woman enjoys the magician's presentation. She takes part in a display of his magic and likes the experience: 'It's wonderful! You should try! Like a dreamy feeling...really!' By stepping into the black magician's world of action, the young woman comes to see beyond her white perspective on African magic. But her white companions disapprove of her voluntary participation because 'one of the disciples might have come before Christ like that. There was the peace of absolute trust in it. It stirred a needle of fear [...] To see it was beautiful would make us [the white people] dangerous'. (*Magician,* 258)

Like the young white woman's experience of crossing physical and mental barriers in 'The African Magician' (1965), Mannie Swemmer in 'Abroad' from the collection *Livingstone's Companions* (1972) discovers life beyond apartheid by crossing the border between South Africa and Northern Rhodesia, renamed Zambia after independence from the colonisers in 1970. This visit to a sovereign African country opens a chain of new experiences for him. Born in Bontebokspruit and proud of his

Scottish origins in South Africa, Mannie has contributed a great deal to the construction of Northern Rhodesia through his services in the public sector in the early 1930s. At the Zambian border, he notices two officers, one English and the other, a black man in the same uniform. In the hotel, he is offered a room to share with an Indian businessman from abroad as no rooms are available due to the anniversary of the new country. Mannie then visits a bar and finds people of mixed origins socialising together under the same roof. A young black man, Thompson Gwebo gives him back the South African two rand note which, by mistake, falls out of Mannie's pocket on the bar floor. Obliged, Mannie offers him a drink. During the conversation, it emerges that Thompson is the brother of one of the Under Ministers in Zambia and has previously studied in South Africa. Thompson now works for the Ministry of Local Government in the new country. As Mannie and Thompson communicate about past experiences of their lives in Africa, the hooligans in the pub interrupt their conversation. Thompson has to drive them away with the help of two black policemen in 'white gloves'. (*Abroad*, 290) From the pub, Mannie comes back late to the hotel and is not let into the room by the Indian. He is now offered a room that is empty but which is usually shared by the blacks in the hotel. Mannie strongly objects to this arrangement:

> The coolie, alright, I didn't say anything. But don't put me with an African, now, man! I mean. I've only just got here, give me a bit of time. You can't expect to put me in with a native, right away, first thing. (*Abroad*, 291)

This experience of a different life in Zambia makes Mannie aware of the dismantling of physical and mental barriers in the new order in Africa.

The struggle against discrimination is summed up in a dream of wild imagery in 'A Lion on the Free Way' from the collection *A Soldier's Embrace* (1980). The story is about the narrator's attempt to make sense of his dream about a lion in the zoo. As he is conscious of his incoherent recollections of his sleepy state of mind, so is the black man who, like the lion in the dream, becomes aware of his yawning state of existence in his South African world. The narrator recollects his vision: 'Open up! open up! What hammered on the door of sleep? Who's that? [...] anyone who lives within a mile of the zoo hears lions on summer nights. A tourist can be fooled. Africa already.' (*Lion*, 24) This dream becomes a frontier place for the narrator to reflect upon the status of the blacks in the struggle against apartheid in South Africa. The lion in the zoo, Africa, and the consciousness of the state of sleep blend in the dream. The narrator has lately read in the newspapers about black men marching on the road for freedom and independence which he links up to the lion of his dream. The image of the black strikers fits in with the lion image: '[…] black centipede with thousands of waving legs advancing. The panting grows louder […] he's out on the freeway.' (*Lion*, 27) The most notable impulse the narrator comes across during the borderland experience in the dream is of being warned which is either a prophecy or a direction for the future: as the lion is the king amongst animals, so is the black man in Africa.

Similarly, the protagonist's pregnancy with a baby inside her belly and the process of delivering him to the world in 'For Dear Life' from the same collection *A Soldier's Embrace* (1980) are symbolic of the birth of identity consciousness amongst the black people in South Africa. The unborn baby listens to her mother's worry: 'No one will know who you are; not even you. Only we, who are forgetting each other, will know who you never were. Even possibilities pass. I don't cry and I don't bleed.' (*FDL*, 71) Here, the dream in 'A Lion On The Free Way' (1980) is replaced by the vision of an unborn child. He is affected by the harsh realities of his mother's outer world whilst still inside her belly. He feels the revelation of his mother's expectation of a secure future, thus signifying a sense of identity and involvement with the place to which he will belong after his birth. The unborn is both the victim and the survivor who enters the human world with a sense of commitment; 'I begin again':

> In my swollen sex, obscene for my size, in my newly-pressed-in-to-shape cranium containing the seed-pearls of my brain cells, in my minute hands creased as bank-notes or immigration papers […] meeting violence with violence, casting myself out like Jonah from the heaving host whale […] swimming for dear life […] Behind me, the torn membranes of my moorings […] I find eyes […] the ancient Mediterranean sun smithereens against me. (*FDL*, 72)

In 1976, the black students in the Soweto township protested against inferior education and the use of Afrikaans as a medium of instruction in schools. (Schrire, 1992, 227) The process of the baby's coming from one world to another in the story represents the transitory era before the Soweto uprisings in which the blacks moved away from passive resistance towards an active struggle against apartheid.

The Late Bourgeois World (1966) presents the events of one day, a Saturday, in the protagonists' lives. Whilst sharing her breakfast with Graham, her lawyer boyfriend, Elizabeth receives a telegram saying that Max, her ex-husband, has driven his car into the sea and drowned himself along with his secret writings on 'the methodology of African socialism'. (LBW, 89) Elizabeth hurriedly visits her son Bobo in his boarding school to inform him about his father's death. Then she spends the rest of the afternoon alone before leaving for an old people's home to greet her grandmother on her eighty-seventh birthday. Graham visits her briefly in the evening when she is busy cooking for her black activist friend, Luke, who visits her late at night. In this succession of events, Gordimer brings to light the transformation in Elizabeth's personality after her contemplation over her political alienation and social marginalisation in her South African life. Even after the divorce from Max, her revolutionist husband, Elizabeth stands by him in his fight against apartheid and provides her full support when he is in prison. Max's defiance of the colour bar leads to his becoming a member of a 'communist cell'. (LBW, 39) He makes a bomb and blows up a post office, an act for which he is tried in court. He is sentenced to five years imprisonment but he gets himself out of prison after fifteen months by becoming a state witness, thus betraying all those who stood by him. After Max's suicide, Elizabeth actively involved herself in the blacks' struggle for freedom and equal rights for all South Africans.

Particular attention is paid to terminology that had been in practice for ethnic identities in South Africa. Elizabeth in *The Late Bourgeois World* notices that Max's mother 'spoke Xhosa' with her black servants and 'Afrikaans' with her 'Cape Coloured cook'. Max's mother regards them 'as if they were my own'. (LBW, 33) She is very much conscious of her being a 'Boer girl', the 'descendent of an old Cape Dutch family who had intermarried with English speaking people'. (LBW, 34) Max's father who has been a 'prominent United Party M.P.' (LBW, 42) for quite a time, comes from 'an English family that emigrated to South Africa when the gold mines started up'. (LBW, 34) This intermarriage between an Afrikaner girl, that is, Max's mother and a man of English origins, that is, Max's father, represents the historical reunion of the two white classes in the face of African reality:

> When Mrs Van Den Sandt spoke of 'we South Africans', she meant the Afrikaans and English-speaking white people, and when Theo Van Den Sandt called for 'a united South Africa, going forward to an era of progress and prosperity for all' he meant the unity of the same two white groups. (LBW, 40)

Mannie Swemmer in 'Abroad' reveals a similar consciousness of his status as a white person in Africa: 'There were quite a few nicely-dressed natives about, behaving themselves [...] And everywhere, Europeans in cars. 'Ah, but the old trees are still going strong!' (*Abroad*, 282–283) This reflects upon the political scenario of the 1970s when the whites reluctantly started to formally accept the blacks as 'natives' and themselves as 'settlers' thus enforcing perennial discrimination on racial grounds. Mannie mocks at the birth of Zambia: 'Gambia, Zambia! These fancy names, with the new kaffir government' thus confirmed the race consciousness of the white people in Africa. (*Abroad*, 278) This is also captured in the comment of the police officer's wife in 'The African Magician' who notices a scribble chalked on the barge below the boat. It hailed the coming of the country's independence from white man's rule. She says: 'They are mad, truly. They think they can run a country. They are just like monkeys, you know. We've taught them a few tricks. Really, they are monkeys out from there.' (*Magician*, 248) Doris Lessing in *African Laughter* comments:

> Once I had wondered why Europeans were so obsessed with their racial superiority, and if it was a compensation for their having been so backward, so uncouth, while the civilisations of the Middle East and the East glittered and despised theirs. The European arrogance was only the boastfulness of the nouveau riche? Pride in white skin was because there was nothing much else to be proud of? (1992, 133)

Gordimer's frequently leads the protagonists to observe the whites like Max's parents behaving towards the natives of the South African land in an act of 'essentialising blackness' (Bhabha, 1990, 3):

> For the rest—the ten or eleven million 'natives'—their labour was directed in various Acts of no interest outside Parliament, and their lives were incidental to their labour since until the white man came they knew nothing better than a mud hut in the veld. (LBW, 40)

In Fanon's terminology also, this Othering is the process by which the blacks were interpreted by the white colonisers in South African society. They labelled the blacks as the *Other* to socially construct them as removed, distant and lesser individuals who were serviceable to cater for the needs, values, interests, and experiences of the white coloniser, thus obliterating the black man's genuine self. Gordimer calls her struggle against apartheid 'my war': 'The colour bar is wrong and utterly indefensible.' (Ross, 1965, 34)

The Late Bourgeois World reflects a shift towards revolutionary attitudes within the banned African National Congress and its adjacent white movements. This novel is based on the sabotage efforts of the

African resistance movement, a group of young white men connected to the Liberal Party who resorted to violence in 1964 and whose actions served to discredit the Liberal Party in the eyes of white South Africa. The necessity for violent action and the implicit rejection of the constitutional programme for change may be seen as a comment upon the political sterility of liberalism. In this setting, Elizabeth says: 'There was a move amongst politically active Africans to keep out of white houses, no matter who's they were, and to reject friendship and even intimacy with whites as a part of white privilege.' (LBW, 89) The close political alliance between liberal and leftist elements between the whites and the blacks broke down and polarisation between the two races became more and more pronounced in the 1960s South Africa.

In a succession of memories, Elizabeth remembers her being pregnant at the time of the Defiance Campaign in 1952. She recalls the Sharpeville tragedy of 1960 when demonstrators against the Pass laws were killed by the white police, the making of the South African Republic in 1961 when all constitutional rights were placed in the hands of the white minority, the formation of the PAC, the ban on the Communist Party, and the prestige of African nationalism on the international forum for passive campaigns against apartheid in South Africa. In her experience of Max, Elizabeth is appreciative of what he is doing: 'The madness of the brave is the wisdom of life.' (LBW, 5) On one occasion, Max makes a 'frightful' (LBW, 44) speech at his sister's wedding in which he talks to the white guests about the 'moral sclerosis': 'What I'm asking you to look out for is—is moral sclerosis. Hardening of the heart, narrowing of the mind; while the dividends go up.' Elizabeth feels embarrassed at his use of what she thinks is an 'idiotic term' in his speech. (LBW, 48–51). The speech itself is a sincere presentation of Max's thinking, yet it disturbs Elizabeth to see its lack of efficacy, its impotence, and the readiness with which it is absorbed and forgotten by the guests. Having rejected his white bourgeois world, its privileges, and the identity it offers, Max is condemned to loneliness. Elizabeth knows that Max 'might have been a lawyer; but all the professions were part of the white club, whose life membership ticket, his only birth right, he had torn up.' (LBW, 74) Long before he drowns himself, Max is considered dead by his parents because the question of white identity is very important to them.

Besides Max's alienation in his white society, Elizabeth recalls his marginality in the black man's world. He 'marched into an African area prohibited to whites, and he also went to Durban to camp with Africans and Indians on a public square in protest against segregation'. (LBW, 41) She reflects:

> He wanted to come close; and in this country the people—with all the huddled warmth of the phrase—are black. Set aside with whites, even his own chosen kind, he was still left out, he experienced the isolation of his childhood become the isolation of his colour. (LBW, 80–81)

Max's revolutionary ideas cannot be refuted. Elizabeth comments: 'He wasn't content to leave bad things the way they are. If he failed, well, that's better than making no attempt.' (LBW, 26) However, Luke is surprised at Elizabeth for not attending Max's funeral. She doesn't want to because he 'didn't die for them—the people [revolutionary comrades], but perhaps he did more than that. In his attempt to love, he lost even his self-respect, in betrayal. He risked everything for them and lost everything'. (LBW, 93) In this context, Elizabeth makes their son, Bobo, aware of Max's limitations:

> Max was in a mess, he somehow couldn't deal with what happened to him, largely, yes, because of his political actions, but also because [...] in general, he wasn't equal to the demands [...] he took upon himself [...] As if you insisted on playing in the first team when you were only good enough—strong enough for third. (LBW, 27)

As she sees it, 'Max wasn't anybody's hero' (LBW, 26), though 'he suffered a lot for his political views.' (LBW, 28) This conversation helps Bobo to talk about his difficulty in standing up against the apartheid psyche of his white classmates in the boarding school. He tells Elizabeth how the other boys laugh at the smell of 'Kaffirs', 'talking as if they were the only ones who ever smell.' Bobo doesn't want to be sensitive to his classmates' comments and wishes 'we were like other people' who 'don't care'. (LBW, 29–30) Towards the end of the novel, Elizabeth becomes aware of a similar feeling in herself. She is frightened at her decision to provide support for her black friends: 'The slow, even beats of my heart repeat to me, like a clock; afraid, alive, afraid, alive, afraid, alive.' (LBW, 160) This complex situation leads Elizabeth to find her South African life as the late (dead) bourgeois world, a world characterised by the death-throes of the white world: Max 'drowned' on the day 'when a man' from America 'walked about in space'. (LBW, 154) Elizabeth somehow finds a link between Max who 'had succeeded in dying' (LBW, 64) and the living man's walk in the space: 'If you master that beyond as those men up there have done, isn't that the closest we've ever got to mastering death?' (LBW, 154) When Elizabeth asks Graham, 'what could one say this is the age of? What on earth do you think they'll call it in history?' he replies: I've just read a book that refers to ours as the Late Bourgeois World. How does that appeal to you?' (LBW, 114)

At Luke's request to find someone whose bank account can be used to transfer funds from abroad, Elizabeth thinks of using her grandmother's account, thus discovering the possibility to slide into underground black politics. This is her acceptance of radicalism and black leadership when Liberalism and its values seem at an end: 'A sympathetic white woman hasn't got anything to offer [...] good old white Reserve of banks and privileges [...] each will have given what he has [...] perhaps it would be better than what I have had—or got.' (LBW, 159–160) Elizabeth finds herself recalling her grandmother's repeated questioning in her old-age forgetfulness, 'what happened.' (LBW, 105) Something has, indeed, happened: for Elizabeth, 'there are possibilities for (her), certainly; but under what stone do they lie?' (LBW, 5) Helping Luke with the transfer of funds through her grandmother's bank account thus provides Elizabeth with a way out of her social alienation and political isolation in her South African world. Two courses of action of the white liberals are reflected in the novel, one is the act of rebellion that Max has taken and the other is an a-political resignation which Elizabeth takes up.

In *The Late Bourgeois World,* Gordimer broke away from the dominant liberal tradition in white South African literature. One can recognise that the logical and coherent tradition of the realist novel in South Africa is a very narrow, but highly organised one. What begins with Schreiner's novel as the liberal tradition in Southern African English fiction does continue in *Turbott Wolfe*, is endemic to *Cry, the Beloved Country*, is reviewed in Lessing's *The Grass is Singing*, and meets its culmination in later novels. (Gray, 1980, 136)

This is particularly true of *The Late Bourgeois World* which becomes a significant landmark in English South African fiction. With the moral and political despair of its main character, Elizabeth, the novel appears to be the end of a road as if the South African novel about personal relations can go no further in the darkening climate of apartheid. By the time Max's revolutionary work along with black activists is disrupted by police action, that is before he resorts to sabotage, 'he had associated himself for a while with people who wanted to organise a new underground white revolutionary group.' (LBW, 91) The word 'white' indicates his loss of contact with the blacks. It seems as if *The Late Bourgeois World* is a novel about the difficulty, if not the impossibility, of crossing class and racial barriers in the rigid South African social formation; and in which those who do not respect the demands for allegiance and complicity required of them by the white ruling class establishment are fated to suffer social isolation and political impotence in their South African society.

After *The Late Bourgeois World*, Gordimer takes a new direction in her writing; a world of radicals and revolutionary situations becomes her subject matter in *A Guest of Honour*, representing the heightened tensions of contemporary Africa. In this novel, Gordimer inculcates her experience of the rest of Africa because there are tremendous similarities in the countries in Africa, including South Africa. Gordimer admits: 'I tried to do something I had never done before [...] I tried to write a political novel [...] tried to put flesh on what have become to be known as the dry bones of political life.' (Cassere, 1972, 57) If *The Late Bourgeois World* expresses the impasse of liberal values and the impotence of liberals in South Africa in the 1960s, *A Guest of Honour* (1973) signifies the collapse of liberalism in the 1960s South Africa. It focuses on a failed liberal character, Evelyn James Bray. The story in the novel begins with Adamson Mweta, a black chairman of PIP, the People's Independence Party, taking over the power as the president of a sovereign African country. For the independence celebrations, both black and white activists and life-long supporters of the African Independence movement are invited except for Edward Shinza, a regional black chairman of PIP. Shinza is not considered in the organisation of the cabinet of government ministers because he has serious differences with Mweta over the process 'to build a nation'. (Guest, 118) Mweta has opted to run the government with the machinery and methods that had been handed over by the white colonial officials. Shinza is totally against Mweta's approach because, as he sees it, this will never help the Africans to progress and develop themselves independently. At the Party conference for the Party wing, the UTUC Secretary-General elections, Shinza gives an eloquent speech and wins the election. Differences between the 'two sharply-defined factions' (Guest, 345) in the Party, and the policies of Mweta's government precipitate 'the strikes, lock-outs, and the confused expressions of dissatisfaction that, in the bush, took the form of tribal wrangling'. (Guest, 286) Evelyn James Bray, an Englishman and 'a close contact' (Guest, 4) of the Party's leadership, attempts to sort out the differences and grievances between Mweta and Shinza but to no avail. He attempts to deliver but his efforts cannot make a difference because 'these nice white liberals getting mixed up in things they don't understand. What did he expect?' (Guest, 502) Gordimer's later fiction thus reveals the inadequacy of liberal values to stand up against apartheid in South Africa. 'Everyone knows those whites who want to be allowed to 'love' the blacks out of guilt; and those who want to be allowed to 'love' them as an aberration, a distinction' (LBW, 80–81), the liberals in South Africa were none of them. To escape his death in the ambush, Evelyn feels the same: 'Inside him was an experience exactly the reverse of emptiness, the sense of all forces disengaged and fallen apart, that he had been having all day.' (Guest, 457–458) He realises 'the paradox that playing safe was dangerous' now. (Guest, 391) His accidental death in a road-blocking riot towards the end of the novel symbolises the death of liberalism in South Africa:

> In a number devoted to 'The Decline of Liberalism' in an English monthly journal, he was discussed as an interesting case in point: a man who had passed over from the scepticism and resignation of empirical liberalism to become one of those who are so haunted by the stupidities and evils in human affairs that they are prepared to accept apocalyptic solutions, wade through blood if need be, to bring real change. (Guest, 503)

The action in *A Guest of Honour* is woven through the last year of Evelyn's life when he is invited by Mweta to come along with the latter's accession to power and help in pilot programmes for the development of the newly born African nation. On his arrival from London, Evelyn is warmly received by both the black and the white associates who have known him since the times when he was Colonel and District Commissioner in South Africa under white colonial rule ten years ago. Whilst serving as 'a white colonial servant' (Guest, 4), he becomes friends with the Africans. This leads him to become involved in supporting them in their struggle for independence from white rule. For his active participation in the African struggle, Evelyn had been deported back to London with his family by the then-serving white colonial officials.

However, after ten years, Evelyn gets an opportunity to help his African friends again in the construction of their sovereign country. Evelyn is charged with compiling a report for an education project which is workable in the new set-up of the country. However, with a very limited budget and no infrastructure which may be required for the proper organisation of a scheme, Evelyn 'felt that he himself was not qualified to find the radical solution that was needed; neither was the ministry of education'. (Guest, 101)

Besides, he does not approve of Mweta's strategy of controlling the country and its people with the use of force over them, such as when a young man from Shinza's faction is beaten up and held illegally by government machinery. A member of the Party is also reportedly threatened by the youth of the opposing faction. With a firm belief that he cannot be 'regarded as a very dangerous opponent' (Guest, 392) by Mweta, Evelyn attempts to utilise his influence and contacts to resolve the differences between the radical and moderate factions of the black leadership but in return, he loses his life. In this regard, the title of the novel, *A Guest of Honour* and the quotations which are utilised at the beginning of the novel, one by the Russian writer, Ivan Sergeyevich Turgenev (1818–1883): 'An honourable man will end by not knowing where to live,' and the other quote from the Argentine Marxist, Ernesto 'Che' Guevara (1928–1967)—a major figure of the Cuban Revolution 1953–59: 'Many will call me an adventurer—and that I am, only of a different sort—one of those who risks his skin to prove his platitudes' (Guest, 5), aptly sum up Evelyn's character. Happily married to Olivia, an English woman, and a father of two daughters, he lives and dies for the things he has stood for. Although Evelyn keeps his contact intact with Shinza and his faction even though Mweta regards them as 'rebels in the union' (Guest, 394), Evelyn is believed by Mweta to be a 'conciliator'. (Guest, 504) However, this experience of power and independence by the blacks and the rivalries between them makes Evelyn conscious of the complexity that exists in the concept of borders in a society. On one occasion, he can't help saying: 'Every nation has its private violence [...] after a while one can feel at home and sheltered between almost any borders—you grow accustomed to anything.' (Guest, 187) Besides Evelyn, on another occasion, Shinza also utters: 'Borders! Doesn't mean anything [...] People are wandering over after their goats, every day. You forget we're the same people on both sides.' (Guest, 260) Here, two things seem to be hinted at, one that borders in society are there to be crossed over and secondly, borders don't only exist between the people of different nations but also between the people of the same colour as well.

For Christopher Heywood, *A Guest of Honour* 'explores the consequences of independence in a Central African country which combines Zambian settings with issues related to the problems of Katanga.' (1983, 26) This 'Central African territory' (Guest, 4) in the novel is, however, an imaginary country that goes through a stage of conflict in the march of history towards independence from the English colonials. Gordimer describes:

> It [A Guest of Honour] is about someone who tries to justify his presence in Africa beyond the colour of his skin [...] you have to accept that you are a victim of history. Here is the end of the colonial period, and what you may stand for as an individual—no matter what you do

> or have done—will be swamped in the general whiteness [...] In South Africa, one wears one's skin like a uniform. (Ellis, 1978, 93–4)

In this context, Heywood's study of the novel finds Fanonist aspirations in the opposing faction's radical socialism:

> When I [...] decided to go along with you, Shinza affirms, coming to power wasn't going to be a matter of multiplying the emancipated, while the rest of the people remained a class of affranchised slaves... He referred with a smile to the phrases from Fanon. (Guest, 258)

Shinza is aware of the real problem, that is, extreme poverty amongst the blacks:

> To keep the sort of status quo the Europeans call stability—the stability of overseas investment [...] but we want an instability, James, we want an instability in the poverty and backwardness of this country, we want the people at the top to be a bit poorer for a few years now, so that the real, traditional, rock-bottom poverty, the good old kind that 'never changes' in Africa, can be broken up out of its famous stability at last, at long, long last, dragged up from the shit. (Guest, 260)

Here, Gordimer points at the real African dilemmas, poverty and illiteracy which must be eliminated if Africans have to prosper and compete with the rest of the world in future.

For Heywood, the novel also 'stakes a claim for the contribution of white activists working in the processes leading to independence.' (1983, 25) But at the same time, it reveals that liberal values such as personal freedom and interracial friendship are irrelevant in front of the Pan-African perspective which worked towards the creation of their version of a just society, thus destroying the role of the white progressives in Africa. For Heywood, Evelyn 'remains an outsider, a vehicle for the experience of 'the growing unwelcomeness of the white man in Africa' as Gordimer expressed the problem in her essay, Where Do Whites Fit In? (1959).' (1983, 26) *A Guest of Honour* provides no clear answer to this conflict. However, the novel represents 'the failure of the knowledge of human sciences to make people more humane.' (Guest, 335) In her presentation of Hjalmar Wentz, the German owner of a nightclub in the days of turmoil, Gordimer describes a feature of the late 1960s era: Hjalmar doesn't 'rejoice' over the fact that his son, Stephen is 'a natural colonial—the adaptable kind who enjoys the sort of popularity you get when you run a bar and everybody calls you Steve.' But he understands it 'as a solution to the problem of survival' in South Africa. (Guest, 331)

In *The Conservationist* (1978), Gordimer moves further away from the liberal ideology which had been the nerve-centre of her previous novels. The story in the novel is set in a 'typical Transvaal landscape' (Cons. 22) which is situated twenty-five miles away from Johannesburg. A river runs by one side of this farm whereas, on the other side, there is another farm which is owned by an Afrikaner family, the De Beers. An Indian store and a transport service station for the blacks of the Location nearby are also situated on the main way towards the farm. Even though there exists a vast black Location near the farm, Mehring, a middle-aged white man of Germanic descent and Namibian origin, and an established business tycoon in Johannesburg buys '400 acres of veld, fields and vlei', though 'weed-choked', yet 'beautiful'. (Cons. 20). This rich landscape creates a spell over Mehring. He feels that on the farm, 'the sense of familiarity, of some kind of unwelcome knowledge or knowing, is slow to ebb. As it does, it leaves space in his mind; or uncovers, like the retreat of a high tide, carrying away silt.' (Cons. 37) In comparison to the 'shallow breath of the city', Mehring 'involuntarily' finds himself drawn in a 'keener pleasure' by the serene atmosphere on the farm. (Cons. 9) Every other Sunday on the farm gives Mehring not only a break from his hectic business life in the city but also provides him with a space to reflect upon his sensual attitude towards the women in his life, his arrogant behaviour towards the struggling lives of the blacks in contemporary South Africa, and his moral distance from his adolescent son's sensitive attitude towards black Africa. However, going away from the farm at the end of the day takes away 'the empty space that was clear in him this afternoon' and 'it exists no more than does a city pavement under the comings and goings of passing bodies that make it what it is'. (Cons. 54)

In this way, the South African landscape acts as a frontier place for Mehring where he can reflect upon his innermost thoughts and feelings about the world he lives in. On the farm, his thoughts follow one after another, intermingling one image with the other: his farm, his woman, his business, his losses, his investments, his son, and his servants, come to his mind all juxtaposed in a stream of consciousness. For example, Mehring's wandering mind recollects the memory of the soft texture of 'a wan yellowed leaf' in the fields. It then reminds him of some important point that is missed in his business discussions with the Japanese counterparts. He makes a 'mental note' because he knows that his tape recorder is in the briefcase which is lying in the car. He then takes a nap whilst lying rolled onto his belly over the grass with his memory of 'my bit of veld and my cows'. When he awakes, he becomes aware of 'breathing intimately into the earth': it appears as if the hairs of his 'half-opened eye that borders it and the filaments of dead grass are one.' He also finds sand sticking to his lips. With 'violent jerks, he changes his body position and thinks, 'the abyss is no deeper than a doorstep; the landing, home' and so on. (Cons. 37) At the beginning of the novel, Gordimer quotes a part of a poem from the collection 'The Tattooed Desert' (1971) written by the Arizona writer, Richard Shelton (1933-to date) that resembles the thought process followed by Mehring's consciousness:

> I must have been almost crazy
> to start out alone like that on my bicycle
> pedalling into the tropics carrying
> a medicine for which no one had found
> the disease and hoping
> I would make it in time
> I passed through a paper village under glass
> where the explorers first found
> silence and taught it to speak
> where old men were sitting in front
> of their houses killing sand without mercy
> Brothers, I shouted to them
> tell me who moved the river
> where can I find a good place to drown (Cons. 7)

The content of the poem, as it appears, seems to have no similarity with Mehring's circumstances but in expression and technique, it has relevance: the narrator of the poem appears to be living in a world of imagination at the border between sanity and madness where he can create, one over the other, a reality of his own making. It seems that he finds it safer to stay within such a frontier as he can get away with what he thinks and feels about the state of life around him. In Mehring's case, the landscape creates such an aesthetic space in his mind where he can make his observations, for example, his noticing himself becoming too fixed in his views to see freshly, in comparison to his son who questions the validity of hierarchal social patterns in their compartmentalised South African society. However, his visits to the farm relieve his sexual desires: he recalls his coming across attractive advances made towards him during a friendly meal by a 'good looking' woman who happens to be his friend for fifteen years. He recollects from the experience that he was not perturbed by her affection at all. Instead, it was her teenage daughter with 'whom he wanted to meet and undress in a hotel room.' (Cons. 28) Such sexual images and descriptions in the story reveal the thought process in Mehring's mind which operates or functions with the landscape around him; it drives him to keep clean the farm to the extent that its natural beauty, that is, its spaciousness, is not spoiled by the 'rot' at other places on the land. He finds the suggestion of Antonia, his mistress at the time of the purchase of the farm, appealing, 'why not just buy it and leave it as it is.' (Cons. 20)

The landscape in *The Conservationist* vividly depicts the territorial and linguistic barriers which reduce the existence of its white and black subjects to marginality in each other's world. Mehring's farm is surrounded by a 'barbed wire fence' from all sides. (Cons. 32) The African Location is fenced and wired with an endless boundary. The Indians, too, have built a fence around their house. All these territorial divisions reflect the borders within borders in South African society. Mehring himself actively maintains such boundaries intact: 'On the farm it is time for conservation—buildings to be repaired, fire-breaks cleared, he must go round all the fences with Jacobus. The sort of job they' all never think to do unless you push them to it. A place must be kept up.' (Cons. 68) The irony is that the blacks themselves are engaged by Mehring and by the Indians to build their fences in order 'to keep blacks out'. (Cons. 32)

Such physical barriers in the African landscape represent fear and mistrust in the psyche of both the whites and the blacks against each other. The fence which separates Mehring's farm from the black quarters is more than just a physical barrier. It is a mental barrier, too, psychologically isolating him from the blacks on his farm. Mehring doesn't trust Jacobus, even though he is the boss boy on his farm. Mehring observes that Jacobus knows more about him than he knows about Jacobus. He is sure of Jacobus telling lies to him such as his making a story of the early morning visit of the birds on the farm, he's not doing much about the dead body which is found on the farm, and his misuse of Mehring's tractor and the kitchen on the farm. Mehring also doubts the Indians' polite attitude towards him because he believes that they are buttering him for keeping their shop going in a place that is 'for white people' only. (Cons. 33) The Indians have bribed the white authorities for the possession of the shop, yet they live in constant fear of losing it one way or the other. They have to keep constant vigilance on every happening inside as well as outside their shop.

Economically, the blacks living in the compounds on the farm and the Indians' black employees in the nearby poor quarters behind the Indian store are no better than the blacks at the Location near the farm. Jacobus visits the Indians' black employees in their 'tin houses' where 'broken chairs' and old 'cooking pots' are evidence of their extreme poverty. Even though there are divisions and sub-divisions between the black and the Indian classes, there are times when they overcome their mental blocks: 'The "our" took in the shopkeeper, his ménage, Jacobus himself and the farm people' when they agree that the dead man is no longer their problem as the police have taken it away from them. (Cons. 32)

The blacks on the farm are, however, frightened of Mehring who might call the police and open the investigation again of the unknown black dead body that was found on his farm. On the other end, Mehring is concerned about the blacks' manoeuvres at the Location near his farm: 'There is a high fence all around to keep them from getting in and out except the location gates, but there're great big gaps where they cut the wire and come out at night.' (Cons. 27) The Sergeant in charge of the area is also suspicious of the blacks' activities at the Location. It seems as if life in and around the farm is a society of fear and mistrust where Mehring, Jacobus and the Indians, all in their respective capacities, look for dogs to protect themselves from each other.

Apartheid in South Africa not only determined the kind of lives people should lead but also influenced the kind of person they should become. They become characters like Jacobus who 'didn't talk to the Indian as he did to a white man, nor as he would to one of his people.' Whilst talking to the Indians at the shop, Jacobus recognises his people, the blacks, at the Location as 'trouble for everybody'. (Cons. 31) Sitting amongst his compound fellows, he mocks Mehring by fooling him with incorrect information about the birds, eggs, and dogs but at the same time 'he could not encourage this talk too much—he was himself half on the side of the authority it mocked, he earned his privileges by that authority and also protected them against its source'. (Cons. 29–30) The most severe impact of apartheid in South Africa was physical as it caused people to live in separate units and classes, generating fear and a sense of alienation towards each other.

As no work of art is entirely subjective or objective, Abdul R. JanMohamed in *Manichean Aesthetics: The Politics of Literature in Colonial Africa* (1983, 272) observes the presence of a split narrative in *The Conservationist*: subjective and objective narratives and experiences merging and diluting side by side into one another. Mehring is introduced in the novel as a conservationist who attempts to protect the natural life on the farm. He is after the dogs who hunt the birds on his farm. He is concerned for the guinea fowl eggs that are picked up by the small black children on the farm. He is disturbed by the fire and then the flooding of water on the farm. He later plants trees as well, but his attempt to stay intact with nature may be genuine or maybe that he 'can afford to indulge': a hankering to make contact with the land' to get tax relief from the laws of the land. Moreover, it is ironic that the black presence is completely chucked out by Mehring in his observation of the 'beautiful' South African landscape. (Cons. 20) He gets upset by the presence of the black dead body on his farm and makes sure that it is not visible in the landscape. Mehring asks Jacobus, his houseboy to cover it with a 'tarpaulin or sacks'. (Cons. 19) He is not satisfied until the dead body is removed by the police from its temporary grave on the farm.

Mehring's passion for sexual ecstasy leads him to take risks one of which proves fatal. On a previous occasion, he luckily gets away with his sexual adventure with a teenage white girl in the aeroplane but this time, his obsession with sex throws him into a deep end: he breaks the apartheid law which restricts sexual relationships outside one's colour. He is caught red-handed in a police trap in a sexual encounter with a pale black girl who looks more 'white' than the usual olive colour. The novel meticulously juxtaposes Mehring's death in disgrace with his conservation of the farm where he grows trees, his ambitious business endeavours which make him wealthy, and his detached communication with the poor black world which stands in contrast with his teenage son's fervour against injustices all over black Africa.

The Conservationist deals with a white land-owning capitalist for whom possessions are everything, and whose relationships with the world read like a catalogue of alienations. At the expense of the white man's prosperity in South Africa, the blacks are robbed of their agricultural land in the face of industrial development in Transvaal villages. On the way to the farm in the novel, vast 'mealie fields' are turned into factories and supermarket stores. (Cons. 21) Although these new developments required more black workers, no economic uplift came the black man's way. Instead, the Locations became more crowded, giving way to crime and violence in black society. These places provided shelter to illegal black workers who didn't have passes such as the 'native Witbooi' in the novel. Although he worked on the farm, he had no pass to work in South Africa. He came from Rhodesia illegally and got hold of work at different places by producing his expired work permits and references which were put down on the pages out of exercise books with 'barely-literate signatures of white housewives.' (Cons. 30) Those references somehow equalled the official passes in 1970s South Africa.

The whites, on the other hand, profited from the industrial development in 1970s South Africa. As a chairman of an Investment fund,

Mehring accumulates a great pool of funds which provides enough space for his keeping a farm for leisure purposes. He fully utilises the tax relief incentive which was meant to be created by the Afrikaner government for poor white farmers only so that they wouldn't suffer in the grip of poverty. In contrast, hunger and disease continuously prevailed in the black quarters of South African society.

Besides representing the capitalist sector, Mehring and his farm are suggestive of a microcosm of that part of South African history when the white colonists, like the bloody dogs frequent visits to the farm, came and disturbed the natural course of African life. (Cons. 18) It does not get registered to Mehring that his very own existence on the farm is an intrusion in the natural course of South African life. Instead, he relishes the memory of telling his Japanese, German and Canadian counterparts about his possession of a farm in South Africa: 'I'm not in the Yacht-owning class. I'm afraid (it was charming of him to say), I have my bit of veld and my few cows. And that's all I want.' (Cons. 36) However, the black children in possession of guinea fowl eggs on Mehring's farm generate a very strong presence of black life as an essential part of the South African landscape. And it also belongs to the blacks as well. The novel's vision is one of historical transfer; prophetically *The Conservationist* is situated at the point where white history ends and black history resumes, that is, the rise of the Black Consciousness era in the 1970s South Africa.

As in *A Guest of Honour*, *The Conservationist* investigates the dilemma of survival and alienation which the progressives faced in 1970s South Africa. Mehring, the protagonist in the novel who represents the progressive Afrikaner elite, is estranged from any sort of community and this is reflected in the fact that a large part of the novel consists of his interior monologues. Due to the absence of any authentic relationships with other people, he has no one to talk to. Mehring, is, in fact, 'conditioned by his lack of contact with the people of the country, his lack of contact with the South African inside' him. (Giliomee, 1984, 125) Apartheid effectively managed to isolate the white man. Mehring thus represents the terminal malaise of a whole history and culture and alienation from the land and its people: 'While the transplanted European identity automatically stresses the white community's foreignness to the environment, the dispossessed blacks always have an irrevocable sense of belonging to the land.' (Cons. 9–10)

In contrast to Mehring is the small community of blacks who work on his farm. They are the true caretakers of the land, and their living is characterised by a fidelity to relationships, both to the living and the dead; at the burial of an unknown black man, the final paragraph of the novel reveals:

> The one whom the farm received had no name. He had no family but their women wept a little for him. There was no child of his present but their children were there to live after him. They have put him away to rest, at last; he had come back. He took possessions of this earth, theirs; one of them. (Cons. 252)

The dead body's burial reasserts the social and moral values of the submerged African proletariat. The black dead man is incorporated within the community and the land from which they have been dispossessed. Here, Gordimer prophesies the eventual repossession of South Africa by the blacks: the dispossessed black communities of Highveld Transvaal will inherit the world they have lost. If *The Late Bourgeois World* was the final elegy of that doomed white English-speaking culture lost in its clubrooms, golf courses and coffee bars, *The Conservationist* laments white South Africa which enjoyed booming prosperity and international links of wealth and power in the 1970s era. But the terminal disease has not been shaken; the power of the novel lies in its evocation simultaneously of the strength, resources, poise of its protagonist and the bewildered hopelessness of his position in his South African world.

The Conservationist deals with the impact of a world of barriers in which the characters find themselves confined within immobility: at Mehring's approach, Jacobus stops 'as if there were a line drawn there, ten feet away from the farmer and goes through the formalities of greeting, which include a hand-movement as if he had a hat to remove.' (Cons. 10) This is a vivid presentation of incalculable psychological damage caused by a grid of barriers in the characters' lives in the novel. Mehring finds himself different from the De Beers and the blacks whereas there are noticeable similarities between the latter two groups such as Mehring observes the Afrikaner girl who is motherly towards her smaller sister. This is an African trait in her personality. Moreover, Mehring observes the black people only in the capacity of doing something negative or clumsy in the whole natural environment of the land. In 'the figure of the black man' (Cons. 10), Jacobus appears awkward to him in his out of season dress and shoes. Playing with the birds' eggs by the small black children is an act of serious misconduct for him. The dead body of the black man is viewed as a crime committed by the black Location nearby. The African Location itself is considered a good for nothing place where theft and murder are common everyday matters. The fact that the black existence inside and around the farm is an integral part of the South African landscape is completely overlooked by Mehring in his concern about the extinction of the African natural life from the face of the earth: 'Soon there will be nothing left. In the country. The continent. The Oceans. The sky.' (Cons. 10) Ironically, the extinction of African culture and civilisation does not occur to him. The blacks have been pushed out of their lands for centuries and are now reduced to surviving in unnatural conditions in the nearby African Location. Gordimer presents 'history from inside' (Clingman, 1986, 224) to raise her voice against the occupation of land by the whites in South Africa. At the same time, it is also an attempt to write a history of settlers' consciousness in South Africa.

Besides territorial segregation and racial prejudices, the language barrier plays a significant role in dividing people into different groups in South Africa. In *The Conservationist*, Antonia's professor husband who is carrying out linguistic research on Bushmen in South Africa and aborigines in Australia signifies the richness and complexity that the variety in languages may generate towards each other. For instance, the sergeant uses the words, 'Bantu' (meaning people) and 'Kaffir' (meaning originally non-believer) for the black people at the Location. The use of particular words such as 'farmer', for the white man, because he owns the land, and 'Kraal' (meaning a village hut) for the compounds intensifies the divisions and boundaries. Afrikaans is identified as 'the white man's other language' (Cons. 10), and 'India' (Cons. 33) for the languages spoken by people of sub-continental origin.

Mehring prefers to speak to the police authorities in Afrikaans to show his identification with them. In the same way, the De Beers prefer to speak to Mehring in English, though in a 'strong Afrikaans accent': 'Their insistence on talking to him in English demarcates the limit of his acceptance, out here, outside the city from which he comes and goes.' (Cons. 44) At times, Mehring enjoys this crossing over into the world of another language: after speaking about the dead body to the police in Afrikaans on the phone, Mehring 'replaces the receiver and says in English, Christ Almighty; and snorts a laugh, softly, so that Jacobus shall not hear.' (Cons. 17) Jacobus also finds pleasure in speaking English whilst using the phone in Mehring's absence. All this use of languages for different purposes and in different ways is a channel to identify with a group other than one's own. It also defines one's confinement in South African society: the Indians' 'challenging, aggressive way of speaking was something that means nothing to farm people; a convention of barriers between them and the Indian proprietor; they were used to him.' (Cons. 31)

In contrast to the death and burial of the unknown black man,

Mehring's death is seen as a trivial incident that produces no visible change in the life of his circle. This signifies the degraded image of liberalism in 1970s South Africa. Mehring makes observations about the problems under apartheid but has not the capability to address them. He is simply not able to appreciate the practical support of the blacks by his teenage son, Terry who gives away his clothes to the black employee on the farm. In Mehring's death, Gordimer appears to have dramatized the fate of liberalism in South Africa. Gordimer utters:

> Liberalism has become a dirty word in South Africa. It has never delivered the goods. Too ready to compromise, to see both sides of the question, too polite: too much of a gesture, not enough of a commitment, not radical. (Ellis, 1978, 93)

Mehring's mistress, Antonia in *The Conservationist* promises what she cannot deliver in practice. Mehring is critical of her for flying away into exile after she has been discovered by the apartheid authorities for arranging meetings between the whites and the blacks on her premises. He shows dislike for her liberal progressive ideas which do not stop her from pretending that she is not scared by the 'trouble': 'He'd seen her eyes, staring at nothing while she waited for him before she caught sight of him: staring at fear.' (Cons. 40) But when Mehring himself meets such an experience of terror towards the end of the novel, he takes his own life.

As in *The Conservationist*, Gordimer moves even further away from the liberal ideology in *Burger's Daughter* (1979). It describes a story of an Afrikaner girl, Rosemarie Burger who, after living through her parents' struggle for the rights of the blacks in South Africa, goes through her struggle to break herself apart from her South African world but to no avail. Once she is back from Europe, she finds herself in her parents' shoes and decides to follow their path. Rosa is concerned to perpetuate her dead parents' communist past. She is appalled by the ruthlessness of apartheid and the attitude of liberals who 'didn't do anything' and 'care more for animals than people' in South Africa. (BD, 210) This shows that Gordimer nullifies the liberal tradition in the 1970s era and replaces it with revolutionary Marxism thus predicting the decline of liberalism in South Africa.

The action in the novel is developed by focusing on an Afrikaner family who is tortured and imprisoned for their efforts to improve 'race relations' in their South African world. (BD, 84) Gordimer follows a chronology of the struggle of the family by providing periods that are very important in the history of South Africa such as Lionel Burger is born in 1905, the period when South Africa was recovering from the Anglo-Boer war that ended in 1902, and his daughter, Rosa, is born in May 1948, the month and the year when the Nationalist Afrikaner government came to power. The novel reflects upon historical resistance movements since Lionel Burger's times and the history of struggle, censorship and ban which Rosa lives through in her South African life:

> [...] the lives of Mandela, Sisulu, Mbeki, Kathrada, Kgosana, gull-picked on the Island, Lionel propped wasting to his skull between two warders, the deaths by questioning, bodies fallen from the height of John Vorster Square, deaths by dehydration, babies degutted by enteritis in 'places' of banishment, the lights beating all night on the faces of those in cells [...] you don't know what I saw [...]. (BD, 208)

This struggle of Rosa's family and friends, and Rosa herself, is a microcosm of anti-apartheid movements in South African society.

After Lionel Burger and his wife, Cathy Burger's death, their daughter, Rosa wishes to stay away from what she has been doing so far, that is, secretly working for her imprisoned parents to carry out their mission: 'I had not spoken [...] but I felt—can't explain—released from responsibility for myself, my actions.' (BD, 205) Instead of relieving her from a sense of commitment, Rosa's journey to Europe sends her back to the same world of responsibilities because she realises that 'I am the place in which something has occurred.' (BD, 5) Being Lionel's daughter and an advocate of human rights, she can't keep herself away from being involved in the politics of her South African world.

In Rosa's desire 'to know somewhere else' (BD, 185), that is, to go away from South Africa, Gordimer projects the devastating capacity of apartheid to break down people psychologically. In her departure, Rosa admits her inability to take any longer the injustices people live through in South Africa. The sight of a beaten donkey on the road helps her to define her misery:

> I didn't see the whip. I saw agony. Agony that came from terrible centre seized within the group of donkey, cart, driver, and people behind him. [...] Not seeing the whip, I saw the infliction of pain broken away from the will that creates it; broken loose, a force existing of itself, ravishment without the ravisher, torture without the torturer, rampage, pure cruelty gone beyond control of the humans who have spent thousands of years devising it. (BD, 208)

Rosa notices that the 'pain was no shock' to the donkey. She didn't stop the black man from beating the donkey, though she 'could have stood between them and the suffering—the suffering of the donkey': 'What more can one do?' (BD, 208) Rosa reflects: 'If somebody's going to be brought to account, I am accountable for him, to him, as he is for the donkey.' Rosa leaves South Africa because she doesn't 'know how to live in Lionel's country' which is a world of rigid boundaries. (BD, 210) Brandt Vermeulen, Rosa's influential contact in the Afrikaner government reveals to her how much South Africa has been 'beleaguered by hostile states on her own borders': it 'imprisons and detains only those who actively threaten her safety from within.' As an Afrikaner, Brandt believes in 'ethnic advancement, separate freedoms, multilateral development, plural democracy.' Therefore, Rosa contacts him in 'a place where a meeting is possible between those for whom skin is an absolute value and those for whom it is not a value at all.' (BD, 194–195) Rosa and Brandt don't make their meetings public for the fear of their respective communities. They don't trust each other's friends either. They know that South African society divides them into restricted social identities. Rosa finds her way out of this confined South African world, and manages, with Brandt's help, to get out of the country after her parent's death in prison.

To bring Rosa out of her marginality in her South African world, Gordimer makes her visit Europe, the world outside and then brings her back to the same life but with broadened sympathy and understanding of the apartheid situation this time. During a gathering held by a women organisation for human rights in South Africa, Rosa finds the attitudes of the participants 'too comfortable—too marginal' (BD, 201) towards the problems of their country. Till then, Rosa has been looking for personal freedom in her South African world which, she realises, is not possible until she fights back against the apartheid system in her society.

Burger's Daughter is an appropriate point of departure from the rhythm in which Gordimer has produced her middle novels; *The Late Bourgeois World*, *A Guest of Honour*, and *The Conservationist* explore characters' sense of commitment to the issues of race and identity in their South African life whereas *Burger's Daughter* focuses on the processes of personal and public struggle that the protagonist and her family have to experience in their fight against apartheid. One after another, these novels retrace the intensified impact of apartheid on characters in their everyday life. They feel trapped and crushed between the white and the black worlds, torn apart by the pressure to survive in a harsh environment in the 1960s and 1970s South Africa.

Gordimer's fiction of the struggle era shows the continuity of a pattern that is followed in the early fiction; the characters are led to borderland experiences through physical situations and psychological encounters which make them aware of the forceful working of apartheid in their South African lives. The plot here too is constructed through frontier situations in characters' lives which provide them with an opportunity not only to go through the experience of apartheid but also to work towards bringing change and transformation in their South African society.

It is through the working of physical borderland situations in combination with psychological borderland encounters that Gordimer presents social and political dilemmas of the 1960s and 1970s South Africa in her later fiction. *A Guest of Honour* attempts, in terms of anticipating Bhabha's formulation, to visit the 'beyond' which provides the characters 'a revisionary time' to 're-inscribe our human, historic communality' and to 'touch the future on its hither side'. (Bhabha, 1994, 7) The novel suggests that the black rule in Independent Africa has not led to social and political justice. More human and egalitarian black Africa requires further revolution.

This shift in Gordimer's approach towards the social and political dilemmas of her South African world continued the pattern that she follows in her plots and characterisation in her fiction. As in the early novels, in *The Late Bourgeois World, A Guest of Honour, The Conservationist* and *Burger's Daughter*, the plot is developed in a kind of frontier formed out of places or situations which allow the protagonists to move 'beyond' the racial divide. For Bhabha, the 'beyond' provides a 'terrain for elaborating strategies of self-hood—singular or communal—that initiate new signs of identity, and innovative sites of collaboration, and contestation, in the act of defining the idea of society itself.' (Bhabha, 1994, 1–2) It is a kind of bridge that may be utilised for the articulation of ethnocentric ideas so that people who believe in them can develop a different perspective on themselves. Gordimer too creates, in Bhabha's words, a 'passage' for her characters which 'may get' them 'to other banks' as regards their South African situation. (Bhabha, 1994, 5) So the plot in Gordimer's novels becomes a domain of the 'beyond' in which the protagonist is led to articulate a 'culture' for himself and his society. (Bhabha, 1994, 1)

The protagonists in Gordimer's later fiction are the product of 'frontier' (Heywood, 1983, 24) situations that produce peculiar psychological pressures for them in their South African lives. In Bhabha's terms, the borderland encounters with apartheid lead them to rethink 'questions of identity, social agency and national affiliation' (Bhabha, 1994, 1) for their future course of life in South Africa such as Elizabeth in *The Late Bourgeois*

World. For Bhabha, such agencies are open to a continuous process of redefining themselves and are replaced by new forms of belonging in multicultural communities such as South Africa. This process of transformation intensifies into a revolutionary spirit through the characters' physical and psychological experiences of apartheid in the 1980s and 1990s South Africa. As in the protest and struggle periods of her fiction, the theme defined as borderland in the work of Bhabha continues to exist in action and characterisation as an integral part of Gordimer's fiction of the liberation era.

Struggle (1964–1979)

1964 Mandela and eight Umkhonto leaders were sentenced to life imprisonment after admitting sabotage and preparation for guerrilla warfare.

1965 **Gordimer's fifth short stories collection *Not for Publication* published.**

1966 **Gordimer's fourth novel *The Late Bourgeois World* published.**

1967 The Terrorism Act (1967) provided for indefinite detention.

1968 The Improper Interference Act (1968) outlawed multiracial political parties which disbanded the Liberal Party.

The Parliamentary representation of the Coloureds by the whites was discontinued.

1969 South African Students' Organisation was formed under the leadership of Steve Biko who propounded the doctrine of Black Consciousness.

1972 Black People's Convention was formed to advance Black Consciousness outside schools and colleges.

Gordimer's sixth short stories collection *Livingstone's Companions* published.

1973 Strikes by black workers took place in Durban. Steve Biko along with seven leaders of the Black Consciousness movement was banned.

Gordimer's fifth novel *A Guest of Honour* published.

1974 The UN General Assembly suspended the credentials of the South African delegation and invited the ANC and the PAC (both recognised by the Organisation of African Unity) to participate as observers.

1975 **Gordimer's seventh short stories collection *Selected Stories* published.**

1976 The black students at Soweto who protested against inferior education and the use of Afrikaans as a medium of instruction were fired on by the police.

Countrywide protests resulted in several deaths. The Internal Security Act (1976) was imposed to control the uprisings.

Gordimer's eighth short stories collection *Some Monday for Sure* published.

1977 Steve Biko died after police beatings whilst in detention. The Black Consciousness groups and the *World*, a major black newspaper were outlawed.

The UN Security Council made the 1963 voluntary arms embargo against South Africa mandatory.

1978 **Gordimer's sixth novel *The Conservationist* published.**

1979 The Industrial Relations Act (1979) recognised African trade unions. The Federation of South African Trade Unions was organised, and Congress of South African Students was formed.

Solomon Mshlanga was the first guerrilla to be executed.

Gordimer's seventh novel *Burger's Daughter* published.

Physical borderlands and mental barriers under apartheid were unique and had specific local features and history. The underpinning of physical borderland by apartheid legislation was dismantled in 1994 when hierarchical patterns created since 1948 were redefined. Apartheid ended with the first general election in 1994 and became physically null and void with the coming to power of the black majority in the same year. But the theme of borderland has continued to occur in the action and characterisation in Gordimer's post-apartheid fiction. It recurs in a different form to discuss issues of identity in post-apartheid South Africa. The same goes for the applicability of Bhabha's notion of borderland to Gordimer's presentation of border worlds in her post-apartheid fiction.

Phase Three: Liberation from Apartheid

Continuing the early pattern, the mental probing at facing apartheid's last years appears in Gordimer's later short stories. The Pass laws were repealed in 1986, violence escalated, and a nationwide state of emergency prevailed till the ban was lifted in 1990 by the Afrikaner government on political parties which struggled against apartheid in South Africa such as the ANC and the PAC. The subsequent release of political prisoners, including Nelson Mandela paved way for the political dialogue which put an end to thirty years old armed struggle of the ANC. The black majority rule was established after the ANC won the first free general elections in 1994. (Schrire, 1992, 229–233)

At different levels, the characters in later short stories break down with shame and embarrassment, and at the same time, the process of mental probing leads them to struggle for change and transformation in the South African society. The plot in 'Jump', from the collection *Jump* (1991), is set in a black terrorist's recollection of his recent past with a deep sense of regret for his wrong doings against his fellow countrymen. A sense of guilt overshadows the black man's personality when he reflects on his life: '—all at once, reeled up as the tape is filling its left cylinder on rewind—the experience that explained everything he had ever done since.' (*Jump*, 8) Secret funding by the government of Inkatha and its allied Labour Movement, The United Workers' Union of South Africa, was exposed by the *Weekly Mail* in 1991. It revealed the government's plot to divide and rule the blacks in South Africa. (Schrire, 1992, 232) Apprenticed as draughtsman to an architect, the black man in the story is detained for five weeks in a dirty cell for blacks by the colonial regime because he is thought to be a spy. Later, he joins a secret organisation to restore white rule through compliant black proxies: 'He grew up [...] as an adolescent he bonded with his peers through joining the parachute club, and he jumped—the rite of passage into manhood.' (*Jump*, 7) He is haunted by his act of destruction and exploitation of his black people: 'horror' fills the vacuum in his personality 'trickling, growing, mounting, rolling, swelling'. (*Jump*, 13)

Contrary to the transitory stage in the black man's life in 'Jump', 'Once Upon a Time', from the same collection *Jump* (1991), captures the revolutionary scenario of the 1980s. A white boy receives a book of fairy tales as a Christmas present from his grandmother. She warns the boy and his parents to be vigilant about the outsiders, though they have a trustworthy black maid and a black gardener working for them in the house. Security measures are taken against the riots in the town by putting razor-teeth blades on top of the wall surrounding the house. Whilst dreaming about a fairy-tale character, the sleeping beauty, to kiss her back to life, the boy walks in his sleep one night, climbs the razor-edged wall and cuts himself with resulting bleeding. The story suggests that even bedtime stories for children cannot escape the intrusion of current South African life.

In 'Keeping Fit', from the same collection *Jump* (1991), the white protagonist, during his early morning run, encounters a disturbing murder scene, the killing of a black person from the ANC by Inkatha activists. To save his own life, he crosses the 'fence', into the 'wrong side', the black quarters. Long before the 'shock' at the realisation of the black world, the 'mould in which his dimensions were defined', he strangely begins his run:

> Not quite a highway, the road divided the territory of Alicewood, named for the daughter of a real estate developer, [...] landscaped industrial buffer between the suburb and the black township [...] by a squatter camp which had spread to the boundary of the industries [...] the municipality—had to put up a high corrugated metal fence to shield passing traffic from the right. (*KF*, 229–230)

Running along the fence, he notices division in every sphere of life: 'The cock-crow sounds from over there behind the fence, a place which itself has come about defying context, plan, definition, confusing the peasant's farmyard awakening with the labourer's clock-in at the industries close by.' (*KF*, 231) The fence in the story is a 'barrier' that is there to prevent the white man from getting into the 'wrong side', that is, the black man's world. But suddenly 'the road was no longer the sure boundary between that place and his suburb' because the 'fence was collapsed under the pressure of shelters' and there are 'no more factory buildings but shanties occupied the land'. (*KP*, 233)

On his way back, the white protagonist thinks of thanking the black woman with some money when she provides shelter to him in her shack until the danger is over. But it pricks his conscience for behaving as a coward in the face of a riot. He is ashamed of his act of hiding in the black woman's shack. He recalls her finding him foolish: 'What do you want to come near this place for [...] he heard something else: is there nowhere you think you can't go, does even this rubbish dump belong to you if you need to come hiding here, saving your skin.' (*KF*, 236) He contemplates the whole incident:

> That's how it will happen, always happen everywhere! Keep away. They came over him, not after him, no, but making him join them. At first, he didn't know it, but he was racing with them after blood, after the one who was to lie dying in the road. That's what it means to be caught up, not to know what you are doing, not to be able to stop, say no!—that awful unimagined state that has been with you all the time. (*KF*, 238)

Arriving home, he finds a chick trapped in a drainpipe. The noise of the trapped bird acts as a reminder for him of his own recent experience of being trapped in the black world. He wants his little sons to get the chick out but his wife 'said, just wait for it to die'. He closes his eyes but listens to the 'cheeping' sound which conveys a message to him: 'Die, it would not die. In another darkness, the most insignificant of fragments of life cried out, kept crying out.' (*KF*, 242) The action in the story becomes alive with the protagonist's experience of a set of events that pricks his conscience and breaks him down in shame and embarrassment.

In 'Amnesty', from the same collection *Jump* (1991), Gordimer composes the individual and the community struggle against apartheid into one fibre in the story. It describes the social, political, economic, and moral struggle of black freedom fighters and their families. Amnesty for one year is granted to the narrator's husband. This doesn't relieve her family, her people and herself from their immediate problems; what the black people need for amnesty is freedom—freedom from discrimination, ignorance, poverty, and exploitation in their South African world. Her husband makes her realise the significance of knowledge and awareness: 'Our ignorance is the way we are kept down, this ignorance must go.' (*Amnesty*, 257)

A symbolical image in the relationship of earth, sky and sea runs through the story till the end. The blacks are struggling for a piece of their land and its achievement, they look to the sky that provides a limitless joy of freedom to them. The narrator's husband, before going to jail, 'was signed up to work [...] in a construction company—building glass walls up to the sky.' This suggests the beginning of a dream about freedom by the blacks. They are ready to make the journey over the sea which stands for struggle and adventure, and for openness and roughness to make them strong enough to achieve their goal of freedom. The fact that the narrator's husband is imprisoned on an island is a presentation of the connection of the earth with the sky as well as with the sea: 'There was the sea…all the way to the sky.' (*Amnesty*, 249–250) The sky appears to have various colours, blue, brown, green, white, black, pink, and grey which suggests that the blacks, like these different colours, have now become aware of their existence and can judge the conditions developing around them. The narrator reveals:

> The sun behind me is changing the colours of the sky […] Underneath is a bar of grey, not enough to make rain. It gets longer and darker, it grows […] There is a huge grey rat moving across the sky, eating the sky. (*Amnesty*, 257)

The fundamental right to self-determination has taken the form of a 'huge grey rat' on the South African horizon which can now destroy everything that comes in its way. The narrator in the story is 'aware' of the things that happen around her: 'My mother sings but I don't; I think […] I've been thinking we haven't got a home because there wasn't time…Now I have understood that.' (*Amnesty*, 254) She visualises the violence ahead and waits for peace—peace inside and peace outside.

Similar personas of characters can be found in the stories 'Home' and 'Comrades', from the same collection *Jump* (1991). Active interaction between the process of realisation and transformation is at work in their lives. The protagonist in 'Home' becomes an activist in politics who successfully smuggles out notes from the cell where her brother and mother are jailed. The whole process of their imprisonment changes her from a loving wife of a biologist to an extremist activist. Similarly, Mrs Telford of 'Comrades' who is on the committee of white and black activists entertains hungry black youths of the ANC at her home. She realises that those youths are on their way or in the process to become violent activists soon.

This future scenario is captured in Gordimer's novella *Something Out There* (1984). It focuses on saboteurs in action within South Africa in the 1980s. In revealing fear and anxiety in the lives of the white residents in Johannesburg, Gordimer comments on the political atmosphere of the time:

> Whatever it was, it made a nice change from the usual sort of news, these days. Nothing but strikes, exchanges of insults between factions of what used to be a power to be relied on, disputes over boundaries that had been supposed to divide peace and prosperity between all, rioting students, farmers dissatisfied with low prices, consumers

> paying more for bread and mealie-meal, more insults—these coming in the form of boycotts and censures from abroad, beyond the fished out territorial waters. (Something, 119)

The white saboteurs in the novella manage to escape the police raid whilst the black activists get arrested and killed in later encounters with the Afrikaner authorities. The action is built with the story of a predator that is at loose in the white suburbs. There is a similarity between the acts of sabotage by the activists and the adventures of the baboon at large; both contribute violence and destruction to the white community in Johannesburg. The Sunday paper reports about the baboon as a 'wild animal' and a 'black' thing. For some white people, it is a 'Chimpanzee', for others, it is 'just a large monkey'. (Something, 126) But it is, in reality, an Umkhonto activity: disguised as an Australian white couple and their two black servants, its activists quietly plan the demolition of a power station near Johannesburg. The story reveals that the newspapers in South Africa are prohibited by 'section 4 of the protection of Information Act 1982 and section 29 of the Internal Security Act 1982' to report about the news of the predator with 'censure.' (Something, 196) The Klopper family of Afrikaners get a shock at the revelation that they have provided lodging to the saboteurs. The activists under Afrikaner and European identities (Anna and Charles Rosser) and with their acquired Australian accents can get away with their movements of sabotage at the heart of the white suburban community. A similar scenario is presented in 'Some Are Born to Sweet Delight', from the same collection *Jump* (1991), when the protagonist, Veera gets pregnant by a foreigner, a lodger at her parents' house who turns out to be a terrorist carrying explosives for sabotage activities in and around the country.

Short stories of the later years depict the social and political climate of the liberation era in a succession of intimate glimpses of the white and the black worlds in South Africa. The revolutionary scenario of the 1980s and early 1990s is presented as a world of transition in these short stories. Similarly, physical borderland situations and psychological borderland encounters exist in the variable form in Gordimer's later novels. They reveal a shift in Gordimer's vision from radicalism towards the prophetic view of revolution. They lead her to predict the future of South Africa and celebrate the end of apartheid in South Africa.

Gordimer's later novels cover the liberation era when freedom from apartheid was prophesied or foreseen in an independent South Africa. In *July's People* (1981), she described an imaginary situation that might result in the case of a civil war in South Africa. *Something out There* (1984),

A Sport of Nature (1987) and *My Son's Story* (1990) contain most of the historical accounts of contemporary South Africa, reflecting an increasing pressure on South Africa to go beyond liberalism towards a radical political system. The actions in these narratives are spread over time going back to the 1960s. *None to Accompany Me* (1994) deals with the experience of victory by the blacks in their struggle against apartheid. Their confidence in themselves is further reiterated in *The House Gun* (1998) in the character of a black barrister who defends a white man in a case of murder. And in *The Pick Up* (2001) Gordimer looks at South Africa in the process of getting over the stigma of the colonial system.

The action in *July's People* (1981) is built upon a state of emergency that occurs in the lives of characters when a revolution and military invasion occurs in South Africa. In the novel, a scenario is created in which the areas occupied by the whites in Johannesburg and neighbouring African countries are shown under armed attack by the black activists. The white Smales family—Maureen, Bam and their two children escape death at the hands of black revolutionaries with the help of their houseboy, July, who provides shelter for them in his village.

On their arrival, the chief of the village wants to learn from them how to shoot because he previously did not own a gun. He wants to fight back with weapons if displaced from his place this time. The chief is not sure about Bam Smales' answer that 'I don't shoot people', and there appears a 'short disgusted snort from the black man; a backwash of laughter.' (JP, 120) This breaking of social and racial barriers cannot be overlooked by the Smales in their present set of circumstances. Besides, confrontations between Maureen and July reveal the illusory nature of trust between them and the ludicrousness of Maureen's claims to know him well. Even though July has worked for Maureen in Johannesburg for fifteen years, she does not trust him with the car keys in his village. And this irritates July; for him, it is like taking part in a structure of massive and hurtful inequity. The shallowness of Maureen's trust and intimacy is appalling for July. It unfolds a relation of manipulation between them:

> He had stopped instantly the blinking pantomime of derision. He might take her by the shoulders; they stepped across fifteen years of no-man's land, her words shoved them and they were together, duellists who will feel each other's breath before they turn away to the regulation number of paces, or conspirators who will never escape what each knows of the other. Her triumph dissembles in a face at once open, submissive, eyes emptied for a vision to come, for them both. (JP, 72)

This shows the presence of cruel and explosive undersides in the enforced quasi-intimacy between them. It also reveals the complexity of the relationship between them in the new circumstances: Maureen's attempt to set up some equality between them and yet her reversion to madam-like behaviour. July relishes his newfound power to decide on the Smales' fate, and yet he insists on remaining within the codes of being their servant. Later, when Bam wants to know from July about the headman whom he meets on their way to see the chief, July appears even more irritable:

> It seemed always to amuse July to be the mentor, as if he didn't take too seriously a white wish to comprehend or faculty of comprehension for what he had never needed to know as a black had to understand, take on, the white man's laws and ways. (JP, 112)

This makes both Maureen and Bam unclear about whether July is their saviour or servant. July is not able to drop the use of the word 'madam' (JP, 96) for Maureen and 'master' (JP, 71) for Bam despite their telling him not to do so. However, he has no objection to the change of his name from Mwawate to July by the Smales for their convenience in their previous life.

Through language, Gordimer attempts to restore the black man's dignity in his African world. Maureen shows 'special consideration she had known for his [July's] dignity as a man, while he was by definition a servant, would become his humiliation itself, the one thing there was to say between them that had any meaning.' (JP, 98) Maureen goes further in saying:

> If I offended you, if I hurt your dignity...if she had never before used the word 'dignity' to him it was not because she didn't think he understood the concept, didn't have any—it was only the term itself that might be beyond his grasp of the language. (JP, 72)

Maureen's communication in English, the white man's language, fails when July towards the end breaks into his language. By revealing that the white man's language acts as a barrier between the black and the white understanding of each other's worlds, Gordimer leads Maureen to see that her concept of herself as humane is an illusion with which she has lived all her life.

July's People describes the social and industrial unrest and the strikes of the early 1980s as a 'chronic state of uprising all over the country'. (JP, 2) In 1980, as the Industrial Relations Act of 1979 recognised the formation of African trade unions, countrywide protests by the blacks erupted in South Africa over wages, rents, bus fares and education. The year 1980 is also significant for the resurgence of the ANC's sabotage attacks on South Africa's oil-from-coal installations at Sasolburg. (Schrire, 1992, 228) In the novel, the chief of the village wonders at the Smales running away from Johannesburg: 'He means he wants to hear—from an eyewitness—white—what it is that has taken place at last, after three-hundred-and-fifty years, between black people and white people.' (JP, 116) Removed from their familiar surroundings, the Smales family is displaced into African life. Through their experiences of dispossession of their belongings such as keys and a gun, Gordimer penetrates questions of displacement and suffering which the blacks had lived through, for centuries. Also, she attempts to shed light on the prospect of snatching power and control of the African world from the whites. The novel depicts the crumbling of white power in South Africa; it is presented in Maureen's losing control over July in a world beyond her compartmentalised South African life.

Contrary to *July's People* in which an African setting acts as a frontier or place of transition before a new dawn arises on the political scenario in the 1980s era, home and exile experiences of people's struggle against injustices in the South African world are captured from a frontier or transitory moment in history in *A Sport of Nature* (1987). The action in the novel is focused on Hillela, a white woman who is the reckless daughter of a 'feckless' mother. (Sport, 232) She appears on the scene as an 'adoptive daughter' under Olga, her aunt's guardianship. (Sport, 12) In her school days, she is looked after by Pauline, her other aunt who sends her to a private school with her daughters, Carole and Sasha. Hillela's mother, Ruthie, Olga's and Pauline's sister, is 'forbidden' by Hillela's father, and lives an unknown life with 'another man' in Mozambique. (Sport, 11) Hillela comes to know her mother late in life. Both appear indifferent in their rare contact with each other.

Since her childhood, Hillela knows that 'she was a white child, with choices; that was the irony of it. Young blacks had no choices, only necessity and plenty of ignorance about how to deal with that, in addition.' (Sport, 71) As a teenager, her photograph appears in a Sunday paper dancing with her school friend, Mandy, titled 'Go Dancers'. (Sport, 45) It signifies Hillela's courage to break the norms of her white identity. In her youth, she becomes friends with Don, a Cape Coloured apprentice electrician. She marries Whaila Kgomani, a black man and bears a daughter, Nomzami, from him. By the time the novel ends, Nomzami is ten years old and is sent to London for education. After Whaila's death, Hillela becomes the third wife of an African President, General Reuel.

Throughout her life, Hillela actively works for the banned organisations, helping the blacks in their activities both underground and in exile.

Revisiting South African history of the 1960s, *A Sport of Nature* describes the scenario when most of the activists had no alternative but to go into exile and struggle from there for their rights and place in their South African world. For them, Nairobi, Angola, and Zaire became safe havens for going into exile. Even though the neighbouring African countries were on their way to independence from the white rule during this time, the black voice in South Africa was forcefully curbed by putting the activists behind the bars. Laws against any such political activism such as the Sabotage Act 1962 and the Terrorism Act 1967 empowered the apartheid government to prolong detention without trial. The Legislation Act 1968 outlawed multiracial political parties which disbanded the Liberal Party in South Africa but paved the way for the creation of the Black Consciousness movement under the leadership of Steve Biko. (Schrire, 1992, 225–226)

This shift towards radicalism in the political struggle against apartheid is narrated in parallel with the main action of the story in *A Sport of Nature.* For instance, the novel shows that the Sharpeville peaceful demonstration which turned into the killing of the blacks by the white police in 1960 led to the creation of 'intruders' in the African National Congress:

> I don't want to be equal with Europeans. I want them to call us baas. I wish I can live till we rule, I will do the same to them: I will send the police to demand passes from whites. Their wives are going to wash the clothes for our wives. We don't want to mix with whites, we left the African National Congress because we saw Europeans amongst us. We are fighting for the full rights of Africans. We do not fight to dance and sit with Europeans. (Sport, 73–74)

This summarised the thinking of The Pan Africanist Congress which broke off with the ANC in 1959. The ANC continued its non-anti-white policy and called for a national convention before South Africa was declared a republic in 1961. But the white republic followed the pattern that had emerged under the old Union of South Africa by not providing constitutional rights for the black majority of the land. This led to the creation of Umkhonto we Sizwe, the military wing of the ANC in the same year. (Schrire, 1992, 225) In *A Sport of Nature*, Nelson Mandela was reported as arrested and sentenced to life imprisonment in Robben Island in 1962 for bombings in a post office, the Resettlement Board

Headquarters, and the Bantu Affairs Commissioner's offices in Johannesburg. (Sport, 121) Whaila who is presented as a top Umkhonto official in the novel, states that the ANC was forced to fight by the intransigence of the government and its suppression of the Defiance Campaign of the 1950s:

> That's the stage we reached after the Defiance Campaign. The realisation that we are forced to fight. But it doesn't make the campaign a failure. The Campaign simply proved that there is no way but to fight, because the government doesn't know how to respond to anything else. (Sport, 213)

The novel depicts Umkhonto's activities in foreign countries to prepare and launch sabotage missions in South Africa. When the first group of saboteurs is on its way to South Africa, Hillela asks Whaila what kind of targets the group is going to attack. He says: 'Military installations, power stations—hard targets' not people. But he adds that if the white government continues to kill and persecute black people in the townships, the ANC may later be forced to target white people themselves. (Sport, 241)

Besides this presentation of history, *A Sport of Nature* deals with the theme of race, identity crisis, and the colour barrier by focusing on physical relationships between whites and the blacks in the South African world. Although the laws against cohabitation between the whites and the blacks, and between the whites and the Coloureds were intensified in 1949 (Schrire, 1992, 223), marriages still took place between them. 'Selina Montgomery and Hillela Kgomani—personages in some race joke: there was this black woman married to a white man, and this white woman married to a black man.' (Sport, 237) Earlier, Hillela's acquaintance with a Coloured man is reproached by the school headmistress, yet it doesn't stop Hillela from liking the man:

> She liked particularly his eyes, a greeny-grey with hair-thin splinters of yellow sunburst in the iris, whose charm was that they seemed too luminous for his sallow skin and tarnished curly hair—like lights left burning in a room in daylight. (Sport, 17–18)

Hillela's aunt, Pauline questions the white man's concept of himself as humane in his attitude towards the black life in South Africa. When Carole, her daughter 'came home in tears' because one of the white girls at school 'had said to a black waiter who serves lunch in the school refectory: 'Don't lean your smelly arm over my face',' Pauline utters:

> Exactly! Idiots we've been. No possibility to buy your way out of what this country is. So why pay? Racism is free. Send them to a government school, let them face it as it's written in your glorious rule of law, canonised by the church, a kaffir is a kaffir, God Save White South Africa. (Sport, 28)

Although Pauline and her husband, Joe 'avoid segregated education for their son, Alexander by sending him to a school for all races, over the border in an independent neighbouring black state' (Sport, 27), they lack something fundamental: 'I expected them to have solutions but they only had questions.' (Sport, 368) This comment by Sasha, the imprisoned activist daughter of Pauline describes the limits of white humanity in the South African world. As the action of the novel is set in the era when 'killing is killing, violence is pain and death' on the South African political horizon (Sport, 87), the natural death of Joe towards the end of the story signifies a gradual disappearance of liberal values from the South African society. This paved the way for radical white and black attitudes in the struggle against apartheid in their South African world.

Remarkably, *A Sport of Nature* predicted radical political moves that the white government made within the very short period of 1989–1991. In the closing chapters of the novel, Gordimer depicts the release of Mandela and other long-suffering political prisoners; the unbanning of various opposition political parties including the ANC, long officially regarded as a terrorist organisation; and the opening of dialogue between the government and its former enemies on the dismantling of apartheid and creation of a new South Africa.

If *A Sport of Nature* presents a sweeping panorama of South African political history from the earliest stages of apartheid to its future dissolution, and the arrival of black majority rule in a non-racial state, the history of the apartheid era is interwoven with the story of personal suffering of a Cape Coloured family in *My Son's Story* (1990). It was the last of her novels to be written in the apartheid era.

In his private life, the protagonist Sonny in the novel is happily married to Aila, a quiet simple Coloured girl from his community who bears him two children, a daughter Baby who joins freedom fighters in Lusaka and a son, Will, the narrator of the story. In his public life, Sonny is totally against the policy of violence in the process of uplifting the movement of 'black solidarity'. (Story, 27) After losing his job as a schoolteacher due to his political commitment towards the African struggle, Sonny and his family move out of the township, 'defied the law and settled in amongst whites.' This idea of settling in a 'grey area' is to uplift their standard of living and to work towards the betterment of their children's future. Will recognises the significance of 'self-respect' in his father's life:

> It's been his religion, his godhead. It's never failed him, when he wanted to know what course to take next: his inner signpost, his touchstone. Do what will enable you to keep your self-respect. This is the wisdom he has offered to us—my sister and me. (Story, 13–14)

But 'Needing Hannah', his white-blonde mistress, makes it difficult for him to keep his self-respect in the company of his family. (Story, 61) When he is seen by Will in Hannah's company outside a cinema, Sonny behaves as if 'nothing happened' and Will also keeps it to himself for the sake of peace in the family. (Story, 5) But when Baby cuts her wrists and is found to have been taking drugs, Will comes to realise that his family are aware of Sonny's affair with Hannah. Baby reveals to Will her experience of finding Sonny making love to Hannah in a room during a party. This has been the cause of 'deep unhappiness' in Baby who finds it hard to forget the sight of her much-loved father indulging in sexual activity. (Story, 61)

Like her sister, Will is divided between his love for his father and his hate for the other side of the father who creates so much pain and misery in their family life. He appreciates his father's commitment to 'liberation politics' (Story, 185) but at the same time, he finds him guilty of making his mother miserable in her life. It hurts Will to realise that 'my mother's not in the struggle so my mother is no priority' in his father's life. (Story, 136) Sonny, Will observes, 'lived like so many others whose families are fragmented in the diaspora of exile, code names, underground activity, people for whom a real home and attachments are something for others who will come after.' (Story, 265) He is not able to appreciate Baby's attempt to keep a family life: '—Family life—babies—it does not go too well with activism like theirs. Doesn't really do, anywhere but particularly in exile.' (Story, 170) Will calls his father a 'bastard' in his absence because he does not recognise Aila's sacrifice over his public struggle and his alibis in the name of political commitment to concealing his relationship with Hannah.

Despite the knowledge that Sonny sleeps with Hannah, Aila stays united with him for the sake of a better life. Baby's marriage to a freedom fighter and then the birth of her child provides Aila with great comfort till her detention by the apartheid authorities. She visits them in Lusaka and becomes extremely happy to see her daughter well settled in her new life. This travelling to Lusaka brings about a significant change in Aila's life. She cuts her hair short which signifies the shedding of her previous submissive role in the family. She frequently stays out of the house which makes Sonny and Will think that she is 'becoming social with her own kind of friends' (Story, 178) but Will finds out that it is a 'lie'. (Story, 188) Aila is a 'revolutionary' now (Story, 242):

> [She is] charged with four offences under the Internal Security Act [...] The charges included terrorism and furthering the aims of a banned organisation. Aila was accused of being a member of something called The Transvaal Implementation Machinery, responsible for acts of terror in the region, and connected to a high command named Amos SeboKeng. She was alleged to have acted as a courier between Umkhonto we Sizwe in neighbouring countries and a cell in the Johannesburg area, to have attended meetings where missions for the placing of explosives were planned, and to have concealed terrorist arms on the rented property where she resided illegally. (Story, 233)

Aila reveals her aspiration for the blacks to access power in new South Africa: 'We're going to need qualified people. Bush fighters won't win the economic war.' (Story, 187) Making 'a nice little corner' for herself in her husband's struggle, Aila goes to exile in Sweden: 'I've had enough of it!' (Story, 255) Will recognises his mother's suffering which finally takes her away from them: 'Because of Hannah, Aila was gone. Finished off, that self that was Aila. Hannah destroyed it.' (Story, 243) As a representative of an international human rights organisation in South Africa, Hannah gives moral support to Sonny's family during the period of his detention and imprisonment, and later, she is useful in finding Aila's whereabouts during her detention. But she is the cause of personal suffering in Sonny's family. At the realisation that she is no match for Aila's loyalty and sacrifice towards her family and her community, Hannah takes a decision: 'This won't happen anymore.' (Story, 235) She takes up a job at the UN as a director of refugees in other African countries. Sonny is frustrated at her departure because his affair with Hannah is 'no flattering flirtations or one-night peccadillos of manhood to ignore, in his record.' (Story, 189) Will observes:

> His attraction to Hannah belonged to the distorted place and time in which they—all of them—he, Aila, Hannah lived. With Hannah, there was the sexuality of commitment; for commitment implies danger, and the blind primal instinct is to ensure the species survives in circumstances of danger, even when the individual animal dies or the plant has had its season. (Story, 241–242)

After Hannah departs from his life, 'Sonny is not the man he was.' (Story, 276) 'Taunted by the tags of passion' for Hannah and pricked by the voice of conscience for Aila, Sonny expresses himself in Shakespearean language: 'Beat at this gate that let thy folly in.' (Story, 252) Sonny is a great 'lover of Shakespeare' though he 'never had the right to enter the municipal library and so did not so much as think about it while white people came out before him with books under their arms'. (Story, 12) His passion for Shakespeare leads him to name his son, William. Like Shakespeare's characters, he is larger than real life, thus suffering tremendously for his actions in the end: 'Nothing, nothing was there to stanch the longing for everything he fled.' (Story, 243)

Towards the end of the novel, Sonny's house, like his relationship with Hannah, is gone but it does not kill his hope and determination to get his inherent right to live freely in South Africa. Sonny tells Will: 'This street—this whole country is ours to live in. Fire won't stop me. And it won't stop you.' (Story, 274) And it does not stop Will from writing his account of the story even though, as he sees it, it will never get published. Will says: 'I am a writer and this is my first book—that I can never publish.' (Story, 177) In this realisation of the force of private and public realities of life, Will is Gordimer's mouthpiece in raising a voice against censorship. During Sonny's detention, there is a word limit of five hundred words for family letters. But in those letters, only 'family matters' can be discussed. The rest is censored by the prison authorities. (Story, 55)

My Son's Story depicts segregation as the controlling principle in people's lives in South Africa. The movements of the blacks were restricted inside South Africa, and the apartheid government denied the blacks their right to visit other countries. In the novel, Sonny's passport is withdrawn and is never issued again, Aila, his wife is given one which soon comes under scrutiny, and she is falsely charged under the Internal Security Act 1982. Will doesn't have a passport and Baby has to leave the country illegally. Mentioning the motto 'Broederbond' (a secret society of Afrikaner nationalists) as a 'bad badge' (Story, 12) has much to reveal about the social and political atmosphere of the apartheid era when Sonny is detained by the police for the first time. Then Sonny's going to 'Black Sash' (Story, 101), that is, a women's anti-apartheid movement in South Africa (Schrire, 1992, 224), projects the radical world of anti-apartheid activists. The action in *My Son's Story* is set in a moment when Sonny is reluctant to 'acknowledgement of any kind of disaffection in the movement' against apartheid because 'it was merely a means of letting the government smell blood' in their political life. (*Story*, 180) He 'believed the disaffected should be expelled, better spilt than a schism within'.

(Story, 192) This ideological development portrays the frustration of most of the anti-apartheid activists who were not getting a breakthrough in the process of their non-violent struggle in the 1950s. Later, talk of the DPCS, that is, the Detainees' Parents Support Committee after Sonny's two years' imprisonment, recalls the revolutionary time when anti-apartheid activists were looking forward to the release of Nelson Mandela from prison in 1990: 'We Greet you, Mandela, call us…' The young activists, 'in the rhythm of a walking song' chant these words over the death of 'nine of their comrades' who have sacrificed their lives in the struggle. (Story, 113–115) Although Sonny is fed up with the 'Nazi's law' for the 'purity' of the white race, he struggles to keep the black solidarity from breaking down into opposing factions which will benefit none but the apartheid government in South Africa. (Story, 263)

Where *My Son's Story* describes the resistance against apartheid through the suffering and struggle of a Coloured family, *None to Accompany Me* (1994) focuses on Vera Stark, a white lawyer who is committed in her struggle against discrimination and injustice towards the blacks in South Africa. As an active senior member of a legal foundation, she works for the rights of blacks in South Africa. Although Vera declines 'to take the executive directorship', she 'is a fixture at the Foundation'. (None, 11) Later, she cannot 'avoid' the title 'Deputy Director of the Legal Foundation' when she has 'to serve on the Technical Committee on Constitutional Issues' at the end of apartheid in South Africa. (None, 277) The action in the novel is woven through Vera's interpretation of 'forty-five' years of her private relationships and her public participation as a lawyer in the movement towards representation for blacks. (None,5) When her soldier husband is stationed in Egypt during the War, she enters a relationship with Bennet Stark who works in the English Department at the University. Despite her relationship with Ben, she happens to be sleeping with her former husband as well. That is why she doesn't know 'whether her first child, Ivan, is the son of her divorced husband or of Bennet Stark.' Vera leaves her 'wartime job' as a secretary, takes up a part-time law study programme at the university and makes her services available for a legal foundation. (None, 17) After twelve years of her marriage with Ben, Vera gives birth to a daughter, Annick. She is not able to remain loyal to Ben for long. She again enters a brief sexual affair with a German, Otto Abarbanel because 'Ben had taught her that the possibilities of eroticism were beyond experience with one man, then this meant that the total experience of love-making did not end with him'. Sexual activity is part of Vera's political struggle:

> Vera was a gentile atheist gratified by the idea that her lover was a Jew, orphaned by racism, without a name that was his own—this linked him with the open, daily purpose of her life, the files of displaced communities on her desk and, before her on the other side of it, day after day, the faces of those who had been made wanderers because they were decreed the wrong race. (None, 67)

Ben notices:

> Vera never ever really wanted a husband [...] It was part of her not having wanted a husband, ever, not the first or the second, not needing security [...] Vera is Malte Laurids Brigge's 'one who didn't want to be loved. That inner indifference of spirit': it was written of Vera. [...] He hated—not Vera, but his dependency on loving her. (None, 298–300)

It becomes difficult for Vera to live with Ben 'because I cannot live with someone who can't live without me'. Vera believes that 'when someone gives you so much power over himself he makes you a tyrant.' (None, 310) So all must change: Vera's ability to shred her emotional bond with Ben signifies getting rid of the customs of her old society to pave the way for the birth of a new South Africa. The title of the novel is borrowed from a verse written by Basho, a seventeenth-century Japanese poet: 'None to accompany me on this path:/Nightfall in Autumn.' (None, 1) In the novel, Vera remains focused on defining her identity in the new South Africa and is determined to struggle towards a new life that she has chosen for herself. Towards the end of the novel, Ben joins Ivan in London whereas Vera, after selling her house, moves to the 'annexe' of a black man's house, Zeph Rapulana, 'the smooth-talking representative of the new middle class'. (None, 311)

None To Accompany Me deals with two issues in South African history. Firstly, it focuses upon the whites' territorial segregation of the African land through successive Acts. The Group Areas Act 1950 imposed residential apartheid on South Africa. The urban areas were zoned, the better areas being allotted to the whites. The Native Laws Amendment Act 1952 limited the blacks' right to live permanently in urban areas. The Land Act 1954 imposed a buffer strip of five hundred yards between any black quarter and the white town it served, creating a captive labour force. The blacks were allowed to live in zoned areas but only as migrants. (Ume, 1981, 178) In *None to Accompany Me*, Vera deals with a case in which an Afrikaner is trying to get rid of the black 'squatters' on his property. He refuses to hold any dialogue over the issue with Vera and Zeph Rapulana, 'the squatter camp leader.' (None, 311) He calls those blacks 'trespassers' and wants them to 'pack up their rubbish and get off his land':

> [He] decided to move with the times [...] farmers would have to—in the businessmen's way of speaking—'diversify resources', yes, that's it, get up to the tricks that make those people rich. He applied to the Provincial Administration for permission to establish a black township on one of his holdings. He would convert the farm into cash as a landlord; he would divide it into plots for rent to blacks. He was going to turn their invasion to profit. (None, 22–24)

In this way, the novel restates the white man's occupation of the South African land. Vera's attempt to sell her house and live in a property owned by a black man reiterates the black man's inherent right of ownership over the South African land:

> The tenant. The designation, for the public, suited her well. [...] between Zeph Rapulana and Mrs Stark [...] the matter of land, over which they had come to begin to know one another. It was a consequence in which there were loyalties but no dependencies, in which there was feeling caught in no recognised category, having no need to be questioned. (None, 321)

The 'empty houses' in the white suburbs have much to convey to Vera:

> FOR SALE. ON SHOW. Are these suburban museums, exhibiting a way of life that is ended? Is that why the once house-proud occupants are leaving? Or as they flee do they really have to fear for their lives—in the constitution, Bill of Rights, decrees that are going to change life? (None, 243–244)

Despite the Sharpeville massacre of 1960, the black student uprising of 1976, and the present killings when Vera, in the novel, also gets a bullet wound, she continues to live in the same area without any sense of fear inside her.

Besides the issue of territorial segregation, *None To Accompany Me* explores beyond the white dilemma, into the effects of displacement upon the black people in South Africa. On coming back from exile in England, Sibongile, the emerging black political figure, finds it difficult to put up with the temporary displacement from one room to another until a residence is found for her family:

I can't live like this, I can tell you.

Sibo, you've lived much worse. It didn't kill us.

At the beginning, years ago, yes. It was necessary. In Dar, in Botswana. But now! My God! I'm not running for my life. I'm not running from anybody anymore, I'm not grateful for a bit of shelter, political asylum [...] This's not for you and me. (None, 45)

Sibongile is distressed at the 'sense that [Mpho, her daughter] knows what home is':

> How could a child brought up with her own bedroom, fresh milk delivered at the front door in Notting Hill Gate every morning, tidy people who sorted their newspapers for recycling, be expected to stand more than one night in such a place, gogo or no gogo? Going out across a yard to a toilet used by everyone round about! Heaven knows what she might pick up there! A return to a level of life to which Sibongile, Didymus, had been condemned when they were their child's age—what did a sixteen-year-old born in exile know of what it was like when there was no choice? (None, 50–51)

Contrary to England-born Mpho, the experience of exile and displacement leaves a deep mark upon the identities of both Sibongile, 'daughter of a Zulu mother and Sotho father' and Didymus, from 'the Transkei'. (None, 43) In exile, they are renamed Sally and Didy. Although 'they regained their original names when they came back,' they cannot get rid of 'the personae of Sally and Didy, the code names of their old concourse with whites'. A transformation has occurred in their personalities whilst living abroad for years. Vera reveals to Ben:

> You should see the Hillbrow dump! Not just the dirt Sally goes on about [...] She's years from that kind of slum atmosphere, even though they're her own people...she and Didy have moved away from that cheek-by-jowl existence they were at home in the old days, Chiawelo. (None, 48)

In the novel, Sally and Didy come back from England into an extraordinary period immediately before the first non-racial election and the beginning of majority rule in South Africa. The whites like Vera who were against apartheid in their South African society joined hands with the blacks in the creation of a new South Africa. Gordimer visualises the future of South Africa as the emergence of a multi-racial and multi-cultural society:

> The challenge facing South Africa is the creation of a multi-cultural society within which people of different cultural, ethnic, and religious identities can be a part. We have exiles returning home with different cultural experiences and an African culture that has been excluded from the dominant or official cultural expression of the nation. We need to ensure that the life-giving resources of these cultures are channelled into the new society. (Villa-Vicencio, 1996, 110)

Vera looks after the technicalities of drafting the future constitution for South Africa. Didymus, once a major figure in the resistance, paves the way for his wife, Sibongile who takes her place as a political figure in new South Africa. This projects that significant phase in the late 1980s and the early 1990s South Africa when African activists focused on getting self-determination and freedom for themselves from the ruling white minority, sacrificing their identities for their community's interest at large. *None to Accompany Me* is an appropriate point of departure from the rhythm in which Gordimer has produced her later novels; both *A Sport of Nature* and *My Son's Story* present an overall picture of life under apartheid in South African society. *July's People* describes the violent move towards a future that *None to Accompany Me* records as finally achieved by the blacks in South Africa.

Nadine Gordimer continued her exploration of racial tension and conflict in her short stories and novels of the later years. By compressing all the major events featured in the earlier works in *A Sport of Nature*, Gordimer gives a unified critique of apartheid in a magnified form. In Dominic Head's words, 'it is a book about her previous books.' (Head, 1994, 136) Richard Peck in his essay 'What's a Poor White to do? White South African Option' (1988) suggests that in Hillela's character, Gordimer criticises most strongly the liberals' inability to find a role in South African history, which is multi-ethnic and predominantly black. Similarly, in her displaced life in the 1980s South Africa, Maureen in *July's People* represents the view that the liberals had reduced themselves to the position of making judgments only and whenever it came to taking practical steps towards the construction of a better society in South Africa, they had been unable to do so. And this inability of theirs could no longer be hidden from the outside world: 'It's like when you tell a story showing your importance or erudition and get caught out.' Maureen recollects a memory of her husband, Bam's conduct during a committee session held for the Architects' International Awards ceremony:

> Most of us couldn't speak Spanish so the discussions were carried on in French—showing that you must be able to speak French, as this was no problem to you. 'We each nominated our candidates, then we presented the laudatory argument for our choice'…I listened to you, every time. I heard you. And when someone asked who your candidates were, you couldn't answer. Couldn't remember! Had to fluff. Because what really happened was you simply enjoyed the importance of being there, being a judge, you just supported the candidates somebody else chose. And so you gave that away, too. You were caught out. Come on. I saw it and so did everybody, Come on…-. (JP, 45)

Later in the novel, Maureen again finds Bam and herself 'caught out' at their son's suggestion to inform the police about the stolen gun: 'If I couldn't pick up the phone and call the police whom he and she despised for their brutality and thuggery in the life lived back there, he did not know what else to do.' (JP, 145) Maureen and Bam have an opinion about the police, though they need them desperately in their present circumstances. Gordimer reveals her dislike for the liberal sector in South Africa which tended to allow rhetoric and sentiment to dominate over meaningful action, its eventual self-interestedness, its limited social vision, and its capacity for self-delusion:

> An old story that she [Maureen] had been ashamed—when she married her liberal young husband—of a father who had talked to his 'boys' in a dialect educated blacks who'd never been down a shaft in their lives regarded as an insult to their culture; now he, the husband, was to be submitted to her being ashamed of that shame. (JP, 45)

July's People is the first novel in which Gordimer depicts the decline of white supremacy in South Africa. It is a futuristic novel that features the emergence of black power in South Africa. The action in the novel is set in a society that lies between two orders. An imagined 'interregnum' forms a state of disintegrated consciousness and contradictions: 'The interregnum is not only between two social orders but between two identities, one known and discarded, the other unknown and undetermined.' (Gordimer, 1983, 21) This is inculcated in the destabilisation of the white Smales family, the black revolutionary uprising, and the state of the larger political world in a process of transformation in South

Africa. In the epigraph to *July's People,* Gordimer comments on this political atmosphere in Antonio Gramsci's words: 'The old is dying and the new cannot be born; in this interregnum there arises a great diversity of morbid symptoms.' (JP, 1) Maureen's running towards the sound of the helicopter at the end of the novel is a sign of interregnum thinking. At the same time, 'her flight from her family, her past and July reveals a radical collapse of identity [...] the flight reveals a total inability (of Maureen) to live with the present.' (Smith, 1984, 97–98) For Clingman, however, Maureen 'is running from old structures and relationships [...] she is also running towards her revolutionary destiny'. (1986, 203–204)

July's People offers symbolic portents of the change to come in South Africa from the urgent but revolutionary perspective of the early 1980s. 'I live at 6,000 feet [...] in a society whirling, stamping, swaying with the force of revolutionary change.' (Gordimer, 1983, 21) The novel begins with this push towards a change in South African life: 'People in delirium rise and sink, rise and sink, in and out of lucidity [...] The vehicle was the fever. Chattering metal and raving dance of loose bolts [...].' (JP, 3) The novel shows that it is through the physical and mental borderland experiences of her characters in an interregnum scenario that Gordimer raises explosive questions about trust, honesty, and self-knowledge of each other's worlds. Although Maureen transgresses the master-servant boundaries of the working relationship with July, she is not able to come to terms with July's control of their movements in the village: 'She was unsteady with something that was not anger but a struggle: her inability to enter into a relation of subservience with him that she had never had with Bam.' (JP, 101) Besides, Maureen finds herself aimless and uninterested in the African life of the village. She fails to establish solidarity with the blacks in the village who, in turn, ignore her completely thus leading her to social marginality in the African world.

As regards this social alienation of people in South Africa, Gordimer's later fiction is 'an examination of the construction of identities' (Head, 1994, 122) which was a significant aspect of the apartheid history in South Africa. As the white protagonist in 'Keeping Fit' steps into the black quarters, looking for his safety, he becomes very conscious of his white identity. Fanon in *Black Skin, White Masks* describes the lived experiences of black people whose body image is associated with the absence of human value through the white racial gaze in the colonial world. (1967, 138–140) Quite oppositely, it is the black gaze, here, which reveals a similar impact; the white protagonist in the story is uncomfortable when 'two black children and a black man stared at him':

> A white man! He felt himself only to be a white man, no other identity, no other way to be known: to pull aside a sack and say, I'm in brokerage, give his name, his bona fide address—that was nothing, these qualifications of his existence meant nothing. (*KF*, 233)

Gordimer seems to be confirming her comments when she described the falsity of the notion of native being exotic in the white South African world:

> I realise that my sense that they were exotic was completely false. It was the other way around. I was the exotic element [...] but if you fall into that colonial situation you simply accept that you are there ruling the earth. (Loercher, 1979, 98)

The Jamaican-British cultural theorist Stuart Hall (1932–2014) asserts the notion of historical 'positioning' of identities that does shift over some time. (1996, 445) Gordimer leads the white protagonist in the story to recognise such politics of identity in his set of circumstances.

In 'Jump', a crossing of social and economic barriers physically and mentally makes the black protagonist aware of his status from being a 'single figure' to the position of 'the hero', and then to being 'the criminal'. (*Jump*, 3) In his reflection upon himself, he discovers that his identity as a terrorist is 'positioned' in a set of circumstances but it is not 'necessarily armour-plated against other identities' (Hall, 1987, 45–46); he finds himself identifying with the curtains in the hotel room:

> The curtains are open upon the dark, at night. When he gets up in the morning, he closes them. By now, they are on fire with the sun. The day pressing to enter. But his back is turned; he is an echo in the chamber of what was once the hotel. (*Jump*, 3)

At the beginning of the story, the curtains are not allowing the sunlight to come inside the room. This suggests the black man's preoccupation with his identity as a criminal whilst in the end, he draws the curtains signifying that he is willing to repent for his crime. The jump from one state of identity to another brings him to come to terms with himself. In the portrayal of this marginalised status of a black man on his own as well as in the white community, Gordimer portrays the dilemma of alienation and identity crisis that affected both the South African communities.

Sensitivity towards issues of race and identity in the South African world is a permanent feature of Gordimer's later fiction. It can be observed in the conversation between Whaila and Hillela about the colour of their still-to-be born baby in *A Sport of Nature*:

> The blackness was a glove…something God gave you to wear. Underneath, you must be white like me.—Or pale brownish, it's my Portuguese blood.—White like me; because that's what I was told, when I was being taught not to be prejudiced: underneath, they are all just like us. Nobody said we are just like you.—[…]
>
> If you are white, there, there's always a skin missing. They never say it.
>
> […] I wonder what colour the baby will come out, Whaila? What colour do you want? […]
>
> Our colour. A category that doesn't exist: she would invent it. There are Hotnots and half-castes, two-coffee-one-milk, touch-of-the-tar-brush, pure white, black is beautiful—but a creature made of love, without a label; that's freak. (Sport, 207–208)

At the beginning of the novel, Gordimer quotes a definition which is provided in the Oxford English Dictionary for the word, Sport of Nature: 'Lusus naturae—Sport of Nature. A plant, animal, etc., which exhibits abnormal variation or a departure from the parental stock or type…a spontaneous mutation; a new variety produced in this way.' (Sport, 7) The title of the novel *A Sport of Nature* indicates the racial complexity that was prevalent in South African society: people were classified into white, black, Coloured and Asiatic groups. Gert Prinsloo, an Afrikaner boy, Hillela recalls, is called 'the Boere' by the black boys at school. (Sport, 67) Hillela and Whaila do not wish the identity of their children to be labelled as Coloured because they are a 'new variety' and not a 'mutation' as South African terminology implied. This comes close to Bhabha's idea of flickering identities which suggests that identity and culture are lucid entities. (Bhabha, 1994, 3) The idea applies to the South African situation as well; the Dutch settlers attempted to create a white country for themselves in black South Africa. They did not realise that identities are affected or transformed in the process of life experiences when people go through the process of migration and settlement in a different culture. Looking at a group photograph after a long time, Vera in *None to Accompany Me* thinks about the identities of the people in it:

> But if someone to come along—wait!—and recognise the one whom nobody remembers, immediately another reading of the photograph would be developed. Something else, some other meaning would

> be there, the presence of what was taken on, along the way, then. (None, 3)

There is a process of transformation that keeps on working in defining people's identities from time to time. In the novel, Otto Abarbanel tells Vera about the process of his birth:

> I'm one. My mother was mated like a cow to produce a good German child for Hitler. I don't know who the Aryan stud was. She didn't know. Was never told his name when he was put on her. Artificial insemination for a cow is better, hei'm, it's a syringe, hei'm?—[...] The genes. I'm no Jewish victim. No Jew. I'm a German. [...] The genes are like the ones they have—the men who were beating up kids and shooting them. (None, 69–70)

In drawing a comparison between Hitler and the Afrikaners' policy of racism, Gordimer visualises the status of the latter's identity in new South Africa. In Otto's mutated personality, Gordimer also predicts that the Coloureds are the future of South Africa. Endorsing her view, Bhabha comments on Aila's brave show of a life of her own in *My Son's Story:*

> In her silence, she becomes the unspoken 'totem' of the taboo of the Coloured South African. She displays the unhomely world, [...] The silence that doggedly follows Aila's dwelling now turns into an image of the 'interstices', the in-between hybridity of the history of sexuality and race. (Bhabha, 1994, 14)

Bhabha reiterates that 'the Coloured South African subject represents hybridity, a difference 'within', a subject that inhabits the rim of an 'in-between' reality.' (1994, 13) Gordimer's protagonist in *My Son's Story*, her last novel of the apartheid era, is a Coloured man:

> Halfway between: the schoolteacher lived and carried out his uplifting projects in the community [...] Not defined—and it was this lack of definition in itself that was never to be questioned, but observed like a taboo, something which no-one, while following, ever could admit to. (Story, 21–22)

Bhabha views the novel as a landmark in Gordimer's later fiction since it is the first novel in which she has moved 'beyond' (Bhabha, 1994, 7) her strategy of developing her plots from a white perspective. She attempts 'a new artistic direction' (Head, 1994,160) by selecting a Coloured person to be her protagonist this time. Clingman in *History from Inside* questions Gordimer's attempt to present the story of South Africa from the black perspective:

> Gordimer may write about blacks but there is still a crucial sense in which she is divided from the black world [...] Gordimer, quite simply, is not 'of' the black South African world [...] This basic social limitation is also, in a deep sense, a historical one; a historical gap stands between Gordimer and the black world. (1986, 208)

This is true to a large extent. As compared to Peter Abrahams, Gordimer is inexperienced in the language and cultural habits of the Coloured community, but she has ventured into that arena in this novel. In her capacity as a white writer in South Africa, she dares to go beyond this historical limitation to express their peculiar destiny in her fiction.

Anticipating Bhabha's construction of identity which is flickering, Sonny's 'changing identities' in *My Son's Story* contribute to the process of transformation that occurs in his private and public struggle. Although he 'earned less than a white teacher with the same qualification' (Story, 23), his family is very much proud of his education and respectable position:

> He was the pride of the old people and the generic diminutive by which they had celebrated him as the son, the first-born male, was to stay with him in the changing identities a man passes through, for the rest of his life. (Story, 5–6)

As a young teacher, Sonny meditates upon his existence as a Coloured man in South Africa. His preoccupation with his 'inner self' makes him aware that 'he didn't feel himself inferior—inferior to what, to whom?' (Story, 23) Otherwise, he would have joined the struggle a long time ago like his cousins who are quite active in 'their resistance movement' in Cape Town. (Story, 14) The Cape Coloureds formed The African Political Organisation in 1902 and enjoyed limited voting rights until they were removed from the common electoral roll in 1956. As compared to other Coloureds, they were educated and had more opportunities to contribute to the betterment of their community. (Schrire, 1992, 221–224) The pride in himself leads Sonny to feel 'a sense of responsibility' towards his people 'in another way': 'When you want to tell people something, you have to know how to express it properly. So that they will take you seriously.—And they followed him.' (Story, 26) In *The Location of Culture*,

Bhabha calls this state of Sonny's existence as the 'halfway house of racial and cultural origins' that bridges the 'in-between' diasporic origins of the Coloured South African and turns it into the symbol for the disjunctive, displaced everyday life of the liberation struggle.' (1994, 13)

Earlier in the novel, Sonny's thoughts reflect Fanon's aspirations in his sense of self as a Coloured man. Fanon in *Black Skin, White Masks* argues that the terms black and white are there not to be defined by them but to challenge and get beneath them. (1967, 228–231) As a teacher, Sonny meditates upon the 'distinction between black and real black' to define his identity. (Story, 25) Later, his son, William also seems to be very much conscious of the colour of his skin: 'Baby [his sister] was light-skinned like my mother, not like my father and me.' (Story,61) But the blacks, whether light-skinned or dark-skinned, 'were accustomed to closeness' with each other:

> In queues for transport, for work permits, for housing allocation, for all the stamped paper that authorised their lives; loaded into overcrowded trains and buses to take them back and forth across the veld, fitting a family into one room, they cannot keep the outline of space—another, invisible skin—whites project around themselves, distanced from each other in everything but sexual and parental intimacy. (Story, 110)

In these comments over a black gathering to mourn the death of their nine fellow activists, where a few whites also turn in to show their solidarity, Gordimer reiterates the consciousness of the blacks as people with their standing who were determined to change their destiny in the South African world.

Quite opposite to the blacks' customary closeness with each other, the whites lived in a fear of closeness with the blacks in South Africa. According to Fanon, white colonisers frustrated their wish for assimilation. They guarded the boundary between the Self and the *Other*, even though their several adventures blur it significantly through contacts that include their physical relationships across the racial spectrum. Whenever the *Other* strove to achieve racial and cultural assimilation, the white self-redefined its boundary, dividing the two camps to suit their whims and tenaciously defending it. (Fanon, 1967, 228–229)

In *My Son's Story,* Sonny's physical relationship with Hannah, a white woman, in Bhabha's terms, 'marks a deeper historical displacement. And that is the condition of being "Coloured" in South Africa.' (Bhabha, 1994, 13):

> In this freak displacement, the biological drive of his life, which belonged with his wife and children he'd begotten, was diverted to his lover. He and Hannah begot no child; the revolutionary movement was to be their survivor. The excitement of their mating was for that. (Story, 241–242)

In *None to Accompany Me*, Gordimer sums up this historical displacement in describing Mpho's personality:

> The oyster-shell-pink palms of her slender hands completed the striking colour contrast of matt black skin [...] Her hair, drawn back straightened [...] Congolese style, [...] Out of her mouth came a perky London English. She could not speak an African language, neither the Zulu of her mother nor the Xhosa of her father. (None, 48–49)

Exile in England has produced a cross-pollination of history in Mpho's character:

> Boundaries are changed, ideologies merge, sects, religious and philosophical, create new idols out of combinations of belief, scientific discoveries link cause and effect between the disparate, ethnically jumbled territorial names make a nationality out of many-tongued peoples of different religions, a style of beauty comes out of the clash between domination and resistance. (None, 48–49)

In *The Location of Culture*, Bhabha calls this mixture of identities in a society cultural hybridity: 'The social articulation of difference, from the minority perspective, is a complex, ongoing negotiation that seeks to authorise cultural hybridity that emerges in moments of historical transformation.' (1994, 2) Mpho 'combined the style of *Vogue* with the assertion of Africa. She was a mutation achieving happy appropriation of the aesthetics of opposing species.' (None, 51) Although Mpho is retarded language-wise by the experience of exile, her getting pregnant by Oupa, an older employee at the foundation who spent 'years of deprivation on Robben Island' (None, 172) is evidence of the significance of strange passions and dangers which may accompany the blacks' new access to power.

In Gordimer's later fiction, mental probing remains a necessary stage for transformation in her protagonist's perspective upon himself and on his South African life; Maureen Smales in *July's People* discovers 'the final illusion of white innocence' (Smith, 1984, 93) in her refuge at July's village. Similarly, the white protagonist in 'Keeping Fit' comes to know the impossibility of staying unaffected by the political and social scenario in South Africa. This discovery is made through his act of crossing the fence, the boundary between his white and the black world. This complements Bhabha's idea of crossing the boundaries to visit the other side of life, the 'beyond' (Bhabha, 1994, 7) which helps the individual to know differences amongst cultures, and leads to a new identity for oneself in society.

Gordimer begins the story in *None To Accompany Me* by Marcel Proust (1871–1922), with the French novelist's motivational saying: 'We must never be afraid to go too far, for truth lies beyond.' (None, 1) This statement comes close to Bhabha's idea of locating one's self or defining one's identity in the realm of the beyond. This was required in the changing lives of South Africans when both the whites and the blacks went through a period of transition towards the establishment of a new social and political setup. Vera in *None to Accompany Me* goes far beyond by working through the consequences of a lifetime's commitments to a new kind of relationship with a black man, Zeph Rapulana. In her character, Gordimer perceives: 'Perhaps the passing away of the old regime makes the abandonment of an old personal life also possible.' (None, 315) Annick, Vera's lesbian daughter reveals: 'I mean just what I said: my father's gone to live in London, you move in with another man. [...] What are you experimenting with?' (None, 312–313) In Vera's decision to share a home with a black man in *None To Accompany Me,* Gordimer suggests that the apartheid system must change in the new South Africa.

These later short stories and novels show a continuity of the pattern in Gordimer's development of action and characterisation. The theme defined as borderland in the work of Bhabha exists in the construction of the plot as a physical space in *July's People*. It develops in the narration of historical events as a transitory situation in *A Sport of Nature* and it inculcates itself in border lives of characters such as Sonny in *My Son's Story*, and Vera in *None to Accompany Me*. It is, in Bhabha's terms, the 'beyond' (Bhabha, 1994, 4) that intervenes to establish a boundary in characters' lives in Gordimer's later fiction, revealing Bhabha's idea of interstitial existence, that is, the passage between racial polarities. The characters are led to live through a life of marginality either in exile or at home which grooms them into discovering new roles of life thus initiating new identities for themselves. For instance, the protagonist in *Jump* 'grew up [...] as an adolescent he bonded with his peers through joining the parachute club, and he jumped the rite of passage [in Gennep's fashion] into manhood.' (*Jump*, 7) The experience of life beyond her everyday life introduces Aila in *My Son's Story*, in Bhabha's words, with 'a sense of the new' (Bhabha, 1994, 7) that articulates the future course of action for her. Bhabha observes:

> [As a Coloured woman, it] defines a boundary [for Aila] that is at once inside and outside, the insider's outsideness. The stillness that surrounds her, the gap in her story, her hesitation and passion that speak between the self and its acts—these are moments where the private and public touch in contingency. (1994, 14–15)

At the same time, physical situations or frontier places in Gordimer's plots reveal her 'consciousness of history' (Clingman, 1986, 224) thus signifying the juxtaposition of historical events with the theme of borderland in her fiction. The plot is composed of situations or events from the past and present lives of protagonists that define their future for them. In *None To Accompany Me*, the three sections titled, 'Baggage', 'Transit', and 'Arrivals' keep the story moving from the past into the present and the future. The action in Gordimer's later fiction is built not only upon passionate relationships between characters but also how their past and present lives are 'determined by the struggle to be free' (Story, 276) from the injustices of the South African society.

These novels of the later years show the continuity of a pattern that has been followed by Gordimer in her writing. The process of mental probing works actively in her later novels, for example when Maureen's illusion of herself as humane in *July's People* is shattered. Despite the intrusion of apartheid in their borderland relationships with each other, the characters stay committed to liberating themselves as well as their people from its shackles as in *My Son's Story*. The plot in Gordimer's later novels is built through the characters' struggle to dismantle the old physical and mental barriers in their South African society so that they can socialise with people across the racial spectrum as equals, as in *A Sport of Nature* and *None to Accompany Me*.

Liberation (1980–1994)

1980 The underground ANC carried out sabotage attacks on South Africa's oil-from-coal installations at Sasolburg.

Countrywide protests erupted over wages, rents, bus fares, and education.

Gordimer's ninth short stories collection *A Soldier's Embrace* published.

1981 **Gordimer's eighth novel *July's People* published.**

1982 The underground ANC carried out a sabotage attack on South Africa's nuclear power complex at Koeberg.

1983 The underground ANC carried out a bomb attack outside military headquarters in Pretoria which killed nineteen people.

In response, the government attacked the ANC sanctuaries in Mozambique.

The United Democratic Front, a coalition of anti-apartheid

Organisations sympathetic to the Freedom Charter was launched.

1984 Most widespread and prolonged black uprising since 1976 erupted in Vaal Triangle. The township at Sebokeng was raided by the police and soldiers.

Gordimer's novella *Something out There* was published.

1985 Six top leaders of the United Democratic Front were charged with high treason. A State of emergency was imposed in parts of the country following deaths in townships violence.

The US imposed limited sanctions against South Africa, and foreign banks suspended credit.

The government announced media restrictions in locations covered by the emergency decree.

1986 1.5 million blacks staged the largest stay away in South Africa's history. The United Workers' Union was launched. The Pass laws were repealed.

The government attacked alleged ANC bases in Botswana, Zambia, and Zimbabwe.

Total censorship was imposed on media reports of political protest.

1987 The Black National Union of Mineworkers began a three-week the longest legal strike in South African history.

Violence escalated around Pietermaritzburg between the support of Inkatha and supporters of the United Democratic Front.

Gordimer's ninth novel *A Sport of Nature* published.

1988 The United Democratic Front along with seventeen anti-apartheid organisations were banned.

An estimated three million black workers went on strike for the to protest against anti-labour legislation.

Bombs destroyed the headquarters of the South African Council Churches and several leading anti-apartheid groups in Johannesburg.

1989 Seven members of the ANC were released from long-term imprisonment. Mandela and President Botha had an unprecedented meeting in Cape Town.

Anti-apartheid demonstrations took place in Johannesburg, Pretoria, and Port Elizabeth.

All public beaches were desegregated.

The Pan Africanist Movement, a surrogate for the PAC, was launched.

1990 The ban on political parties was lifted in South Africa, and political prisoners were released. Mandela came out of jail after twenty-seven years of imprisonment. The Separate Amenities Act was repealed.

Fighting between the supporters of Inkatha and the United Democratic Front in Alliance with the ANC spread from Natal to townships around Johannesburg.

The ANC announced a cease-fire, ending the thirty-year-old armed struggle. The political activists in exile returned to South Africa.

The National Party opened membership to all races. Political dialogue between the ANC and the government began.

Gordimer's tenth novel *My Son's Story* was published.

1991 The *Weekly Mail* exposed secret government funding of Inkatha and its allied movements. The rivalry between Inkatha and the ANC ended. The National Party's constitutional proposals and the National Peace Accord were rejected by the ANC and other anti-apartheid organisations. The Native Land Act, The Group Areas Act, and The Population Registration Act were repealed.

The US lifted economic sanctions against South Africa.

Gordimer's tenth short stories collection *Jump and other stories* published.

1992 Codesa, a Conference for a democratic South Africa was held in Kempton Park.

1993 Parliament adopted the Interim South African Constitution.

1994 First free general elections were held.

Mandela was inaugurated as President of South Africa. The Restitution of Land Rights Bill was passed.

The Security Council lifted its 1977 Arms Embargo and other restrictive measures.

South Africa resumed its full membership of the World Health Organisation (WHO) and the Commonwealth, and, was readmitted to UNESCO.

Gordimer's eleventh novel *None to Accompany Me* published.

Gordimer's post-apartheid fiction portrays the lives of people in contemporary South Africa under the black majority rule, and artistically captures people's fears and frustrations which are projected in physical and psychological encounters as experienced in the rhythm of their everyday lives in contemporary South Africa. Since 1994, South Africa moved from the system of apartheid to one of majority rule; the African National Congress (ANC) is in power and has won the subsequent elections in 1999, 2004, 2009, 2014 and 2019. Although the black government pledged and still reiterates to create a fair, safe, and democratic South Africa for all its citizens, corruption and struggle for power gradually has become the norm amongst the black leaders, drifting away from solving major issues like poverty, unemployment, education standards, AIDS outbreak, refugee crisis, and, law and order. Gordimer explores the history of contemporary South Africa through displacement as well as a juxtaposition of the private with the public in her characters' lives. Her fiction records a narrative internal to South African identity which makes her characters aware of prevalent conflicting attitudes in their South African society.

Post-Apartheid

The theme of apartheid is no longer the focus of Gordimer's attention in her post-apartheid fiction. Four novels *The House Gun* (1998), *The Pick Up* (2001), *Get a Life* (2005) and *No Time Like the Present* (2012), and three short stories collections *Loot* (2003), *Beethoven Was One-Sixteenth Black* (2007) and *Life Times* (2010) have been published in the post-apartheid years in which Gordimer explores other avenues of human life such as a murder trial in her twelfth novel, *The House Gun*. Where *None to Accompany Me* (1994) deals with the experience of victory by the blacks in their struggle against apartheid, their confidence in themselves is further reiterated in *The House Gun* (1998) in the character of a black barrister who defends a white man in a case of murder. The action in the novel is set in the era of the black majority rule in South Africa and reveals a change in Gordimer's presentation of her South African society. A psychological thriller, *The House Gun* presents a story about a young man who kills his gay friend with a gun for sleeping with his girlfriend. Similarly, stories from *Loot* (2003) present themes other than apartheid. The title story 'Loot' describes the story of an earthquake. 'Mission Statement' presents the story of a relationship between a white man and a black woman. 'Look-Alikes' is a story about homeless people. 'The Diamond Mine' is about teenage sex life. 'An Emissary' describes people dying of Malaria, and 'Karma' in nine parts, is an ironic and symbolical comment upon life and death. This shift in action and characterisation in Gordimer's post-apartheid fiction marks a boundary between her short stories and novels written during and after the apartheid era.

Set in Johannesburg as well as in an unknown Muslim country in the Far East, *The Pick Up* (2001) is a story about a young white woman, Julie Summers, falling in love with Abdu, an illegal Arab Muslim immigrant. After failed attempts to stop his deportation from South Africa, she decides to leave with him for his home country. Towards the end of the novel, the protagonist declines to accompany her partner who leaves for America, and she prefers to stay back with his family. By deporting her characters to the countries of the Other, Gordimer attempts to look at the whole issue of immigration and settlement at different levels, both privately and publicly:

> 'Relocate,' they say. The couple are 'relocating'. [...] 'Locate: to discover the exact locality of a person or thing; to enter, take possession of.' To discover the exact location of a 'thing' is a simple matter of factual research. To discover the exact location of a person: where to locate the self?[...] To discover and take possession of oneself, is that secretly the meaning of 'relocation' as it is shaped by the tongue and lips in substitution for 'immigration'? (PU, 47)

Focusing on the theme of migration, *The Pick Up* looks at the effects of displacement on people all over the world. There is a development from Gordimer's presentation of borders that existed in South African society under apartheid.

Themes related to race and identity recur in her fiction, but in different forms such as short stories presented in *Beethoven Was One-Sixteenth Black* (2007), and *Life Times* (2010). These stories provide a philosophical comment upon other dimensions of human existence, though weaving history alongside the main action. In 'Mother Tongue', Gordimer presents a love story of a German male and South African female who don't know each other's mother tongue but the love between them keeps them together. In 'Beethoven Was One-Sixteenth Black', the very statement by a white radio presenter makes fifty-two years old Frederick Morris, a white academic and teacher of biology, and an activist of the apartheid era, think about the history of human genes and biological development since the times unknown: 'Once there were blacks wanting to be white. Now whites are wanting to be black. It's the same secret.' (*Beethoven*, 3) In the past, Frederick's grandfather had lived for years on his own in South Africa to make money. Frederick imagines that his grandfather and white men like him might have physical relationships with black women to fulfil their sexual needs. To suggest that Beethoven might have some genetic connection or black man's blood is an ironic comment and realisation of the fact that there can be no final word on the existence and development of history and the human race. Identities flicker as would say Bhabha.

This idea of no 'finality' is explored again, though in a different form, in 'Dreaming of the Dead' (2007, 32). In the story, Gordimer presents a dream in which three dead people, the renowned Palestinian philosopher Edward Said, the South African activist of the apartheid era and editor of a South African newspaper, Anthony Sampson and Susan Sontag who used to run a Chinese restaurant in New York, meet in Susan's restaurant and chat about the world they once lived. Said whose 'invention of the *Other* that's survived the end of the old-style colonialism into globalisation' questions Susan: 'What did you leave unfinished?' Susan replies:

> Everything is unfinished. Finality: that's a mistake. It's the claim of dictatorship. Hegemony. In our turn, always we'll be having to pick up the baggage taking from experience what's good, discarding what's conned us into prizing, if it's destructive. (*DD*, 31–33)

An unusual process of creativity is, indeed, at work in these marginal situations. Gordimer creates a scene for the present with the past to comment on the 'unpredictability of humans' (*AE*, 2007, 140)

In 'History' (2007), the scene is set in the 1940s era—after the revolution and German occupation of Europe; Madame Delancy's French cuisine is replaced by 'Sauerkraut and sausages' when a German businessman buys the restaurant. The caged parrot, Auguste who is used to entertain customers of the French cuisine, behaves strangely in the new set-up:

> Now he's tittering nonsensically...the creature has gone silent. He fidgets about the cage...He yells in anguish, PAPA PAPA PA-PAA! Where is that child from whom this cry came, and is stored, may be for the rest of a hundred years? PA-PAA! Where is the father who was called for in desperate appeal, and did he ever come....The parroting that isn't only that of parrots repeats how we hide from one another's hurts....there is what was overheard, what he shouldn't have overheard....Doesn't go at all. (109–111)

There is continuity in Gordimer's making connections with history in her fiction. In 'Allesverloren' (2007), her historian South African widowed protagonist who, at a conference in England, presents a bottle of South African wine to an Afrikaner settler in London:

> He received it with appreciative pleasure.—All the way from South Africa!...the label, two words run into one, most likely those of a Boer wine farmer after the old war lost to the British, the defeated still spelling in Dutch from which his own language, Afrikaans, derived.—Allesverloren, 'everything lost'—ah, you see, from my Holland side—grandmother—I can translate...—You know the one you knew. Cannot know the other, any other. Allverseloren. (100–101)

Similarly, 'The First Sense' and 'The Third Sense' (2007) explore human dilemmas and complexities of the human mind through a focus on extramarital affairs on one hand and describing contemporary South Africa on the other. Whilst questing her husband's extra-marital affair, the white protagonist in 'The Third Sense', discovers her husband's concern regarding their airline business:

> Those enterprises of old regime white capitalism were not the way to safe success in a mixed economy—politically correct capitalism.
>
> ...If Michael and his partner are white, the cabin attendants, one of the pilots and an engineer are black...She knows what keeps him open-eyed, dead-still in the night: if the national airline takes up the homely routes its resources will ground the Everything in loss. (*TS*, 170)

In a process of 'disorientation' and 'a disturbance of direction' (Bhabha, 1994, 1) in their contemporary lives, Gordimer leads her characters to find new perspectives on themselves and the life around them: 'Zsuzsana has found home. He is in exile.' (*FS*, 154). The action in 'The First Sense' revolves around Ferenc, a young Doctor of Philosophy from Budapest, and his wife, Zsuzsana, a dressmaker from Hungary who migrates to South Africa for a better life. Ference finds a job at a supermarket and sticks to it while Zsuzsana gradually moves away from her dressmaking and progresses in life by travelling abroad on business trips for a property developer agency. She drifts away from Ferenc and divorces him in the end. The story is knitted with the physical struggle of two migrants whose identities are transformed in the process of migration.

Like fiction written in the apartheid era, the presentation of physical and psychological experience is significant in the action and characterisation in Gordimer's post-apartheid fiction; her characters acknowledge new sensibilities about themselves and their South African world. In 'Parking Tax' (2010), the scene is set in a parking area of a contemporary local South African suburb where poor black men have found a job for themselves—to help white people park their cars and load their shopping for some coins in return. Gordimer states:

> These are enterprises of the Informal Sector, now a category in the new theory of the economic structure of the country, which declares that the price of the privilege of recognition is a share of the responsibility in reducing unemployment. The unemployed must rouse—not arise, in protest against their condition—and do something for themselves. (*PT*, 537)

Lucas is one of them. He happens to be on good terms with a young white couple, a media person and his lawyer wife who works 'in a legal aid centre for people who can't afford paid representation in the courts.' (*PT*, 541). He helps them to park their car in the parking. As in Gordimer's other stories, the process of mental probing is actively at work. Getting into a laughter episode with Lucas one Saturday morning—in the parking—makes the couple realise that 'it's not that they're one with the people, the people are one with them':

> They don't have to remark upon it to one another, that would be unconscious admittance of what they were before: bleeding heart syndrome, believing they didn't have any class, let alone feelings of superiority. Now this freedom of spirit is coming in its validity, granted, from the most unlikely quarter, on the other side of the divides. Here was a man, Lucas, organising people who have no recognised place, told they are Informal...In his self-appointed domain of the shopping street, there is—something?—in him that brings coherence. (*PT*, 542)

It makes the white couple observe that blacks in South Africa 'don't have the incentives we have' but 'they have found a way, and we haven't'. It 'shamed' the white lawyer to see the black Lucas not having proper employment and him to protect her—the white person—from exploitation by the Informal Sector: once a poor black man approaches her in the parking area to ask not for money but a tin of sardines. She was about to give him a tin of tuna when Lucas stops her from doing so because the poor man is in habit of selling the tin of fish to buy a drink for himself. Her realisation that 'Nothing's changed' is an ironic comment on the economic exploitation which continues to exist in South African society; for blacks, 'Without property, the principle of ownership?' is questioned in the story. (*PT*, 542—544) Through the construction of fictionalised situations in her stories, Gordimer attempts to raise her voice against corruption and economic exploitation in contemporary South Africa.

Physical situations and psychological encounters exist in the variable form in Gordimer's post-apartheid novels. In *Get a Life* (2005), Gordimer presents contemporary South Africa juxtaposed in a story about human fear of destruction, contamination, alienation, and solitude as experienced by Paul Bannerman, an ecologist who is diagnosed with cancer. The prescribed radioactive treatment requires him to live in isolation until his body gets free from the radiation. To protect his young wife, Berenice and his three years old son, Nicholas from the effects of radiation, Paul moves to his parents' house where a part of the house is designated for his stay in isolation. This fragile existence causes him to see beyond; he is struck by the contradictions in values between his work as a conservationist and that of his wife, an advertising agency executive.

The strange nature of Paul's condition leads his mother, Lyndsay to face her fear: her husband Adrian will leave her one day. On his trip abroad after retirement, Adrian falls in love with a thirty-five years old Norwegian woman Hilde and informs Lyndsay in his correspondence. In the past, Lyndsay had an extramarital affair for four years as a young civil rights lawyer and on confession, Adrian had responded: 'I thought you were going to tell me you were leaving.' (Get, 128). Adrian did not leave her at that time 'but it was an amputation, excision...Four years taken from his maleness...Four years thrown in the trash where contaminated paper plates go'. (Get, 80). Lyndsay shares the information with her son Paul but does not raise the subject with Adrian in her correspondence and pretends that everything is normal between them.

In this process of telling the private story of Paul and his family's struggle against their fears and frustrations, Gordimer presents the state of public life in contemporary South Africa. Paul and Berenice socialise across the racial spectrum: 'The mix of a few friends from the Agency includes a black photographer with its Afro-American girlfriend and a lesbian copywriter (white) who is surprised by the arrival of the dishy husband's bush mates, Thapelo and Derek.' (Get, 111) Lyndsay has a social worker contact, Charlene who is 'coloured, one in whose broad face, a composite image of the Khoi Khoi, San, Malay, Dutch, English, German and only the past knows what else, was pleasingly mixed.' (Get, 141). Charlene works for the local government social welfare department to look after abandoned babies infected with HIV and AIDS. She helps Lyndsay adopt an HIV positive black child, Klara who is allowed to play with her grandson Nicholas. In Paul and Berenice mix house gatherings, children 'hug lovingly':

> The private schools they go to, these days, have black and white pupils and all the complexions and features characteristic of in-between colours; there is nothing unexpected for them in this gathering. (Get, 112)

History is reminded when Berenice meets Adrian for lunch in a local restaurant:

> It was in a suburb where white civil servants, mainly Afrikaners, had lived neatly around their Apostolic and Dutch Reformed churches, and had been deserted by them when after their regime had been

> defeated, black people had the right to move in as neighbours. Then it had become a place where all that had been clandestine, the mixing of blacks and whites, not necessarily the political activists who had won that freedom, was open. (Get, 44)

When Paul is shifted to his parents' house, he is looked after by a Zulu housemaid from Transkei, Primrose. He thanks her in the Zulu Language for her service. (Get, 22) Later in the novel, Paul is happy to see his son learning to speak Setswana—'a new generation that might produce white multilinguists.' (Get, 125) Paul is a conservationist who is against the government's plan to construct a nuclear reactor and toll road in the wild coast area:

> If you thrust a toll highway through the centre of endemism, the great botanical marvel...heavy minerals...sand dunes...isn't that the morality of survival...exploitation of...our rich resources...It's been pledged...the end of poverty...Survival...Civilisation goes against nature...what I do, I am. Protect. Preserve. (Get, 168)

Paul, with his research colleagues Thapelo and Derek, is frustrated at the irony that fifty-one per cent of the black-owned company has allocated dunes mining projects to the Australians in which the blacks have only fifteen per cent share—'fifteen per cent is a bribe?...a laugh at this bit of black empowerment...Get a life. The Agency admonishment.' (Get, 183). They observe:

> Bribery is going to serve them even better. The option they've given to a black empowerment company that represents the very community, the traditional leaders we counted on, the people we've been lobbying to protest misuse of their land, threat to their subsistence. A fifty per cent stake in the mining deal, ten million dollars. Ten millions! How does that divide up amongst—how many people?...ten million dollars shareholders...who'll get the dividends—? (Get, 145)

The title of the novel, *Get A Life* itself describes the need for righteousness in South African society at both private and public levels: 'You will never understand what it means to be straight, my innocent darling. Get a life!' (Get, 111)

Towards the end of the novel, the government puts to halt its plans to construct the 'pebble-bed nuclear plant' (Get, 186) and the highway in 'Pondoland marine protected area' (Get, 144). Paul is relieved at his baby's birth as a normal child even though he has gone through the radioactive treatment. His time in isolation—his displaced life where he dwells, though for some time, and then return with an aptitude, in Bhabha's words, 'to touch the future on its hither side' (1994, 7). Displacement is a necessary process to get to the moment of transit, to the moment of realisation and transformation in Gordimer's fiction. In this process, Gordimer's characters find themselves introduced to a sense of purpose—get a life—for them: Lyndsay adopts Klara, an HIV positive child. Adrian mates with Hilde. Berenice gives birth to a healthy baby despite Paul's fear of contamination and decay. Paul recovers from his illness and focuses on his work as a conservationist. In the adoption of a black child and the birth of a white child, Gordimer visualises the juxtaposition and integration of black and white societies in South Africa. It serves to create and guess in her imaginary plot the future of South Africa.

As 'destruction takes on many states of existence' in *Get A Life* (Get, 186), *No Time Like the Present* (2012) presents sharp psychological insights into the political complexities of contemporary South Africa which are presented in the story of a couple attempting to make a living in new South Africa. Years of resistance, the struggle, and the liberation phases of South African history are juxtaposed into one fibre. Brought together in exile by a shared devotion to political struggle against apartheid, the couple find themselves caught in bourgeois dilemmas as a wealthy middle-class family in South Africa where injustice is still rife, and violence still threatens the lives of the prosperous. In telling the couple's story, Gordimer depicts the social and political climate of the liberation era in a succession of intimate glimpses of the white and the black worlds in South Africa; during Nelson Mandela's presidency in the years 1994–1999, the government of National Unity was established; the cabinet was made up of twelve ANC representatives, six from the National Party, and three from the KwaZulu-Natal Inkatha Freedom Party (IFP)—historically the voice of Zulu nationalism. Economically, the government embarked on the Reconstruction and Development Programme (RDP) to address the socio-economic consequences of apartheid, including alleviating poverty and addressing the massive shortfalls in social services across the country. The Truth and Reconciliation Commission (TRC) was established to expose the crimes of the apartheid era. It operated by allowing victims to tell their stories and by allowing perpetrators to confess their guilt, with amnesty on offer to those who made a full confession. Those who chose not to appear before the commission faced criminal prosecution if proven guilty by the authorities. Whilst some soldiers, police, and ordinary citizens confessed their crimes, few of those who had given the orders presented themselves. State President P.W. Botha and then-Deputy President Thabo Mbeki refused to appear before the Commission. In 1995, South Africa hosted and won the 1995 Rugby World Cup. Nelson Mandela wore a Springbok rugby jersey to present the William Webb Ellis Cup to South African captain Francois Pienaar, a symbolic image of reconciliation between the races.

In the years 1999–2008, the ANC's majority increased under the Mbeki presidency which allowed to alter the constitution. The Democratic Party (DP) had traditionally functioned as a stronghold of liberal whites and now gained new support from conservatives disenchanted with the National Party (NP), and from some middle-class blacks. Mbeki emphatically denied the HIV crisis in South Africa which invited global criticism, and his conspicuous failure to condemn the deteriorating situation in neighbouring Zimbabwe unnerved both South African landowners and foreign investors. In 2005, corruption allegations related to a national arms deal surfaced against the country's Deputy President, Jacob Zuma. His financial advisor, Schabir Shaik, was convicted of corruption and fraud. Popular support for Mbeki suffered from the feeling that his government's economic policies had failed to generate inclusive development. Though the Black Economic Empowerment programme was implemented in 2003 to redress the inequalities of the apartheid era, it was criticised as benefiting mostly a narrow stratum of previously disadvantaged groups and made crime a massive problem in South Africa. Also, an estimated 250,000 white South Africans emigrated at the plight of white farmers who were murdered in attacks since 1991.

In 2007, all leadership positions within the ANC went to former Deputy President, Jacob Zuma's supporters, representing a major power shift within the ruling party. Tensions within the ANC led to Mbeki's resignation in 2008, and several prominent members defected to form separate parties such as the Congress of the People (COPE), under the leadership of Mosiuoa Lekota, Mbhazima Shilowa and Mluleki George, and the Economic Freedom Fighters (EFF) led by Julius Malema which supports land reform. The ANC majority gradually reduced under Zuma's presidency in the following years.

In *No Time Like the Present*, the scene is set in contemporary South Africa when the power struggle of black politicians and the embarrassing stories of corruption allegations and the rape trial of Jacob Zuma comes into public. Steven Reed whose father was a Scot and mother Jewish, and, his wife, a black lawyer Jabulile Gumede move to live in a suburb with their young daughter, Sindiswa. They were activists in the past—Steven worked in a paint manufacturing factory, and Jabulile was a schoolteacher in a missionary school under apartheid. After the liberation, she establishes herself as an attorney and Steven becomes a university lecturer of chemistry in new South Africa. Their new status makes them aware of the fact that freedom—the better life for all—that was fought for and promised—is created but still challenged by political and racial tensions in South Africa. The vast and growing gap between affluence and mass poverty continues to exist in their South African world; Steven is frustrated at the government education policies which are not making any difference to black youths and their development, and Jabulile is disappointed with no jobs for young and educated black South Africans. They plan to leave South Africa for Australia but don't go in the end—the solution is not to run away to Australia but to stay and fight back. The action in the novel is woven together with Jabulile and Steven's passionate relationships, and how their past and present lives are determined by the struggle to bring change in education standards and employment prospects for the blacks in South Africa.

Gordimer presents themes related to race and identity in *No Time Like the Present* in a different form. When Jonathan seeks advice from his brother Steven about the best University faculty of engineering for his son and the prospect of his settling abroad, Gordimer contemplates:

> Home is transferable. It always has been. Long before tribes coming down from the equatorial North, the Dutch following the reconnaissance of the Dutch East India Company, the French and their viniculture, the English colonial governors, the indentured Indians for the whites' sugar plantations, the Scottish mining engineers, the Jews from Czarist Russian racism and later Nazi Germany's persecution, the Italians who took a liking to the country during their spell as prisoners of war here, the Greeks whose odyssey launched by poverty brought them—all these and others of distant origins made home, this South Africa. You can make of somebody else's your home anywhere. It's human history. (Present, 273)

In South African history, the white settlers attempted to create a white country for themselves in black South Africa. They did not realise that identities transform—flicker—in the process of migration and settlement in a different culture. A process of transformation is always at work to keep identity and culture as lucid entities. Bhabha's notion of borderland remains active in Gordimer's post-apartheid fiction:

> A boundary is not that at which something stops but from which something begins its 'presencing' such as the articulation of 'dissident histories and voices—women, the colonised, minority groups, the bearers of policed sexualities, the history of post-colonial migration, the narratives of cultural and political diaspora, the major social displacements of peasant and aboriginal communities, the poetics of exile, the grim prose of political and economic refugees. (Bhabha, 1994, 5)

It seems that South Africa without apartheid has become an interesting place to discover the life of the *Other*. In exploring an opportunity to relocate and move to Australia in *No Time Like the Present,* Steven comes to a realisation:

> RECONCILIATION...the Native Title Act 1993 which recognises native land ownership throughout Australia. In 2008, the Australian Prime Minister apologised to the Indigenous people for the 'Stolen Generation': the Indigenous children who between 1910 and 1970 were forcibly removed from their families, inflicting profound suffering and loss in...Education, health, housing...White South Africans didn't apologise to black South Africans for the abuse suffered by blacks from whites, seventeenth century to apartheid's final perfection...Humans lived in Australia 60,000 years ago. The San, humans living in what is now South Africa 200,000 years ago, joined by the Khoi Iron Age people...have managed to survive under whites that saw them as hardly humans... (Present, 277)

Steven is caught in a split historical position—as produced in the articulation of cultural differences: a white person living in privilege in South Africa, yet espousing the causes of the deprived black South African masses. The idea of relocating to Australia acts as a physical space for both Steven and Jabulile to go beyond the polarities of the *Self* and the *Other*:

> Ah...I don't want to go—no echo there also in the decision of their future? They don't need even to suppress the subject, there's no distance between them...pointing the hair about her head—Medea!—he's amused. But the reference is unlikely to have visual meaning for Jabu, just as in Zulu image or metaphor often her reference has no meaning—match—for him...But if references not known between them at home are sign of the intimately irreconcilable, coming from

their different 'cultures', aren't they, haven't they been from the beginning the fascination of what's called the Other! (Present, 320)

Steven always 'enjoyed himself' in his visits to Jabulile's KwaZulu village where he 'felt at home. In her home. In place....A reconciliation brought about by Jabu, by life with her?' (Present, 270) At the beginning of the novel, Gordimer quotes from South African national poet Keorapetse Kgositsile's (1938–2018) 'Wounded Dreams':

> Though the present remains
> A dangerous place to live
> Cynicism would be a reckless luxury.

For both Steven and Jabulile, their preparation to migrate to South Africa acts as an intervening space—the 'third space' (Bhabha, 1994, 36)—and gives 'a revisionary time' to them to return to their existing life with 'a sense of the new' (Bhabha, 1994, 7). In this process, they find themselves introduced to a new sense that leads to attaining new avenues of knowledge and understanding of their South African world. There is a continuity of a pattern that has been followed by Gordimer in her presentation of physical and psychological experience in the novel; exploring through cultural and psychological dimensions, *No Time Like the Present* presents marginal situations and events from the past and present lives of the protagonists that define their future for them.

The title of the novel, *No Time Like the Present* itself reveals Gordimer's 'consciousness of history' (Clingman, 1986, 224) thus signifying the difficulty of choices that people face in contemporary South Africa. Jabulile is not at home with her black people:

> It is killingly difficult to accept a priority between choice of existences in the meanly allotted human span. Oh, stuff the philosophy. There is her heritage KwaZulu Africa as exemplified in her father with whom she is bonded although parted from the poster she came upon on the fence. (Present, 271)

Once proud of her father as headmaster and her mentor, Jabulile is disappointed at his support of Jacob Zuma to become the next President. In her character, Gordimer reflects profound disillusionment. It intensifies Jabulile's disappointment to see that black South Africans are still suffering from poverty and unemployment. At the same time, Steve identifies low standards of education in black South Africa because it is crippled by the fact that the apartheid generation was denied a decent education.

No Time Like the Present is closely entwined with current issues in South Africa—AIDS outbreak, law and order, an influx of refugees from neighbouring countries and widespread corruption:

> UBUNTU. One of the African words everyone, all of us, any colour, we know—we know it means something like we are all each other—shouting—Say it! Say it! Say it for what it is. Turned out to be! What we've produced! What we're producing! Corruption's our culture. The Spirit of the Nation... (Present, 421)

The black government with its Protection of State Information Bill—The Secrecy Bill is a sham designed to hide widespread corruption, by giving any organ of the state the ability to decide what constitutes the protection of state information; ministers will be able to prosecute and jail offenders—worse than anything under apartheid. The powers the government is taking to curb the press are far wider now and the powers given to the minister of state security are greater—No Time Like the Present, says Gordimer.

In her interview published in *The Sydney Morning Herald* (2012), Gordimer admits: 'We were naive, because we focused on removing the apartheid government and never thought deeply enough about what would follow.' The robbery incident at Jabulile and Steven's house and their old housekeeper Withu being attacked by the looters in *No Time Like the Present* is a reminder of Gordimer's own experience of a robbery at her place in 2006; during the robbery, she and her housekeeper were dragged upstairs, and her housekeeper was punched and kicked. When Gordimer shouted at the robbers that the housekeeper was old enough to be their grandmother, they stopped. Both women were locked in a cupboard as the robbers left. Gordimer reaction to the experience was: 'Oh well, it's my turn to experience what so many others have.' (ibid) Gordimer's view was that the young men who robbed her were sent by gangs when what they needed were work and education. In *No Time Like the Present*, Steven's reaction to the robbery experience is: 'That was what was happening while we were reconciling with Africa in the bush.' (Present, 388)

In *How Long Will South Africa Survive?* (2015), the British Journalist R W Johnson asserts that liberation has failed as the black majority rule is incapable of governing South Africa as a free democratic country. Gordimer refutes this opinion:

> People who criticise us forget that Europe had 400 years to get it right and you still have many problems [...] we have provided thousands of houses to people living in shacks, that people have got running water in their houses who never had it before. Today I see a white person and a black person kissing in the park. These are small things that Europeans take for granted. For us, it is enormous. (Allfree, 2007)

Loyal to the end, Gordimer projects the progress made under the ANC government and at the same time, recognises the need to work towards better political and economic systems in the country. In *The Sydney Morning Herald* interview (2012), Gordimer responds to the question, 'Would she have preferred a quieter life?': the normal life, the one that never was?'—she wouldn't. Gordimer fought—unafraid—to the end with the hope to win the new challenges in post-apartheid South Africa. Jabulile and Steven in her last novel, *No Time Like the Present* decide not to leave and continue their struggle to build South Africa.

Post-Apartheid (1995–2014)

1995 The Constitutional Court was formally opened. Winnie Mandela, Deputy Minister of Arts, Culture, Science and Technology was dismissed from her post.

Names of three of South Africa's nine provinces changed: Pretoria Witwatersrand and Vereeniging become Gauteng; Orange Free State becomes the Free State and the Northern Transvaal becomes the Northern Province.

The Truth and Reconciliation Commission (TRC) was established. Identification Amendment Act No.47 amended the 1986 Identification Act to compile a new population register.

The Public Protector's Office was established.

National local government elections were won by the ANC, securing 66.37% of the votes cast.

1996 President Mandela's marriage to Winnie Mandela was formally ended.

Parliament established the Human Rights Commission.

Five members of the Afrikaner Resistance Movement (AWB) were sentenced to twenty-six years imprisonment each for their part in a bombing campaign in which twenty people were killed and hundreds injured, aimed at disrupting the 1994 elections.

The National Party left the Government of National Unity headed by Nelson Mandela to become the Official Opposition, its first time out of government since 1948.

Mandela confirmed that he will not stand for re-election in 1999 and supported Deputy President Thabo Mbeki as his successor.

The new Constitution of the Republic of South Africa was adopted.

The Independent Electoral Commission (IEC) was established.

The first census was conducted; South Africa had a population of 43 million people, 22 million of them women.

1997 On the TRC forum, five security police officers confessed to the 1977 murder of Black Consciousness leader Steve Biko and made a formal amnesty application.

The Constitution of the Republic of South Africa came into effect. The new Federation of Unions of South Africa (FEDUSA) was officially launched.

Winnie Mandela was re-elected as president of ANC'S Women's League.

Eugene Terre'Blanche, leader of the Afrikaner Weerstands Beweging (AWB) was sentenced to six years in jail for attempted murder and brutal assault of his worker, Paul Motshabi. Former President F.W. de Klerk announced his retirement from politics and his leading role in the New National Party.

President Mandela stepped down as leader of the African National Congress and was succeeded by Deputy President Thabo Mbeki.

1998 Siphiwe Nyanda became the first black to head the South African National Defence Force.

At the age of 80, President Mandela married Graca Machel, the widow of a Mozambican president and black liberation leader Samora Machel.

Former President P.W. Botha was fined and given a suspended one-year jail sentence for ignoring a subpoena to testify about apartheid atrocities in front of the TRC.

Gordimer Twelfth novel *The House Gun was* published.

1999 Four police officers charged with the fatal beating of Steve Biko were denied amnesty.

The ANC won South Africa's second democratic election.

Thabo Mbeki was sworn in as South Africa's secondpost-apartheid president. He appointed Jacob Zuma, who was the chairperson of the ANC, as deputy president.

Allan Boesak, a leading anti-apartheid activist, was sentenced to six years in prison for theft and fraud of stealing money from foreign donors intended for the Foundation for Peace and Justice.

President Mandela handed the Schmidtsdrift San communities—Xun and! Khwe tribes—almost 13,000 of farmland, including Platfontein, near Kimberley.

The ANC government signed a peace pact with the arch-rival Inkatha Freedom Party.

The TRC granted amnesty to Eugene Terre'Blanche after he made a full disclosure for his apartheid-era crimes.

2000 Delegates walked out at President Mbeki's statement at the 13th International AIDS Conference in Durban that poverty was a greater enemy than the AIDS virus.

The ANC won municipal elections.

2001 The ANC government unveiled World AIDS Day 2001 campaign.

The first World Conference Against Racism. Racial Discrimination, Xenophobia and Related Intolerance (WCAR) was held.

The ANC government ordered the demolition of shacks on the occupied land in Bredell.

Marike de Klerk, former wife of former President F.W. de Klerk was found stabbed and strangled in her luxury apartment near Cape Town.

Gordimer's thirteenth novel *The Pick Up* published.

2002 South Africa's parliament passed the Minerals and Petroleum Resource Development Act 2002 which aimed at transforming the country's mining industry by giving the government control of mineral rights.

A series of bomb blasts rocked the township of Soweto. The Boeremag (Afrikaner Power) was believed responsible.

2003 In its final report, the TRC recommended that the government pay compensation totalling $348 million to more than 21,000 victims of apartheid-era abuses.

Winnie Mandela was sentenced to four years in prison for her conviction on fraud and theft charges.

Gordimer's eleventh short stories collection *Loot and Other Stories* published.

2004 President Thabo Mbeki signed the Broad-Based Black Economic Empowerment Act. It imposed a host of obligations on companies that wished to do business with the government.

South Africa held its third democratic election, marking a decade of democracy. The ANC received 67.7% of the votes.

President Thabo Mbeki was elected unopposed for a second term.

The country celebrated its 10th anniversary as a democratic state at the Union Buildings, Pretoria.

2005 The municipal council in Pretoria voted to rename the capital to Tshwane.

President Thabo nominated Pius Langa to become the first black justice to hold office.

Mbeki dismissed his deputy, Jacob Zuma, after he was implicated in a corruption scandal, and, appointed Phumzile Mlambo-Ngcuka, his minister for minerals and energy to replace Zuma.

Brett Kebble (41), a mining entrepreneur and cultural philanthropist, who had links with the African National Congress was found shot to death in Johannesburg.

Mark Scott-Crossley, a white farmer convicted in the murder of one of his former black workers, was sentenced to life in prison.

South Africa's former deputy president Jacob Zuma was indicted on corruption charges in a scandal involving his financial adviser Schabir Shaik and two French arms companies. The ANC accepted the withdrawal of Jacob Zuma, its popular deputy president from leadership duties for the duration of his rape trial.

Gordimer's fourteenth novel *Get a Life* published.

2006 In the Local Government elections, the ANC won the majority of seats nationwide.

The court found Jacob Zuma not guilty of rape, paving his way to becoming the ANC president at the Polokwane Conference in 2007.

2007 South Africa officially assumed its seat as a non-permanent member of the United Nations Security Council.

Marais Viljoen, former president of South Africa (1979–1984), passed away.

Former law and order minister Adriaan Vlok and former police chief Johan van der Merwe, together with former Major-General Christoffel Smith and colonels Gert Otto and Johannes Van Staden, received suspended sentences after pleading guilty in the Pretoria High Court on charges of attempting to murder anti-apartheid activist Rev Frank Chikane, by poison in 1989.

Jacob Zuma defeated President Thabo Mbeki at the party convention and moved into position to become president in 2009.

The National Prosecuting Authority served Jacob Zuma an indictment to stand trial in the High Court on various counts of racketeering, money laundering, corruption and fraud.

Gordimer's twelfth short stories collection *Beethoven Was One-Sixteenth Black* published.

2008 South African National Police Commissioner Jackie Selebi resigned as president of Interpol and planned to fight corruption allegations.

A series of xenophobic attacks against mainly foreign nationals started nationwide. Within three weeks of violence 62 people including South Africans were killed.

Thabo Mbeki resigned from his position as President of South Africa nine months before his second term of office expired.

South Africa's parliament elected Kgalema Motlanthe, former trade unionist, freedom fighter and deputy leader of the ruling ANC, as interim president of the country.

The Congress of the People (COPE) was founded in Bloemfontein by former ANC members Mosiuoa Lekota, Mbhazima Shilowa and Mluleki George to contest the 2009 general election.

2009 Helen Suzman, a South African anti-apartheid activist, died at the age of 91. She won international acclaim as one of the few white lawmakers to fight against the injustices of racist rule and was nominated twice for the Nobel Peace Prize.

The National Prosecuting Authority (NPA) dropped corruption charges against Jacob Zuma, saying the case had been manipulated for political reasons and clearing the way for him to become the next president without the looming threat of a trial.

South Africans voted in the fourth democratic general elections. ANC won 277 votes in the 400-member National Assembly. Jacob Zuma was sworn in as president of the Republic of South Africa in the Union Building in Pretoria.

Former President Nelson Mandela's 91st birthday also marked the inaugural Mandela Day. President Jacob Zuma announced on World AIDS Day in Pretoria that all HIV-positive babies under the age of one will receive anti-retroviral drugs as part of a huge expansion of treatment.

2010 Eugene Terre'Blanche (69), the leader of the right-wing Afrikaner Weerstandsbeweging (AWB), was attacked and killed by a 21-year-old man and a 15-year-old boy who worked for him on his farm outside Ventersdorp, about 68 miles northwest of Johannesburg, following a dispute over pay. The alleged attackers were arrested and charged with murder.

Frederik Van Zyl Slabbert (70), academic, political analyst and anti-apartheid activist in the apartheid-era Parliament, died. The former South African legislator helped chart a way out of apartheid by leading fellow whites into talks with exiled black South African leaders.

Basic Education Minister Angie Motshekga announced that pupils will have the option of learning their mother language in their first three years of schooling. Children were currently taught either in English or Afrikaans, both languages inherited from the eras of colonialism and apartheid.

President Jacob Zuma announced that South Africa would stop recognising half the nation's traditional kings and queens, dismissing them as artificial creations of the apartheid regime.

Former National Police Commissioner Jackie Selebi (60) was sentenced to 15 years in prison on corruption-related charges after he was found guilty in 2009 of receiving bribes to turn a blind eye to drug trafficking, making him one of the most senior officials to be convicted of corruption in the democratic era.

South Africa's Home Affairs Department announced the withdrawal of special status granted in 2009 to illegal Zimbabwean immigrants who fled their country's economic meltdown and political violence.

Gordimer's thirteenth and the last short stories collection *Life Times* published.

2011 South Africa's government Communication department rectified media censorship of government information.

Crime Intelligence Head Richard Mdluli handed himself over to the police and appeared in court after a warrant for his arrest in connection with the 1999 murder of Oupa Ramogibe was issued. Former South African General and Defence Minister Magnus Malan (81) died.

The Equality Court convicted ANC youth leader Julius Malema (30) of hate speech and in effect bans the singing of the song, 'Shoot the Boer.' ANC suspended Malema for five years after a disciplinary committee found him guilty of bringing the party into disrepute and sowing divisions.

Crime Intelligence Head Richard Mdluli handed himself over to authorities and appeared in the Commercial Crimes Court in Pretoria on fraud and corruption charges. The Specialised Commercial Crime Court later provisionally withdrew the charges against him.

2012 South Africa's Supreme Court ruled in favour of the Democratic Alliance that the National Prosecuting Authority must allow a review of a 2009 decision by its head Mokotedi Mpshe who dropped charges of corruption, racketeering, tax evasion and money laundering against President Jacob Zuma.

General Bheki Cele was sacked by President Jacob Zuma for alleged offences of fraud and corruption in the handling of leases for police headquarters that were signed at far above market rates.

Members of the white extremist group 'The Boeremag organisation' were found guilty of high treason and plotting to kill Nelson Mandela and trying to overthrow the government.

Anglo American Platinum (Amplats) fired 12,000 striking South African miners after a protracted strike over wages. Police opened fire on workers at a platinum mine in Marikana, killing at least 34 people, leaving at least 78 injured and arresting more than 200 others.

Julius Malema was charged with money laundering over a government tender awarded to a company partly owned by his family trust. The case was a politically motivated attempt to silence Malema's campaign against President Jacob Zuma, in particular over the Marikana shootings.

Bulldozers accompanied by South Africa Police Services destroyed homes in Lenasia Township in Johannesburg that authorities say were constructed on illegally sold land, despite efforts by protesters to stop the demolition.

Four white men Mark Trollip, Johan Prinsloo, Martin Keevy and Hein Boonzaaier were arrested and faced treason and terrorism charges over an alleged plot that include plans to attack the African National Congress political party conference in Mangaung, North West and kill President Jacob Zuma and others.

Gordimer's fifteenth and last novel *No Time Like the Present* was published.

2013 South African government authorised the deployment of South African soldiers to the Central African Republic (CAR) as part of a military cooperation agreement between the two countries to help the country's army as it faces a threat from a coalition of rebel groups. Neighbouring countries Cameroon, Gabon and the Republic of Congo sent troops to help stabilise the country confronted by the rebellion.

South African police arrested Etienne Kabila as a ringleader of a group of Congolese rebels who face charges of allegedly plotting a war to unseat Congolese President Joseph Kabila.

Former Vice-Chancellor of University of Cape Town Dr Mamphela Ramphele, an academic and co-founder of the nation's Black Conscious Movement, announced the creation of Agang, a new political party 'to build the South Africa of our dreams'. Dirk Coetzee (57), a former commander of the Vlakplaas covert police unit during the apartheid era in South Africa, died.

Coetzee had fled South Africa in 1989. He pledged allegiance to the ANC in exile and told the Harms Commission in Britain how he had watched his colleagues murder the student activist Sizwe Kondile and the human rights lawyer Griffiths Mxenge. He returned in 1993 and was a witness at the trial of former police Colonel Eugene de Kock. In testimony to the Truth and Reconciliation Commission, Coetzee confessed to plotting the 1981 murder of attorney Griffiths Mxenge.

South Africa withdrew its troops in the Central African Republic. The National Assembly passed the Protection of State Information Bill.

Julius Malema, former head of the ANC's Youth League, launched his Economic Freedom Fighters (EFF) party in Marikana. Malema formed the EFF following his expulsion from the governing African National Congress (ANC) in 2012 after a bitter fall-out with President Jacob Zuma.

Mike du Toit, along with four others, was sentenced to 35 years in jail for his role as a mastermind behind the 2002 right-wing extremist plot to kill former President Nelson Mandela and drive blacks out of the country. The rest of the 20 militia members on trial received 10 and 30 years sentences depending on their degree of involvement in the plot. The judge suspended 10 years of the sentences for some and took into account the time behind bars during the trial.

South Africa observed the centenary of the Natives Land Act of 1913. The Act became law on 19 June 1913, restricting black people from buying or occupying land in South Africa except as employees.

South Africa's first democratically elected President Nelson Mandela died at the age of 95.

2014 South Africa's main opposition Democratic Alliance party headed by Helen Zille announced its intention to merge with the smaller Agang group to jointly challenge the ruling ANC party.

The Public Protector Thuli Madonsela found that some of the R246 million taxpayer-funded refurbishments at President Jacob Zuma's Nkandla residence are unlawful and orders him to repay part of the cost.

South Africans voted in the fifth democratic and the ANC was officially declared the winner of South Africa's 2014 general election after securing 62.15% of the national vote.

President Jacob Zuma was sworn in at the start of his second term at the Union Buildings.

Albie Sachs (79), the South African judge who survived a bomb attack and rose to fame for his role in the anti-apartheid struggle, was awarded the Tang Prize, touted as Asia's version of the Nobel Prize, for his contributions to human rights and justice.

South Africa's Supreme Court of Appeals ordered the National Prosecuting Authority to release taped phone conversations about corruption charges against President Jacob Zuma.

Nadine Gordimer (90), a Nobel literature laureate (1991) and anti-apartheid activist, died.

The theme of borderland is an integral ingredient of action and characterisation in Gordimer's fiction. It is a stylistic and thematic tool to portray South African society in her fiction. The construction of fictionalised borderlands provides Gordimer with an opportunity to raise her voice against apartheid in South Africa. There is a continuity in its presentation which demonstrates the centrality of its deployment as a narrative strategy in her fiction. Through shared colonial and post-colonial experience, it forms an important literary device for Gordimer to describe South African life in her fiction. Like the carnivals of the nineteenth century which allowed space for the characters to criticise the kings, revealing themselves in ways as they wanted to be, Gordimer's fiction provides a space for her characters to vividly express the polarisation between the coloniser and the colonised in the South African world. It makes them contemplate hierarchical social patterns and questions their validity in their everyday South African life.

Race, Identity and The Theme of Borderland

A border or boundary is a symbol—a surrounding line or exterior limit of a country or a region through which nations and localities define themselves. Whereas a borderland is a neutral zone—an area near the borderline separating two countries or an area of overlap between two entities. It generates a 'territorial passage' (Gennep, 1960, 3) that alters one's identity from a citizen into a foreigner. Although the borderland is relatively a small area, it can be a meeting place of every kind of landscape, from hill to valley, forest to plain. It is not only a spatial fact with sociological effects but also a sociological fact that forms space. It defines at once territorial limits and socio-cultural space. For instance, a psychological space is created in the borderland between reality and myth to experience both history and fiction resting beside each other in the American writer Terri Windling's (1958–to date) urban fantasy series *Bordertown: A Chronicle of the Borderlands* (1986). In the liminal environment of a border town between Elflands (a fictional place) and The World (a shared universe), neither magic nor technology functions normally, and, when juxtaposed, unpredictable combinations of the two emerge, that is, a disenfranchised culture of gang violence, generation gaps, class conflict, miscegenation and race relations. The borderland here creates a psychological as well as political space between two or more cultures in which different people mingle and blend their cultures.

In *The Space Between* (2006), the Indian American writer Thrity Umrigar (1961-to date) provides a powerful social commentary on the issues of poverty, domestic violence, class, education, women's rights, AIDS, privilege and wealth, through a space—a borderland—between distance and intimacy that exists in a twenty years-long relationship of her two female characters, Sera Dubash a Parsi housewife with a privileged affluent Mumbai life, and, Bhima Gopal—a poor old servant. Both women drink tea together, Bhima squatting on the floor and Sera sits on the table; even though Bhima is thought of as one of the family, she is not allowed to sit on the furniture she polishes, has separate utensils to drink and eat, and a separate bar of soap to wash. In their chat on a personal level over a cup of tea, the novel sheds light on the class difference and hypocrisy prevalent in modern Indian society.

Set against the backdrop of the British rule and the Indian Independence movement in the 1920s, *A Passage to India* (1924) is one other good example in this regard. The English author, Edward Morgan Forster (1879–1970) explores the themes of humanism and cultural conflict; Adela, an English woman on a visit to India gets hallucinated inside the Marabar caves—a fictitious place modelled on the Barabar caves in Bihar. Adela thinks that she has been assaulted by Aziz, an Indian Muslim doctor, even though he is in an entirely different cave at the time of the incident. Marabar caves here provide a space—a borderland—for the writer to highlight the racial tensions and prejudices between the colonised Indians and the coloniser British.

In the South African context, the concept of borderland is important as it deals with the severe physical impact of apartheid on its white and black communities. It affected them through being forced to live in separate units and classes and generated fear and a sense of alienation towards each other. Writers such as the French-Tunisian writer Albert Memmi (1920–2020) in *The Coloniser and the Colonised* (1974) and Fanon Frantz in *Black Skin White Masks* (1967) have demonstrated how the myth of an unbridgeable gap between the black and the white races was created during the colonial period in history; the European exile caused the African displacement, forcing them to leave their tribal lands and to live apart even from their families. Crossing borders in the age of navigation muddled the earlier categorisations of white, black, and Coloured peoples and created identity crises in the post-colonial world. In twentieth-century South Africa, segregation and apartheid regulated a restricted social experience and identity, imposing different types of borders based on colour. When a writer like Gordimer was placed under constraints in a society like South Africa, she invented an unusual marginal world full of activities such as in *Occasion for Loving* (1963), *Burger's Daughter* (1979) and *My Son's Story* (1990) where her characters transform and discover their new selves to deal with the working of apartheid in South Africa. An unusual process of creativity is, indeed, at work in Gordimer's borderland, subverting issues of rigid boundaries which exist in her South African world.

Like Gordimer, the white South African writer Beverley Naidoo grew up under apartheid laws that gave privilege to white children. Black children were sent to separate, inferior schools; apartheid denied all children the right to grow up together with equality, justice, and respect. In her interview with Paromita Pain (2006), Beverley reveals how writing about issues of ethnicity, gender and violence has provided her with an opportunity to cross boundaries and imagine herself into the lives of characters often very different from herself. Her first novel, *Journey to Jo'burg* (1985) was banned under the apartheid rule; it describes a story of two children who endure enormous odds to reach their mother living and working far away from them.

In *Brave Borderland* (1935), the British writer, H. Drummond Gauld's reveals how the history of a country is largely that of its frontiers and events deriving therefrom. South African society is built on extreme margins, the political border, the border fence, the cultural boundary, the linguistic barrier, and the colour barrier. Cultural boundaries have been maintained in South Africa through devices like ritual initiations, secret activities, and legal barriers which restricted knowledge to group members and shielded white culture from African influences; the cultural distinctiveness can exist as long as two different societies remain separate from each other. This sense of cultural difference created a barrier in the minds of the white minority which led them to guard their political power and privileges in South Africa. In this context, the French historian Fustel de Coulanges (1830–1889) in *The Ancient City: A study on the Religion, Laws and Institutions of Greece and Rome* (1864) discusses how certain rituals, beliefs, everyday rites, and memory consecrated the sacred bounds of ancient cities and fortified cultural, geographical, and territorial boundaries between them. Such practices were boundary maintaining mechanisms that expressed and sustained the corporate identity of various groups in a society.

A culture is a body of customs, beliefs, and social institutions which overlooks the fact that people and society change at different levels for different reasons and that different cultures get influenced by each other through people's interactions; instead of remaining separate from each other, identities become juxtaposed in cultural diversity phenomenon, losing hold of cultural differences that previously have been validated and constructed on racial, religious, or political grounds. Every person is multicultural through the cultural metamorphosis that constantly takes place in every society. To deal with culture intertwined with multicultural categories of ethnicity, race, class, religion, gender, and sexual orientation, Bhabha in *The Location of Culture* (1994), stresses the need to establish hybrid intellectual spaces to describe heterogeneous peoples and places as one human world; hybridity challenges the ideological homogeneous concepts of colonialism, that is, viewing the human world as composed of separate and unequal peoples' cultures. The fact is that human cultures are neither coherent nor homogeneous; the cultural differences get reframed into multiculturalism as an individual's identity is in a continuous process of redefining itself in a multicultural society.

For Marx, culture is not an independent reality but it is inseparable from the historical conditions in which human beings create their material lives; the relations of dominance and subordination (exploitation) which govern the social and economic order of a country determine the whole cultural life of the society. This Marxist understanding of the class struggle as the motor of history is partially justifiable in the South African context where the division between the haves and the have-nots was marked by race. Economic explanations become insufficient for understanding the racial features of colonised societies like South Africa; capitalism was installed, there, through the coastal trade and the enforced labour of the black peoples. Race relations were crucial for the white colonisers in making available a labour force in South Africa.

In this regard, the last Prime Minister of the Cape Colony (1908–1910), John Xavier Merriman (1841–1926) remarked in 1908 that race consciousness is created by colonial hierarchies. (Ranger, 1983, 213) Indicting this colonial brutality, Aimé Césaire (1913–2008), the Afro-Caribbean writer and the founding member of the 1930s Negritude movement, claims in 'Discourse on Colonialism' (1950) that colonialism not only exploits but dehumanises and objectifies the colonised subject, as it degrades the coloniser himself. He explains this by a dark equation: 'colonisation = thingification.' (Pinkham,1972, 21) The white superiority complex had been its principal psychological tool to distract the colonised people from thinking about doing things in their way. In *Tamas* (1988), a novel set in the 1947 riots at the time of the partition of the Indian Sub-continent, the Indian writer Bhisham Sahni (1915–2003) presents an English Deputy Commissioner who is known for his shrewdness in handling the Hindus' and Muslims' violent confrontations. He is regarded as more sensible by the Indians in comparison to their judgements. They equate his far-sightedness with the ancient prophet figure Khizr who was well-known for his righteousness, great wisdom, and mystic knowledge; in various Islamic and non-Islamic traditions, Khizr is described as a God's messenger who guards the sea, teaches secret knowledge, and aids those in distress. However, the Deputy Commissioner's wife is appalled by the British policy—her husband's strategy of staying away from interfering with the Hindus and Muslims' religious affairs. She questions: 'Didn't human values mean anything anymore?' (*Tamas*, 107) In Nadine Gordimer's *The Lying Days* (1953), a novel set in the early apartheid years, the black girl in Helen's class attempts to write down every word of the lecture given by the white teacher. She is sure that she has a lot of catching up to do to get educated in a white way, yet she never succeeds. This psychological impact of racism was no less devastating for the colonised people than the plundering of their resources.

As a white South African writer, Gordimer's detached observation of her South African world is symbolic of a colonial vision; to be colonial means living in a strange land, and this applies even when the colonial's family has lived for generations in a foreign country. Of course, it is home but it is also alien, a place of deep cultural differences for them. This means that the white settler cannot, ultimately, transcend his foreignness; he cannot become part of Africa because his skin is white, and his ways are essentially European. In *Prospero & Caliban: The Psychology of Colonisation* (1956), the French psychoanalyst Octave Mannoni (1899–1989) attributes a basic inferiority complex to the coloniser. Though his analysis is focused on the Malagasy natives of Madagascar who were colonised by Europeans. He argues that the inferiority complex constitutes the main driving force of the colonisers which sets them apart from all other peoples in the world. The struggle with this complex, Mannoni argues, underlies European initiative, independence, creativity, and dominance. In her fiction, Gordimer brings into focus this white man's desire to believe in the gulf between him and the black man. This enables him to view the latter as an ignorant savage in contrast with his enlightened, civilising Self. This appears in the attitude of the white protagonist's European companions on the ship to Africa in *A World of Strangers* (1958), and the arrogance of the white travellers in 'The African Magician' (1965).

The colonial experience is, indeed, a history of madness. This appears in Joseph Conrad's *Heart of Darkness* (1902) in which the white characters become a spectre of madness: Kurtz goes mad whereas Marlow is in constant danger of losing his identity. This constant threat leads Marlow to retain his sanity by clinging to a European framework including the starched white shirt he insists on wearing daily. In *The Grass is Singing* (1950), Doris Lessing looks at the elements of social hierarchy, self-alienation, emotions, and psychological pressures which make their way in her white protagonist's life who prefers to behave as gentrified. Similarly, Alice Walker in *The Colour Purple* (1982) has approached the question of race and colour with a classic defence of negritude in American society. These novels show that race has formed a powerful ideological element in colonial and post-colonial history, as it affects the coloniser and the colonised.

Social divisions based on race have determined numerous colonial and post-colonial writings. For instance, *A Morning at the Office* (1964) in which the Guyanese writer, Edgar Mittelholzer (1909–1965) deals with psychological, physical, and mental barriers in a colonial setting and vividly describes a black youth's feelings of inferiority amongst white superiors. Edward Said in *Orientalism* (1978) calls the maintenance of such divisions a form of radical realism which seeks to institute Europe in superiority over its *Other*. According to him, Orientalism was a form of 'radical realism' which sought to institute Europe in 'flexible positional superiority over its Others [...] Orientalist discourse delivers an Other which is both an object of knowledge and surveillance and an object of libidinous impulses.' (1978, 2–3) This had been the effect of colonialism that broke its society into divisions. European colonialism propagated the concept of the *Self*, that is, the coloniser, and the *Other*, that is, the colonised. The former is related to everything which is superior in civilisation and the latter is considered savage. A physical line of demarcation is drawn between the *Self* and the *Other* from the very early times of colonisation which led to a mental block against each other's worlds. The physical boundary between the *Self* and the *Other* became a frontier where people from both sides used to gather. At first, the whites acted as masters and the blacks as slaves and servants. However, physical communication led the whites to enter into sexual relationships with the blacks. The resulting Coloured society produced a hybrid culture that acted as a bridge between the white and the black worlds. In this context, Homi Bhabha in *The Location of Culture* presents'unhomeliness' as a condition of being Coloured in South Africa. (1994, 13) He refers to the different houses in Gordimer's *My Son's Story* (1990) as symbolic of the compartmentalised South African society in which members of a Coloured family have to struggle to find a home for marginalised people like themselves.

Bhabha sees racism as a 'hangover' from a pre-modern episteme rather than recognising it as 'part of the historical traditions of civic and liberal humanism that create ideological matrices of national aspiration, together with their concepts of 'a people' and its imagined community.' (1994, 250) He questions Frantz Fanon's model of fixed colonial identity, that is, the *Self* and the *Other* polarities. Fanon saw the mind of the oppressed as being set in which he called a Manichean mould in which everything about the colonisers is regarded as evil and everything about the oppressed as good; Fanon's revolutionaries despise compromise and reconciliation. Christopher Heywood in his study of Gordimer's fiction (1983) discovers Fanon's aspirations being followed by Gordimer in her fiction such as in 'Some Monday for Sure' (1976), *Occasion for Loving* (1963), and *July's people* (1981). Since the 1960s, South Africa had become a place of violence that finally led to revolutionary changes in its political and social life. Gordimer's fiction records the mode of the era in *A Sport of Nature* (1987) and *My Son's Story* (1990).

In his rejection of Fanon who re-maps race and class divisions in *The Wretched of the Earth* as expressions of the relationship between the coloniser and the colonised on to one another (1963, 32), Bhabha believes that the colonial relationship is structured on both sides by forms of 'multiple and contradictory belief.' (1994, 75). Bhabha seeks to emphasise the mutuality and negotiations across the colonial divide. For him, the relationship between the coloniser and the colonised is more complex than Fanon implies, principally because the circulation of contradictory patterns of psychic effect in colonial relations (desire for, as well as fear of the Other) undermines their assumptions that the identities and positioning of the coloniser and the colonised exist in stable and unitary terms which are also absolutely distinct from, and necessarily in conflict with, each other. Bhabha claims that all cultures are impure, mixed and hybrid. (Bhabha, 1994, 2) Hybridity is a concept that Bhabha uses to describe the liberatory potential of the difference between and within cultures, which displaces, transforms, and subverts colonial norms in a way that is liberating for those oppressed. Historically, the emergence of cultural, religious, and ethnic Diasporas created new forms of identities in South African society such as the Afrikaners, the Coloureds, and the blacks. In her fiction, Gordimer constructs, in Benedict Anderson's terms, imagined communities to describe these forms of cultural hybridity which are shaped out of history and at the same time, in Frantz Fanon terms, reveals the struggle for the creation of a human world—that is a world of reciprocal recognitions.

The notion of borderland provides an opportunity for the quest for identity in modern fiction. The English poet Mathew Arnold (1822–1888) and the American-British poet T S Eliot (1888–1957), in their respective capacities, were concerned with the sense of self and loss of identity in the modern world. The English writer D H Lawrence's (1885–1930) sense of identity and sexuality led him to look for the reconstruction of self in the world. The Irish writer Samuel Beckett's (1906–1989) concept of zero identity has shaped the twentieth-century literary arena. Whereas the writings by South Africans, both black and white writers, present the modern literary consciousness of Africa: the former in search of an African's image and the latter in search of the white man's belonging to Africa. In Bessie Head's *A Question of Power* (1973), the central figure finds herself alienated from her environment, faces a crisis of identity, and feels neither at home in South Africa nor Botswana. Her anguish lies in that she does not feel properly African. Here, in this case, Bessie Head offers a diagnosis, that is, an unwarranted assertion of power produces madness but so too does unwarranted subservience to it. Peter Abrahams, a Cape Coloured himself, deals with the existence of the Coloured community in South African society in *The Path of Thunder* (1948). As the dominant reality of apartheid does not allow any alternative except to claim identity with whites, the Coloured characters are driven to a form of madness and death in the novel. Nadine Gordimer combined the vision of these writers and created a mode of urban realism to explore and comment on the apartheid era in her fiction. Where J M Coetzee represents the reality of the body in *Life and Times of Michael K* (1983) and *Foe* (1987), Mongane Serote's *To Every Birth its Blood* (1981) represents the collective black social body which prepares the ground for its future, Njabula Ndebele in *Fools* (1983) combines a sense of the township community as a social body, Gordimer's protagonist in *July's People* (1981) escapes from mental as well as a social breakdown by running towards the future.

Gordimer categorically deals with the physical impact of apartheid on people in South Africa in *A World of Strangers* (1958), *Occasion for Loving* (1963) and *Burger's Daughter* (1979). Physical borders and mental barriers generate a restricted social experience and identity, producing anxiety of limits in the forms of madness and hallucination in characters' lives in these novels. In this regard, breaking down her characters with shame is a process necessary for greater awareness. Madness is seen as a state of great potential, a dynamic process leading to change. In psychological terms, there is a very thin borderline between sane and insane worlds. The people who happen to visit that margin between the two entities develop a different outlook on themselves and the life around them. Similarly, Gordimer's characters undergo a world of borders where they confront the most feared and hated aspects of their selves. The experience provides them with another perspective on themselves and their South African world.

The concept of a borderland has achieved a prominent position in the psycho-analytical presentation of events and characters in fiction such as found in Doris Lessing's *The Grass is Singing* (1950). The novel deals with the story of a young white woman who has to live through poverty and social hardships and who suffers the psychological threats which are part of her white society. It becomes increasingly difficult for her to come to terms with the fact that she has found herself sexually attracted by the black Moses who is a servant in her house. Mary gradually loses the soundness of her mind which ultimately becomes the cause of her death towards the end of the novel. As a white person, she is profoundly alienated from the African continent and avoids any real contact with it. She hates it. She whips Moses, the black house boy in the fields, but when he comes inside the house, she is frightened of him. Her fear that the bush is creeping in towards her to get her is a kind of a threat to the Africans which may do the same as she does to them. Here, sexuality becomes a symbolic marker of colonialism because it upholds the boundaries to prevent miscegenation from taking place in a white woman's life. Lessing's character reveals the intensity of the struggle over the limits in colonial society. The central character in Alan Paton's *Cry the Beloved Country* (1948) lives at the margins of two opposite worlds, one real and the other, the world of thoughts. The experience leads Paton's character to a fearful vision: soon the black people will start hating the white people in South Africa and it would be then too late for the latter to become friends with the former. In Gordimer's fiction too, this frontier acts as the little house on the prairie or a treasure island which represents the characters' insecurities and instabilities. The symbol finds its way in different forms, sometimes appearing as a theme and at other times, taking control of the text as in *A World of Strangers* (1958) and in 'The Train from Rhodesia' (1949). It may exist in the construction of a plot such as places or physical spaces where the main action of the story takes place or it may become a trait or a flaw in a character's personality for people who live on the edges between two conflicting worlds of action, as in Jessie in *Occasion for Loving* (1963).

Several other writers have taken their characters to the border between madness and sanity to achieve greater awareness about their inner selves as well as the world outside. Mongane Serote in *To Every Birth Its Blood* (1981) deals with the madness of the present that is experienced by the central character, Tsi Molope. He is caught up in a world of degradation and breakdown, with no escape. When the character joins an underground political organisation, he discovers the unknown present for blacks like him. This new realism defines a rational future for him and becomes a point of return to his sanity. Similarly, Mtutuzeli Matshoba in *Call Me Not a Man* (1979) presents a glimpse of the experience of the past: 'The wall became symbolic of the wall of man-made laws that demarcates the black man from the rest of the mankind and makes him the doormat of the races. At that stage, I felt a new strength [...].' (CMNM, 53) The black character keeps on surviving even in the worst of circumstances which generate, for him, a spirit of hope that physical and mental barriers can be broken and he, as a black, will be a free man one day. Olive Schreiner in *The Story of an* African *Farm* (1883) and Nadine Gordimer almost throughout her fiction have utilised similar kinds of techniques in the development of the action in their narratives. The act of meditation which is woven into the development of events in *The Story of an* African *Farm* leads the characters to raise queries about their religious thinking. The active thought-process in Gordimer's *The Conservationist* (1978) allows Mehring, the main character little time to mend his ways. He commits suicide in the end. These characters rigorously oscillate between the world of reality and the world of their thoughts which becomes a study of their inner selves. The theme of borderland in Gordimer's fiction is, both literary and metaphorically, a site for construction and articulation of identities, a place betwixt and between cultures, a vague and undetermined place created by an unnatural boundary or a border fence; cultural, political, linguistic, and social boundaries between the whites and the blacks were maintained, indeed, invented in South Africa. Gordimer's borderland explores how these boundaries intersect with the individual lives of people in South Africa. It is in the actions of her characters living in time and place that these forces are embodied, interpreted, contested, and negotiated in her fiction.

Bhabha's theoretical work on borderland in *The Location of Culture* is related to the issues of race, borders, and identities in Gordimer's fiction. Bhabha defines his notion of borderland by explaining it in several ways such as the domain of the beyond, the liminal or the third space. He also names it as the 'interstices'. (1994, 2) It means a minute opening or crevice between things such as the space between adjacent atoms in a crystal lattice. Liminality is derived from the Latin word, *limen*, a threshold. This is a quality of the second stage of a ritual in the theories of the Dutch-German-French ethnographer Arnold van Gennep (1873–1957) and British anthropologist Victor Turner (1920–83); a rite of passage is a ceremony or ritual of the passage which occurs when an individual leaves one group to enter another; it involves a significant change of status in society. This rite of passage has three phases: *Separation*, that is, the rites of separation from a previous world, *Liminality*, that is, the pre-liminal rites—those (liminal or threshold) rites executed during the transitional stage, and, *Incorporation*, that is the post liminal rites—the ceremonies of incorporation into the new world. So the change is accomplished by separating the individual from the previous social group; followed by a period during which one is betwixt and between neither one status nor the other (the liminal stage); and the following period during which one's new social status is confirmed. The liminal state is characterised by ambiguity, openness, and indeterminacy. One's sense of identity dissolves to some extent, bringing about disorientation. Liminality is a period of transition during which normal limits to thought, self-understanding and behaviour are relaxed, opening way to something new. Liminal zones in Gordimer's fiction are peripheral positions in marginal spaces where new exciting and empowering forms of identity may be articulated such as in *July's People* (1981). This resonates Bhabha's description of identity which is differential, lucid and, in theory at least, infinitely displaceable. Whilst talking about margins in a minority discourse, about the space of people and halfway populations, and discussing the cultural temporality of the nation as a social reality, Bhabha emphasises, in *Nation and Narration* (1990), the need to rethink questions of identity, social agency and national affiliation. These entities, he notes, are in the continuous process of redefining themselves. Identities go through a process of transformation in every society such as the evolved Afrikaners' identity and the development of the apartheid system in South African society. This justifies Stuart Hall's assertion that identities are not firmly anchored or fixed to the spot, but are not entirely free-floating:

> Every identity is placed, positioned, in a culture, a language, a history [...] It insists on specificity, on conjuncture. But it is not necessarily armour-plated against other identities. It is not tied to fixed, permanent, unalterable oppositions. It is not wholly defined by exclusion. (1987, 45–46)

Gordimer's fiction projects this liminal status of identities in her characters' shift from liberal to radical approaches towards the struggle against apartheid such as in *The Late Bourgeois World* (1966) and in breaking of the polarised and compartmentalised South African society out of the social and colour barriers such as in *None to Accompany Me* (1994).

Like Bhabha, the beyond signifies a spatial distance in Gordimer's fiction. It marks progress and promises the future, but the very experience of the beyond makes her characters displaced and they cannot return to the present, they cannot be the same people again. They step into the beyond but then return to the present transformed. The white protagonist in *A World of Strangers* (1958) and the black character in *Occasion for Loving* (1963), for instance, are affected by the experience of their socialising across the racial spectrum. Also, displacement is a necessary process to get to the moment of transit, to the moment of realisation and transformation in Gordimer's fiction such as in *July's People* (1981). The protagonist's displaced life in an African village brings her up against the illusion of white innocence. Bhabha's notion of borderland provides not only an intervening space but also gives 'a revisionary time' (Bhabha, 1994, 7) to people who return to the present with a sense of the new, that is, the new-sense that provides an ongoing negotiating process for personhood and helps marginalised people and communities to build their restless identities. In *July's People* (1981), Gordimer displaces her characters in a spatial distance where they dwell, though for some time, in society beyond their South African world, and then return with an aptitude, in Bhabha's words, 'to touch the future on its hither side' (1994, 7) in their present South African society. In this process, the characters find themselves introduced to a sense of the new, that is, the utilisation of available resources for syncretism, juxtaposition, and integration of black and white societies in South Africa. The presentation of such a world in her borderland serves to create and guess in her imaginary plots the future of South Africa. Bhabha's 'third space' (1994,1) is the linguistic split and an overlap between the subject of the statement and the subject who speaks, reads, and identifies with it; the subject written into a statement and the person speaking, reading, or identifying with that subject position inhabit two very different cultural and discursive environments. There is therefore both a join and a divide between these two subjects, a linguistic space that both joins and divides. Bhabha calls this in-between space, the third space.

This third space has affinities with the notion of potential space found in the theory of play developed by English psycho-analyst D W Winnicot (1896–1971) in *Playing and Reality* (1971). Winnicot contends that cultural experience begins with creative living first manifested in play. It is the play that helps to bridge the gap between mother and child, in the transition between the child viewing herself as part of the mother and realising herself as distinct from the mother. Play is a third area that is neither inner or personal psychic reality nor the external world but rather the potential space between the individual and the environment. For Bhabha, Winnicot's potential space considers the relation of the Self to the Other in a way that does not isolate either but shows how difference, even within the *Self*, is related to the *Other*. Through play, the child is both joined to and separated from the world around it. The potential space is that space in which paradoxically one both finds and creates the world. It is a space in which there is an interplay between me and not-me, where I and not-me are both merged, and always emergent as distinct. In Nadine Gordimer's fiction, a similar kind of physical space, that is, the 'third space' (Bhabha, 1994, 1) is provided to the characters through borderland situations. It presents a society that goes beyond the polarities of the *Self* and the *Other.* In the South African context, however, this seems inapplicable in front of the prevalent apartheid in every sphere of South African life. But it successfully gets itself depicted in the lucidity of characters' identities in borderland situations and encounters in Gordimer's fiction. For Bhabha, the notion of borderland is an aesthetic discipline to attain new avenues of knowledge and understanding of one's identity in his or her society. Gordimer's fiction steps into a similar space where her characters acknowledge new sensibilities about themselves and their South African world as in *A World of Strangers*, *Burger's Daughter* and *July's People*.

PART II: MEMOIR

Stellenbosch (16–21 May 2005)

The Afrikaner-dominant city of Stellenbosch was my starting point to explore the past South African world of apartheid where it was conceived and developed as a racist ideology. There was a story to tell—from intellectual to a layman—of the apartheid era. A new South Africa is emerging out of the identity and power politics of the white South African rulers that previously generated a world of legal boundaries in the form of apartheid depriving the non-white South African subjects of their land and basic human rights for centuries.

My encounter with South African society didn't have to wait till I would have reached Stellenbosch. On a British Airways night flight from London to Cape Town, the person sitting next to me on the plane was an Afrikaner, a Boer, Theo Geyser. He was very amused at my survey of his Boer features: he had blue eyes but no red hair. The Afrikaners have a distinguished variety of blue and dark eyes, and red and blonde hair which have occurred due to the fusion between different European races. Professor Annie Gagiano at Stellenbosch University, as a proud Afrikaner, confirmed this distinction in our conversation later.

An enriching conversation took place with Theo about apartheid and the society in South Africa. He suggested replacing the word *Coloured* with the word *brown* in my terminology for the people of colour in South Africa. Theo also believed that South Africa is different in spirit from what one can gather from books. He agreed that Stellenbosch is the right place to begin my fieldwork as it had been the centre of apartheid; the philosophy of apartheid was propagated and developed there. According to Professor Annie, it is difficult to substantiate whether apartheid as a philosophy was propounded in Stellenbosch but as most of the early apartheid founders, prime ministers and other dignitaries did study in the University of Stellenbosch—most of the buildings on the campus had been named after them—so one can assume so.

Theo admitted that the Afrikaners were fully responsible for the formal creation of apartheid society in South Africa, though they were wrong in their approach. Apartheid had made a mess of everybody's life in South Africa. It was cruel and something very unnatural. Theo recommended visiting one of the squatter camps during my stay to see for myself what apartheid had done to most people in South Africa. But Theo insisted that the Afrikaners themselves had suffered too in their South African lives; his grandmother fought in the Anglo-Boer war against the English, and she had harsh things to talk about the concentration camps and the way the English looted their houses, killed, and abducted their children and raped their women. After the war, most of the Afrikaners as Boers were very poor. Theo himself was born on a farm in Stellenbosch and has lived there all his life. As an Afrikaner, he can trace his origins to German and French. He had been studying in Europe for some time, research in philosophy and theology. I envied him for understanding and knowing so well the deconstruction theory as developed by the Algerian-born French philosopher Jacques Derrida (1930–2004). He also seemed very much interested in the German philosopher Friedrich Wilhelm Nietzsche's life (1844–1900) and his philosophy of denying the self-ego and rising above it so that a peaceful world can be created. Later, Santa Hofmeyer-Joubert, my host in Stellenbosch, informed me that Theo leads a religious group in the Church who are very active in exploring the problems of self through spiritual and meditative activities.

By profession, Theo was a musician. During apartheid in the seventies, he was banned from travelling abroad for making revolutionary music against the oppression that existed in South African society. He then ran a private charity in support of poor black South Africans. He was not happy with the way the present black majority rule was running the government; according to Theo, the personal interests of the blacks in power who suddenly have become rich dominate the issues which need urgent attention such as housing, medication, and employment for most of the poor South Africans. They have simply forgotten what they once stood for. Previously, it was apartheid to blame for the suffering of the people of colour in South Africa. Now, even though the apartheid system is no longer working, still, the present rulers prefer to run the government through the same colonial management giving way to corruption and nepotism which is much higher than it used to be under the apartheid government. But Theo was full of praise for Nelson Mandela and wished that he should have governed South Africa for some more time. Theo, however, agreed that it would not be fair to look for a change in a short period of ten years' black majority rule when the damage done by apartheid is so extensive that it requires much more time than expected to get rid of the colonial ways in South African life. Before going to sleep on the plane, I happened to watch the film Hotel Rowanda. Somehow, I found the rivalries and battles between the Hutus and Tutsi tribes of Rwanda similar to the struggle between the English and the Afrikaners for power and control in South Africa.

Landing in the morning, Theo pointed out the areas in Cape Town which were townships. From that height in the sky, the houses looked like small boxes of similar shapes built at a particular area of the land.

Later, I had a good look at them along with the squatter camps and shacks which occupy the sides of the motorway leading to Stellenbosch. At the immigration desk at the airport, the black female officer asked which Pakistan I belong to, East or West. I was surprised at her question because as far as I knew there has always been one Pakistan. First-hand knowledge: when it comes to identity, classification is very important in South African society. The officer had to fill in this information, otherwise, the computer will not let her proceed further. The electronic record of the immigration desk needed correction; geographically, Pakistan had two separate parts, East and West (I come from West) but it was never two separate countries. I told her that East Pakistan had become Bangladesh a long time ago in 1970. The black officer seemed not impressed by the information, kept doing her job and let me go. At the customs, my baggage was checked by an Asian Muslim officer. So it was a piece of evidence that the Muslim community exists in South Africa about which Gordimer knew little. Santa was surprised at receiving her guest that is me, in European dress; somehow she was under the impression that she is going to meet a conventional Muslim girl—maybe with a headscarf. Seventy-one years old Santa was exceptionally active and without a single wrinkle on her face: Afrikaner genes or South African weather! She later confessed the secret of her youth: two glasses of wine every day.

The thirty minutes' drive from Cape Town to Stellenbosch was an experience. As informed by Theo, the first noticeable sight was the shacks. There were unending rows of shacks on both sides of the road as one leaves Cape Town for Stellenbosch. Santa was a little uncomfortable and seemed a bit embarrassed at this reality of her South African world. 'This should not have happened' was her first comment. She informed that most of the black population living in these shacks were brought here from Transkei (Eastern Cape Province) by the ANC to win the votes of the Xhosa tribe in the election. She revealed that it is amazing to see how well-dressed people come to work from these shacks. They have communal toilets and no proper bath facilities. Their cleanliness and good hygiene are commendable despite the lack of proper sanitation. The people in shacks and squatter camps have been offered places in the townships but they refused to go there because the roofs of the houses constructed in townships are not good enough to protect them either against heat in summer or cold in winter; in summer, the township buildings become hotter and in winter they become colder due to bad construction. In comparison, the shacks are more airy and comfortable.

One feels an odd vastness in the South African landscape—a vast space to create. Like visiting his farm makes Mehring conscious of the vastness in the landscape in Gordimer's *The Conservationist*, one does feel carried away by the space factor in the South African landscape. Therefore, most houses in South Africa are in one-storey construction because there is enough space to build and create on as much land as one wants to. Stellenbosch is a valley of beautiful mountains and huge vineyards. The town was less crowded. It reminded me of Ghalanai, a small town in a valley that is covered by the mountains from all sides in the border tribal area—a kind of buffer zone between Pakistan and Afghanistan. In that valley, the mountains have army—militia posts on each peak to guard the valley on both sides. Whenever a vehicle has to stop at the check-post to get into the valley, one can enjoy seeing the stunningly beautiful valley, especially in evening lights. On that point of entry, I always enjoyed complimenting my father who was the administrator of that valley, with Shakespeare's character, King Lear's style, *Here lies my kingdom*. My father's eyes used to smile back at the comment. I felt the same as I entered Stellenbosch. Suddenly one gets a feeling that one is in a valley, a place of natural beauty with green and dry mountains existing side by side. The huge mountains and their landscape make their strong presence felt; humans look very small in front of them. Keeping my Muslim background in mind, Santa enquired if I would be interested to visit one of these vineyards. I was very amused by her comment.

One can see black people walking at the side of the road. They still travel by foot. A black woman was standing by the road to hitchhike. This reminded me of Gordimer's story in which a black man is given a lift by a liberal white South African woman and her English guest who is driving the car. When the black man is dropped off, the white characters tend not to look back in contemplation that he might be waving at them—liberal dilemma—to be or not to be. I asked Santa to tell me about the separate seating area for the whites and the blacks in the buses. Santa said that those buses were a common feature of big cities like Cape Town and Johannesburg. But in Stellenbosch, there was never a good transport system. Taxis, and small vans have been popular but they are not safe. Yes, there were separate seating areas for the whites and the blacks in the public transport system. At traffic lights on the roads in South Africa, black traders attempt to sell fruit and accessories. I was amused to hear Santa saying *Dankie* to the seller every time. It sounded as if she is responding to their offer by calling them a donkey. *Dankie* in Afrikaans means *Thank you*.

It is interesting to recall what Santa told me in small statements about her South Africa during that journey. As per her knowledge and experience, she answered my questions, and she was very clear in what she was saying:

- Afrikaans became an official language eighty years ago. Due to the rift between the English and the Afrikaners, it couldn't be done so earlier.
- South Africa is called a Rainbow country because of the diversity that exists in every sphere of South African life.
- To call the natives Kafir was not meant bad. When I told Santa that it is an Arabic word meaning non-believer, she was really surprised because she thought it was just a slang word.
- Xhosa is a tribe that lives in Transkei in the Western Cape. Mandela is a Xhosa.
- Hottentots and Bushmen used to live in the Northern Cape.
- Mbeki stays more out of the country—seems worried more about solving problems for the greater Africa than the ones at home. He doesn't go against Mugabe of Zimbabwe because he is older than him. In African culture, it is considered bad manners to challenge the decision of one who is older than you. Mandela is against Mugabe and has criticised him in public for his aggressive policies. Mandela has also denounced Mbeki for his HIV policy. Mbeki's government does not consider Aids a serious problem in South Africa. His health policy provides minimum medical support to Aids victims. Instead, people are advised to pay attention to their hygiene which will cure them of the disease. Here Santa told me about the recent cult amongst the Africans that if one can have sex with a virgin, it will cure him of the Aids problem. So many young girls are under threat; it was in the news that some Africans had carried out this cult by utilising their female children to get rid of their Aids problem.
- It is not only the whites who own the mining business in present South Africa. The owner of the biggest mine in South Africa is a black woman nowadays.
- Santa tells from her own experience that the Coloured are very nice and polite people but you cannot trust them as you can trust a black man.

- I was also informed that the media was not previously as developed as it is now. On the farms, the radio reception was not very good. Newspapers used to arrive late sometimes two days later; if people didn't have opportunities to know things on time, how far would it bc fair to blame poor struggling Afrikaners of rural areas for the apartheid that was groomed and created by the Afrikaners who lived urban? I didn't know whether to agree with her or not. I just listened.

Over a deliciously South African bean soup in traditional bowls with one handle, I had an interesting conversation with Santa. She summed up what she has been telling so far: Santa's mother was born in 1916 just after the Anglo-Boer war was over. Santa herself lived her earlier days of life on a farm in Orange Free State. Her father was a teacher and principal of a school which catered for white children in that area. Her grandfather was also a teacher who went from Cape Town to Orange Free State to spread education amongst the white masses. It was only in their house that radio existed, and other white people of the area used to come and listen to the news on the radio in her house. Santa was talking about the period 1928—that is, after the Anglo-Boer war when Boers were defeated, and the English won the war and went after gold and diamond mining. What the Boers built in one hundred and fifty years for themselves in South Africa, the English destroyed it and completely took it over for political and economic reasons.

During and after the Anglo-Boer war, the English victors set the concentration camps where women and children were raped and tortured. The Boers were reduced to poverty and hunger. Poor whites used to work in Santa's parents' house. Later, Santa took me to meet her mother who lived in an old people's home in Stellenbosch. To my surprise, she looked much younger than Santa—not a single wrinkle on her face despite poor health! Santa's mother also confirmed the poverty that existed amongst the Afrikaners after the Anglo-Boer war and revealed that they had fed hungry Boer children several times at their school from their pocket with cheese, bread, and milk.

In WW1 and 11, the Boers were on the side of the Germans. Hitler was a hero for them. His voice was very impressionistic on the radio. Santa still remembered Hitler's voice. He made powerful speeches about the purity of race which appealed to the Boers who hated English as Hitler hated the Jews. Hitler was a big influence, and it was only later that the Boers discovered the concentration camps set up by Hitler in which many Jews were killed and tortured just like the English did to the Boers during the war-time. The Boers were embarrassed for what they stood for but it was too late then; Jan Christian Smuts (1870–1950), the Afrikaner army General and a statesman later supported English in the war. When World War 1 was fought, the memory of their mothers and sisters being taken to the concentration camp by the English in the Anglo-Boer war was still alive in the minds of most of the Boers. That is why they were in favour of siding Hitler against the English in the war. This gave way to the idea of apartheid (racism—separate lives) amongst the Boer intellectuals of the time who seemed very impressed by Hitler's idea of purity of race.

Santa herself grew up with Sotho people who used to work on their farm in Orange Free State. That part of South Africa had and still has a Sotho population. In her times, there were not many *Coloured* people around in that area. On the farms, these Sothos lived in labour cottages which were made of clay and bricks and constructed next to each other. Santa told me that the natives don't like to live in a single house that is not in close quarters with the other house. They always prefer to stay or live together. She recalled an incident from her childhood when she had stepped out of the house without telling her parents to visit the black quarters to listen to their singing. It was the only time her father gave her corporal punishment for leaving the house without his permission. Santa said that the Sotho people are, in her words, 'very sweet', polite and submissive people, unlike Zulus who were warriors. They are very well-behaved people. Also, they keep their houses very clean and tidy. I found it interesting to notice Santa repeatedly saying how the Boers trained them in different skills. Santa unconsciously used the word 'trained' on several occasions in her conversation about black people. It kept on reminding me of Fanon's presentation of the coloniser's psyche which always believed that he was superior. For Santa, her parents, and the other Afrikaners like them had always kept a paternal attitude towards the labourers on their farms—we trained them—we gave them uniforms—we taught them manners—this amused me to no end. Santa admitted that she found it very strange when the blacks came up with the idea that they have their own culture. However, she agreed that the natives of the South African land were not heathens as believed by early white settlers. They were believers and had their code of ethics for how to behave and how not to behave but which the whites couldn't understand because the missionaries came, and they wanted to teach them Christianity.

I told Santa how much I was moved by reading Katherine Heywood's book *Cape Hills in the Sunlight* (1964). The Afrikaners had their difficult times when they had to trek inland from place to place. They, no doubt, deserve due recognition for the struggle in the development of the land they lived on. I told her that I found one of Professor Christopher's drawings in his mother's book. Many people know Professor Christopher an authority on the history of South African Literature but less know that he is a very good painter too. In Santa's collection of things of arts and books, I have seen postcards superbly painted by him. Why do you like to travel to Europe so often, I asked Santa. Her answer was: 'I love to go back to Europe, that's true, maybe our roots are there.' But I also saw her reading Die Burger, the Afrikaner newspaper and she keenly watched Afrikaner's soaps on the TV. I wondered at what point people accept that their identity has now changed.

Santa later accompanied me to the Stellenbosch village museum which displays four different periods of Dutch settlement by preserving houses from the periods 1709, 1789, 1803 and 1850. These houses project how and under what circumstances the Dutch settlers used to live in South Africa. How and where they used to store their food and everyday necessities of life. What types of utensils, pots, cutlery, chinaware, and furniture were in fashion and what was the quality of their general life. In the 1709 display, there were bamboo and a lemon tree at the back of the house which was permanent features of the household those days. The Dutch settlers used to preserve dry fish by hanging them on the ceiling. The 1789 displays a magistrate's house. The English influence is visible in décor in later period houses. Santa informed that Cape Malay people have not been only the best chefs but also very good furniture makers. Most of the displays of woodwork and design of furniture in these houses are excellent examples of their art of work. There was also a room on display that showed where the slaves used to live and how the feet of the slaves were put in chains—like the police handcuffs—who tended to run away. This visit to the museum was one of the best experiences of my life, going back to the history of four centuries ago. It is amazing to know how the Dutch managed to bring the necessities and luxuries of the European lifestyle through ships to Africa.

Santa cooked *mealimeal* with vegetables at my request for our dinner together. I had read about *mealimeal* in the books only—the staple diet of black South Africans. They eat it with spinach and vegetables. *Mealimeal* is made with white corn flour and is soggy in appearance. Its taste reminded me of *Bajara* roti—a popular bread made with white corn flour and consumed with spinach (preferably) in rural areas in Pakistan.

Traditional African mealie meal grinder and soup bowl

Meeting Academics/Professionals at the University of Stellenbosch

The University of Stellenbosch is a place of impressive big, beautiful buildings and has an aura of its own. Students and academics from different ethnic backgrounds are visible utilising the facility side by side with one another. Professor Annie Gagiano, perfect in her appearance as an Afrikaner woman—blue eyes and blonde hair—welcomed into her office at the Department of English at Stellenbosch University. Like Santa, she spoke English with an accent and revealed the strength of an Afrikaner woman in her. She has lived all her life in Stellenbosch and loves the place very much. The view of mountains from her office window was very romantic; she said that she adores this view when the fog veils and then unveils the peak of the mountains at various times. Regarding the status of Afrikaners in South African society, Annie explained that a rift and struggle for power between the English and the Afrikaners existed since the early times of their first contact with each other and it still prevails in new South Africa. She is not a great supporter of Afrikanerdom but she always speaks for the contribution of Afrikaners like Brown Fisher who sacrificed their lives in the struggle against apartheid. That is why, despite criticism from various sections of her South African society, Annie had been at the forefront of the campaign which led to honouring Brown Fisher with a Doctorate in recognition of his efforts to bring a change in South African society. About Stellenbosch, as being the birthplace of apartheid, Annie was of the view that it is difficult to pinpoint any particular site of birth but it is a fact that most of the apartheid supporters were Dutch in origin and who became politicians afterwards had studied in Stellenbosch. Annie admitted that there had been a distinct minority of Afrikaners who were against apartheid but not the majority. The reason simply was that resistance against apartheid could make people's lives uncomfortable, so most of them preferred to stay away or ignore what the apartheid government was doing with the non-white people in South Africa.

Regarding apartheid and racism in South African society, Annie recommended the poems written in the 1820s; Michael Chapman has published a paper book of South African poetry in this regard. There are many other accounts available in South African Literature which reveal the history of racism since the times of early European settlers such as the role and contribution of Christian missionaries who were profoundly racists. That is why, for Annie, apartheid is an ethos, that is, a distinctive character, spirit, and attitudes of a people—the Afrikaners—who lived through the colonial culture or era. As regards, the dispute over the land between the white settlers and the natives of South Africa that had been a big issue since the early times, here one should not forget, that Annie stressed the point, that such claims over the land had been a reason for big fights even in between the natives of the land such as the land dispute between the Koikoi tribe and Bantu people. Antie Krog's *Change of Tongue* and *Country of My Skull* are worth reading texts to understand the complexity of the South African situation that prevailed and still exists amongst different races in South Africa. Charles Eglington is worth reading in this regard.

For Annie, liberalism, like apartheid, was an ethos too. She also believed that the liberals were the real beneficiaries of the Truth and Reconciliation project in new South Africa. She gave the example of Rosa in Gordimer's *Burger's Daughter* who is a liberal character and her entry to radicalism is dependent on when transformation happens in her character. Annie revealed that, during apartheid, young black South Africans had resentment against the Liberal Party for its slide away and keeping them out from its membership; Helen Suzmen, the chairperson of the Liberal Party asked its members of different ethnic origins—non-white liberals—to resign so that the Party can survive under the apartheid Law that allowed the creation of a party on one racial grouping only.

On the question of Gordimer not knowing much about the Muslim community in South Africa but whenever she created Muslim characters—though rarely, she has presented them very well such as in *The Pick Up*, Annie said that Gordimer has lived all her life in the North of South Africa where there is less Muslim presence in everyday life as compared to the Western Cape where Muslims are settled in a big community. In terminology, the Cape Malay community who originally came from Malaysia as slaves is classified as Muslims in racial grouping in South Africa. So, Gordimer rarely would have come across any real Muslim character. But we should not ignore the fact that Gordimer is a well-read woman who does her proper homework before starting her writing project. Here, Annie revealed that Muslim society has gone through a distinctive change with the demise of apartheid in recent years. In this regard, South African writer, and filmmaker Rayda Jacobs (1947-to date) is a promising Muslim writer who has done well in her collection of short stories *Post-cards from South Africa* (2004).

About the reception of Gordimer's work at home in South Africa, though she is an internationally acclaimed writer, Annie was of the view that prophets had never been valued by their community, so Gordimer had to go through the same dilemma in her own South African society. This has made her cold and distant in her attitude towards the masses in general. Her Jewish identity could also be one of the factors in this regard. Annie had read most of Gordimer's works and she liked *My Son's Story* and *The Pick-Up*. She said that Zoe Wicomb's 'David's Story' is a direct reference to *My Son's Story*. And that resented Wicomb—the way Gordimer portrayed his story in her novel. Annie had read in the newspapers about the recent row between the biographer Ronald Roberts and Gordimer over the publication of her biography. Her view on the subject was that Gordimer is a much-acclaimed figure and sometimes people like Roberts creates drama to get undue publicity. Annie believed that the authentic South African critics of Gordimer's work are Stephen Clingman who now lives in the USA, Catherine Wagner, Hermione Lee, and Dorothy Driver who supervised Ph.D. research work of Meg Samuelson, a lecturer at the Department then. Annie also revealed that Gordimer is close in her friendship with Mongane Wally Serote (1944-to date), the black South African writer in English.

In our scheduled one-to-one sitting, Professor Derek Klopper, Head of the English Department at the University of Stellenbosch initially appeared a bit distant in his conversation but later he opened and explained that there are painful memories of apartheid times and whenever one is asked to speak about them, one cannot help himself from not getting sensitive about that horrible era in South African history. Derek confirmed that the English did loot during the Anglo-Boer war and had set up concentration camps to destroy the world that Afrikaners created for themselves after a long struggle against the natives in South Africa. Then Derek spoke about his personal experience of living through apartheid. He was born and brought up in an Afrikaner family. Apartheid was a system of life then and he was part of it until he came to know about the Civil Rights Movement in America. This made him conscious of his South African world. Gordimer's characters also become conscious of what is happening around them through an incident or at a certain moment in their life. Most of the time and in many cases, people generally are not conscious of their surroundings. A person who is born and brought up under a certain system then accepts it as a normal life until something happens to register whether he is on the right or wrong side of the world. Derek remembered that when the UN challenged and considered South Africa' conquest of Namibia as illegal, it also made people aware of the oppression and injustice which were carried out by the apartheid government inside South Africa. In his student life, Derek participated in resisting politics and joined the Pretoria anti-conscription campaign which later became associated with UDF—the United Democratic Front. It amused Derek to tell that he was also in that group of students who attempted to Africanise South African literature. In this regard, Derek finds poetry—a non-essential way of thinking—and music as good sources for establishing a connection with the non-white people in South Africa. This reminded me of Theo.

About Gordimer's work, Derek believed that she deals with issues related to identity politics in her work such as language and identity discussed in *The Pick-Up*. Identity and its limitations have always been a factor in the creation of borders in societies everywhere in the world. In this regard, Anita Gosh and Salman Rushdie have talked about psychic borders in their work. In Travel writing, one can find similar accounts of the spaces which have inter-subjective locations such as the Eastern Cape which was, historically, the meeting and confronting place between Europe and Africa—the bordering that separates and connects at the same time. For Derek, the true people of South Africa now are the people of the Western Cape, and he would call them, the 'Coloured Afrikaners'. That evening, over a cup of tea with South African Rusks—a kind of local biscuits, I kept on thinking about how far the Afrikaners could be held responsible for the racial complexity in the South African world.

During my visits to Stellenbosch University, I was invited by Dr Dan Lehman, a visiting American Professor at the Department to speak about my area of work in an undergraduate seminar; the text under study was Antie Krog's *A Change of Tongue* with special reference to the theme of cross borders in South African society.

As an exercise, R. P. Gaylard, a then lecturer in English at the University introduced the idea of notebook emptying; the students referred to Najibulo Ndebele's *Cry of Winnie Mandela* to stress the importance of collective memory in a society like South Africa. I noticed that the undergraduate overseas students in the seminar hardly knew about Nelson Mandela's contribution to South African society except that he is a great leader.

I also had the chance to meet three young English lecturers at the University for lunch: Meg Samuelson (then Dorothy Driver's Ph.D. student), Lucy Graham (then a Ph.D. student at Oxford), and Chris Warres (recently finished his Ph.D. at Cambridge). They were surprised to find me looking into the issues which have become things of the past. Like the students of the undergraduate class, they belonged to the new South Africa—not interested in reflecting on the mistakes and blunders of older generations. During my lunch with them in a cafe, I could not stop myself from imagining as if I was sitting with Gordimer's characters and not the real people. In appearance, Lucy appeared to me like Jessie in *Occasion for Loving* and Chris as Toby in *A World of Strangers* but both didn't have the traits of the characters I looked for.

The next day, a brief session took place with a promising young South African Muslim writer of Asian origin and critic of Bhabha's work, Dr Ashraf Jamal—somehow I found Dr Jamal another Bhabha in the making. He appeared very aloof; it came across as if he was not interested in his religion and his identity as a South African of Asian origin. He was born in South Africa but grew up abroad until he came back to do his Ph.D. at the University of Natal; his Ph.D. thesis was on 'Predicaments of Culture' which explored Bhabha's ideology of culture and identity. I am asked to contact Liz Gunner at Pietermaritzburg who can send me a copy of Stephen Helgersson's thesis on Nadine Gordimer, Coetzee, and Ndebele (Publication of University of Natal Press). I am also advised to investigate the work of Glenn Cowley which might be relevant to my area of study.

My last one-to-one sitting at Stellenbosch University was with Shaun Viljoen, a *Coloured* lecturer in English who was then in the process of finishing his Ph.D. on the works of black South African writer Richard Moore Rive (1931–1989). To speak about Rive's relationship with Gordimer, Viljoen said that Gordimer has been a liberal humanist who believed in racial harmony. According to his reading, Gordimer's best work is 'Something Out There'. She artistically creates the fear of the blacks. She is concerned with what makes us human, what constitutes human—and that is what she focuses on. Viljoen's comment reminded me of the way Gordimer presents the response of the white woman to her husband's inhuman attitude towards the black boy in 'Train From Rhodesia'. In real life, Viljoen was classified as *Coloured*. During apartheid days, it was tremendously difficult for people of colour to find ways to progress and compete but he was lucky enough not to go through much hardship. Viljoen was not comfortable answering the question of whether he ever felt inferior to the whites in South Africa. But he admitted that there were psychological pressures that do dominate one's mind whilst in contact with people across the racial spectrum. This reminded me of the young black attendant who let me in every time with great respect and without checking my letter of permission to enter the library. His name was Qobolakhe Botha. He explained that his surname means Mowo, meaning greetings. He could tell that he was black and a Xhosa. I asked him whether he had experience with the Bantu schooling system but such education didn't exist in his school as far as he knew. Neither he had an answer to why native and local languages were neglected or not spoken as English and Afrikaans. It is a pity to see the psychological effects of apartheid written on black and *Coloured* faces. I wondered whether the politeness in their behaviour, in general, was an act of submissiveness or lack of confidence in themselves or their culture and language or if there was something else. Earlier, in my curiosity to examine my ability to differentiate between a Cape Malay and other groups of *Coloured* people, I asked one of the library staff whether he was a Cape Malay. He didn't know his origins except that he was born *Coloured*. It made clear to me that, firstly, all Cape Malay don't look alike. Secondly, it doesn't matter whether they came from Indonesia, Malaysia or Asia, most of them have lost their identities; they now regard or think of themselves as *Coloured*. One another experience was meeting Patricia, the *Coloured* staff who looked after the photocopy section in the library. During a brief friendly chat with her about her origins, she couldn't tell any other identity of hers other than being classified as *Coloured*.

Professor Wium van Zyl—University of Western Cape

University of Western Cape campus is simple in architecture but it is spread over a vast area of land into various buildings. Under apartheid, the University catered for the education of blacks and *Coloured* only but now one can see the white students as well, utilising the campus side by side with their *Coloured* and black classmates. I was a bit amazed to see that most of the students had cars. Professor of Dutch and Afrikaans at the University of Western Cape, Professor Wium van Zyl took me around to see various parts of the University, including the monument which is placed in the middle in front of the main building on the campus in memory of the 1970s uprisings. Reading the material in most of the subjects in Arts and Literature is available in the library at the University. Over a cup of tea in the University Cafeteria, Professor Wium spoke about his experience and knowledge of the apartheid era. Like Professor Annie, he had a strong Afrikaner accent and an Afrikaner appearance—blue eyes and blonde hair. He was of the view that one must not forget that racism existed in every sphere of life in South Africa—not only between the whites and the blacks but also within these individual races. In this regard, the Afrikaners had a vision—a dream—to create a white South Africa for themselves. They were damn serious about the separate development for all the races in South Africa. The making of this University is one such good example. Apartheid is an extension of that dream. But they misjudged the prevailing situation and landed everybody into trouble. Elsa Joubert's *The Long Journey of Poppie Nongenu* which is translated from Afrikaans in 1978, tells how the character Poppie lived in the Cape and helps to understand an Afrikaner's life.

For Professor Wium, apartheid was an evil ideology but at the same time, he admitted that it was very difficult for an Afrikaner to go against his community. Though he was never personally harassed either by his community or by the non-white people in their struggle against apartheid, he had witnessed some very disturbing events on the premises of this University such as the clash of students with police in the 1970s uprisings. Also, it had been the white settler's way of life for centuries to either kill or hunt the natives for their economic and political interests. Since earlier times, the white colonisers found the natives of South Africa difficult to enslave in one form or the other. The slaves were brought to South Africa from abroad. Gradually, the white settlers managed to establish control over the natives of South Africa due to extreme poverty in the latter's quarters which led them to submit to the cheap labour offered by the white colonisers. Over the destruction of native culture and civilisation in the hands of the Western Imperial society, Professor Wium agreed that the colonisation of South Africa by the Europeans had drastically affected its local society. The language and customs of the coloniser took over, giving way to the death of many native languages and traditions. The Khoikhoi and the Hottentot language did die but Xhosa survived which is spoken in the Western Cape. Zulu which is spoken in Natal and Sotho which is spoken in Orange Free State also survived. Professor Wium explained that these languages have been taught in schools and universities even during the apartheid era under its separate development programme of action. According to Professor Wium, the Afrikaans has survived over the years and will also survive in future because it belongs to them in other words, the people in the street feel a sense of belonging towards the language; they are proud of Afrikaans. Most speakers of the language were and are *Coloured* Afrikaners. This sounded like Professor Derek Klopper who believed that the *Coloured* Afrikaners are the true people of present South Africa. Professor Wium was born and brought up in a farmer's family but there had always been books in their house to read. This led him to become an academic in Afrikaner Literature. For him, the future of Afrikaner literature is very bright in new South Africa. Good poets and writers are coming up who were not able to get their due recognition during the apartheid era.

Yusuf Abrahams—Cape Peninsula University of Technology

Santa drove me to visit Yusuf Abrahams, the Director of Marketing, Communication and Development at the Cape Peninsula, University of Technology. The name of the University is misleading but the University does have Language departments as well and is a well-built place with beautiful architecture. Under the Separate Universities Act 1963, it was built to cater for the education of the *Coloured* people only. Now it is open for students of all ethnic origins but I could see only black and *Coloured* faces utilising the University facility in the company of each other. Yusuf explained that it would take a longer time for South Africans of different origins to come to terms with themselves and accept each other outside the apartheid setup of life. Also as compared to Western Cape where one finds strong English and Jewish influence, people on this side of the world are mostly of *Coloured* and black origins.

Yusuf took us around to show various sections of the building including the IT unit which is very impressive. The University is well-equipped to meet the academic requirements of its students. I was very happy to find confidence in the faces of black and *Coloured* students. Yusuf revealed that these students love their university. They feel a sense of belonging towards its premises and equipment. That is why, in times of protest, the University was never damaged. Although the students struggled against apartheid in violent ways, they always felt a sense of their responsibility to protect its premises against destruction.

Over a cup of the South African blend of Rooibos tea in his office, I couldn't hide my curiosity to find more about the Cape Muslim community. As a Cape *Coloured* person, Yusuf revealed that Muslims played a minor role in the struggle against apartheid in South Africa. He could only recall the name of Imam Abdalla Haroon who was very active in the resistance politics in South Africa. The Cape Malay community was all Muslims of Indonesian and Malaysian origins. Muslims from Indonesia were mostly Imams and Intellectuals whereas Malaysian Muslims have slave origins. Muslims of the Indian Sub-continent who settled in Cape Town came to South Africa under entrenched labour. The best chefs in South Africa are from the Cape Malay community since old times. The chefs used to cook for the Afrikaners and modified it according to the taste of their masters. This blending gave an extra touch to their cooking.

Yusuf very proudly said that the Afrikaners were not only taken over by Cape Malay in food but in language as well. The Afrikaans has taken a big influence from Javanese and Cape Malay's language, Malayo. This reminded me again of Derek saying—that the true people of South Africa are the *Coloured* community. Yusuf told an amusing story about the apartheid days. In the fifties, the apartheid council at the Cape announced to win the votes of the Cape Malay community that they would be given the right to franchise after the election. The Cape Malay community baked cakes and distributed them in rejuvenation. When the apartheid authorities changed their mind after winning the election, the Cape Malay people again baked and distributed the cakes but this time, the cake had two sides, one white and one black—meaning two-faced government.

Yusuf himself has slave origins and originally came from Indonesia. Due to the bit comfortable economic position of his family, he did not suffer much as a child living through apartheid. His parents were able to provide him with a better education compared to other children in his community. He was also lucky not to study under the Bantu education system; it was introduced when he had already finished his education. Yusuf was against apartheid during his university days but he admitted that it was not easy then to become part of the resistance movement under the apartheid government. Fear was created by harsh punishments by the authorities and people, in general, were scared for the safety of themselves and their families.

Yusuf agreed that the question of identity had been and still is a very important matter in South African society. Under apartheid laws, people were classified into several racial groups. Non-White people were made conscious of their separate identities by the introduction of such classification. This led to the rise of black consciousness in the society which was then very difficult to handle by the apartheid authorities. Classified as Cape Malay, Yusuf didn't feel intellectually inferior to the white people or people of other ethnic origins; Yusuf was amongst those South Africans who have inborn confidence in themselves despite deprivation and insecurities in their lives. He was cheerful and a light-hearted person, and, amused at the thought of how come they have lived through and survived apartheid in their lives. Yusuf agreed to meet us again along with his wife for another session at Sunday lunch in Cape Town.

A Visit to the Spier and the Delheim Farm

Traditional Bell used by the Dutch masters to make the slaves aware of their work and break times—Stellenbosch (2005)

On the outskirts of Stellenbosch, Santa briefly stopped the car at the Spier, a tourist spot now but once it was Santa's home. The Spier is a huge farmhouse with Dutch-style gable buildings which belonged to Santa's late husband in the past. The buildings along with their antiques which are approximately three centuries old are open to the public. Santa took me around and showed me how the Dutch used to live in old times. The yellow wood which is a South African brand but which nowadays is very expensive wood due to its shortage in the market was used in the décor of the master's house. The younger house which is a building next to the main building used to be the residence of the eldest son of the family. Some of the halls in the buildings are nowadays used as conference rooms. Old-style two-wheel horse-drawn carriages were also on display.

There were huge green grounds around the buildings. About the recent development of restaurants, bars, and shops in these gardens to attract tourists, Santa was of the view that such an introduction of modern life has affected the natural beauty of the farm. A big stream flowed at the side of the main building cutting through the grounds. There was a traditional slave bell near the main house on the farm. In old times, it was used to make the slaves aware of their work and break times. Near the parking area at the entrance to the farm, the traditional bush is planted on the pathways to project to a foreigner like me how the bush looks in reality.

A church bell nearby rang twelve times and we knew it was noon. We set off for lunch at the Delheim farm. It belonged to Santa's family friends. In the past, she used to work for them in establishing the restaurant on the farm where we were going to have lunch that afternoon. Delheim is a beautiful farm of huge vineyards which is surrounded by green mountains from all sides. The owner of the farm grows and brews grapes into fine wine which sells all over the world. Santa took me around and showed me how the wine has been made over the years—how it is tested and tasted in a variety of ways. In the restaurant, we met Nora, the daughter of the owner of the farm who deals with the marketing of the wine, her husband, Erhardt, a professional photographer and their two young sons. They had two timid dogs, though I was uncomfortable with their presence around us. Meeting Nora and her family reminded me of the characters in Gordimer's *A World of Strangers*. I felt like Toby sitting amongst a well-educated, well and well-travelled Afrikaans and English-speaking white class. Later Santa took me to their other farm where they lived. To my surprise, they could fluently speak both languages without an accent. They ran a restaurant on the farm for the tourists. Santa took me to the Kitchen section to meet the staff whom she trained for the job in the past. It was interesting to know that the *Coloured* people don't like to work with the blacks in the same place because they regard the latter as belonging to the lower class. The same racial prejudice exists in blacks as well. That is why I could see the kitchen of that restaurant run by the *Coloured* chefs only. The blacks were employed as attendants only in the same restaurant.

During my conversations with Nora and Erhardt, I came to know that Nora had a Dutch mother and a German father. She told me that they have to work very hard to maintain the farm and the business going. She started the conversation with the acceptance of the reality of apartheid in her world and how bad she felt to see people surviving in shacks and squatters in all kinds of weather. Something bad has happened in her South African society which should have not happened in the first place.

I found Erhardt a real Afrikaner. He was of the view that there exist a variety of tribes all over Africa. Most of them had their kings, language, culture, and traditions. He gave an example of Swaziland, about the Zulu and Xhosa tribes which had always resisted amalgamating or juxtaposing in one another's cultures and did not accept each other's dominance either. They had always preferred to keep their separate identities. So if the whites tried to do the same in Africa, why were they so fussed about it? Erhardt admitted that there did happen evil things but the intention of the Afrikaners was not bad. They just wanted to create a white world for themselves. What's the harm in having your separate world or keeping your separate identity? I could see lots of European and foreign plants and trees fully flourishing in the garden of their farm restaurant. I was amused when earlier, Erhardt inquired about my moral duty towards my country; he wanted to know why I reside in the United Kingdom and have no immediate intention of contributing to my people's intellectual progress. I wondered who is questioning whom!

At lunch, I went for Cape Malay Chicken and traditional cheesecake. I was informed that all Cape Malay dishes use Halal meat. After lunch, we went to see a wine cellar and then a little drive in the area around. Santa informed how the farmers are trying to manage with fewer labourers on the farms because the farmer has to be very careful in taking someone into employment. According to the new Farm Labour laws, the farmers have to keep the labourer for the rest of his life when he is grown old. The farmers don't like it because the old labourers then start keeping families on the farm to look after them. The farmers can't strike the labourers of their employment as they used to do in the past.

On our way back, the sight of vineyard farms along with the shacks is an interesting combination of rich and poor lives in the South African landscape. Santa drove through the black and the *Coloured* townships near Stellenbosch. These were separate developments away from the main town. In comparison to the *Coloured* townships, the black areas were in poor condition.

Shacks were constructed one after another in odd lines. People were selling food and other domestic items sitting outside in front of these shacks. I was surprised to see a Television and a sofa inside a shack. I recalled Toby noticing the black painter and his wife in *A World of Strangers* who attempt to keep a standard of living in their shack house. Toby also visits Shabeens with his black friends in such a locality. I asked Santa about the Shabeens but she was a bit reluctant to go further inside the township at that time of the evening.

Santa's neighbours cooked the meal and brought it to Santa's table to enjoy it together on my last day in Stellenbosch. They came across open-minded South Africans. One was a middle-aged Afrikaner lady who was very much interested in music and Sufism. The other was a middle-aged journalist of Scottish origin with prince Charles' eyes and had a *Coloured* daughter Emani from her West Indian boyfriend—a good mix of white, black, and *Coloured* in a family. We had an interesting conversation about the classification of people in South Africa in different categories. To my surprise, I came to realise that I have overlooked the fact that Hottentots and Bushmen were not classified into any category in the Racial Grouping Act 1950. The journalist friend of Santa had spent some time living in Johannesburg. She could recall the times when people could not meet openly across the racial divide. The apartheid authorities used to keep a strict watch on the manoeuvres of people into each other's world. When she was pregnant with Emani some ten years ago, she had to leave Johannesburg because apartheid politics was threatening to destroy her personal life. Santa agreed that although there were restrictions on friendships between the white and non-white people, still people kept in touch with each other in one way or the other; she gave an example when some *Coloured* friends were openly invited to a wedding in her family. Now they meet openly in new South Africa without apartheid.

Delheim Vineyards Farm—Stellenbosch (2005)

Cape Town (22–23 May 2005)

Home to the Cape Coloured community, Cape Town is the largest city of Western Cape province in South Africa. In its character as the oldest and the second-largest city after Johannesburg, it projects the history of racial classification and land possession by the white rulers who amounted to only 10 per cent of the total South African population. The non-white population suffered deprivation of their land and discrimination based on the colour of their skin during the apartheid era.

Just before noon, we set off from Stellenbosch to visit Sheikh Yusuf's Dargah in Macassar and then meet Yusuf Abrahams and his wife Cass Abrahams for lunch in Cape Town. Macassar is a small *Coloured* township near Stellenbosch. Most of its population are Muslims. The uphill junctions at the road leading to the town reminded me of the road uphill from Islamabad to Murree Hills in Pakistan. It was a beautiful relaxing journey of half an hour. Sheikh Yusuf was a renowned spiritual Muslim scholar who came from Ceylon to South Africa in the seventeenth century. He quietly spread Islam amongst the people of colour including the slaves. His tomb is situated on top of a small hill and its green pyramid stands out amongst surrounding constructions. Muslims visit his tomb to pay tribute to him for his contribution to creating an Islamic community in South Africa.

Muslim Spiritual Sheikh Yusuf Dargah—Macassar 2005

Later, Yusuf Abrahams explained that in those days in the seventeenth century, slaves who embraced Islam quietly visited Sheikh Yusuf at night so as not to offend their Christian masters. Intellectuals and Islamic scholars who had command of the Arabic language came from Mali to spread Islam in South Africa. The first translation of the Holy Quran from Arabic was done in the Afrikaans language. In some of the mosques in Cape Town, the Khutba (Friday sermon) is delivered in Afrikaans too. Yusuf said that it is amazing to see the huge number of Muslims who come for the Friday prayers in the mosques in Cape Town.

Inside the one-room Dargah—Sheikh Yusuf Tomb 2005

At entering Cape Town, the harbour and its ships remind one of the times when the Europeans arrived on this spot centuries ago. The Cape of Good Hope is at the far end of this main harbour. Robin Island is visible as a small spot in the sea. A boat ride is available for tourists nowadays to visit the Island. Nearby the harbour, a castle of colonial times is noticeable on the other side of the road. And how one could miss the presence of huge mountains near the side of the harbour. The famous Table Mountain with a flat surface on the top is a beauty. A chairlift takes the visitors up there to enjoy walking on the flat surface of the mountain and view Cape Town from that height. There is another peak next to Table Mountain and it is called Lion's Head because it looks like a lion's head. And on the other side of Table Mountain, there is a mountain which is called Signal Hill. In colonial times, guns were placed on top of this mountain. Whenever there was a sighting of the enemy nearby, the fire from the guns from that height used to signal and warn people against the danger in Cape Town. Also, as a small spot on the way to climb this mountain, one can notice the existence of a tomb near the top area. Santa told me that a spiritual Muslim from old times is buried there.

As we approached Cape Town, the shacks were visible on both sides of the road. Santa said that these shacks, in local terminology, are called *Kayalitsha* (a township in Western Cape). In comparison to the shacks, the townships and the squatter camps are developments of the 1980s era. We passed by the hospital where the world's first heart surgery took place. Santa pointed at the huge part of the land with gardens and trees that ran along the road. It was once the property of Cecil Rhodes who donated it to the Cape Town Council as a gift to the people of the land. Rhodes has well contributed land and money to finance the University of Cape Town as well as the Western Cape University. His house is now the official residence of the President of South Africa.

Santa took me to see Mount Nelson hotel, one of the famous places in Cape Town. Dignitaries like Mandela had been on its guest list. We stopped by the Clarks book shop in the famous Adderley Street and visited the mall to see the big statues on the roundabouts which are placed there in the memory of the first white settlement in Cape Town. Santa drove around a square which was the actual place of the landing of Riebeek's ship. Van Riebeek originally planted trees on the premises of present-day Company Gardens. It reminded me of the fence—the border demarcated with this plantation between the white settlers and the rest of South Africa. Van Riebeek's statue stands right in front of the main gate of the Company Gardens—guarding his boundary of the plantation as usual!

We went for lunch to a big fish market in Cape Town's huge shopping centre. At Santa's request, the attendant showed me the variety of fish available in the restaurant. I came to know that the most popular fish in South Africa is Snoek. Hake fish also sells well. I asked Yusuf and his wife, Cass whether they know that Muslims cannot eat fish that has no scales on their skin; I had heard about this from my elders in Pakistan but never got the chance to confirm the name and type of the fish that is forbidden. Both Yusuf and Cass were not aware of any such holy instruction. That is why, perhaps, Muslims of Cape Malay eat snoek which is without scales.

Cass had brought along an album of their only son's wedding which took place recently. Looking through the photographs, I could see the influence of Asian and African culture in their customs and ceremonies of the wedding. Similar had been the case with food recipes. Over some time, a blend of African, Asian and Afrikaners ways of cooking have given a new taste to the present South African food. Cass herself made the dishes for her son's wedding. She is, I was told, one of the best chefs in Cape Town and her book *The Culture of Cuisine of the Cape Malays* (1998) has been selling well in the market.

In this session, I got clear in my head about the administrative system in South Africa; I was somehow under the impression that Johannesburg had been the centre of political activity but this was not the case. Though Johannesburg is a popular city internationally, the political control in South Africa is spread over the whole country: Pretoria is the Judiciary capital, Cape Town has the Parliament, Orange Free State (Bloemfontein) has the Legislative Assembly. I also came to know about the geographical divide between the Western Cape which I visited and the Eastern Cape which covers areas of East London, Port Elizabeth, and Transkei.

Over the question of racial complexity in South Africa, Yusuf and Cass, as Coloureds, had a lot to reveal. Yusuf himself was a direct descendant of the slave community in South Africa. He could trace his origins back to the slavery period of the colonial era. Cass, a convert to Islam, was a Coloured from German and Mulatto origins. Mulatto slaves were the product of the physical relationships between the Dutch and the blacks including the slaves. Despite race consciousness, intermarriages between the Coloured and the blacks and amongst Cape Malay, Bengali, Indonesian and Malaysian people took place. Yusuf added that the Cape Malay community is close to Afrikaners in language and culture. Cass agreed that the Coloured acted as a buffer society between the white and the black worlds in South Africa. But she made an interesting revelation about the non-white people who wished to classify themselves as whites under the apartheid law in the 1960s and 1970s; they needed to fulfil three conditions.

Firstly, the person competing for the classification must pass the 'Pencil test'. It means that if a pencil doesn't stay where it was put in the hair and slips or falls, the person has passed the test. Amongst the Africans in general, the Khoisan tribe had the traditional short curly hair. Secondly, the person must have white colour skin. And lastly, he must have grown up in a white suburb.

Both Yusuf and Cass believed that apartheid laws were stupid. The white and non-white people were friends—had relationships for generations—but the law of the land said that you cannot sit and eat together. You cannot meet in public places. Gordimer has written several stories and novels in which personal friendships between both the white and the non-white people break down due to the apartheid laws in their everyday life; in fact, the characters get caught and punished for their physical relationships. Without a permit, people in South Africa couldn't visit each other; Cass, Yusuf and Santa had been friends for years but they had to get a permit whenever they wished to meet each other. Here Santa recalled an incident of her times when she had to write a letter of permission for an Indian because Indians were not allowed to stay on the farms more than twenty-four hours.

Cass was of the view that South African society had a layer of borders and boundaries between its people since colonial times. There had been already a boundary of religion and tribalism between the people and on top of it, another boundary was imposed in the form of apartheid which was a total transgression. There was a strong reaction but people reacted in their ways. As privileged, the white people took the whole system of life for granted. We questioned, Cass said. Santa could recall his own experience of aggression amongst the *Coloured* staff at the school nursery against the participation of the white people in the community uplift scheme in 1975.

Yusuf believed that apartheid was a clever scheme. The Separate Amenities Act was introduced which means no kind of sports can take place between the white and non-white people in South Africa. Properties were frozen by the Groups Areas Act meaning the inhabitants of District Six had to leave their homes where they lived for generations. They were mostly tenants of Jewish landowners who didn't protect them well. The pretext of separate development was a cunning idea. It allowed the white community to keep the non-white people away from amalgamating into their culture and society. Simon Town, a place near Cape Town is another sight of forced removals but District Six has become a symbol of the oppression of the non-white people by the white community in South Africa.

Cass was a biology teacher and had taught in ghetto schools for 17 years. She had seen the resistance amongst the students against apartheid. She had watched them changing into violent protestors. It upset her to find recourse to drugs and illegitimate pregnancy amongst her good students. The 1970s uprisings led her to an emotional breakdown. She was traumatised and had to leave the job. She couldn't take it anymore. Then there was another kind of psychological misery she had to live through when she was asked to move her home under the Groups Areas Act. The place where she lived with her family was declared an area for whites only. Yusuf also remembered their misery and desperation at not providing their school-going children with a satisfying answer to why they are not allowed to go and play in the parks which are reserved for the whites only. Cass told me that she and her community now feel more full people in new South Africa without apartheid.

However, Cass said that she always felt sorry for the white people in both old and new South Africa. They have marginalised themselves in every way. Apartheid was a disadvantage for everyone. The white community, though materially and physically privileged, are isolated from other communities in South Africa. They did not amalgamate like the non-white people with one another. Both Yusuf and Cass agreed that all of us in South Africa had disadvantages one way or the other because of the apartheid system of life.

Bokaap

After lunch, Yusuf took us on a drive to see the Bokaap area of Cape Town. On the way, I could notice big palm trees which are not indigenous but are grown on both sides of almost every main road in Cape Town. I asked Yusuf about the yellow buses and the separate seat arrangement for the white people in those buses. I was told that the yellow buses are now mostly taken over the small vans. Separate buses and separate seat systems had been more common in Johannesburg. When asked what he thinks of then-President Thabo Mbeki, Yusuf considered him a statesman. Much has improved under the ANC government. Yusuf was aware of the criticism of the slow rate of development but you cannot expect ANC to clean the mess left over by apartheid policies in just ten years. Such matters need more time. I told Yusuf about a BBC report in which a black person living in a shack gave a similar answer to the question of what he would say to not getting the promised housing after the ANC came to power. To the white reporter's shock, the black man said that he was very happy with what the ANC is doing for the country; there had been a lot of economic depravity for a long time amongst the masses and it will take time for them to recover from it.

Bokaap is a huge *Coloured* Muslim township—the Malay quarters—at the heart of Cape Town. In the past, slaves used to live there. It is built on a steep hill. From the road on top of the hill, one can see the whole of Cape Town. Yusuf drove us up and into the streets to show what the locality looked like. His relatives still live there. He showed the mosques in the area, including the oldest one where he used to come and still come for prayers on big religious occasions. There is a small museum in the Bokaap as well which had a record of the history of the area. Yusuf parked the car and we went around to see some inside streets. Cass wanted me to notice the walls of most of the houses painted in bright colours. However, I was more fascinated by the pattern of the houses constructed next to each other. There is hardly any space between the houses. Was it cultural or shortage of land that led people of colour to live so close to each other? Perhaps, both. However, it is pathetic that only 13 per cent of the land is owned by non-white people in South Africa. Most of the land is the white man's property who is only 10 per cent of the total population of South Africa.

Bokaap is nowadays considered one of the fashionable areas in Cape

Town. I am told that the price of its properties is on the rise as people from abroad have invested in building the area for residential as well as the commercial sector. Yusuf led us to a modern cafeteria in a recently constructed shopping arcade inside the Bokaap town-ship. Over a cup of tea and a piece of apple crumble cake, Yusuf pointed out that surprisingly, Bokaap is the only township in Cape Town where forced removals didn't take place. Most of the Muslim communities settled here are educated and affluent people. Yusuf then went into remembering the days of struggle under apartheid. Nobody across the colour line could sit together like we were having tea that day. Andre Brink, Richard Rive and James Mathews used to visit him secretly. As young people, all of them were struggling against apartheid in their respective capacities. In his university days, Yusuf recalled the incident of Dr Yusuf Dadu, the chairman of the Pan Africanist movement when he was taken into custody for reading the ANC freedom charter in front of the students in the University. He was picked up by the police and banned from meeting people in public. Luckily, one of his old students oversaw the police station Dr Dadu was taken for imprisonment. Instead of putting a charge against his teacher, the police inspector apologised and set him free. He knew that a peaceful person like Dr Dadu could never be a threat to society at large.

As a young man, Yusuf himself was an active member of the Pan-Africanist movement for some time. In this regard, he was sent to Cairo under the pretext of studying at Al-Azhar University. He had gone through difficult times. He was imprisoned too. Somehow, Yusuf preferred not to go into details. Probably, it must be disturbing to recall painful memories of those difficult days under the apartheid system of life. We left Bokaap on a lighter note: Cass was telling us about the gays who are becoming the second largest community in South Africa. And Santa was teasing Yusuf about the Muslim tradition of having four wives. He reminded Santa that the Zulu tribe has also the tradition of having more wives. But Yusuf was not happy with the inheritance problems which result due to the children from more than one marriage.

A Visit to District Six Museum

A handout was given to the visitors at the reception of the museum which had the following information:

- District Six was named the sixth district of Cape Town in 1867. Established as a vibrant mixed community of freed slaves, merchants, artisans, labourers, and immigrants, it was closely linked to the city and port. By the beginning of the 20th century, the process of removals and marginalisation started. The first to be 'resettled' were 'Africans', forcibly removed from the area in 1901. As the more prosperous community members moved to the suburbs, the district became the neglected ward of Cape Town. In 1966, under the Group Areas Act of 1950, District Six was declared a 'white' area. By 1982, the life of that community was over and 60,000 people were forcibly removed, their houses flattened by bulldozers, to a barren outlying area aptly known as the Cape Flats. The District Six museum was born on December 10, 1994, to work with the memories and the experiences of those affected. [...] The museum portrays the history of Apartheid and its effects on the 'ordinary' people through an intimate look at their stories. It is a celebration of local triumph which resonates with all people who have experienced marginalisation. [...] Through documenting, the exhibition deepens our knowledge of District Six, while using memory as a vehicle for healing. The exhibition is a richly textured exploration which involves the visitors' response to the multi-layered history of the area. The voices and stories of ex-residents are the major resource and departure points for the exhibition's themes.

Looking through various displays in the museum—posters—and photographs—is a disturbing experience. A map of the buildings in District Six before the forced removals is drawn in dummy architecture in the main hall of the museum on the floor. Preserved nameplates of the then streets hang in the shape of a ladder from the ceiling. Residents' memory of their homes is embroidered in words on big pieces of clothes hanging from the ceiling. Amongst them, there was a big piece of cloth with residents' names and addresses written in ink and colour who used to live in District Six. I looked through the collection of information:

- District Six was declared as a white group area in 1966. Residents were moved under the Groups Areas Act 1950—a segregated city—separate townships.
- Demolition was completed in 1984—a white area was declared in 1982.—42 sites of removal since 1901, then in 1927, 1932–36, 1957, and 1963.
- Pass laws—1760—applied to the slaves then—afterwards—over some time—to control African People—1952 Native Laws Amendment Act—1955 Native Urban Areas Amendment Act was introduced to control the influx of labourers.
- Coloured people preference policy was abolished in 1984.
- 1986—the identity of fingerprints was introduced.
- Albertus Fransman in the early 1940s was one of the founders of the Communist party.
- The Industrial and Commercial Workers Union was founded in 1919, formed by a man Clements Kadalie from Nyasaland, known today as Malawi.
- 1834 was the Emancipation Day end of slavery but the law required then 4 years of apprenticeship.
- The Bantustan policies increasingly placed the rural population into ethnically defined homelands.
- Forced removals—1886 then 1901 then 1923 to control the influx.
- The 1940s—more concerned with the growth of uncontrolled black settlements.
- During the 1930s—the Slum Act was to clear the land.
- Soweto—the homeland of many former freehold areas of Sophia town.
- Departure and Displacement—the pain and misery of the residents are displayed in photographs and words—digging deep experience—tears kept rolling in my eyes.

One of the staff at the District museum explained that this site of the museum was originally an old church that was built in 1880. A picture of the Church of those times also hangs on the wall. The church was mostly used by the Coloured community before the removals.

In the museum, there is a display of household items to project how an average *Coloured* person used to live in District Six before the forced removals. I was amazed to look at the classic taste the *Coloured* had in the selection of furniture and chinaware. A local white teacher who was visiting the museum with a badge of school students added to my knowledge that the non-white people always imitated the white people in their everyday life. Her point can be taken as far as the decor is concerned but when it comes to the standards of hygiene, the non-white people, in comparison, were and are far ahead; impressive cleanliness is maintained even inside shacks and squatters. They used to decorate their old-style communal lavatories with flowers and scents to keep the undesirable odours away. The non-white people are in general house-proud community.

Later Santa said that the District Six museum is not just one example but similarly forced removals of the non-white people from their homes took place all over the country under apartheid laws. Most of the properties in District Six before the removals belonged to the Jews who rented them out to the local community but they never spent money on the maintenance of those properties. As a result, the condition of the area gradually deteriorated and the resulting bad atmosphere led to disease and sickness in the community at District Six.

That day, Santa took me for a meal to Lazari restaurant in Portioli which was once an area for whites only in Cape Town. From the big glass window of the restaurant, I saw a car full of young white people passed by on the road. It was driven very fast by a blonde girl. Somehow Gordimer's characterisation clicked in my mind.

Meeting Academics/Professionals at the University of Cape Town

Professor Geffrey Haresnape, retired from his services at the University of Cape Town and his wife, Leslie, a retired schoolteacher were my hosts for a day in Cape Town. We went to the University of Cape Town first. The University is impressively built in a huge area with both old and new campuses. A big statue of Cecil Rhodes (removed in 2015) was placed in front of the main building. There is a big garden in front of the main building which was, for the first time, utilised for the University convocation ceremony in which Nelson Mandela was given an honorary degree of doctorate after his release from prison. Table Mountain with its surrounding peaks looks very close to the main building of the University. Covered by the fog from time to time, the peaks give special effects to the whole scenery in the landscape. Professor Geffrey told an interesting story which had been famous amongst the local people about one of the peaks which was afterwards named the Devil's Peak. In old times, the natives used to believe that there was a Devil on the peak who smoked in huge quantities. That is why, most of the time, the peak is covered in smoke. A black man who was also a heavy smoker climbed the peak in his attempt to challenge the Devil that he could make more smoke than him. Nobody knows what happened next but it is believed that that black man never found the Devil up there. On our way to the library, Professor Geffrey spoke on several areas:

- Durban which is in Natal is an area of early English settlement.
- Like 'Africana', Professor Geffrey is in favour of coining the word 'Anglicana' for the English side of the South African world. This reminded me of Professor Christopher Heywood's favourite word 'Creole' which he has used for the people of South Africa in his recent book, *History of South African Literature* (2004).
- There have been similarities between the Anglo-Boer war in South Africa and the Anglo-French war in Canada. In both countries, the English set up the concentration camps after getting power and control of the area from the Boers and the French respectively.
- Koikoi were the indigenous people of Cape Town.
- District Six is a black spot.

- Professor Geffrey suggested that Pauline Smith, William Plomer and Royal Cambell are worth reading writers to understand the history of South African society.
- Richard Rive's story 'You Made Me Black' is worth reading to understand the racial complexity that exists in South Africa.
- Katherine Mansfield is one other good storyteller.
- Coetzee had studied with Professor Geffrey. He migrated to Australia which has offended South Africans very much.
- Tatumkula Afrikana is a famous Cape poet nowadays.

Professor Geffrey was the Editor of the South African Journal 'Contrast' for a couple of years. He told me how difficult it was to publish material against apartheid in those days. Still, 'Contrast' was very active in resistance politics. Professor Geffrey argued that he has always questioned whether it is colonialism or racism is to blame for the development of the ideology of apartheid amongst the white community in South Africa. I told Professor Geffrey an amusing saying about the superiority complex of the white race: when God attempted to make a human being for the first time, He put the structure of man which He made with clay into a hot oven to dry it well. It was His first attempt to create such a thing, so the body of a human being somehow got burnt. That has become the people of black colour. The second time he tried to make the human being, He overcooked the body. So this has become the people of brown colour. The third time God was able to get the temperature right in the oven and so the white man was made. Here Professor Geffrey added to change the version of the last attempt: when the third time God attempted to create the man, the human structure of clay was left undercooked. So this has become the white man. We had a good laugh. At that moment, the memory of the poem 'African Shakespeare' that I once read online some time ago created a lot of amusement in my mind:

> Dear white fella,
> Couple of things you should know
> When I born, I black
> When I grow up, I black
> When I go in sun, I black
> When I cold, I black
> When I scared, I black
> When I sick, I black

And when I die, I still black.
You white fella,
When you born, you pink
When you grow up, you white
When you go in sun, you red
When you cold, you blue
When you scared, you yellow
When you sick, you green
And when you die, you grey
And you have the cheek to call me coloured?

The UCT has a big library with an archive section as well. In one section of the reading rooms, there is a robot structured statue standing with a pillar in the memory of the ancient Hottentot woman who was taken to Europe by the white colonisers and exhibited there in a cage as a sub-human. I had read about the incident and had seen the photographs in the books of South African history but somehow the sight of that statue was more appalling. I asked Professor Geffrey how one could think of the colonisers as coming from a so-called civilised Europe when they were not able to understand the simple fact that the physical structure that black Hottentot women had, was considered a beauty in African culture. When an African baby girl is born, the women of the household keep shaping the body of the new-born with massage and other ways so that it gets the buttocks as bigger as possible. According to the African culture, such a structure of the body makes the woman more physically attractive to men. I told Professor Geffrey that my mind simply does not accept the explanation given by the European exhibitors of the time that as there was a shortage of water, the Hottentot women used to store water in their buttocks. Big nonsense. Professor Geffrey suggested reading George Orwell's story 'Shooting an Elephant' which, according to him, describes real South Africa.

Geffrey took me to the archive section where we met Tania, one of the senior staff of the library. Coming from a Jewish family, Tania had been very active in resistance politics in her younger life. She openly opposed apartheid and supported the non-white people in their struggle against all kinds of oppression in their everyday life. She was shocked at the views I had come across in Stellenbosch about the apartheid and the justification the Afrikaners gave about creating a white country in South Africa. According to Tania, the white community has to take full responsibility for the apartheid in South Africa. She asked me to read the history of Frontier Wars which took place between the Dutch and the natives of

South Africa in 1781. The accounts of the war tell how cruel the white colonisers were and how much they had destroyed African life everywhere they went to South Africa. Tania said that Bushmen were hunted down by the Afrikaners like animals.

We had to say goodbye to Tania in between such an interesting conversation as we were getting late for our lunch with Gail Finhan, the lecturer in English at the University of Cape Town. Gail was more interested in knowing my area of study and how far I have developed my research than talking about her experiences of apartheid. However, she did say that forty years of apartheid is like a black spot in the history of South Africa. It had isolated people, making them marginalised leading to keyhole experiences of each other's world such as described by Gordimer in her story 'Ah, Woe Is Me'. Gail agreed that the white ethics of the white community under apartheid is questionable. She was hopeful that at least in new South Africa, the white people, like her, don't have to live with the guilt anymore.

Simon Town

Author in Simon Town with Emeritus Professor Geffrey Haresnape—(2005)

On the way from Cape Town to Simon Town, one can notice a plantation of chestnut trees along the mountainous road which looks beautiful. Simon Town is a small town near the sea that had a small harbour where the British fleet was stationed till the National Party came to power in 1948. There used to be a big *Coloured* township with nice brick cottages which had been wiped out under the forced removals in 1967. Leslie pointed at the places where that township used to be in the past.

There is a local museum which has a record of the history of the area. We had a small walk near the harbour to look at the historical sites with information plates which reveal the history of the area in brief words. I found Simon Town picturesque with huge mountains on one side and the sea on the other. It had been an army town and still carries an aura of the past.

Professor Geffrey decided to take us further around the mountain towards the sight of the Natural Reserve. It was a beautiful drive by the side of the mountain and the sea on the other side. We passed by beaches including the Fishhook beach. After Musenberg, a small town where Rhodes died, there is a beach where the British fleet landed for the first time on South African soil. We passed by a Masonry where the colonisers used to keep the slaves in the past. Professor Geffrey told that the Bokaap museum had more information about the slaves in South Africa. It led us to discuss how much the Afrikaans had been influenced by the languages of the non-white people in South Africa. The first translation of the Holy Quran in South Africa was in Afrikaans. We came back to Cape Town via a different route so that I can visit Lavender Hill, a black township that is a very run-down area on the outskirts of Cape Town. Leslie used to teach there in a school. Leslie and teachers like her had tried to educate the non-white children about their rights and duties towards themselves and their society but they did it with strategy and in a very quiet manner. As a teacher, it always hurt her to see non-white children with a lack of confidence in themselves due to their low position in society. She couldn't help them out and it was frustrating. Apartheid laws were very strong.

Author at lunch with Leslie, wife of Professor Haresnape (left) and English Lecturer Gail Finhan (middle)—University of Cape Town (2005)

Over the partisan politics between the King of the Zulu tribe and the ANC, I told Professor Geffrey and Leslie that we do have the same kind of tribalism still prevalent in Pakistan. Like the tribal kings in South Africa, the tribal elders in Pakistan were given monetary support to keep them under control. Before its incorporation in Pakistan in 2019, the tribal mountainous belt acted as the buffer zone between Pakistan and Afghanistan; the tribal elders would take financial grants from both sides and were not loyal to either. Professor Geffrey informed that Transkei in South Africa was that tribal zone in which the apartheid government attempted to bring a change in the shape of Bantustan. I could relate to the social and political developments of South African society: we did and still have the same big gap between the rich and the poor in Pakistan. Due to poverty, child labour is still common. In villages, people to date work in bonded labour because they cannot pay back the debt to the landowner. There has been a quota system in place for the people of poor and under-developed areas similar to what South Africa had labour reserved area for the *Coloured* and the blacks.

Since her retirement, Leslie was very active in Church activities. She is against all kinds of violence in society; no religion in the world preaches violence. It is we who interpret it differently for our selfish reasons. We agreed that the bloodline of both the prophets, Jesus and Mohammad, comes from the same Prophet, Abraham (Peace be upon them): Prophet Jesus was the descendant of Isaac who was Prophet Abraham's son, and, Prophet Mohammad was the descendant of Ismail who was also Prophet Abraham's son—their mothers were different—Prophet Abraham's first wife Sarah gave birth to Isaac and Ismail was born to his second wife, Hajra. This makes one contemplate why do the priest and mullah not tell and promote that we are one family—an extension of each other—brothers and cousins of the same origin?

Table Mountain view from the city centre—Cape Town (2005)

Looking at the excellent view of Table Mountain from my hotel's window, I meditated over the developments so far; after an exciting stay in Stellenbosch where I came to know the Afrikaner side of the apartheid story, and, an interesting visit to Cape Town which provided an opportunity to see the Cape Coloured community at close quarters, my last port of call was Johannesburg where I was hoping to meet Gordimer and see the world she lived all her life.

On my departure from Cape Town to Johannesburg, it was difficult to say goodbye to Santa who had been not only a perfect host but an excellent human being to know and be friends with. Being a seasoned person, she was very articulated. Once Petra, my German hostel-mate at Lancaster University in 1988, told me that she hated saying goodbyes because they make you feel miserable as if you are losing some part of your life. I felt the same whilst saying goodbye to Santa.

Author in Cuisine with Santa Joubert—Cape Town (2005)

Johannesburg (24 May–2 June 2005)

I met Nadine Gordimer in Johannesburg and explored the South African liberal English society that she has projected in her fictional world. The question of why Liberalism had become a dirty word in South Africa was addressed in my conversations with Jonathan Paton, Jill Wentzel, Rowland Smith, and Ahmed Essop.

Jonathan Paton and his wife Margaret (2005)

Jonathan Paton (1939–2006) was my host in Johannesburg. His father Alan Paton (1903–1988) founded the Liberal party in South Africa in 1953. Even though his health was not sound, Jonathan came to collect me from the airport. Johannesburg airport is a huge complex as compared to London Heathrow airport. It takes a good amount of time either to get in or come out of the airport. On the way to his residence, Jonathan broke the news: Gordimer is not willing to give an interview. Long before my travelling to South Africa, I had been trying to make an appointment for a sitting with her. In this regard, Collin Smuts, one of Gordimer and Jonathan's mutual friends, approached her but to no avail. Jonathan had revealed his reluctance to call her himself in the first place. Due to a row between Gordimer and his late father in the past, Jonathan's relationship with Gordimer had not been cordial since then; he couldn't condole Gordimer at her husband's death in 2001. A day before my arrival, Jonathan did eventually contact Gordimer over the telephone to convince her if I only could meet her—no interview—but Gordimer's answer was still in the negative. Maureen Isaacson, a journalist by profession and a close friend of Gordimer also couldn't help us further. When I found out that Gordimer is travelling abroad in a couple of days, it pricked my heart to think that I am in Johannesburg and won't be able to meet or see Gordimer. Jonathan suggested that I should request Gordimer in person on the phone which I did that evening.

During our journey to Jonathan's residence, I tried to look around to see and record the atmosphere of how Johannesburg looked but I just couldn't. Jonathan was explaining that he lives on the eastern side of the city and we will later visit the western and northern parts of the city which have been very fashionable white areas. Margaret, Jonathan's wife received us at the gate. It was a nice big bungalow. My room was right opposite Jonathan's study. I could see the swimming pool at the far end of the garden from my window. Most of the houses in the suburbs have swimming pools. As it was sunny, we had lunch in the garden. But I could feel the chill in the air as compared to Stellenbosch and Cape Town. Jonathan was amused to know that his voice on the phone made an opposite image of the man I met today. I informed him about my area of research and the experience that I had in Stellenbosch and Cape Town. He told an amusing story about him and his friends: once having a meal with Gordimer as young liberals, they strongly believed that July, Gordimer's servant at her place in Park Town then who served them food, was the persona of the main character in her novel *July's People*. We retired to our rooms for the afternoon nap, the luxury I miss in London. I couldn't sleep, so I decided to unpack and settle myself in my room.

Later in the afternoon, we had a session to finalise the scheduled visits and appointments. Jonathan kept dialling Gordimer's phone number but there was no response. So we knew that she was not at home. Meanwhile, Jonathan decided to have a drink and asked if it is okay to consume alcohol in my presence. This led to an interesting conversation about Muslim and Pakistani culture and our family backgrounds. An hour later, we tried again and this time, Gordimer picked up the phone. Jonathan quickly handed over the receiver to me. I couldn't find words for a while as I heard her voice. I didn't believe I was talking to her in person. With some difficulty, I found my voice to start the conversation telling her that I am taken over by the moment right now. As I introduced myself and referred to Jonathan's previous call, she became a bit furious and told me that I must respect her privacy. I informed her that I have been studying her work for the last ten years and she has been my inspiration and I would like to have a photograph if not the interview. Gordimer suddenly sounded very rude and said that it is more important to concentrate on my research than having a photograph with her. I again requested if she could spare me a few minutes only. It would be a pity as I had come to Johannesburg and I didn't meet her. But Gordimer was adamant that she cannot see me, said good night very coldly, and put the phone down. Why would she say no to just one photograph? It puzzled Jonathan and Margaret too. Gordimer's attitude reminded my earlier analysis of her distant and detached style of work which I now with great confidence reiterate was correct. That evening, Jonathan called Gordimer's close friends, Collin Smuts and Ahmed Essop, an acclaimed South African Muslim writer in English, informing them over the phone about what Gordimer did to me. Ahmed Essop (1931–2019) tried to cheer me up on the phone by saying that if someone would have asked him for a photograph, he would have done it with pleasure. He sounded a cheerful person, not intense and distant in his voice as Gordimer was. Ahmed agreed to see us for lunch on Sunday.

Jonathan's daughter Pam and her husband Rob (2005)

At dinner, I met Pam, Jonathan's lovely daughter who lived next door. By profession, she was a belle dance and drama teacher. She also found Gordimer's response to a single photograph a bit out of place. Jonathan explained that Gordimer has acquired an isolationist attitude for some time now. Professor Christopher Heywood had already alerted me long before I visited South Africa that Gordimer had become very difficult to approach since her husband had passed away. At this point, Jonathan changed the subject in his attempt to relieve me from my misery of no chance of meeting Gordimer. He asked what I think of Salman Rushdie. I told him that I am not impressed by how he writes and what he says and at times, he appears a kind of pseudo-intellectual to me. Jonathan told the story of how much Gordimer wanted him to come to South Africa and then she had to withdraw the invitation because the South African Muslims threatened to harm her and kill Rushdie if he ever came to South Africa. I was told that Ahmed Essop has done some research on Rushdie which is yet to be published but it would be interesting to know more from him about Rushdie's work. That evening, I retired to my room to go to bed early. I slept. Suddenly I was very tired.

Wednesday 25 May 2005—the day I met Gordimer

Author with Nadine Gordimer at her house in Johannesburg (2005)

Jonathan took me for a drive to see the white suburbs of Johannesburg. I decided to take the chance and ring the bell of Gordimer's house on Frere Road in Park Town. Jonathan preferred to stay away from this adventure of mine. He parked the car at the back street and waited for me till I am over with my five per cent chance of meeting Gordimer. I walked to the front of the house and found a black servant and a dog by the gate. I asked him if this was Gordimer's house, though I knew it very well. He said she is not at home but I can sit inside and wait for her as she is coming back soon. I decided to wait by the gate. No point going in without an appointment. It might offend her. The dog started barking at me as if it knew how much I fear its kind. The black servant stood by the gate for some time and then he went in. I took some photographs of the house from different sides, not believing that I am standing in front of Gordimer's house. I started praying to God: please help. I saw Gordimer driving back to her house. She looked very small and very old in her new small silver car. She didn't look at me, drove inside the garage, asked the servant, perhaps about me, and came to the gate with her dog to enquire if she could help me. My heart was throbbing: I remembered Jonathan saying not to take it to your heart if she is rude to you. The moment I introduced myself, she said: I have told you I don't like to be photographed. I told her again that she is my inspiration and I have been working on her fiction for the last ten years. I have come to South Africa to meet her. I cannot go without seeing her. Gordimer still said no. She said she cannot do it. I must respect her privacy. I kept on insisting that I am not asking for a sitting or interview, I request just one photograph. She still said no. I became emotional and pleaded: Please Madam, let me have this honour. She asked why I want a photograph. I said I just want to keep it with myself as a memory that I met you. She enquired if I am going to use it for any other purpose. Of course, not. I had no such intention. Can you put this in writing? Gordimer asked. I quickly nodded in agreement and to my good luck, Gordimer gave in: you are very stubborn. Come in. Her dog walked beside me as I entered the gate. Gordimer saw my hesitation and led the dog away. I was taken into the garden via the kitchen and dining room. I waited till she came back after checking her messages on the answering machine. I quickly asked what she would like me to put in writing. She said: it's alright, I can see you are not that type of person. When I requested if her servant can take our photograph, she became upset: that is going to be a problem. You don't have anyone with you to take the photograph? Jonathan was outside but I was not supposed to reveal it. I will tell the servant how to take it, I said. Gordimer got more upset: no, no, he has never taken a photo in his whole life. You wait here, I see if I could ask my neighbour.

I was happy and tears flowed in my eyes as I gazed around. She had a beautiful garden inside the house. I didn't know how to respond to where I am. A big lifetime experience. I just gazed at everything to keep it remember in my memory forever—dark wooden floors—whitewashed veranda with plants of big leaves—countless pots with plants on the right side of where I was standing and a nicely trimmed garden in front of my eyes. When Gordimer came back with her neighbour, Michael, and his wife, she was in a different mood. She was now very cheerful and lively. Michael happily took some photographs, leading us from one side of the veranda to another to get appropriate light for the photographs. During that time, Gordimer asked me which country I come from and how old I am. I was mesmerised by the experience as if I were in a dream talking to Gordimer in person. I told Gordimer how I did my first M.Phil. presentation on her short story 'Amnesty', and how it led me to discover more about her and her fiction. She listened attentively and seemed impressed. She told me about her new publication which is going to be on the market soon and would like to know what I think about it. Sitting next to her for the photograph, I told her that it is a lifetime experience for me and I feel honoured to be photographed with her. She looked into my tearful eyes and smiled at me. It was, indeed, a great moment in my life.

Author in conversation with Nadine Gordimer

To keep my word, I decided to leave soon after this brief photo session. Gordimer wanted to know how I came here and how I will go. I said that my friends dropped me and they are coming to pick me up. She asked me to sit in her dining room and rang them. She sounded a bit worried as it had never been safe for a foreigner like me to travel alone in Johannesburg. She insisted that I should wait inside the house until they come to pick me up. I preferred to wait in the kitchen. Before retiring to attend to other matters, Gordimer shook hands, wished good luck for producing a good piece of research, and asked me to send her a copy of my work at completion. I thanked her once again for her time. Before she went inside, Gordimer asked: I hope you don't think that I was rude to you? I said: no, not at all—what else could I say. As she disappeared behind the kitchen door, I fiddled with my mobile for a moment and asked the servant to let me go out of the gate. I quickly walked towards the back street where Jonathan was waiting for me in the car. I didn't know how to show my happiness. I kept on thanking Jonathan for making my day. He didn't believe what happened. He congratulated me for my courage to take the risk and get it done on my own. I was over the moon. I was not listening anymore. My mission was complete, it seemed. The goal was achieved and I was very happy. This made Jonathan relax—I finally managed to meet Gordimer. We drove back home in rejuvenation. Jonathan showed me the popular Johannesburg flats but I was not fully paying attention. I was thinking of sending an email to Dr Chandramohan, my mentor and then my Ph.D. supervisor, to inform him that the unexpected has finally happened. That was not Gordimer who changes her mind so frequently; some miracle had occurred. It was Dr Chandramohan's idea to visit her without an appointment and request a photograph if she doesn't agree to a formal interview. That night, I prayed and thanked God for making my dream become a reality.

The Jewish and Christian societies in Johannesburg

I accompanied Jonathan to a Jewish Church where he was invited to speak about Alan Paton's life and times before a small gathering of old Jewish people, mostly women. Jonathan delivered an absorbing lecture about his father's life. Jonathan introduced his talk by saying what it was like as Paton's son and announced the title of his speech, 'Alan Paton and other Animals' which amused the audience.

Alan Paton was born in 1903 in Natal which was a British colony then. Paton's father was a very authoritative person who was very strict with his children. Paton was a bright student and did his matriculation at the age of fifteen. As a trained teacher, he was sent to teach in Ecopo (Ixopa, a Xhosa word). There he fell in love with a married woman whose husband was on death bed suffering from TB. He passed away within six months of their love affair. Jonathan was comfortable to tell that her mother lived in guilt for some time even after her marriage to his dad. It diffused with the birth of Jonathan in her life.

Alan Paton converted to the Anglican faith under the influence of his wife. The other person who had made a deep impact on Paton's life was Jan Hendrik Hofmeyer (1894–1948). Paton later wrote a biography about him as well. Hofmeyer was an extraordinarily talented man who did his matriculation at the age of 12 years, BA at the age of 15, MA at the age of 19 from Oxford University, and became Vice-Chancellor of the Wits University at the age of 23. But he had a very dominating mother who even went to Oxford with him when he was studying there. Hofmeyer had liberal views and wanted the United Party to be liberal in the 1930s. At that time, Smuts was on the front in WW1 and Hofmeyer was the Minister of Education. He asked Paton to reform prison at Depkloop into a reformatory. Paton took up the assignment and did very well. He took away the guns and removed the fences from the prison because he believed that by giving freedom of movement and expression to the prisoners, there comes a sense of responsibility which finally led them to improve their behaviour. Henry Verwood disliked Alan Paton for what he was doing at Depkloop—the Liberal party was a party of all races. In his speech, Jonathan revealed his concern about the way Paton's house at the Depkloop is abandoned and left to decay and destruction in no time.

Paton took some time off from his work and went to Scandinavia, England, and United States to visit reformatories there. It was during this trip that Paton wrote *Cry The Beloved Country*. At that time, he was very much under the influence of the interpretation of the English version of the Bible (King James VIII) and the verses from the Zulu. He finished the book to the end when he arrived in the United States; he kept on writing everywhere he went, even on the trains. The story flowed in his mind. *Cry The Beloved Country* was translated into 23 languages. Paton always gave a signed copy of his books to Jonathan. He finished writing his last book in April 1988 which was published in 1987, the only book he couldn't sign for Jonathan as he passed away by then. Paton had altogether seven Honorary Doctors from all over the world.

Jonathan remembers his father as an authoritarian person who was not a good listener. After the death of his first wife, Paton was married to his secretary till his death. She now lives in England. All the original manuscripts of Paton's work now exist with her. The royalty of Paton's work is equally divided between his grandchildren. Paton kept his both sons Jonathan and David cut out of inheritance because David left his wife against Paton's wishes. Jonathan was punished too along with his brother. Alan Paton was without a passport for ten years. He and his works were never banned but his phones were always taped and the mail always interfered.

The Jewish audience enjoyed the talk and asked a couple of questions. Over the tea afterwards, I met Jewish women. There was one who migrated from Latvia with her family, now a widow, her late husband was a doctor in Cape Town. She had recently moved to Johannesburg and was not happy there because people were not sincere in that big city. To my shock, hardly anyone of them knew Gordimer. I found one Jewish woman whom I met in the washroom and who managed to gossip, in front of an outsider like me, about the breaking of Gordimer's first marriage; this Jewish woman had met Gordimer once at the airport when Gordimer was very rude to her. Jonathan later told that Gordimer is not a popular and known person in her community. On our way back, Jonathan took me to show Nelson Mandela's huge bronze statue in the Sandton city plaza.

At Pam's birthday party in the evening, I met people from the Anglican Church. Pam's sister-in-law, Joy whose husband was a priest in the church, talked about the role of the church in the 80s when it actively participated in the struggle against apartheid. However, Joy admitted that white people benefited from the apartheid system. Later, I spoke with the black housemaid in Jonathan's house, Rachel, and her husband, Isaac who were also invited to the birthday party. They were a bit reluctant to talk about apartheid and the new South Africa but then Rachel opened:

she was happy with the new labour laws. Her husband was paid well. Isaac told how hard it used to be to travel from his village two hundred miles away and come to work in Johannesburg. Rachel recalled a story of her being put into prison because she didn't have the pass to enter the white area and how she spent the night in jail with her sick baby in her lap. I found Rachel behaving like a duck, very calm on the surface but underneath a lot of disturbance, a lot of lava, anger, and bitterness which need to come out. Rachel appeared happy but a bit shy when I asked her to pose for a photo with me. Rachel had a certain kind of pride in herself. I liked it.

Nelson Mandela statue in Nelson Mandela Square—Johannesburg (2005)

In conversation with Jonathan Paton and his wife Margaret

I had a short sitting with Margaret in the kitchen during our late breakfast together. Margaret belonged to the Anglican Church all her life and was not comfortable with the current shift of the theologists and priests towards moderation of Christian values in the light of a changing world. We landed in an interesting conversation about the consciousness of skin colour in Asian and South African cultures. Margaret was amused to know that in Pakistan, people prefer having the white colour of their skin instead of their standard brown complexion. I told her the amusing fact of my sister's marriage that took place mainly because of her white skin colour. It didn't matter whether she had other traits in her personality—though she has many luckily—but as long as she was white, she was more than acceptable to the boy and his family. I told Margaret that when I came to the United Kingdom for the first time, I was shocked to find Western people fancying to have darker skin. The darker skin is considered beautiful; white people plan to go to holiday destinations where they can get themselves tanned or coloured. In South African society too, non-white people are very conscious of their skin colour. Margaret found it funny to see black women bleaching themselves to look fairer than their natural colour. I told Margaret about my experience of the black women wearing wigs of straight hair because they are not comfortable showing their natural bushy hair.

Author with the maidservant Rachel in Jonathan's house (2005)

Somehow we ended up discussing Rachel, the black housemaid in Margaret's house. Margaret observed that Rachel wasn't satisfied with what she was given. Margaret spoke highly of her as a domestic and as a person but she felt hurt that Rachel never appreciated when she gave her a gift or present on occasion. She always expects more. Margaret was unable to understand why Rachel wanted to buy a dishwasher for her village home—the white man's life!—before she retires from her domestic job at their house. It irritated Margaret when Rachel made sarcastic remarks in her frustration. However, Margaret understood that one cannot expect a person to be virtuous when he or she has to live at the line of poverty all his or her life. How could one expect the people of colour not to mistrust the white people or become suspicious of them when they see the latter living with a better lifestyle? Margaret admitted that Rachel would have made progress in her life if she had the same opportunities as she had as a white person in South African society.

Earlier, when Margaret was talking about the modernisation of the church, we came up to the discussion about the lack of awareness of the general white population about the African life around them. She said that liberals like Alan Paton made efforts to create awareness amongst people against the inhuman values of their South African society. But the white Nationalists took this liberal stance as an exaggeration and propaganda of the left-wing and the communist party. In this context, Margaret told a story of her childhood to reveal how white people approached African life. Once she asked her mother as a child why their black gardener doesn't live with his own family. Doesn't he miss them? Her mother responded: they are different and they don't feel like us. Margaret held the white people responsible for the mess and violence that occurred in their South African society: how could one expect people to behave when you force them to live without or far from their families? How could one expect a healthy progression in society if people are deprived of their basic needs and necessities? It was the reading of her father-in-law Alan Paton's *Cry The Beloved Country* that made Margaret very much conscious of her lack of knowledge and understanding of the other side of her South African world.

During this brief conversation, Margaret also revealed that the Dutch Reformed Church was responsible for instilling in the psyche of the white colonists that God had made white people rule and the people of colour to be ruled. That is why people of her mother's generation could not think beyond this interpretation of life for themselves. Also, it benefited them enormously in every part of life. Although the Anglican Church was always uncomfortable with what was happening in society, people like

Margaret lived with guilt. I was impressed to see Margaret participating with charity workers in support of Aids victims; she provided materials that they would need to look after young babies and children who suffer from Aids. I was told that the gardener at Margaret's house suffered from Aids and had unknowingly transmitted the disease to his wife. In Margaret's opinion, it was pathetic to see the government completely ignoring the fact that Aids is a serious problem in South Africa.

Author with Jonathan's granddaughter Nina—Johannesburg (2005)

Later in the afternoon, I met Nina, six-year-old grandchild of Jonathan and Margaret. For her age, she was very well-mannered and soon became friends with me. I came to notice that she was not conscious of her white colour at all. She did not treat me differently because I was brown. She kept on clinging to me and preferred to hold my hand when we went out shopping. However, her step-brother who is older than her and who is brown due to his mixed parentage is very much conscious of his skin colour. Margaret later told me that he doesn't like the skin of his colour: he wants to be white. This made one aware of the colour complexities which exist in societies everywhere in the world. In South African society, colour barriers affect those people psyche more who are on the *Other* side such as Nina's step-brother. In the market, wooden statues of wise men and working women amused me to no end; in traditional African society, a man has the status of a philosopher in the family who would spend most of his time thinking, and a woman works in the fields and does domestic work. On our way back, Margaret drove past Nelson Mandela's official residence where he met the public and dignitaries during his rule as President of South Africa.

Over a glass of his evening drink and my cup of tea, I had an interesting session with Jonathan. I wanted to know about the role and importance of PEN in the South African world of writers. It was a forum for the writers to express themselves but it got political with time. The conservative members were asked to resign and then PEN had been dominated by the black writers afterwards. For Jonathan, South African Literature cannot be defined without Peter Abrahams, Alan Paton, Ahmed Essop, Alex La Guma, J M Coetzee, Eskia Mphahlele, Richard Rive, and Herman Charles Bosman. Coetzee focused on the extermination of Bushman and Hottentots by the Afrikaners in his early fiction. *Waiting for the Barbarians* (1980)—a good piece of work by Coetzee is about the end of apartheid and the power of blacks; the barbarian is a sardonic comment on the power of blacks in South Africa. Coetzee's *Life and Times of Michael K* (1983) travels through the bleak landscape. Coetzee's approach is pessimistic and presents a very bleak picture of South Africa. La Guma has written a novella about District Six. He joined the communist party and never came back. Eskia Mphahlele had to leave South Africa on an exit permit like Nat Nakasa who committed suicide but Mphahlele returned to South Africa after his request to come back was granted by the apartheid government. This offended hard-line blacks and anti-apartheid activists. Mphahlele doesn't appreciate Alan Paton and criticises Paton for not creating black characters as round characters. He believed that Paton was white and doesn't know about the black world, so he cannot represent the black world through a keyhole experience. Richard Rive was a black writer, a gay person who got killed. He was almost like Steve Biko, very dark-skinned but he spoke English like an English man. He was a militant person. His early writings—short stories present the early days of apartheid. Bosman was a good story writer but is misunderstood because of his Kaffir terminology.

About Muslim writers in South Africa, Jonathan was of the view that no other Muslim writer is of Essop's class mainly because he is prepared to satirise Muslims in his work. In Johannesburg, generally, people don't know about Muslims. Their identity had been of the traders; there were some Muslim tailors in the oriental plaza. Overall, Muslims were wealthier merchants in the clothing business. Apart from these traders, Muslims were isolated in Johannesburg; being part of marginalised South African society, they lived in the Muslim township, Lenasia near Johannesburg.

However, in Durban, Muslims, Indians, and the whites did meet socially and were not isolated as in Johannesburg. The Durban Indian community—mostly Hindus range from lawyers and doctors to the very poor. Gordimer didn't have first-hand knowledge of Muslim life but she did good research work to portray Muslim characters in *The Pick Up*. Jonathan suggested that next time I visit South Africa, I must go and visit Natal and meet Fatima Meer (1928–2010) in Durban. She has written about Muslims in South Africa. Jonathan has also recommended looking at a *Coloured* Muslim writer and then a professor at the Western Cape University, Adam Small's (1936–2016) plays about the Coloured community.

What exactly had happened between Alan and Gordimer? Jonathan said that all came in public. Gordimer's comment that *Liberalism is a dirty word in South Africa* made Alan Paton very upset. *Absolute nonsense*, she said and Paton attacked Gordimer in Sunday Times. There was an angry exchange of letters between Alan and Gordimer and both stood their ground. On his death, Gordimer said that it is a great pity that Paton had devoted his life to the cause which went no way. Jonathan was upset that it was his father who used to say that I want to stab the white people in South Africa in the heart. How could she say such a thing?

Jonathan believes that Alan Paton was a philosopher. He used to say that liberals cannot be written off…as if they had done nothing. […] we are accused—even by a person so eminent as Nadine Gordimer—of making promising that we could never keep. I do not remember any of these promises. We promised blood and toil and tears and sweat, and it is what many of us got […] we were abhorred by the right and despised by the left.' (Paton, 1988, 117).

The liberal party died its death because political parties could only legally exist as one racial group as per the laws under apartheid. Helen Suzman (1917–2009) belonged to the progressive liberals who were a less militant group and who could be classified as mild. They ask the black members to resign so that the party could survive. Liberal Party was allowed a seat in the parliament under the apartheid government. Suzman's group became the only liberal voice that with time, gradually, got softer. Jill Wentzel has talked about this in her book *Liberal Slide Away* (1995). So liberals were the major in-between society—the borderland characters; Gordimer does present liberals of all sorts, progressive, militant, leftists—ANC supporters and the right wings who propagated the idea of a qualified franchise.

Jonathan said that he is a liberal like his father. He joined the Liberal Party very early in his life and was an active participant in the University of Natal. He showed me an old photograph of Liberal party members and I could locate him in the photo. In his university days, his job was, as an organiser, to visit door to door to convince people to join the Party. Once he had a hard time when he knocked at the door of an Afrikaner who then shouted back at him in abusive language. Jonathan was proud to share that his father, Alan Paton was always appreciative of what he (Jonathan) did for the Party. Jonathan recalled that *Contact* was the Liberal Party paper which no longer exists. Amongst contemporary Johannesburg newspapers such as Citizen, Die Vaderland, The Star, and Sunday Times, Mail & Guardian weekly is considered as a left-wing newspaper in present South Africa. I am told that this weekly has been under fire by the government for its blunt criticism of ANC policies—a grim reminder of censorship under apartheid in new South Africa. Jonathan added that censorship is still actively practised in the neighbouring country, Zimbabwe under the rule of Robert Mugabe (1924–2019).

That evening, Pam and her husband Rob joined us for supper at Jonathan's house. Rob gave me a website to look at exhibition photos related to the apartheid era. He shared his experience of becoming aware of apartheid when he went to study at the University of Stellenbosch. Most of the students were Afrikaners there. Coming from an English background, he felt isolated and marginalised. That was the point of realisation that apartheid is evil. This led him to look at South African life with different eyes. Rob said that he has been a liberal, consciously or unconsciously, all his life. Pam said that she has lived through apartheid and she can see that a change is now coming into society. Previously, children across colour could not study together in one school. But now the government is making sure that every school has a multi-cultural badge of students. Things are improving but people still need to be educated on how to amalgamate and live in peace in new South Africa. Here, Jonathan added that Mandela should have stayed longer in power. It seemed Mbeki and his cabinet were not popular even in the English community of South Africa—the minister Shabeer's case of bribes and corruption was in highlights those days.

In conversation with Jill Wentzel

Author with Jill Wentzel in her house—Johannesburg (2005)

Jonathan accompanied me to Jill Wentzel's house for our scheduled meeting for half an hour at noon. On our way, Jonathan spoke about Jill's contribution to the establishment of the Liberal Party in South Africa. She was very active in the liberal politics against apartheid and worked for the Institute of Race Relations till her retirement. Jill welcomed us into her spacious house and led us to sit and enjoy drinking grape juice near the swimming pool outside in the sun. As I was introducing myself and my area of work, Jill came up with all her answers to the questions I was about to ask; my focus of discussion was to find out her views about the divisions in the Liberal Party and the psychological effects of apartheid on people in South Africa. Jill asked me to read her book *Liberal Slide Away*. Jonathan has kindly let me his copy to read it because the book is out of print now. For Jill, apartheid was a source of anxiety that led people, like her, to work towards a liberal society for herself and the people in South Africa. To probe that deep hurt that is, apartheid, people needed space to speak and the Liberal Party provided such a forum and platform to people of different races. Yes, liberals were the in-between society, Jill agreed. Then she mentioned the consciousness of white guilt that existed amongst the liberals during the apartheid period; it was this guilt of being white and privileged that led many of them to appreciate the humanistic values of a liberal world. She and many others like her found relief from this white guilt in new South Africa. Jill very honestly admitted that liberals were not angels. They had their weak spots, they had their ups and downs. Most of the white liberals did live comfortably under apartheid as compared to the black and coloured liberals; though they were against the system, they lived very much the same way as most whites lived. At the question of the gradual division of the Liberal Party into factions, she agreed that there were divisions but those people were individuals only. Initially and basically, all of them were liberals in principle. There were rich liberals like John Haris who used to pour a pool of funds into the Party's establishment. In the early days of apartheid, liberals were not that disturbed by the security police as the way they were approached in later days: there was a hotchpotch; both liberals and communists were all thrown together in the same category by the security police. They were mostly treated as prisoners of war during the 60s era—the African resistance movement was against the communists as well. It was after the 1960s when ANC decided to go towards the politics of violence, there appeared a violent group in liberal politics. Though at times, the liberals and the communists were at daggers with each other, still they decently fought against apartheid. The 1960s was the time of real violence. By the early 70s, people were completely ignoring Pass laws. It was the time when illegal strikes were going out of momentum because of the change in the demographic situation; the employees were legally trained blacks and people of colour. Jill asked me to read *The Silent Revolution* by John Kaneberman.

To comment on Gordimer's work, Jill had little to say. She found Gordimer a bit distant in her association with the liberal world. Of course, Gordimer always avoided being labelled with any world. Jill liked Gordimer's early work to which she can relate but she found herself bored with her later fiction. Jill remembered meeting Gordimer a couple of times and her visits to the Sash Movement sessions a few times but apart from this, she hardly found Gordimer participating in the liberal activities during or after apartheid. When Jill was the Vice President of the Black Sash, Gordimer didn't give them any funds but she did come to support them. Jill said that the Institute of Race Relations is a record, the best living record in detail of what apartheid was doing or did to people in South Africa. In the beginning, the liberals were actively running the Institute but then they became arrogant and the communists took over. After the 80s, the Institute found it difficult to maintain its reputation in front of the growing corruption in its quarters. The surveys at the Institute are factual information. So there is not much available on how people would have suffered emotionally. So for the information on psychological breakdowns, Jill suggested that I would have to depend on South African writers in fiction.

Before we ended the conversation, Jill showed interest in my work and would like to read my novel when it is ready. I shared with her how I started working on a novel under the influence of William Golding's *Lord of the Flies* and left it unfinished in my university days. She said that it had been ages since she read something new. Jill showed her interest in literature produced in Pakistan when I mentioned my father's works in poetry and journalism. I was over the moon after I met Jill that afternoon. I told Jonathan that now I have the confidence to say that I know something about the factions amongst the liberals under apartheid. My mind was much clearer about the world of liberals in South Africa.

Meeting Rowland Smith, Carole Gindenhuys and Collin Smuts

Author in Jonathan's house with Rowland Smith—Johannesburg (2005)

Rowland Smith, one of the main critics of Gordimer's work, was in town visiting his mother from Canada. He kindly agreed to a brief morning sitting at Jonathan's place. He showed interest in my area of study and I was pleased to know from him that there is a punch in my subject matter. Rowland Smith finds Gordimer a highly intelligent woman. She has been extremely courteous and friendly with him. About Alan Paton's row with Gordimer over her stance that liberals were observers, Rowland was of the view that the liberals in South Africa were ineffectual. I liked his use of the word, 'ineffectual'. That is what we get in Gordimer's *Occasion for Loving* where the characters don't alter but still get affected in different ways. Gordimer's *A Guest of Honour* is another such good example: highly goodwill and sympathetic understanding inappropriate of liberalism. Gordimer's *The Late Bourgeois World* had that anonymous ineffectual use of the signature. It presents a world judgemental about liberalism. There were two sides of the problem in the novel—two ineffectual sides—one the dead husband and the other old grandmother. In Gordimer's *Burger's Daughter*, Rosa goes to Europe and discovers the pleasure-seeking French Bourgeois world. Rowland didn't have much time so I asked him to suggest any writers I may be reading to enrich my area of research. He said: Margaret Atwood and Alice Munro's short stories.

Carole Gindenhuys, a physical educationist now and had the honour of being the first woman to become the captain of a cricket team in South Africa met us in a café for lunch. She was very hospitable. She said that she would make sure that next time, she would cook. Jonathan and she had to discuss some educational matters, so I kept listening until Carole had time to answer a couple of my questions. I asked how she feels in new South Africa. She said: very good. The blacks forgave us, the elections took place, and we went to queue for the voting side by side, it was a big experience, there was a joy and we were happy. I asked the same question which I previously had asked Jonathan, as a white person, if she feels marginalised in new South Africa. She had the same answer: as belonging to the old generation, we have no such problem but the young white South Africans might have as now there is more competition. Carole then shared her own experience of segregation in sports. She had an Asian student, Rubina khan, a potential tennis player but she was never given a chance to play and she ended up becoming the court girl who picks up the balls in between the games. Rubina is now a sports admin at Wits University. This was just one example but there were many cases when students are barred from doing things just because of the colour of their skin.

Carole admitted that when she was young, she was not brave enough to query what was happening around her but she always questioned why they cannot play cricket with teams across the racial divide. Then Jonathan asked her to tell the story of her reluctantly shaking hands with the apartheid dignitaries as a captain of her team in 1974. I asked her how would she like to be identified—a liberal white, a radical white, or a South African? She said I will call myself South African. Carole was very enthusiastic about Pakistani cricketers and knew more about them as compared to me. She was a fan of Shoaib Akhtar and wanted to know about Imran Khan's wedding to Jemima. I enjoyed meeting Carole, a dedicated sincere human being.

I met Collin Smuts later in the evening. *Coloured* in origin, he appeared to be a heavy drinker. He used to work for the Cultural forum which was very active in resistance politics. He was an organiser of a resistance meeting under the writers' forum in 1982. In 1997, he organised a seminar on South African writers from all over the country. He was in the Congress of South African writers in 1989 but then he decided to leave after being a treasurer there for some time. He then ran an art school for children in the townships. Being a close friend, he was the third person whom Gordimer asked to speak at her husband's funeral. It was Collin who organised the Nobel Prize-Winning reception for her. People from all spheres of life including writers were invited to the celebration. Desmond Tutu also came to the party. Collin informed that people call Gordimer his white auntie; she is a big mama to him.

Author in Jonathan's house with Collin Smuts—Johannesburg (2005)

Collin provided information I mostly knew: Gordimer writes from 7 am to 1 pm daily—Monday to Friday. Verna Hunt is her secretary nowadays. Gordimer doesn't like it if some white person turns up uninvited to her party but for the non-white people, there is no such rule; everybody is welcomed. However, Gordimer stops them, that is, the guests and friends in the house from drinking at 8 pm. But on the day of her Nobel Prize-Winning, she didn't stop anyone from drinking till late. Collin revealed that Gordimer is very close to her son, Hugo. She is not in a cordial relationship with her daughter who decided to marry a waiter in France. It upset Gordimer to know that her daughter lives in a council flat in France—divorced with two children residing on a farm in Italy. Collin said that people objected to his inviting Gordimer as a guest to the African Arts Trust forum. To attract an audience, it was important, Collin gave justification: who would have come to listen to Ahmed Dangor? Collins recalled an incident when he along with Gordimer and Zakes Mda were once stuck in no man's land between the South African border and Botswana. Gordimer behaved like a little comrade. On other occasions too, whenever he was short of money, he borrowed money from her. Many times, she paid for the school in times of need.

Collin revealed that Gordimer has utilised real situations for the plot and action in her stories and novels such as in *A World of Strangers*. She used to visit the flats in Johannesburg which were described in the novel. But Gordimer has the habit of not admitting it straight away. The same is the case with *Burger's Daughter*. Collin was of the view that Gordimer has been neglected by the publishers in South Africa. She felt let down by them. Now, one South African publishing company has agreed to publish Robert Suresh Ronalds' controversial biography on her. Collin shared that he didn't like Suresh from day one and kept on warning Gordimer that he might harm her reputation. But still, Gordimer trusted him and let him investigate her record of files. It was an authorised biography but Suresh broke his promise and went ahead with the publication of the material to which she strongly objected. Suresh is originally from Trinidad and comes from a prominent lawyers' family. Himself a lawyer by profession, he appears to be a very ambitious person. Nowadays, he is working on writing a biography of Mbeki. We had to stop our conversation here as Collin had an appointment to attend.

In conversation with Ahmed Essop

A half an hour drive from Patons' house in Johannesburg, Lenasia is a township built for separate Asian development. On the outskirts of the settlement, the sight of several shacks and squatters kept alive the memory of apartheid. The lanes and streets in Lenasia were marked with the names of animals s such as Alboitrus, Vulture, and Essop lived in Lark street. Essop and his wife Fareeda wholeheartedly welcomed me along with Jonathan and Margaret for Sunday Lunch. They were very hospitable in their Asian way, with fresh Mango drinks followed by grand Asian lunch and desserts, and, then afternoon tea was served with a variety of cakes and biscuits.

Author with Ahmed Essop in his house—Lenasia 2005

Our conversation started with my reporting on how I finally met Gordimer. Essop agreed that Gordimer is a very difficult person to deal with. He told an incident when she was very rude to his wife for no reason but at the same time, he recalled her as a very lively person in her earlier days when they met for lunch at each other's houses. Gordimer has a set schedule for the day and she doesn't want to meet people in the mornings and without appointments. She is also very unpredictable in her behaviour. The most recent example is her row with Roberts for not permitting him to publish in his biography her comment about Ruth First whom Gordimer named as a 'left bitch'. Essop showed us cuttings of Ruth's photo in the papers. She was, indeed, an attractive woman of her times. Essop was very much impressed and influenced by Ruth as a child when she took them to debates and discussions at the Red Square where Mandela also used to come. Essop supported Ruth First's views and like many other fellow students of his time such as Can Themba, Nat Nkosi, and Lewis Nkosi—the Drum Generation; she was quite aware of the suppression. Essop told that his character Roseland in his story 'The Third Prophesy' is, in fact, the persona of Ruth First. Essop also informed that Coetzee is more difficult to communicate with than Gordimer. Once he agreed to an interview and when the interviewer arrived, Coetzee picked up a book and started reading completely ignoring the existence of another person in the room. Like me and Jonathan, Essop was also not a great fan of Coetzee. According to Ahmed, Coetzee completely ignores other facets of life such as physical pleasures and much other everyday life satisfaction, and wholly focuses on misery as if this is the only thing in life. I shared with Essop that Professor Klopper also said in a seminar that Coetzee likes to be miserable all the time.

During Lunch, Essop spoke about his background how his father came from Gujrat (India) to South Africa in 1931 when he was two years old. He was lucky enough to have very good teachers at a boarding school run by a wealthy Muslim merchant for the Asian community in South Africa. Despite extreme poverty in their early days, he had good food plus good clothing, and some money as well which were part of the package in studying at that institution. He was nine when he was put to this schooling and since then his writing and creating skills were groomed by the excellent art and literature teachers in the school. This led us to discuss the early Asian settlers who contributed to education such as Sheikh Yusuf. In this regard, Essop has recently completed a biography on Suleiman Mohamed Nana, a respected intellectual amongst the early settlers. Essop was happy to collect and restore the lost material that ever existed about the life of such a great personality. This biography is a property of the Institute of Education and is not for commercial sale.

Essop told very interesting and amusing stories of his childhood days how the teachers at school used to encourage the students to develop their aesthetic skills. One of their much-loved teachers was offended by the misconduct of a student in public but he didn't want to criticise him for his action. Instead, he uttered, 'It takes all sorts of people to make the world' As an educationist, Essop was not satisfied with the way students are taught and graded nowadays. It seems silly to him to teach William

Shakespeare's *Macbeth* and Nadine Gordimer's *July's People* to students at the matriculation level. They simply find it boring because they are too young to understand the intensity that exists in these texts. For refusing to follow the State Education rules of teaching, Essop was suspended for a year and then it took another two years in the courts to get reinstated. But he did not go back to teaching. He was not happy because he was not paid back his salary which dates back to his years out of work. Essop and his family survived because the teachers' association helped them from time to time and also he did business here and there. Essop was amused to tell that he earned more whilst doing little as a businessman whereas he earned little for the work he did as an educationist. He believed that those days of suspension from work were, in fact, a blessing in disguise because then he was able to give time to his writing. He produced most of his work during that time.

Ahmed Essop and his wife Fareeda—Lenasia 2005

Essop's mother tongue is Gujrati and Fareeda's Urdu. They understand but they cannot speak in their mother tongue. They regard English as their language now. Both husband and wife have never been to India and have little to relate to that Asian culture and traditions. Their link to their parentage makes them conscious of their Indian ancestry who spoke the same language and keep up with their Indian lifestyles. This reminded me of the extinction of most native languages in the face of Afrikaans and English languages in South Africa: linguistic identities flickered and were affected by colonialism drastically. For Essop and Fareeda, South Africa was their home. In his conversation, Essop also revealed that there was no classification between Muslims and Hindus as such. All of us were considered Asians who had no rights to own or acquire the lands or do any other occupation. So mostly the Asians were constrained to become a businessman. That is why most of the Asians turned up shopkeepers and merchants in South Africa and then a few took up jobs as teachers in the later period.

After lunch, I tried to work out my discussion with Essop in two sections. The first part was fully concentrated on Gordimer and the other was focused on Essop for which I requested if I could record his voice and he happily agreed.

I introduced three different areas of focus in my research, the presentation of the liberal world, of physical borderlands, and the psychological effect of the borderland encounters in Gordimer's fiction. However, I started by asking how he would grade Gordimer and how come he is in her good books. Essop spoke highly of her writing skills and of her courage to review his writings. This led us to discuss her limited knowledge of the Muslim community. Here, Essop stressed that writers like Gordimer are imaginative people.

He agreed that she hardly presents Muslim characters in her stories. The only story he could recollect was 'Chip of Ruby' in which Gordimer has focused on a South African Muslim character, Mrs Bamgee, and then later in her novel *The Pick Up*, she focuses on a Muslim character who is not a South African.

When asked if Essop would agree to Gordimer's stand that Liberalism was a dirty word in South Africa because the liberals preferred to act as observers during the apartheid era, Jonathan reacted very strongly to my question which was put to Essop for an answer—after-effects of the heavy lunch, I suppose!. Jonathan wanted me to specify which group of liberals I was talking about, the aggressive liberals like his father, Alan Paton who founded the Liberal Party in 1953, or the passive liberals like Suzman, or the militant ones like John Haris, or that group of liberals who had to live with apartheid against their wishes after the end of the Liberal party in 1968. I felt caught by my sweeping statement but Essop quickly came to my rescue: there were several groups in the Liberal Party and the left-wing politics was very much divided into small groups of intellectuals. Essop did not agree with Gordimer's presentation of the liberal world as observers only. He gave examples of liberals like John Haris, a very good-natured person and a very close friend who put his life at risk in his struggle against apartheid. He planted a bomb at a public place that killed several white people. Essop couldn't believe that Haris can ever do such a thing and to his satisfaction, he found out afterwards that Haris did not put the bomb at the public place but it was accidentally brought there by someone (God knows who!) who might not have known that it was a bomb. Haris did plant the bomb but it was not a public sight. He was hanged for his militant liberalism. This reminded me of Max in Gordimer's *The Late Bourgeois World*. I agreed with Essop that there is always a difference in experience and it depends on a lot from which perspective one is looking at the situation. As a liberal and living in an Asian township, Essop's interpretation plus experience of apartheid would always be different from people like Gordimer, for example, who lives in the white suburb, the posh Park Town—generating key-hole interpretations of each other's worlds.

I reluctantly took the initiative to ask—in Jonathan's presence—whether liberals felt marginalised during the apartheid era. Jonathan provided the answer as expected. Yes, they became marginalised towards the end of the Liberal party in South Africa due to the extremism of Afrikaner nationalism and the Black Consciousness movement but the fact cannot be ignored that the liberals were the only community that was a good mix of all colours. Essop agreed with Jonathan that it was a liberal ideal that provided space for different communities and non-whites to come closer and struggle against the oppression in society.

Moving on to the issue of physical borderlands, Essop talked about his own experience of moving to Lenasia Township. The Groups Areas Act forced different communities into separate homelands, so they were shifted to Lenasia as a part of separate development from an Indian suburb near Wits University. About psychological breakdowns, Essop was of the view that we have to depend on writers like Gordimer to record the effects of apartheid on people in South Africa. People reacted to apartheid in different ways. People like Ruth First, Jenny Curtis who was sent a letter bomb, Ahmed Timol who was thrown out of the window—these anti-apartheid activists sacrificed their lives for bringing a healthy change in society. Alan Paton's *The People Wept* (1957) reveals the misery people lived through apartheid. Essop's own stories 'Haji' (1978) and 'Emperor' (1984) also shed light on psychological issues of life in South African society.

In the following brief session, I focused on three main areas, the Asian/Muslim writers in South Africa and their future, Ahmed Essop's identity in the South African world, and the role of Gandhi's politics and social work in South Africa. Essop referred to Ahmed Dangor, Yusuf Patel, Farooq Azmat, and Ronnie Garvender from Natal as promising Asian writers in contemporary writing in English. He also mentioned the recent emergence of Cape Muslim writers on the literary horizon who are worth reading. I asked about the literary response, the white or English response to his work: was it fair, did he ever feel discriminated? Essop's response was negative. He had fair treatment and was satisfied with the way his work has been approached, reviewed, and acclaimed in the literary circles in South Africa and worldwide.

When asked how he would define identity, particularly his own, Essop said that he is an Indian South African. I rephrased my question and brought in Bhabha's definition of flickering identities to lead Essop to say more about identity issues; as he kept 'Indian' attached with the South African identification, I expected him to say more but to no avail. It, however, tempted Jonathan to utter that identities keep on changing. I wanted to hear this from Essop instead. We moved on to discuss the role of Gandhi in South African politics; Gandhi had been quite a controversial figure in Indian sub-continent politics for his passive resistance policy at the time of partition and for which he was murdered in 1948 at the age of 78. Essop admired Gandhi for his passive resistance politics for twenty years in South Africa: passive resister is a friend of everyone and enemy of none. Essop recalled the spilt in the Indian Congress Movement between extremists and moderates in the 1960s; Dr Yusuf Mohamed Dadoo (1900–1983) was abandoned and the Party negotiated with General Smuts to keep the movement alive during the apartheid era.

Essop came up as a great admirer of Salman Rushdie, especially of his work, *The Satanic Verses*. He had been working on an article on Rushdie then. Essop claimed that Gordimer is a dense writer; once read, nobody would like to read her piece of work again. But with Rushdie, one can read him again and again; it is an enriching experience every time. Essop's views on Islam were quite controversial. He believed that whatever the Holy Quran says is an allegory; it can be interpreted in more than one way. For him, Prophet Jesus (peace be upon him) died on the cross and was not risen alive to the skies by God as both Muslims and Christians believe. There is no such thing as the day of judgement and nobody is getting the 'Hurs' (beautiful virgin women) in paradise for their good deeds in this world. On our way back home, I shared with Jonathan that I always think whatever I wish and don't get, I would get it in the world after: I wish to have long hair but due to my genetic makeup, it is not possible. So it means I won't be getting long hair at departure to the next world. Jonathan laughed: it seems so! It was my first time interviewing a renowned figure like Ahmed Essop. And it was his first time too to be interviewed for his fictional work. I thoroughly enjoyed the experience and could hope that Ahmed Essop did as well.

University of Witwatersrand

Gordimer studied for some time at the Witwatersrand University which organises Nadine Gordimer Lecture in her honour every year. I was invited by Dr David Attwell, the Head of the English Department at the Wits to attend a colloquium on 'Present & Future Directions in South African Literary Studies'. To my surprise, three academics from Stellenbosch University whom I met before were also amongst the speakers. Dr Dirk Klopper, the Head of the English Department at Stellenbosch University looked at Coetzee's *Boyhood* and *Youth*. He presented a comparison between James Joyce and Coetzee's writing as autobiographical fiction, and his language of the journal and aesthetic proving that Coetzee addresses reciprocity; there is a language of desire and reciprocity that exist side by side in his fiction. Then the speaker went into the indeterminacy of autobiographical writing and how much Coetzee and his characters enjoy and feel good at being miserable. I enjoyed his presentation.

Dr Ashraf Jamal's presentation on 'Thinking the Hybrid Moment: Writing South Africa' was also very impressive. Like Bhabha, he likes to present and deal with ideas in difficult terminology—he is in fact, Bhabha junior—and I found myself at a time lost in what he said. He talked about obscurity in Bhabha who believes that just we don't understand anything, it doesn't mean it cannot be accommodating. Then he went to talk about stupidity, that is, black stupidity—Foucault's Black Stupidity. Dr Jamal quoted from Bhabha's essay 'The Post-colonial and the Post-modern' the idea of a hybrid moment which is neither signifier nor signified; the hybrid moment resides in the interstitial [...] in the beyond. I could gather that he was talking about the creative space where there could be immense possibilities of hybridity. He came to the point that South Africa is constructed and continuously has constructed itself in different ways. Then he went to language and its banalities which was out of my understanding. Then he came back to South Africa, presenting its people as some *Other* people suggesting to take South Africa as a black whole. Then he brought in Foucault to know the truth from the false; we are in a post-colonial world. Then he talked about paradigms and projectories. He then went on to talk about transition, liminality, and homogeneity suggesting that Bhabha's hybrid moment fits in South African literature. Talking about the dangerous fluidity of identities, he brought in Foucault's idea of Flash. Then he quotes from Bhabha's 'the World and the Home': what is said seem to resist what is said, where literature lies sublime [...] symbolism [...] something is beyond control but [...]'—I missed the thread what he was trying to say. Then Dr Jamal talked about South Africa and its history of suffering. There is a sense of fascination and loathing for South Africa. He believes that we must embrace obscurity. He also believes that stupidity is healthy. South African literature needs reorientation. He then quotes from Bhabha's 'Aura and Aora' and talks about a part dream and part analysis, the signifier and the signified. Dr Jamal no doubt gave an excellent presentation but it was beyond my understanding.

However, Shane Graham's (Lecturer at Wits) presentation 'Towards a Spatial-Materialist Reading of South African Fiction' which was about the space and the notion of time and space, and Meg Samuelson's (Lecturer at Stellenbosch) paper on 'The City Beyond the Border: The Case for a (Trans) National Literature' in which she talks about social, corporal and ontological borders between life and death, were a bit hard to digest due to my lack of interest in the subject. But I enjoyed David Attwell's interesting presentation on 'South Africa in Post-colonial Theory'. He began talking about the process of orientation, then went on to reveal how the empire writes back its history. He believes that anti-colonialism is a global and international project. In this regard, verses from South African writer, Mongane Serote's poetry were brought in which the black man's child becomes the figure of decolonisation. Then David talked about two conditions or generalities of South African post-coloniality. One textual and layered character and another history of industrial modernisation. He referred to Nadine Gordimer what she says about black writers and literature. Then David went to conclude by commenting on the theory of trans-culturalism and the inadequacy of the binary forces; Transculturalisation followed by reconstruction as it applies to South African post-coloniality, defines the whole national culture.

During the tea break, I had the opportunity to have a brief chat with Shane Graham and David Attwell about my area of work. I came to gather from their conversation and my previous contact with the academics at Stellenbosch and Cape Town that Coetzee is much praised in the current literary world as compared to Gordimer. I came back home from the Wits with relevant material for my research work as well as some fruitful secondary information:

- Ahmed Essop was an active P.E.N. member.
- Alan Paton and Peter Abrahams were amongst the pioneers of shaping English literary consciousness towards the struggle against apartheid in South African society. (Dark Testament).
- Ruth First was a staunch communist and was murdered.
- The Congress of Democrats were mostly Jewish—previous communist party.
- South African PEN (augurated in 1978) Conference took place on 8–9 September 1979.
- The TV came to South Africa in 1976.
- Newspaper 1785 (Saturday, January edition).
- 1913 Land Act: 70% of the population on 13% of the land.
- Freedom Charter was adopted in 1955.
- Sol Plaatjie was one of the founding father of ANC (formed on 8 January 1912 in Mangaung, Bloemfontein.
- Gordimer's Lecture at Wits and Paton's Lecture at the Natal University are organised annually.
- Individual Interviews: Julie Frederikse collection. Historical Papers. The University of Wits.
- Congo was a Belgian colony.
- Save the Beloved Country by Alan Paton. Ed. Hans Strydom and David Jones. Melville: Hans Strydom Publishers, 1987.

After a productive day at the Wits, it was a joy to watch the English comedy—*Kumars at 42* on South African Television in the evening; foreign programmes and Hollywood films on black American culture are not only popular but have influenced the young South Africans in language and custom.

A house next door with a gable front is quite noticeable from the entrance gate of Jonathan's house. It reminded me of Stellenbosch where most of the old houses had gable architecture, the reminder of Dutch rule in South Africa. I noticed foreign plantations on the sides of the roads and in people's houses. I was told that trees in Johannesburg are the largest man-made forest in the world. Jonathan said that most of the plantation in Johannesburg is Australian in origin. The discovery of gold in 1886 and then its mining made many white people rich and led them to stay in South Africa. They could afford to bring in large shipments of the plants and grow them as the labour was very cheap then. We drove on the motorway which at many places provides the dividing line between the white and black areas. One can see the mounds of yellow soil from place to place as well as the old digging machines as a reminder that once gold mining was carried out in these areas. Taxis—small vans—are a common feature of modern South African life but they are not safe. Most of these vehicles don't get serviced. The rash drivers drive them aggressively, making them over-crowded and over-loaded which has led to cause serious accidents.

On the way, I took the liberty to ask Jonathan if he ever did feel marginalised as a white liberal person in South African society. He said he didn't and he doesn't: I belong to South Africa. Jonathan was born in Natal where there was a very small community of Afrikaners who were pro-apartheid. Though Jonathan moved to Johannesburg at a young age, his heart was very much in Natal. He added that a road is named after his father, Alan Paton in Natal and there is an Alan Paton Lecture which takes place every year at the University of Natal. The Wits University arranges a similar Lecture seminar every year in Gordimer's honour.

We passed by the school Jonathan went to. He said that young boys like to play rugby in South Africa. At the Reformatory which now seemed an army colony, we visited the house in which Jonathan lived as a child with his family. Even though the house was in shatters (the house seemed abandoned for ages), Jonathan could tell where he played on the stoep and where the rooms were. He showed me the places where plover birds used to nestle near the house. We took photographs for the record. Jonathan was disappointed to see his father's house at Depk-loop in such a run-down condition. Alan Paton was the Principal of

Depkloop Reformatory from 1935 to 1948. He contributed to the welfare of his South African community by turning the prison at Depkloop into a reformatory centre. Jonathan then described his experiences of studying at Cambridge and how the times have changed now: at that time, there was an obsession with sex, that is, the white man sleeping with the black woman. He enjoyed teaching but he was never a theory person. As a student too, he struggled with understanding the rules of different literary methods.

Jonathan Paton in front of the remains of Depkloop Reformatory (2005)

Soweto Township is far from Johannesburg. I was shocked to know how much travelling the blacks had to do to come to work in Johannesburg. Jonathan said that the apartheid government deliberately did not build shops in Soweto so that the blacks had to come to Johannesburg to work and to shop. They used to get up very early and travelled by bus. Jonathan was not sure about the current minimum wage but he could tell that it is in between eight hundred and one thousand rands—£37 to 46 per month—still less. Jonathan talked about the Booysens town when we drove by the Gold Reef City, a created place to represent old Johannesburg which has become a famous tourist attraction. I was interested to know about Sophia town which I have read about in Gordimer's *A World of Strangers*. Jonathan explained that many townships were created outside Johannesburg such as Sophia town, Alexandria, and Orlanda which is a part of Soweto. Most of the blacks lived in slums and were removed to Orlando in 1932; Bishop Tutu lived in Orlando for quite a time.

Standard one-storey township house—Soweto (2005)

Soweto is a huge township with countless small one-storey houses, some in good condition but most with extended shacks revealing poverty to no end. We passed by a huge electricity plant, right in the heart of the Soweto township which catered electricity for the white areas. But the blacks, Jonathan told me, did not have electricity in the townships for a long time. Jonathan drove through the street where Winnie Mandela's house still existed. Jonathan knew her very well and had financially supported her once when she didn't have the funds to pay for her children's education. Jonathan said that she doesn't have a good reputation in the political world. I knew that she was involved in murder cases but I was shocked to know through Jonathan that she had a relationship with other men when Mandela was in prison and that she likes to spend money on her manicure more than anything else. Jonathan told how difficult it was for Mandela to come to terms with this reality. On the question of my meeting Mandela, I am told that Mandela is not in good health, therefore, not contactable. Jonathan and Margaret were lucky enough to meet him recently through Helen Suzmen's special request.

Jonathan drove me to see the road where the uprisings took place in 1976. It was the site of the shooting of Hector Pietersen, a fifteen years old black student who was first to be shot by the police during the protest procession on 16 June 1976. Hundreds of young people died during such uprisings. The students protested that Afrikaans must be abolished in the education system. Afrikaans was declared as an official language in 1925. Half of their subjects were in English and others in Afrikaans. They were finding it hard to compete and complete their education. On the question of the implementation of the Bantu education system which was introduced in 1953, Jonathan said that resistance against Bantu education increasingly grew because the blacks were not given the right version of history. The Bantu system generated the view that the white and the black people arrived in South Africa at the same time and portrayed the blacks as inferior to the white people and responsible for their backwardness. I came to know through Jonathan that several languages were spoken in Soweto amongst which Zulu and Sotho were the dominant ones. This variety of languages led to the creation of a mixed language, Tsotsi, a Sotho word meaning bad person.

Hector Pietersen's monument outside the museum was a disturbing sight. Inside the museum, the record of the 1976 uprisings in photographs, videos of the forced removals, the display of Steve Biko's death in detention, and the presentations of oppression move one to tears. Jonathan told that Biko's head hit hard with the wall during the investigation by the police which made him unconscious straight away and later led to his death. This revelation came out in the Truth and Reconciliation sessions when one of the policemen came forward to speak the truth. I couldn't bear to listen and watch the video presentation of poetry sung by an African artist whilst beating the drum in front of an audience. I didn't know the language but it felt as if the voice and the beat of the drum were telling the story of pain and misery.

Union Building—Pretoria 2005

The next day, Jonathan took me to visit the Voortrekker museum near Pretoria and the Union building in Pretoria. Though the legislative assembly sits in Cape Town and the President's official residence is also situated in Cape, still, Pretoria has the status of the Capital from where the country is officially run by the government in power. There has been a debate to move everything to Cape but people still want to keep the Union building which is a history. Also, it is a work of superb architecture, built on a huge piece of land with an extraordinary plantation in front of the main area of the building. The Voortrekker museum is another monument. It categorically displays and represents the history of Afrikaners' culture who trekked inland and how they established themselves after fighting fierce battles with the natives of the land. The role of women in the trek is commendable. The monument revealed the history of the Afrikaners' struggle and settlement in different periods of their trek till the English took over in the early 19th century. The English came and disturbed the set-up which Afrikaners made for years. They abolished slavery and put Afrikaners in a difficult economic position. The Afrikaners hated English for undermining their efforts to build their life in South Africa. Jonathan told me that Alan Paton once grew a beard and tried to live like a Boer but then concluded that liberalism is the best option for all the people in South Africa.

Author beside a waterfall in Walter Sisulu National Botanical Gardens—Johannesburg (2005)

Walter Sisulu National Botanical gardens near Johannesburg are an experience. It is a vast piece of natural land which is nurtured further with varieties of local plants and trees and surrounded by mountains and a big waterfall. The atmosphere of the place is kept as it was centuries ago when the Europeans arrived in South Africa. There, one can have the feel of the landscape how it looked like when the colonisers settled in Johannesburg. On the question of the famous Kruger Park built in 1898 which is quite far from Johannesburg and is spread over two hundred miles, Jonathan remarked that the making of that park is the only appreciable thing President Kruger (1825–1904) did during his rule in South Africa.

Traditional African wooden images of female as a worker and male as a person of wisdom—Johannesburg (2005)

Over lunch in the gardens, I had an interesting conversation with Jonathan and Margaret about the people and society in South Africa and how the natives of the land and their culture could not survive in front of the colonial society. I showed them two letter-opener black wooden spatulas that I had bought in the market. On one corner of each flap, a human head was carved, one male and the other female; signifying that the African man stands for intellectual—a thinker who plans, and the African woman has a worker status in African society who does manual work. Jonathan was amused at this display. A writer of a book on South African history, Jonathan explained that Sothos were easy to subjugate than Zulus. Due to their aggressive behaviour, the people of Swaziland survived as a compact tribal country. Otherwise, most African cultures were affected by contact with European civilisation. I asked that there is an assumption about the Africans that they are lazy people; they only plant and grow as much as they need for today and they are not bothered about what will happen tomorrow. I was corrected: it doesn't imply that Africans are lazy but they are just like that. This had been their attitude towards life. This had been their culture for centuries until they are colonised.

Like my first afternoon at the Patons, I had lunch with Margaret in the sunny garden on the day of my departure from Johannesburg—a Papaya and Avocado sandwich with a cup of tea—healthy South African food. Later, Margaret drove me to the hospital to say goodbye to Jonathan; he was admitted in the morning as his ongoing medical condition—lung malfunctioning—needed treatment. I still remember his affectionate eyes, looking at me from behind the oxygen mask. He was full of regret that he won't be able to see me off. I told him that I am short of words to express my gratitude for his precious time and generous support throughout my stay in Johannesburg. We shook hands and wished each other to stay in touch. I didn't know that it was our last meeting; Jonathan passed away a year later in 2006. As the flight took off in the evening for London, I realised that along with my research on the theme of borderland in Gordimer's fiction, I had lived in borderland weather too. It was neither hot nor cold—something in-between—transitory—throughout my period of stay in South Africa.

CONCLUSION

Anti-racist message from the seventh century continues to appeal to date:

> *All humankind is from Adam and Eve, white person has no superiority over black human being nor black man has any superiority over white man, except by piety and good deeds.*
>
> *(Prophet Mohammed—Peace Be Upon Him, Farewell Pilgrimage Sermon, the ninth day of annual rites of Haj, Uranah valley of Mount Arafat, Makkah, 623 AD)*

I conclude with Gordimer's words:

> My challenge, as a writer, is to understand what life is about through each changing set of circumstances. For this to happen it is necessary to reach beyond ourselves, seeking to discover who we are from another perspective, from the point of view of others. (Villa-Vicencio, 1996,106–110)

This invites her protagonists to free themselves from prejudice and ideological control like Mary Logan's advice that she gives to her daughter Cassie in *Roll of Thunder, Hear My Cry* (1976):

> Baby, we have no choice of what colour we are born or who our parents are or whether we're rich or poor. What we do have is some choice over what we make of our lives once we're here. (RTHC, 142)

Gordimer made the choice and struggled all her life for a just and decent new order in South Africa—a non-racial democracy under majority rule in her native land. Gordimer was 'truly colour-blind' (Godwin, 1998); her scrupulous sense of fairness motivated her to oppose racism in South Africa and worldwide. Gordimer has, indeed, utilised her writing talent to fight against apartheid. Till her death, aged 90, she remained committed to a society where imposed racially-biased consciousness would give way to a world within which each person shall be free to be him or herself—a world where 'to live together with dignity for all; to meet difference with compassion, and to address human rights from the standpoint of those often precluded from the outset.' (Bhabha, 2019)

My mentor, Professor Christopher Heywood, a critical analyst of South African Literature had warmly commented on my project to write this book:

> Imagine you are a guide in Paradise to a new contingent of phantoms who are keen to know more about Nadine Gordimer the woman, her society, and her writings, and to interview her spirit. (2017)

Professor Heywood had reservations about the media's labelling Nadine Gordimer (1923–2014) as *Lady of Letters*—the title which was popular for her in the literary circles after she won the Nobel Prize for Literature.

At her death in Johannesburg on July 13, 2014, historian, and journalist, Ángel Gurría-Quintana paid a tribute to Gordimer in his column 'Taking Tea with Nadine Gordimer' (2014) by remembering her as the grand and great lady of South African letters. Professor Heywood was of the view that one must be careful in the usage of titles *Sir or Madam/lady* because these English words have derogative connotations: not only a woman of repute and high position but the head woman in the courtesan world is also called a lady or madam. Similarly, the white colonisers awarded such titles along with huge areas of land to those individuals who showed their subordination and loyalty, helped them gain their political and economic interests and protected them against the local insurgence in the colonies such as the Indian subcontinent—then the British colony; in a post-colonial society of Pakistan—the country of my birth that came into existence at the end of British rule in 1947, it was and still is a custom to address people of rich class and higher position with *Sir* or *Madam*.

Recipient of honorary doctorates and major literary prizes worldwide, Gordimer responded to the 1991 Academy's ovation of her being a magnificent epic writer:

> I am just a writer. I write about the mysteries of life in my home place, a place that happens to be imbued in all its details and scenes with one of the most horrible problems in the world: racism. (Villa-Vicencio, 1996, 105)

Established in 1901 by the inventor of dynamite, Alfred Bernhard Nobel (1833–1896), the Swedish Academy awards individual achievements which have been of very great benefit to humanity. Winning the Prize was a tribute to Gordimer's role in exposing the horrors of apartheid; her fiction focuses on the impact of apartheid on the lives of all South Africans, regardless of colour. It artistically records her sensitive observations of polarised South African society that was divided by race into the privileged and the dispossessed. The characters reveal the tensions and stresses of life in a racially divided society and the corrupting and corrosive effects of the apartheid system. If South Africa was her contextual location, apartheid was the canvas in her fiction:

> It can be no other way [...] I do not choose apartheid or oppression as a subject. I don't go out and look for it. I write about what I [...] I absorb from the life I live, [...] It's the air I breathe and the food I eat, it's the bus I get on and the cinema I go to. My whole life is implicit

with it and so it comes naturally into my writing. (Villa-Vicencio, 1996, 108)

Both her stories and novels depict an acute analysis of prevalent institutionalised racial discrimination and oppression in South African society; her characters provide a moral insight into South African consciousness—reflecting, confronting and making connections with various stages of South African history since the late 1940s: pre-apartheid racism followed by apartheid segregation and then post-apartheid non-polarisation when the legacy of apartheid was reversed and racism failed as a system paving way for liberal humanism. The wider theme of borderland and the broadening idea of third space provides an opportunity for Gordimer to describe the situations which create guilt and moral dilemma, imbalance her characters and then transform them to get to a different perspective on their South African life.

BIBLIOGRAPHY

List of Nadine Gordimer's Fiction

(1949) *Face to Face*. Johannesburg: Silver Leaf Books.

(1953) *The Soft Voice of the Serpent*. London: Victor Gollancz.

(1953) *The Lying Days*. London: Victor Gollancz.

(1956) *Six Feet of the Country*. London: Victor Gollancz.

(1958) *A World of Strangers*. London: Victor Gollancz.

(1960) *Friday's Footprint*. London: Victor Gollancz.

(1963) *Occasion for Loving*. London: Victor Gollancz.

(1965) *Not for Publication*. London: Victor Gollancz.

(1966) *The Late Bourgeois World*. London: Victor Gollancz.

(1972) *Livingstone's Companions*. London: Jonathan Cape.

(1973) *A Guest of Honour*. London: Jonathan Cape.

(1975) *Selected Stories*. London: Jonathan Cape.

(1976) *Some Monday for Sure*. London: Heinemann.

(1978) *The Conservationist*. London: Jonathan Cape.

(1979) *Burger's Daughter*. London: Jonathan Cape.

(1980) *A Soldier's Embrace*. London: Jonathan Cape.

(1980) *Town and Country Lovers*. Los Angeles: Sylvester & Orphanos.

(1981) *July's People*. London: Jonathan Cape.

(1984) 'Letter from His Father,' *The Three Penny*, 18: 3–6.

(1984) *Something Out There*. London: Jonathan Cape.

(1987) *A Sport of Nature*. London: Jonathan Cape.

(1990) *My Son's Story*. London: Bloomsbury.

(1991) *Jump and Other Stories*. London: Bloomsbury.

(1994) *None to Accompany Me*. London: Bloomsbury.

(1998) *The House Gun*. London: Bloomsbury.

(2001) *The Pick Up*. London: Bloomsbury.

(2003) *Loot and Other Stories*. London: Bloomsbury.

(2005) *Get a Life*. London: Bloomsbury.

(2007) *Beethoven Was One-Sixteenth Black*. London: Macmillan.

(2010) *Life Times*. London: Bloomsbury.

(2012) *No Time Like the Present*. New York: Farrar, Straus and Giroux.

List of Nadine Gordimer's Non-Fiction and Speeches

(1959) *Where Do Whites Fit In?* The Twentieth Century, *4,326–331*

(1965) A Writer in South Africa. *The London Magazine*, 5 (2), 21–28

(1966) One Man Living Through It. *The New Classic,* 2 (1), 11–16

(1967) How Not To Know the African. *Contrast,* 15, 44–49

(1967) *South African Writing Today*. Harmondsworth: Penguin.

(1970) Censorship and the Primary Homeland. *Reality1,* 6, 12–15

(1970) The Interpreters: Some Themes and Directions in African Literature. *The Kenyon Review,* 32 (128), 9–26

(1970) Themes and Attitudes in Modern African Writing. *The Michigan Quarterly Review,* 9 (4), 221–230

(1971) The Metaphor of Exile. *South African Outlook,* 101, 12

(1971) White Proctorship and Black Disinvolvement. *Reality3,* 5, 14–16

(1972) Apartheid and the Primary Homeland. *Index on Censorship,* I, 25–29

(1972) Origins and Direction: The Theme of African Literature. *Lecture,* University of Cape Town.

(1973) 98 kinds of Censorship. *American Pen,* 5 (4), 16–21

(1973) *The Black Interpreters: Notes on African Writing*. Johannesburg: Ravan.

(1973) The Novel and the Nation in South Africa. In: Killam, G D (ed) *African Writers on African Writing*. Evanston: Northwestern University Press, 1996 33–52.

(1973) *On the Mines.* Cape Town: Struik.

(1974) Literature and Politics in South Africa. *Southern Review,* 7, 205–227

(1974) Apartheid and Censorship. In: Paton, Jonathan (ed) *The Grey Ones*. Johannesburg: Ravan, 1974.

(1975) At the Crossroads of Cultures. *London Times Literary Supplement,* 1227

(1976) Writers in South Africa: The New Black Poets. In: Smith, Rowland (ed) *Exile and Tradition*. London: Longman, 1976 132–151.

(1977) Nadine Gordimer: the Politics of Race. *World Literature Written in English,*16, 256–262.

(1977) From Apartheid to Afrocentrism. *South African Outlook,* 107, 181–83

(1979) Nadine Gordimer's *A World of Strangers*: Strains in South African Liberalism. *English Studies in Africa,* 22, 45–54

(1979) Relevance and Commitment. In: White, L and Couzens, T (ed) *Literature and Society in South Africa*. Essex: Longman, 1984 162.

(1982) Modern African Writing. In: Robert, Martin (ed) *The Writer's Craft: Hopwood Lectures 1965–81*. Ann Arbor: University of Michigan Press, 1982 286.

(1983) Living in the Interregnum. *New York Review*, 1, 21–26 (1986) *Lifetimes: Under Apartheid. London:* Jonathan Cape.

(1988) The Essential Gesture: Writing, Politics and Places. In: Clingman, Stephen (ed) *The Essential Gesture*. London: Penguin, 1988.

(1989) The Gap between the Writer and the Reader. *The New York Review*, 336 (14), 59–61

(1991) *Crimes of Conscience*. Oxford: Heinemann.

(1992) *Why haven't you written?* Harmondsworth: Penguin. (1993) Codes of Culture. *Bucknell Review*, 37 (1), 21–29

(1995) *Writing and Being*. Cambridge: Harvard University Press.

(1999) *Living in Hope and History: Notes on our Century*. London: Bloomsbury.

List of Nadine Gordimer's Interviews and Conversations

(1962) Terkel, Studs. An Interview with Gordimer. In Bazin, Nancy Topping and Seymour, Marilyn Dallman (ed) *Conversations with Nadine Gordimer*. Jackson: University Press of Mississippi, 1990 12–31.

(1963) Terkel, Studs. Nadine Gordimer. *Chicago Perspective, 12,* 42–49.

(1965) Ravenscroft, Arthur. A Writer in South Africa: Nadine Gordimer. *London Magazine,* 5, 20–28.

(1965) Ross, Alan. An Interview with Gordimer. In: Bazin, Nancy Topping and Seymour, Marilyn Dallman (ed) *Conversations with Nadine Gordimer*. Jackson: University Press of Mississippi, 1990 34–41.

(1969) Salkey, Andrew. Nadine Gordimer Talks to Andrew Salkey. *Listener,* 184–185.

(1969) De Beer, Mona. Nadine Writes from a Position of Involvement. *London Times*, 7.

(1970) Burrows, E.G. An Interview with Nadine Gordimer. *The Michigan Quarterly Review,* 9 (4), 231–234.

(1972) Cassere, Diane. An Interview with Gordimer. In: Bazin, Nancy Topping and Seymour, Marilyn Dallman (ed) *Conversations with Nadine Gordimer*. Jackson: University Press of Mississippi, 1990 56–57.

(1972) Gray, Stephen. Writing in South Africa: Nadine Gordimer Interviewed. *New Nation,* 2–3.

(1976) Bragg, Melvyn. The Solitude of a White Writer. *Listener*, 514.

(1977) Schwartz, Pat. An Interview with Gordimer. In Bazin, Nancy Topping and Seymour, Marilyn Dallman (ed) *Conversations with Nadine Gordimer*. Jackson: University Press of Mississippi, 1990 78–83.

(1978) Ellis, Nesta Wyn. An Interview with Gordimer. In: Bazin, Nancy Topping and Seymour, Marilyn Dallman (ed) *Conversations with Nadine Gordimer*. Jackson: University Press of Mississippi, 1990 87–95.

(1979) Loercher, Diana. An Interview with Gordimer. In: Bazin, Nancy Topping and Seymour, Marilyn Dallman (ed) *Conversations with Nadine Gordimer*. Jackson: University Press of Mississippi, 1990 96–100.

(1980) Riis, Johannes. Nadine Gordimer. *Kunapipi,* 2, 20–26.

(1980) Servan Schreiber, C. Learning to Live with Injustice. *World Press Review,*30–34.

(1981) Gardner, Susan. A Story for This Place and Time: An Interview with Nadine Gordimer about *Burger's Daughter*. *Kunapipi,* 3 (2), 99–112.

(1981) Kakutani, Machiko. Nadine Gordimer, South African Witness. *New York Times,* 11.

(1981) Morris, Edmund. A Visit with Nadine Gordimer. *New York Times,* 26–27.

(1981) Gray, Stephen. An Interview with Nadine Gordimer. *Contemporary Literature,* 22 (3), 263–271

(1984) Boyers, Robert et al. A Conversation with Nadine Gordimer. *Salmagundi, 62,* 3–31.

(1987) *Writers in Conversation*. Video. Nadine Gordimer with Margaret Walters. London: Institute of Contemporary Arts.

(1991) Sharansky, Natan. A Conversation between Nobel Prize Winner Nadine Gordimer and Natan Sharansky. *Jerusalem Report,* 24 October 1991, pp. 5–7.

(1996) Villa-Vicencio, Charles. 'Nadine Gordimer: A Vocation to Write.' In: *The Spirit of Freedom: South African Leaders on Religion and Politics*. Berkeley: University of California Press.

(1998) Brink, Andre. An Interview with Nadine Gordimer. In: Oliphant, Andries Walter (ed) *A Writing Life: Celebrating Nadine Gordimer*. London: Viking, 1998 419–425.

(1998) Godwin, Peter. An Interview with Gordimer: Cape Crusader. *The Observer Review*,2:1.

(2003) Nadine Gordimer in Conversation with Hermione Lee. *Wasafiri,* 39.

(2005) A conversation with Nadine Gordimer. *Haaretz,* 11:14.

(2007) Allfree, Claire. An Interview with Nadine Gordimer. *MetroLife,* 11: 29. www.metro.co.uk

(2012) Cartwright, Justin. An Interview with Nadine Gordimer: Into the Fire. *The Sydney Morning Herald,* 4:14.

(2014) Gurría-Quintana, Ángel. Taking tea with Nadine Gordimer. *Prospect,* 7: 21.

(2014) Frazer, Jenni. 'Prickly' Gordimer, anti-apartheid star. *The JC,* 7: 12.

Other Cited Works

Abrahams, Peter (1948) *The Path of Thunder*. Cape Town: David Philip.

(1954) *Tell Freedom*. London: Faber.

Achebe, Chinua (1958) *Things Fall Apart*. London: Heinemann.

(1989). *Hopes and Impediments: Selected Essays*. New York: Doubleday.

Affiah, Kwame Anthony (1992) *In My Father's House: Africa in the Philosophy of Culture*. London: Methuen.

Afrika, Tatamkhula (1994) *The Innocents*. Cape Town: David Philip.

Ahmed, Ajaz (1992) *In Theory: Classes, Nations, Literatures*. London: Verso.

(2007) *In our Time: Empire, Politics, Culture*. London: Verso.

Anderson, Benedict (1991) *Imagined Communities*. London: Verso.

Arnold Mathew (1892) *Essays in Criticism*. London: Macmillan.

Ashcroft, Bill and Griffiths, Gareth and Tiffin, Helen (1989) *The Empire Writes Back*. London: Routledge.

Attridge, Derek and Jolly, Rosemary (1998) *Writing South Africa: Literature, Apartheid and Democracy*. Cambridge: Cambridge University Press.

Baldwin, James (1963) *The Fire Next Time*. London: Michael Joseph.

(1976) *The Devil Finds Work*. New York: Dell.

Bardolph, Jacqueline (2001) *Telling Stories: Postcolonial Short Fiction in English*. Amsterdam: Rodopi.

Beckett, Samuel (1986) *The Complete Dramatic Works*. London: Faber.

Behr, Mark (1993) *The Smell of Apples*. South Africa: Abacus.

Beinart, William and Dubow, Saul (1995) *Segregation and Apartheid in 20th Century South Africa*. London: Routledge.

Bennet, Tony (1979) *Formalism and Marxism*. London: Routledge.

Bennett, Andrew and Royle Nicholas (1995) *An Introduction to Literature, Criticism and Theory: Key Critical Concepts*. Hemel Hempstead: Harvester Wheatsheaf.

Berger, Maurice (1999) *White Lies, Race and the Myths of Whiteness*. New York: Giroux.

Berghe, Pierre van den (1979) *The Liberal Dilemma in South Africa*. New York: St Martin's Press.

Bernstein, Hilda (1986) *Death is Part of the Process*. London: Grafton.

Bhabha, Homi K (1983) Difference, Discrimination and the Discourse of Colonialism. In: Barker F *et al* (ed) *The Politics of Theory*. Colchester: University of Essex Press, 1983 194–211.

(1990) *Nation and Narration*. London: Routledge.

(1991) Race, Time and The Revision of Modernity. *The Oxford Literary Review*, 9, 193–219

(1994) *The Location of Culture*. London: Routledge.

(1994) Frontlines / Borderposts. In: Bammer, Angelika (ed) *Displacements: Cultural Identities in Question*. Bloomington: Indiana University Press, 1994 269–272.

(1996) Postmodernism / Postcolonialism. In: Nelson, R and Shiff, R (ed) *Critical Terms for Art History*. Chicago: University of Chicago Press, 1996.

(2019) 'Why We Need a New, Emotive Language of Human Rights.' London: Institute for Contemporary Arts.

Biko, Steve (1978) *I Write What I Like*. London: Heinemann.

Boehmer, Elleke (1995) *Colonial and Postcolonial Literature*. Oxford: Oxford University Press.

Bongie, Chris (1998) *Islands and Exiles: The Creole Identities of Postcolonial Literature*. Stanford: Stanford University Press.

Bongie, Chris (1998) *Islands and Exiles: The Creole Identities of Postcolonial Literature*. Stanford: Stanford University Press.

Bonner, Philip and Delius, Peter and Posel, Deborah (1993) *Apartheid's Genesis 1935–1962*. Johannesburg: Witwatersrand University Press.

Bosman, Herman Charles (1949) *Mafeking Road*. Johannesburg: Central News Agency.

Boulton, Eva (1894) *Borderland Fancies*. London: The Leadenhall Press.

Bridges, J H (1865) *A General View of Positivism: Auguste Comte*. Trans. London: Trubner.

Brink, Andre (1979) *A Dry White Season*. Great Britain: Minerva.

(1982) *A Chain of Voices*. London: Faber.

Brodber, Erna (1988) *Myal*. London: New Beacon Books.

Butler, Guy (1975) *Selected Poems of Guy Butler*. Johannesburg: Donker.

Campbell, Joseph (1949) *The Hero with a Thousand Faces*. New York: Pantheon.

Campbell, Roy (1968) *Selected Poetry*. London: The Bodley Head.

Capra, Dominick La (1991) *The Bounds of Race: Perspectives on Hegemony and Resistance*. London: Cornell University Press.

Chandramohan, Balasubramanyam (1992) *A Study in Trans-ethnicity in Modern South Africa: the writings of Alex La Guma 1925-85*. Lampeter: Mellen Research University Press.

Chapman, Michael (1989) *The Drum Decade: Stories from the 1950s*. Pietermaritzburg: University of Natal Press.

Clingman, Stephen (1986) *The Novels of Nadine Gordimer: History from the Inside*. London: Allen & Unwin.

Coetzee, J M (1980) *Waiting for the Barbarians*. London: Secker & Warburg.

(1983) *The Life and Times of Michael K*. London: Secker & Warburg.

(1987) *Foe*. Harmondsworth: Penguin.

Conrad, Joseph (1902) *Heart of Darkness*. London: Harper Collins.

Cooke, John (1985) *The Novels of Nadine Gordimer: Private Lives/Public Landscapes*. Baton Rouge: Louisiana State University Press.

Cope, Jack (1986) *Selected Stories*. Cape Town: David Philip.

Coulanges, Fustel de (1896) *The Ancient City: A Study on the Religion, Laws and Institutions of Greece and Rome*. Trans. W Small. Boston: Lee & Shepard.

Cronon, Edmund David (1955) Black Moses: *The Story of Marcus Garvey and the Universal Negro Improvement Association*. Madison: University of Wisconsin Press.

Dangor, Achmat (1983) *Bulldozer*. Johannesburg: Ravan.

Davidson, Basil (1983) *Modern Africa: A Social and Political History*. London: Longman.

Dholomo, Rolfes Reginald Raymond (1928) *An African Tragedy*. Lovedale: Lovedale Press.

Donald, Munro and Cosmo, Pieterse (1969) *Protest and Conflict in African Literature*. London: Heinemann.

Douglass, Frederick (1881) The Colour Line. *North American Review*. Vol. 132, No. 295: 567–577.

Dover, Cedrick (1937) *Half Caste*. London: Secker & Warburg.

Drucker, Peter (2012) 'Byron and Ottoman love: Orientalism, Europeanisation and same-sex sexualities in the early nineteenth-century Levant.' *Journal of European Studies*. vol. 42, No, 2: 140–57.

Du Bois, W E B (1903) *The Souls of Black Folks*. Chicago: A C McClurg.

Eagleton, Terry (1976) *Marxism and Literary Criticism*. London: Methuen.

Eisenach, Eldon J (1981) *Two World of Liberalism: Religion and Politics in Hobbs, Locke and Mill*. Chicago: University of Chicago Press.

Eliot, T S (1971) *The Wasteland*. London: Faber.

Essop, Ahmed (1978) *The Hajji and Other Stories*. Johannesburg: Ravan.

Ettin, Andrew Vogel (1992) *Betrayals of the Body Politic: The Literary Commitments of Nadine Gordimer*. Charlottesville: University Press of Virginia.

Fanon, Frantz (1963) *The Wretched of the Earth*. Trans. C Farrington. New York: Grove Press.

(1967) *Black Skin, White Masks*. Trans. Charles Lam Markmann. New York: Grove Press.

February, Vernon (1981) *Mind Your Colour*: London: Kegan Paul.

Forster, E M (1924) *A Passage of India*. London: Edward Arnold.

(1927) *Aspects of the Novel*. London: Penguin.

Frankenberg, Ruth (1993) *White Women, Race Matters: The Social Construction of Whiteness*. London: Routledge.

Fredrickson, George M (1981) *White Supremacy: A Comparative Study in American and South African History*. New York: Oxford University Press.

Foucault, Michel (1986) Of Other Spaces. *Diacritics, 22–27*

Fugard, Athol (1963) *The Blood Knot*. Johannesburg: Simondium Publishers.

Gauld, H. Drummond (1935) *Brave Borderland*. London: Thomas Nelson.

Gennep, Arnold Van (1960) *The Rites of Passage*. London: Routledge.

Gerhart, Gail (1978) *Black Power in South Africa: The Evolution of an Ideology*. Berkeley: University of California Press.

Giliomee, Hermann (1984) Changing Everything Except the Way We Think. *Leadership*, 3 (3), 125

Gilroy, Paul (2000) *Against Race: Imagining Political Culture Beyond the Colour Line*. Cambridge: Belknap Press of Harvard University.

Goldberg, D Theo (1990) *Anatomy of Racism*. Minneapolis: University of Minnesota Press.

Golding, William (1980) *Rites of Passage*. London: Faber.

Goonetilleke, D D R A (2001) *Perspectives on Post-colonial Literature*. London: Skoob Books.

Gray, John (1980) *South African Literature: An Introduction*. Cape Town: David Philip.

(1989) *Liberalisms: Essays in Political Philosophy*. London: Routledge.

Haggard, H Rider (1887) *King Solomon's Mines*. London: Cassell & Co.

Hale, Grace Elizabeth (1998) *Making Whiteness, the Culture of Segregation in the South 1840–1940*. New York: Pantheon.

Hall, Gary and Wortham, Simon (1996) An Interview with Homi Bhabha. *Angelaki*, 2 (2), 59–63

Hall, Stuart (1987) Minimal Selves. In: Procter, James (ed) *Stuart Hall*. London: Routledge, 2004 44–46.

(1994) Cultural Identity and Diaspora. In: Williams P and Chrisman L (ed) *Colonial Discourse and Postcolonial Theory*. New York: Columbia University Press, 1994 392–403.

(1996) New Ethnicities. In: Morley, D and Chen, K (ed) *Stuart Hall: Critical Dialogue in Cultural Studies*. London: Routledge, 1996 441–449.

Haresnape, Geoffrey (1999) *African Tales from Shakespeare*. Hout Bay: Gariep.

Harrison, David (1981) *The White Tribe of Africa: South Africa in Perspective.* Berkeley: University of California Press.

Haugh, Robert (1974) *Nadine Gordimer*. New York: Twayne.

Head, Bessie (1973) *A Question of Power*. London: Davis Poynter.

Head, Dominic (1994) *Nadine Gordimer*. Cambridge: Cambridge University Press.

Hegel, G W F (1956). The Philosophy of History. Trans. J. Sibree. New York: Dover Books.

(1979) *Phenomenology of Spirit*. Trans. A W Miller. Oxford: Clarendon.

Helms, Janet E (1990) *Black and White Racial Identity: Theory, Research and Practice*. London: Greenwood.

Hepple, Alex (1974) *Press under Apartheid*. London: Defence & Aid Fund.

Heywood, Christopher (1983) *Nadine Gordimer*. Windsor: Profile Books.

(2004) *A History of South African Literature*. Cambridge: Cambridge University Press.

Hooks, Bell (1990) *Yearning: Race, Gender and Cultural Politics*. Boston: South End Press.

(1992) Representing Whiteness in the Black Imagination. In: Grossberg, Lawrence (ed) *Cultural Studies*. New York: Routledge, 1992.

(1992) *Black Looks: Race and Representation*. Boston: South End Press.

(1994) *Outlaw Culture: Resisting Representations*. London: Routledge.

Hope, Christopher (1988) *White Boy Running*. London: Abacus.

Jacobson, Dan (1955) *The Trap*. London: Weidenfeld & Nicolson.

(1956) *A Dance in the Sun*. London: Weidenfeld & Nicolson.

(1971) *A Way of Life and Other Stories. London*: Longman.

JanMohamed, Abdul R (1983) *Manichean Aesthetics: The Politics of Literature in Colonial Africa*. Amherst: Massachusetts University Press.

Johnson R W (2015) *How Long Will South Africa Survive?* London: Hurst & Company.

Johnson, David (1994) *The Idea of a Liberal Theory: A Critique and Reconstruction*. New Jersey: Princeton University Press.

Jones, A M. (1799) *The works of Sir William Jones*. London: Evans.

Jordon, Winthrop (1968) *White over Black: American Attitudes towards the Negro 1550–1812*. Chapel Hill: University of North Carolina Press.

Kahn, Joel S (1997) *Culture, Multiculture, Postculture*. London: SAGE.

Keith, Michael and Pile, Steve (1993) *Place and Politics of Identity*. London: Routledge.

Khan, Imran (2011) *Pakistan: A Personal History*. London: Bantam Press. Khushwant Singh (1956) *Train to Pakistan*. New York: Grove Press.

King, Bruce (1993) *The Later Fiction of Nadine Gordimer*. Basingstoke: Macmillan.

Koundoura, Maria and Rai, Amit (1993) An Interview with Homi Bhabha. *Stanford Humanities Review*, 3 (1), 1–6

Kunene, Mazisi (1970) *Zulu Poems*. London: Deutsch.

(1979) *Emperor Shaka the Great: A Zulu Epic*. London: Heinemann.

La Guma, Alex (1962) *A Walk In The Night*. Ibadan: Mbari.

(1967) *The Stone Country*. Berlin: Seven Seas.

(1972) *Apartheid: A Collection of Writings on South African Racism by South Africans*. London: Lawrence and Wishart.

(1975) South African Writing under Apartheid. *Lotus*, 23, 11–21

(1979) *Time Of The Butcherbird*. London: Heinemann.

Lambley, Peter (1980) *The Psychology of Apartheid*. London: Secker & Warburg.

Langbaum, Robert (1977) *The Mysteries of Identity: A theme in Modern Literature*. New York: Oxford University Press.

Lattimore, Richmond (1951) *The Iliad by Homer* Trans. Chicago: University of Chicago Press.

Lawrence, D H (1968) *Complete Works*. Geneva: Edito-Service.

Lessing, Doris (1950) *The Grass is Singing*. London: Michael Joseph.

(1992) *African Laughter*. London: Harper Collins.

Lewis, David L (1993) *W E B Du Bois 1868–1919: Biography of a Race*. New York: Henry Holt.

Lipsitz, George (1998) *The Possessive Investment in Whiteness*. Philadelphia: Temple University Press.

Lodge, T (1983) *Black Politics in South Africa since 1945*. London: Longman.

Loomba, Ania (1998) *Colonialism/Postcolonialism*. London: Routledge.

Low, Gail Ching-Liang (1996) *White Skins/Black Masks: Representation and Colonialism*. London: Routledge.

Lukacs, Georg (1962) *The Historical Novel*. Trans. H and S Mitchell. Harmondsworth: Penguin.

(1999) *In Defence of History and Class Consciousness*. Trans. Esther Leslie. New York: Verso.

Luthuli, Albert John (1962) *Let My People Go*. London: Collins. Malan, M A (1962) *South African History*. Cape Town: Maskew Miller.

Malan, Rian (1991) *My Traitor's Heart*. Great Britain: Vintage.

Mallaby, Sebastian (1992) *After Apartheid*. London: Faber.

Mandela, Nelson (1990) *No Easy Walk to Freedom*. Oxford: Heinemann.

Manning, D J (1979) *Liberalism*. London: J M Dent & Sons.

Mannoni, O (1956) *Prospero & Caliban: The Psychology of Colonisation*. Trans. Pamela Powesland. London: Methuen.

Marquard, Leo (1965) *Liberalism in South Africa*. Johannesburg: Institute of Race Relations.

Marx, K (1961) *Capital*. Volume 1. Moscow: Foreign Languages Publishing House.

Matshoba, Mtutuzeli (1979) *Call Me Not a Man*. Johannesburg: Ravan.

McKnight, Kathryn Joy (2009) *Afro-Latino Voices: Narratives from the Early Modern Ibero-Atlantic World 1550–1812*. Indianapolis: Hacket Publishing Company. p. 59.

Mda, Zakes (1997) *Ways of Dying*. Cape Town: Oxford University Press.

Memmi, Albert (1974) *The Coloniser and the Colonised*. Trans. Howard Green. London: Souvenir.

Merrett, Christopher (1994) *A Culture of Censorship: Secrecy and Intellectual Repression in South Africa*. Cape Town: David Philip.

Miller, Jacques Alain (1986) *The Ethics of Psychoanalysis 1959–60*. Trans. Dennis Porter. New York: W Norton & Company.

Millin, Sarah Gertrude (1922) *Adam's Rest*. London: Collins.

(1924) *God's Step Children*. London: Constable.

(1951) *The People of South Africa*. London: Constable.

Mitchell W J T (1995) Translator Translated: An Interview with Homi Bhabha. *Artforum*, 33 (7), 80–84

Mittelholzer, Edgar (1964) *A Morning at the Office*. Harmondsworth: Penguin.

Mofolo, Thomas (1949) *Chaka the Zulu*. London: Oxford University Press.

Moore, Sebastian (1985) *The Quest for Identity through Oedipus to Christ*. London: Longman.

Morel, E D (1920) *The Black Man's Burden: The White Man in Africa from the Fifteenth Century to World War 1*. Great Britain: Modern Reader Paperbacks.

Motsisi, Casey (1980) *Selected Writings of Casey Motsisi*. Johannesburg: Ravan.

Mphahlele, Ezekiel (1959) *Down Second Avenue.* London: Faber.

(1962) *The African Image*. London: Faber.

(1984) *Afrika My Music: An Autobiography 1957–1983*. Johannesburg: Ravan.

Munger, Edwin (1967) *Afrikaner and African Nationalism*. Oxford: Oxford University Press.

Naidoo, Beverley (1985) *Journey to Jo'burg*. London: HarperCollins.

Nakasa, Nathaniel (1963) Writing in South Africa. *The Classic*, I, 56–63

(1975) *The World of Nat Nakasa*. Johannesburg: Ravan.

Ndebele, Njabulo (1983) *Fools*. Johannesburg: Ravan.

(1991) *Rediscovery of the Ordinary: Essays on South African Literature and Culture*. Johannesburg: Congress of South African Writers.

Nelson, Cary and Grossberg, Lawrence (1988) *Marxism and the Interpretation of Culture*. Chicago: University of Illinois Press.

Newman, Judie (1995) *The Ballistic Bard: Post-colonial Fictions*. London: Arnold.

(1988) *Contemporary Writers: Nadine Gordimer*. London: Routledge. Ngugi, wa Thiong'o (1965) *The River Between*. London: Heinemann.

Nkosi, Lewis (1986) *Mating Birds*. London: Constable.

Nkrumah, Kwame (1963) *Africa Must Unite*. London: Heinemann.

Oderberg, David S (1993) *The Metaphysics of Identity over Time*. Basingstoke: Macmillan.

O'Reilly, Christopher (2001) *Post-colonial Literature*. Cambridge: Cambridge University Press.

Ousmane, Sembene (1969) *God's Bits of Wood*. London: Heinemann.

Padayachee, Deena (2003) *What's Love Got to Do with It? and Other Stories*. Dormerton: USM Publishers.

Pain, Paromita (2006) Crossing Boundaries: An Interview with Beverley Naidoo. http://www.thehindu.com/thehindu/Ir/2006/02/05

Parker, Kenneth (1978) *The South African Novel in English*. New York: Africana.

Parry, Benita (2000) *Postcolonial Theory and Criticism*. Cambridge: Brewer.

Paton, Alan (1948) *Cry the Beloved Country*. London: Jonathan Cape.

(1988) *Journey Continued. An Autobiography*. Oxford: Oxford University Press.

Patterson, S (1953) *Colour and Culture in South Africa*. London: Routledge.

Pease, Howard (1893) *Borderland Studies*. Newcastle on Tyne: Mawson.

Peck, Richard (1988) What's a Poor White to Do? : White South African Options in *A Sport of Nature*. *ARIEL*, 19.

Pinkham, Joan (1972) 'Discourse on Colonialism' by Aimé Césaire. Trans. London: Monthly Review Press.

Plaatje, Solomon Tshekisko (1930) *Mhudi*. Lovedale: Lovedale Press.

Plomer, William (1925) *Turbott Wolfe*. London: L & V Woolf.

Pratt, Mary Louise (1992) *Imperial Eyes: Travel Writing and Transculturation*. London: Routledge.

Pringle, Thomas (1834) *African Sketches*. London: E Moxon.

(1881) *Afar in the Desert and Other Stories*. London: Longman.

Rabinsow, Paul (1984) *The Foucault Reader*. New York: Pantheon.

Ranger, T (1982) Race and Tribe in Southern Africa: European Ideas and African Acceptance. In: Ross R (ed) *Racism and Colonialism*. The Hague: Martinus Nijhoff Publishers, 1982.

(1983) *The Invention of Tradition*. Cambridge: Cambridge University Press.

Rive, Richard (1964) *Emergency*. London: Faber.

(1981) *Writing Black*. Cape Town: David Philip.

(1983) The Liberal Tradition in South African Literature. *Contrast*, 14 (3) 19–31

(1983) *Advance, Retreat: Selected Short Stories*. Cape Town: David Philip.

Roberts, Ronald Suresh (2005) *No Cold Kitchen: A Biography of Nadine Gordimer*. Johannesburg: STE Publishers.

Robertson, Janet (1971) *Liberalism in South Africa 1948–1963*. Oxford: Clarendon.

Rodney, Walter (1972) *How Europe Underdeveloped Africa*. London: Bogle.

Roux, E (1948) *Time Longer than Rope*. London: Victor Gollancz.

Sachs, Albie (1990) *Protecting Human Rights in a New South Africa*. Cape Town: Oxford University Press.

Sachs, Bernard (1961) *The Road from Sharpeville*. London: Dobson.

Sahni, Bhisham (1988) *Tamas*. Trans. Jai Ratan. New York: Penguin.

Said, Edward (1978) *Orientalism*. London: Routledge.

(1993) *Culture and Imperialism*. London: Chatto & Windus.

Schreiner, Olive (1883) *The Story of an African Farm*. London: Hutchinson.

Schrire, Robert (1992) *Adapt or Die: The End of White Politics in South Africa*. London: Hurst.

Scott, Jonathan (1994) *The Invention of White Race: Racial Oppression and Social Control*. New York: Verso.

Selden, Raman (1988) *The Theory of Criticism*. New York: Longman.

Serote, Mongane (1981) *To Every Birth Its Blood*. Johannesburg: Ravan.

Shimoni, Gideon (2003) *Community and Conscience: The Jews in Apartheid South Africa*. Glosderry: David Philip Publishers.

Silverman, Kaja (1992) *Male Subjectivities at the Margin*. New York: Routledge.

Slater, J Herbert (1915) *Problems of the Borderland*. London: William Rider & Son.

Smith, Pauline (1925) *Little Karoo*. London: Jonathan Cape.

Smith, Rowland (1980) Living for the Future: Nadine Gordimer's *Burger's Daughter. World Literature Written in English,* 19 (2), 163–173.

(1984) Masters and Servants: Nadine Gordimer's *July's People* and the Themes of her Fiction. *Salmagundi,* 62, 93–107.

(1990) *Critical Essays on Nadine Gordimer.* Boston: G K Hall.

(1994).The Voyage Out: Exile, Escape and Obligation in Nadine Gordimer's Fiction. *Matatu*,11, 51–57.

Snodgrass, Mary Ellen (1997) *Encyclopaedia of Frontier Literature*. California: Santa Barbara.

Soyinka, Wole (2001) 'Chinua Achebe of Bard College.' *The Journal of Blacks in Higher Education*. Autumn 33 (33): 28–29.

Sparks, Allister (1990) *The Mind of South Africa: The Story of the Rise and the Fall of Apartheid*. London: Heinemann.

Spivak, Gayatri Chakravorty (1988). 'Can the Subaltern Speak?' In Nelson, Cary; Grossberg, Lawrence (eds.). *Marxism and the Interpretation of Culture.* Basingstoke: Macmillan. pp. 271–313.

Stead, William Thomas Ed. (1902) *The Last Will and Testament of Cecil John Rhodes*. London: Willaim London: William Clowes & Sons Limited. p.58.

Suzman, Arthur (1960) *Race Classification and Definition in the Legislation of the Union of South Africa 1910–1960*. Johannesburg: Institute of Race Relations.

Talking Ideas: Discussing Postcolonial Culture (1994). Video.

Peter Osbourne, Stuart Hall, Homi Bhabha and Paul Gilroy. London: Institute of Contemporary Arts.

Taylor, Mildred D. (2011) *Roll of Thunder, Hear My Cry.* London: Penguin.

Theal, George M'Call (1902) *The Beginning of South African History.* London: T. Fisher Unwin.

Themba, Can (1972) *The Will to Die*. London: Heinemann.

Thomas, Nicholas (1994) *Colonialism's Culture*. Princeton: Princeton University Press.

Tiffin, C and Lawson, A (1994) *Describing Empire, Postcolonialism and Textuality.* London: Routledge.

Tucker, Martin (1965) Colour and Guilt. *Africa Today*, 12 (2), 13–14.

(1967) *Africa in Modern Literature*. New York: Frederick Ungar.

Tully, Mark (1992) *No Full Stops in India*. London: Penguin.

(1996) *The Heart of India*. London: Penguin.

Turner, Victor (1974) *The Ritual Process: Structure and Anti-structure*. Harmondsworth: Penguin.

Uledi Kamanga, Brighton James (2002) *Cracks in the Wall: Nadine Gordimer's Fiction and the Irony of Apartheid*. Asmara, Eritrea: Africa World Press.

Ume, Karu E (1981) The Origin of Apartheid in South Africa: A Review. *Journal of African Studies*, 8 (4), 176–181.

Umrigar, Thrity (2006) *The Space Between Us*. New York: William Morrow.

Vale, P, Hamilton, L and Prinsloo, E H (2014) *Intellectual Traditions in South Africa: Ideas, Individuals and Institutions*. Pietermaritzburg: University of KwaZulu-Natal Press.

Vaughan, M (1993) Madness and Colonialism: Colonialism as Madness. *Paideuma*, 39, 45–55

Vigne, Randolph (1997) *Liberals against Apartheid: A History of the Liberal Party of South Africa 1953–68*. London: Macmillan.

Vincent, Theodore G (1973) *Voices of a Black Nation*. San Francisco: Ramparts.

Wade, Michael (1993) *White on Black in South Africa*. Basingstoke: Macmillan.

Walcott, Derek (1990) *Omeros*. New York: Farrar, Straus & Giroux.

Walker, Alice (1982) *The Colour Purple*. London: Women's Press.

Ward, David (1989) *Chronicles of Darkness*. London: Routledge.

Webster, Mary Morrison (1954) Trends in South African Literature. *Forum*, 19–20

Wentzel, Jill (1995) *The Liberal Slideaway*. Johannesburg: South African Institute of Race Relations.

White, Charles (1799) *An Account of the Regular Gradation in Man, and in different Animals and Vegetables*. London: C. Dilly.

Wicomb, Zoe (1987) *You Can't Get Lost in Cape Town*. Great Britain: Virago.

Williams, Patrick and Chrisman, Laura (1993) *Colonial Discourse and Postcolonial Theory*. Hemel Hempstead: Harvester Wheatsheaf.

Wilson, M and Thompson, L (1969) *The Oxford History of South Africa*. Oxford: Clarendon.

Windling, Terri (1986) *Bordertown: A Chronicle of the Borderlands*. New York: TOR Books.

Winnicot, D W (1971) *Playing and Reality*. London: Tavistock.

Wolff, Robert Paul (1969) *The Poverty of Liberalism*. Boston: Beacon Press.

Wright, Richard (1940) *Native Son*. New York: Harper.

Young, Robert (1990) *White Mythologies*. London: Routledge.

(1995) *Colonial Desire: Hybridity in Theory, Culture and Race*. London: Routledge.

APPENDIX: SELECTED LETTERS

Letter 1: NG to Matheus Uys Krige, 18 January 1947

225. K.L. G.34)

BALMORAL HOTEL

DURBAN.

P.O. Box 935.

TELEGRAPHIC ADDRESS:
"BAROLMORAL," DURBAN.

18th. January, 1947.
NATAL, SOUTH AFRICA.

My dear Uys;

You cannot imagine how delighted I was to receive your letter. Unfortunately it took weeks to reach me, as it had to be forwarded twice – once from "Vandag" to Springs, and then from Springs to Durban. Now at last I have it.

As you see, I am still in Durban; it seems I have been here forever, not because I am bored or weary of the life, but only because on a holiday I lose all sense of time and remain suspended in a kind of dream until the train dumps me down in

2.

Springs and I awaken to myself again. I have had a good time and have enjoyed being on my own – away from the family –. The Cape sounds wonderful; you must surely have been sorry to leave.

I do so appreciate your having contrived to read the stories before you left Johannesburg. I know how rushed you were. The young Afrikaans woman I worked pretty hard on, but at the conclusion I felt that she did not emerge nearly so clearly as I should have wished. The old lady is better done, I think; rounder. Didn't you perhaps feel that there was a certain lack of vitality in the younger woman? I want to know how this strikes you, because I had in mind a particular kind of uncomplaining, inherent vitality that belongs to a woman with her sort of ugly face.

3.

DURBAN.

P.O. Box 935.

TELEGRAPHIC ADDRESS:
"BAROLMORAL," DURBAN.

NATAL, SOUTH AFRICA.

There should be an echo of her father somewhere in her, otherwise her defeat by the half-dead old lady loses some of its firmness. It should be an ironic, even slightly evil, defeat of life by death.

But enough of it. I should like to talk to you about it, when I come home, if I may? I am relieved and glad that, on the whole, you liked it. I wonder what Mr Plomer thought — well, I shall know soon.

This afternoon I bought "New Writing" and read a story by a South African named Oliver Walker. It was extremely poor; badly constructed and trite, except for the end. I really think I shall send them something again.

-4-

I have asked all over Durban for your book, but no one has it yet. Is it still on the way from England? I am looking forward to it, and wish it would hurry up and come. Part of my wishes to you for the New Year (if it's not too late to wish you every happiness in 1947) are that the book will be a great success everywhere and that it will be a terrific best-seller. And may this year be a good one for you and your family and your work. — Thank you so very much for your wishes to me, and — at the risk of being a bore and saying again something I think I can't say often enough — may I tell you once more how glad I am to be able to consider myself your friend, and how grateful I am to you for your wonderful kindness, and interest in me. It means a great deal to me.

I am coming home next week, and look forward to a talk with you soon.

Sincerely,
Nadine Gordimer

A. 14/5/50

27 Mount Willmar,
Isipingo Street,
Bellevue,
Johannesburg.
23rd March, 1950.

My dear Uys,

No-one seems to have heard from you yet, so I am sure you must still be busy getting settled in — that is why I have hesitated to write although I've wanted to. To-day, however, I had a phone-call from the young boy Lionel Abrahams asking me for the story which he gave me to read ... and I realised with dismay that I'd given it to you that afternoon at Gleneagles and you'd gone off to the Cape

before you could give it back.
Have you still got it, safe and sound? — it's called "A Bunch of Daisies". I certainly hope so. I'm really worried about it. So please be a dear and find a moment to read it and return it to me — Lionel A. is a hopeless cripple and a very courageous person, and is thrilled at the idea of your seeing something of his.

Are you working well, I wonder? I do hope so, and that Lydia is well again and life less harassing in the country. I am growing more Buddha-like daily and shall be glad to leave the flat for a house and garden. I miss you, am longing to hear news of you, so do write to me when you have time. Love from us both to both of you — Nadine.

P.T.O.

P.S. Charles is coming to lunch to-morrow, so I hope to get your address from him!

M.

Letter 3: NG to Matheus Uys Krige, 16 May 1950

A. 30/8/50

Nadine Gordimer

~~Johannesburg.~~

77 Rustenburg Road,
Emmarentia,
Johannesburg.
16th May, 1950.

My dear Uys,

How good to get your letter. I was so pleased to have news of you that I put it away — and a whole month goes comfortably by with the feeling that it is there when I want it . . . As you can see by the new address, we have moved into the house on the hill. I just seemed to fall into place here; in a few days settled down to work as if I'd never lived anywhere else. It's quite beautiful — a wild garden full of birds and lizards, and at night a real fire. The one whole

-2-

Nadine Gordimer

Johannesburg.

wall of the livingroom is made of glass and it slides back to let the garden in — I do wish you could see it; I know you'd love it.

You ask about the baby and the story competition — well at the moment it's a battle for time between them. The baby may be born any hour (literally!) and I am waiting frantically to have two new stories ready in time for the competition. Unfortunately I had nothing worthwhile on hand that had not already been published — I think that both you and your mate stand a very good chance of getting somewhere — pity that you are debarred by previous publication from sending in 'The Coffin'; I'm sure it would have scored.

I'm so glad Harper's are going to

3.

Nadine Gordimer

Johannesburg.

publish it, though. Success with them is not something at which to snap one's fingers, believe me. Curious that they should ask you to re-write the changing wagon scene; do you remember the afternoon we discussed the story and I told you that that piece bothered me? To me it was the one part of the story that was blurred; though the reasons you give for it are valid, they are not *apparent* in the story. In what number was "Death of a Zulu" published? I do want to get it if I can.

Gloomy thought apropos the story competition: it will probably be won by some startling piece of amateur melodrama.... And all our subtleties will waste their perfume etc. on the desert air.!!

Please give our love to Lydia;

4.

Nadine Gordimer

Johannesburg.

wonderful to hear that she's better. And she will probably find life in Capetown stimulating. How is Cliff the hermit crab liking the confines of his own shell after a month? Your letter sounded so strongly confident of continued joy in your own company! Admittedly, it's delightful company, but I doubt if you're the one to appreciate it.

Tuesday 23rd.

I've left this unfinished for a whole week, but I'm still here and the infant still hasn't plucked up enough courage to emerge into this cold J.H.B. world. On top of it, I've been in bed with shocking 'flu for three days and am awfully bored with *myself*.

To return to what I didn't say last week — I'm relieved to hear that you've got Abraham's story, but feel

5.

Nadine Gordimer

Johannesburg.

guilty about having burdened you with the obligation to read it. – I know how everyone pesters you with manuscripts.

There has only been one good thing about this delay with the baby: I was able to go and see Johan Nel in "King Oedipus" last week. He was magnificent – God, how these Greeks knew men, and how actable their plays still are.

Write to me soon; and good luck to you – I hope to hear you're producing great things there. Saw Charles the other night and he seems to be liking his new advertising job. He sent you a message, but it was too complicated for me to reproduce – something about don't give him up: apropos some article he's supposed to be doing?

Blessings and much love –

Nadine.

P.T.O!!

P.S. What do you think of my
fearful tattooed notepaper — a present
from a well-meaning friend, so please
excuse it!

19/9/50

77 [illegible] Road, Emmarentia
Johannesburg.
19th September 1950.

My dear Uys;

I have just this minute received and read your letter — how's this for promptness, eh! But I'm not trying to heap coals of fire on your head, old dear; it's just that I'm so delighted to hear from you that I want to reply at once. As for forgiving you — well I want to be forgiven too, for not having written to you when the results of the story competition came out. As a matter of fact I did start to write to you last week, but there are so many interruptions in my life these days that the letter never got beyond the third page — I have it here in my desk still.

Anyway, what I wanted to say was congratulations, congratulations! You old genius you — I was really thrilled when I opened the paper and saw your dear familiar face under the announcement of the winners. It quite made up for the disappointment of not getting anywhere myself. I am terribly eager to read the story — do let me? Also the other one that you would rather have won. — Incidentally, I think that that's always the sort of thing that happens in competitions of this nature. I shouldn't let it worry

.3. Nadine Gordimer

Johannesburg.

me, if I were you, for after all in a thing like this it's the money that counts — as you've always said, in S.A. prestige is easy to come by, but it's seldom that people remember that writers eat, too. I do hope that your story will do well in the international tests — that would be wonderful. A sidelight — I think it's pretty good, you being able to beat the so-called "English" S.A. writers at their own game and in their own language.

Charles tells me that American magazines are showing great interest in your work and are asking for more! I do hope that you are going to take advantage of the opportunity and write up some of the ideas that have been waiting their chance in your head for years now. At last I too have got my foot in in America — two days ago a cable came from my agent telling me that "A Watcher of the Dead" has been accepted by the "New Yorker". You can imagine how delighted I am. Now too, I feel I want to follow up this start with more and new stories, but I must echo your wail — "Time, time..." You can imagine how little time I get to work, with a young baby to look after. So whilst I am enchanted with my child and want to enjoy her, I get furious and frustrated with having to spend my days as a nurse-maid. It is so difficult to live and work at the

5.

same time; particularly if one is a woman. In many ways it is more of a curse than a gift for any woman to have talent and work of her own to do. — And yet when I fret because I haven't got time to write, I feel guilty towards my child — so what is one to do? Everyone says consolingly: "You are young. You need to mature, what does it matter if you don't write for a year." But after all, life is short (I haven't even got a grannie aged 94 to encourage me!!) and there is always the nagging fear that one's writing will "go off", won't be any good anymore. And how I regret my laziness and the time wasted in the past, when I had all the day to work in!

Thanks so much for finding out about my story from Brett Young.

So it did get as far as here; I wondered, because it was returned weeks later than my other one (apparently thrown out at once). Incidentally, it (the one going now) had some asinine "corrections" marked on it which first annoyed and then amused me; surely he could not have been responsible.

Also many thanks for the critique of Abrahams' story. He will be most grateful.

We don't, of course, go out at night as freely as we used to, but we see Charles quite often. I had a little dinner party the other night and he was here. He is fine, and writing a lot. To-night we are going to see "Hassan" — very good, I believe, and a great success for Lydia. I hope to have a word with her

.7. Nadine Gordimer

Johannesburg.

back-stage, after the performance.

How are the children? Strange to think that now I have one, too! We have named her Oriane, after the Duchesse de Guermantes in Proust. At the moment it is too big and beautiful a name for a round little baby, but she will grow up into it, I am sure!

Ulys my dear, when are you coming to our part of the world again? Soon, soon, I hope. Our best love to you — and do write again soon.

Nadine.

P.T.O!

P.S. About Paton — I did like him so much. And the story which reached the finals of the competition: it was based on an incident he related to me and said — " — I have always wanted to write that into a story but I never shall — you have it as a present and write it". And I did!

N.

Letter 5: NG to Matheus Uys Krige, 6 November 1950

A. 19/3/51
and earlier

Nadine Gordimer
Johannesburg.

507 Cleveleys,
Hannaben Street,
Cyrildene – Jhb.
6th November 1950.

My dear Uys,

I've just re-read your letter and was shocked to see that it's dated six weeks back – seems I only got it the other day. Many thanks for it, and for sending me "The Charcoal Burner."

Your story – I pounced on it and read it with quite a remarkable variety of reactions: all confirmed or

(2)

Briefly, I think it completely satisfying and successful on a certain level; an excellent short story of a certain type. But I can't say that that type interests me much as an achievement; and I know that to achieve a success on that level is too easy for you for it to interest you much, or satisfy you completely.

In more detail: first, I don't care for the anecdotal presentation. It (the story itself) is a wild beautiful incident — I don't like it (blast this pen!) told to me over coffee before the fire, like a yarn in a club. I know that that was a device to make the denouement come easily, but I don't think it was necessary. The story-

③ **Nadine Gordimer**

Johannesburg.

could and should stand alone, told directly. As a matter of fact, the very stirring, restrained emotion of the scene in the Allied Screening Commission office (excellently written – the way the meaning of the circle against the names comes out, no anticipatory "give-away" to the reader, natural, simple, the way momentous statements really do hit one – anyone can tell you're a playwright!) – this fine and final scene is where one wants to be left. To be dragged back to the fire and the coffee and the Englishman keeping a stiff upper lip as he flicks the ash dramatically from his cigarette – that, for me, is anti-climatic and artistically mistaken.

The story itself has all you

wonderful gift for creating intensely
"living" men and women, used, I should
say, rather carelessly. The very fact
that they are so vital when they
have been merely slapped together
makes one shake one's head, regretting
what they might have been had you
given them some of your subtlety,
another, closer look from your keen
eye. When I examine the three
Italians carefully, I marvel at the
impression they make (for they
~~ter~~ certainly do that) because they
are built up out of a few heroic
clichés, little else. There is a lack
of — what shall I say? — really
sensitive observation, really telling
touches, the way a person looks,
something apparently irrelevant said,
that seize up the actual outward

(5)

Nadine Gordimer

Johannesburg.

sometimes even become its whole meaning. (The sort of thing that gives the "Coffin" its force and charm.)

Then the style is mostly commonplace. The particular cadence of your phrasing, full, poetic, sensuous, is only evident here and there.

But let me hasten to say, Uys dear, that this is all very much the criticism of one writer to another – all very close and minute and workman-like. Looking at it purely as a reader, it is always interesting, has a real beauty, and gives one the sort of sense of the strong simple goodness of life that one gets when reading Silone's "Bread and Wine". All I can say is that even at your worst-best, you're still bloody good!

(6).

You know, I think you would be perfectly justified in continuing to send stories ~~direct~~ directly to the magazines with which you yourself had already established contact before appointing this man your agent. I admit the situation is a delicate one, but I personally would do so without compunction, although I don't think it would be fair to send stories to any other magazines. My situation is a little different. You see, I didn't place any stories at all on my own efforts — my agent was entirely responsible. So I suppose that in all decency, I can't go sending stuff to the "New Yorker" direct; I have to continue to do so through my agent, who made the contact in the first place.

Incidentally, I'm very satisfied

7.

Nadine Gordimer

Johannesburg.

with my agent — she's now sold another story, this time to the "Yale Review". They promise publication in six months, and are paying me 75 dollars. A small fee for American magazines, but the agent says that I'm very lucky to get into a journal which carries such prestige (!) So I'm more than pleased. Two out five stories have now been sold.

Of course, they're asking me for more. And my God, how it breaks my heart because I've got so little time to write. I'm back in a flat again now, and you can imagine what it's like, with a five-months-old baby to care for. The only answer is for me to work at night. But I'm so bloody tired

8.

by then that I can't keep my eyes open, let alone think at night. I'm really terribly depressed and miserable about the whole thing. Now, just when I'm really making headway I'm expected to resign myself to not writing. I've just managed, under enormous difficulty and with constant interruptions, to finish one short story. I'm afraid to read it; God knows what it's like.

Well, my dear, I mustn't drone on any longer. Do write soon, and tell me if there is any hope of seeing you up here soon. Gerald sends his love and so, I'm sure, would Oriane, if she could. She's very sweet, quite bright, and resembles her Mama in looks.

Love
Nadine.

P.S. Have sent "Charcoal Burners" on to your friend.

Letter 6: NG to Matheus Uys Krige, 2 July 1951

507 Cleveleys,
Hannaben Street,
Cyrildene,
JOHANNESBURG.

2nd July, 1951.

My dear Uys,

Charles phoned me a few weeks back with a message from you, saying that you might be able to get some of our stories considered by an Italian trilingual magazine.. Unfortunately all sorts of things cropped up in between—it would take too long to explain!—and I8ve only now been able to collect the enclosed three stories. By the way, could you return "The Prisoner" and "Another Part of The Sky" to me at once, as I haven't copies of either, and need them?

I was pleased to get a message from you through Lily Rabking and hope the promised letter will follow soon?

With love to you and Lydia—

Nadine

P.S. My story is in the 9th June issue of the New Yorker.

Letter 7: Matheus Uys Krige to NG, 10 July 1951

"Dawn",
Rouwkoop Road,
Rondebosch.
10th July, 1951.

My dear Nadine,

I've been carrying about a letter in my head or my heart --- preferably the latter --- for the last six weeks or so. Ever since I got those two charming, spontaneous and heart-warming letters from you at one and the same time. (I have just gone through all my correspondence in order to find them and reply to them, but they have got lost in that maze!) Many thanks for those two letters. But soon after I received them, I was almost swept off my feet by the onrush of events, to put it rather pompously. I took part in the War Veterans' Movement, spoke here, flew to P.E., spoke there to 20,000 people, came back with the "Steel Commando", spoke at George and then spoke here again to 50,000 people. It was a pretty unnerving experience. Vast crowds hit you right in the stomach when you're not used to speaking to them. You've got to learn to control both yourself and them. And that will only come with experience. I also gave a number of lectures and talks, to smaller audiences, thank God. And I prepared them very thoroughly as I've never prepared lectures before. Since I was paid for them. You see, how conscientious I am. (Only I neglect my friends.) Then I also became involved in Lydia's play. Or rather Lorca's play. The play was a great success. And it was a personal triumph for Lydia. The newspapers were enthusiastic, and severe critics say that it was Lydia's best role to date. I am enclosing an article an article I wrote for the Cape Times. It has been cut by more than a thousand words, so don't worry about its disunity or lack of proportion. But please send both clippings back.

I read both stories with great interest several times. I liked The Prisoner very much. I did not like Another Part of the Sky, as I told your young friend whom I liked very much. He is a very sensible and intelligent person. I liked them both, and spent two very pleasant afternoons with them. How are they? Did they give you all my personal messages?

Both stories ~~xxxxx~~ set off so many trains of thought in my mind my brain for some time was more like Johannesburg station on a public holiday than a small conglomeration of grey matter. It's an old trouble with me: my friends work give me so many vivid reactions I get frightened of putting them down on paper. Not because I don't want to speak my mind, but merely because I have so much to say and my time is so limited.
I shall ready both stories again today and then perhaps give you a few summary views, or perhaps I'll speak to you about it when I see you again. In any case, you'll have them back very soon now.

I'm enclosing a paragraph about you that appeared in the Cape Argus the other evening. I am delighted at your success Now you must go straight on and "exploit" those American contacts. It is a very fine initial success, you couldn't have hoped for a better one and nothing in the wide world should stop you now from going from strength to strength, and at the same time earning some money. Which is damned important, as you know only too well yourself. Will you be publishing a book of short stories in the U.S.A.? And will it be a new one? And what has happened to the novel? Both Harpers and Collins have asked me for a novel. But I need a year in which to write it -- and how would we all live in the meantime?

Perhaps you have seen the English anthology from the fine Italian review, *Botteghe Oscure*. It has had a very good press in Britain and elsewhere. Charles reviewed it for the *Forum*. Its editor has asked for several South African short stories. I immediately thought of you, Charles, Antony Delius and a few others. I thought we should give them your best short story, but I think it must be a story that has not appeared in the U.S.A. If it has appeared here, it doesn't matter in the least. Which story of yours do you consider the best for this purpose?

A famous French monthly, *Les Cahiers du Sud*, wants to publish an all - South African number. I met its editor 18 years ago in Marseilles when he had just launched his review. It had already a great reputation in France before the war and it has maintained its high standards ever since. Madeleine Masson, who leaves for France in a few weeks time, will hand all the Mss. over to the editor. I shall give her oneof your stories. I don't think it matters in this instance whether the story has been published or not. The story will, of course, be translated into French. We have some very able translator friends in Paris. What about The Prisoner for Les Cahiers du Sud? Have you copies for me of the two stories that appeared in the American quarterlies? I would like to make the very best choice for these two important publications. As time is the essence of the contract, please let me have every story of yours you think is pretty good and I haven't seen.

Do you ever see Herman Bosman these days? If so, please do me a big favour. Show him this letter and get him to co-operate. And convince him, with that wonderful tact I know you have, and that it is only my appalling lack of time --- and no disregard for him --- that has prevented me from writing to him. And that he should consider this letter as much his as yours. And give him my best regards please. I think he owes me a letter or a note, I am not sure ...

On Friday I was just about to start a letter to you when it was time for my typist to go. So I felt a bit sore when on coming home last night, I found your letter and the three stories. "Sore" in the sense that I would have liked to have written to you before getting that letter. Naturally I was very happy to hear from you. To get the stories. And also the photo. Which is charming. The little girl is very attractive and has a distinct Nadiné expression on her dear little face. So give her a big hug and kiss for me. And also for Gerald, Fuerte, Abrazo. I am looking forward to reading all your stories either this afternoon or this evening. I've dictated this letter at breakneck speed, so you must overlook its being so diffuse and slapdash. Our love to you all

Letter 8: NG to Matheus Uys Krige, 10 March 1952

NADINE GORDIMER

3 Northview,
Bezuidenhout Street,
Bellevue,
Johannesburg.
10th March, 1952.

My dear Uys,

Gerald came back two days ago with all the good news about your trip to Europe, and also the request for my agents' address. It is:

SIDNEY SATENSTEIN 75 VARICK STREET,
NEW YORK CITY, N.Y. U.S.A. Tell him that I recommended him to you, won't you? – I have found him very alive, and scrupulously business-like, although as friendly as Americans usually are.

I can't tell you how pleased I am that you're really getting out of S.A. again at last; I'm sure it is just the stimulation and refreshment you need and

2.

will be immensely valuable to your writing. How I wish to God I could get away from this life of mine in Johannesburg; for it's still essentially a domestic life with all the tedium and none of the compensations of a normal one. I drag along in a continual state of miserable unhappiness. I'm lonely, and worried about money and my work. The only thing that gives me any pleasure is Oriane.

The novel is a nightmare to me. I have written 65,000 words of it and it gets more mountainously difficult every day. When I read it over it seems tame and not eventful enough. I am supposed to hand it over complete in July...

Of course if I didn't have a baby I would take what money I have and go to Europe, but there is no one I'd care to leave her with (my mother won't take her) so what can I do? Also I

3.

am living on the advances of the novel, which worries the life out of me, — cause the money gets finished and the novel doesn't. And I must admit I hate being poor and not ever being able to invite friends round because it means buying a bottle of brandy.

Well, enough of my troubles, I'll be depressing you. ~~It~~ Unfortunately I missed seeing Lydia the other night; Charles phoned up and said she was coming round and would I come. But it so happened that I couldn't that night. I hope I'll get the chance to see her some other time. And of course I must see Lysistrata.

Ly. says again sailing about 26th of this month, so I shall understand if I don't get a reply to this before you leave — I just wanted to get Lindsay's address to you at once. But I shall look forward to hearing from you when you are away, so <u>please</u> don't disappoint me?

4.

My dear, I do hope you're going to have a wonderful time, and shall think of you often. When you write, do tell me the details of this scholarship and what your working plans are.

So in the meantime, good luck and bon voyage and my love to you—

Nadine

P.S. I shall also write to Sidney and tell him you're getting in touch with him.

N.

Letter 9: NG to Matheus Uys Krige, 8 February 1956

Stellenbosch

A. 28/2 55

Denver,
Transvaal.
8th February, 1956.

My dear Uys,

It always seems to take us six months to answer each other's letters, but I don't think this is to be taken as a gauge of our affection for each other. We think and talk of you often, and I was so glad to have your long letter — six weeks, three months ago? Now it's a year since we had that short holiday in Cape Town with the Sackses, and a year since we've seen you.

The most important event in our life in the interim was, of course, the baby — a son, as you thought. He's an enchanting little creature, this Hugo Cassirer (named after Reinhold's father) now ten months old, fat and sweet. But I hope you'll see him soon, because we are coming to Hermanus for three weeks from the 4th of March. Someone has lent us a cottage there, and we are coming en famille, by car. I haven't seen the house — or been to Hermanus before, for that matter — but R. says that there are plenty of beds. Won't you and Lidia come for one of the weekends while we are there? A visit would be worth ten letters, don't

2

you agree? I know that last year I was here, but the fact was that I was so weighted down with young I scarcely had the energy to see anyone!

I've had a busy year, and have done quite a bit of work. A new collection of stories – written over the past two-and-a-half years – is coming out in England and America later this year. R. has been working hard, too, and has to go to Rhodesia much too often for our liking. Then, last October, his brother and sister-in-law from Denmark came here on a holiday and disrupted our normal routine very pleasantly.

We were delighted to know of Lydia's success in "Medea"; heard of it, indeed, from everyone who saw her. Has she been doing anything new, lately? I wonder if either of you has bumped into Cedric Messina, our friend from the S.A.B.C. who is in C.T. to produce a series of radio plays? I thought Lydia might, since she does radio work.

What are you doing now? Thinking back to your letter (I don't know where I've put it) I remember with concern – I was distressed about it at the time, and now am more distressed because I should have written to you then – that you said that things were not going well and that you were first about keeping the wolf from the door. I hope to goodness that this will be a better year for you. At the risk of putting my nose in where it isn't wanted, I feel I must say again what I've been saying to you on and off for years: please, stop wasting your time and energy on plays and literary contests in South Africa. You simply cannot make any sort of a living here. You must resign (?) yourself to the bread-and-butter necessity of writing short things and writing in English. When, when, WHEN are you going to put down on paper those stories you tell so enchantingly? It's a damn disgrace (and no-one's fault but your own, I may say) that "Death of a Zulu" is the only story you've published – outside your book – in America.

Dear Uys, forgive the scolding. R. is beside me, writing letters too, and we both send our love and greetings to you and Lydia.

Till Hermanus?

Affectionately,

Nadine

Letter 10: NG to Matheus Uys Krige, 3 October 1960

7 Frere Road,
Parktown West,
Johannesburg.

3rd October, 1960.

Dear Uys,

I wonder if you feel, as I do, that you would like to make a protest, as a writer, against the Censorship Bill? I realise that most of us already are associated with opposition to the Bill, in our individual political or other affiliations, but it seems to me that a writer has a special responsibility not only to the written word but to the freedom of imagination and the world of ideas. Wouldn't it be a good idea if a group of us issued a statement along these lines?

I am writing to make this suggestion to Alan Paton, Harry Bloom, Jack Cope, Mary Renault, Daphne Rooke, Hans Hofmeyer, Ronald Byron, Geoffrey Jenkins and Tom Hopkinson. Mary R. and Tom H. are not South Africans, but since they live and write here, there seems to be no reason why they should not speak up if they wish to. It would be very nice to include South African writers who no longer live here—Dan Jacobson and Ezekiel Mphahlele, for example—but I have a strong feeling that the protest ought to come from those of us whose daily lives are subject to South African legislation.

I do hope that you will let me have a quick note giving your reactions to the idea of a statement. The statement itself, I imagine, should be drafted by two of the proposed signatories, and then presented to the rest for their approval.

With all good wishes,

Love Nadine

Letter 11: NG to Matheus Uys Krige, 1 November 1961

Stellenbosch

1st November, 1961.

225. K4.G.3 (3)

Dearest Uys,

Many thanks for the lovely letter; more than half the pleasure in a thing like this award is the feeling that friends who have always been interested in you and who believe in you, are glad for you. Thanks for the cuttings, too; I should not have seen them at all if you hadn't sent them, since no-one else thought of it. I have been very upset by the report of my interview with the London representative of "Die Burger" (Saturday 21st October). I don't know if you saw it: it made me out to be violently anti-Afrikaner, among other things..! I have sent a letter of protest, giving the truthful version of the interview; I hope that they publish it prominently. Why is it that people twist your words and simply cannot believe that ~~becausexyouxarexx~~ you are anti-apartheid but not anti-Afrikaner? (I find this maddening in England, too, where even intelligent people seem to think that all Afrikaans people are made in the image of Dr Verwoerd.)

I can't begin to tell you what I felt about America—it would overflow a letter. But when we meet (and it's about time we did) we'll have a long gab. In Brief, I could never, never live there; that's one thing I'm sure about, though, like you, my feelings about the places and people are mixed and contradictory.

I did not know that your sister had died; how awful. Which sister was it? I am so sorry...

What are you working on, and when shall we see you up here? I've been away such a lot this year and done so little work—I don't think I can hope to come to the Cape until next year. Please apologise to Jack, for me; I rushed off to England without answering his letter.

I didn't see Leila in America, because she was still in Jamaica, then. I stayed in Los Angeles with Yvor's mother; a splendid woman. The Smitters had onedisaster after another in Jamaica, lost a great deal of money, and now have gone back to New York.

I am very excited about Athol Fugard's new play "The Blood Knot" (hideous title) which is starting a three-week run here next week. It's a marvellous piece of work; I hope you'll get a chance to see it in Cape Town.

R. is fine and so are the children; Pippa at boarding-school and Oriane as big as I am, and Hugo in the toothless stage between six and seven. Is Eulalia married? I haven't seen Lydia for months. Much love, and best wishes to Jack.

Affectionately

Nadine

Letter 12: NG to Matheus Uys Krige, 7 July 1965

7 Frere Road,
Parktown West,
Johannesburg.

7th July, 1965.

Dearest Uys,

Many thanks for sending us the radio script. We both read it carefully, but agree that we should prefer to use your poem ENCOUNTER (from the anthology TOWARD THE SUN) rather than an excerpt or poem from the script. May we have your permission? We'll write to the publishers of the other anthology, once we have the O.K. from you. Except for a few late decisions and some odds and ends, our anthology is virtually in shape now, so far as collecting material is concerned. Now comes the editing and arranging, etc, which should take us about a month. I've found it a great deal of work and shall be glad when it's been mailed to Penguin.

Many thanks for the personal letter that came with the script, and please forgive me for not answering it adequately now. That's my grouse against the anthology: I simply haven't time to write my personal letters. We are all fine; Reinie more in Zambia than in JHB, which is awful for me, but staff difficulties are so great up there that his presence is called for. I've been up with him three times in the past year, twice done the long trek by car, and plan to go up again for a few days in August. My book of stories has had a good reception in the U.S. and England; the review copies seem to have got lost on the way here, however, since although the book's in all the shops, the papers keep ringing me up to know where their copies are. As if I hawked the thing myself.

Hope all goes well with you; by the way, do you ever let the Onrus house? We'd love to hire it sometime. Any chance over December or January?

Best love, as always,

Nadine

Letter 13: NG to Matheus Uys Krige, 17 November 1965

7 Frere Road,
Parktown West,
Johannesburg.

17th November, 1965.

My dear Uys,

Lionel and I were sorry to hear that you were upset at the idea of our using the poem "Encounter" in the anthology, and so of course we have withdrawn it. You said originally you would be agreeabl[e] to have us take an excerpt from "The Way Out", and that is what we are now going to do. Would you give us permission to use Chapter 26 (Maskew Miller revised edition) from the beginning on page 204 to the end of the paragraph "knowledge and understanding or else perish." on page 207. This 2,500 word extract is complete in itself, as you will see if you look it up. We'd like to give it the title of the book ~~itself~~ rather than the chapter title ("Cannonade"); the conclusions in the last paragraph concern the only "way out" not only through enemy lines, but out of man's situation in general. Please let us have a postcard saying "yes"

Forgive this short note. I am up to my eyes in work and the letters pile up so, on the side. Reinie has spent this whole year trooping back and forth betwee[n] JHB and Zambia, occasionally with me in tow. We are all going up for Christmas (he has to work, so in order to be together, the family must follow). Much excitement because Burchard and Brigitte (from Cairo during the war, now living in Zurich—South of France—London) have suddenly written to say they are coming to spend a holiday with us, arriving early December. I must get the anthology off before them.

Love from us both,

Nadine

Letter 14: NG to Matheus Uys Krige, 29 November 1965

7 Frere Road,
Parktown West,
Johannesburg.

29th November, 1965.

My dear Uys,

I don't know where you got the information that we were making our choice from your total works (certainly not from my letters to you), but of course this was quite wrong; the scope of our anthology specifically excludes any writing not in English. Not even translations, unless they fall under the special category of English versions done by the author himself. Otherwise imagine the immense labour of getting adquate translations to choose from, from Afrikaans, African languages, perhaps even Gujerati and Tamil! Since Afrikaans is one of the two important literary languages of this country, we decided that we should like to include a couple of token examples of Afrikaans writing. But they would have to be translations or original works in English, the translations to be made by the authors themselves; hence the inclusion of Jan Rabie's "The Stone Flower" and something by U.K.

Now about that something, cher maître—the Fascist Bombers poem has made us change our minds again! We both find it so moving and altogether excellent that we want to use it instead of the piece of The Way Out. Is this all right? Very many thanks for coming up with this poem on the stroke of midnight.

Although The Soldier has remarkable atmosphere, I must say quite honestly that I find the vocabulary cliché-ridden ("infinite dusk" "boundless earth" "aching lack"). By the way, if Fascist Bombers is a translation rather than original poem, it certainly reads like an original.

Briggite and Burchard now say they are coming on December9, and leaving on January 3. But we are supposed to take them up to Zambia with us from before Christmas until they fly off direct from there, so I'm afraid you'll miss them. But we hope to be back about the 10th Jan., so please let us know when you arrive.

We are all so upset about Bram. I saw the daughters and Paul last week; that boy looks tragically ill. Ours is a sad country, eh?

All our affectionate wishes for a Happy Christmas and New Year, dear Uys. See you in January, I hope.

Love Nadine

Letter 15: NG to Matheus Uys Krige, 18 February 1975

A. A. 4/6/75

7 Frere Road,
Parktown West,
Johannesburg.

18th February, 1975

My dear Uys,

I did so enjoy and appreciate your lovely letter, with its generous pleasure at my having received the Booker, and the thoughtfulness in collecting and enclosing cuttings I'd otherwise not have seen. Believe me, not all my fellow writers in South Africa were moved to congratulate me... The time I've taken to write to you is no (negative) measure of my thanks.

It was good, for us, to see something of you in October-November. I liked Ty and his wife very much, too; next time you come, they must visit our house with you. I always feel after ten minutes in your company the old spell and revelation that I got from early meetings with you when I was a young girl—a sense that we inhabit then and now an inner world in common. And it will always be there, just as—miracle!—it was there for me to find myself in, partly through you. What am I saying? That we are writers and care more about the daily splendid struggle with ideas and words than anything that concerns others.

Enslin has just been here again. I'm ashamed to say I find less and less in common with <u>him.</u> (Don't ever let him know.) Is it his extreme age—and my irritation with its petty manifestations, foreshadowing what my own old age will be like? Or is it, as I sometimes think, that basically he is a charming amateur—was always a charming, very talented amateur—and there was never any passion in his work to sustain his personality through old age. Probably I'm romanticising or shaping a theory to suit myself—his arteries are hardening, that's all.

I've been reading Robert Liddell's book about Cavafy, with mixed feelings. After waiting so many years for a "life", it could have been expected to be better, less a product of the Alexandrian-Egyptian homosexual Englishman club mentality. Because it's written from the "inside" of that persistent milieu (persistent even in the Dispersion) it's tantalisingly limited; much is left out, or assumed, rather, that would have emerged if it had been written by a diligent and fascinated outsider. But at least the book has sent me back to the poems (in the Mavrogodatis translations).

I'm glad your play came to life so vividly again. That's something special, that only a playwright can experience; the play is an old garment hanging in the wardrobe, and suddenly a new interpretation inhabits it, fills out the creases, flaunts the style and colour of it. And to be able to hear that it makes people laugh! And then quiets them in the intensity of attention. That's the only good form of wielding power.

I'll pass on your message to Racilia—can you imagine, I don't know her address, either; I always telephone her. She is trying to wangle a trip to the Cape at the same time that Reinie has his (or rather Nederburg winery has its) Sotheby-auctioned wine sale. I'll be away, as my stint at Columbia university is due--I'm leaving in five days for New York. I send you much love, dear Uys, anyway, and am determined to get to the Cape, and thence to Onrus to see you and Jack, later this year. Stephen (Gray) sends his best to you; talking of making people laugh, he's just written a wild and funny novel. The Evelyn Waugh in it is somewhat swamped by a more American, crueller sense of the absurd, but that may slough away in subsequent books. About time we produced a satirist.

Affectionately

Nadine

PS. Oriane – my daughter – is fine & expecting a first child in June. It will be a Franco-South African production, a Catholic-Jewish mixture with a dash of Italian and (distantly) Roumanian blood!

N

Reinhold sends his love.

Letter 16: NG to Matheus Uys Krige, 22 February 1976

A. A. 10/4/76

225. KL. G 3(3)

2193

7 Frere Road
Parktown West
Johannesburg.
22nd February 1976

My dear Uys,

Yesterday Reinhold and I heard over the radio of the death of your mother. It doesn't matter how old one's mother is — to all of us there is something awful about that particular loss. The umbilical cord perhaps is never quite severed until then. And I know you were close to your mother at many periods in your life. We send you our affectionate thoughts.

I was sorry indeed not to have you at Onrus that weekend. Jack and the Rabies were kind and entertaining — the fire provided a typically Cape ending to our visit. Jack's property must be looking pretty bleak; I must say I should find the summer dangers, the fear of every spark, rather trying if I lived in your part of the world. At least, up on our plateau, the winter dangers is offset by crisp nights and mornings! But all this belongs to a South African controversy that must have started when the first ox wagon reached the Highveld...

I do hope you are over that bad patch, physically and that maybe this time the medical tests showed what line of treatment you should follow. Aren't the Eliots a nice couple (of very definite individuals!) It was a good place to meet again. Take care of yourself.

Love

Nadine